Fictions of Femininity

Fictions of Femininity

LITERARY INVENTIONS OF GENDER IN
JAPANESE COURT WOMEN'S MEMOIRS

Edith Sarra

STANFORD UNIVERSITY PRESS
STANFORD, CALIFORNIA

Stanford University Press
Stanford, California
© 1999 by the Board of Trustees of the
Leland Stanford Junior University
Printed in the United States of America

CIP data appear at the end of the book

For Terashima Shōichi

☞ Acknowledgments

I have been graced by a wealth of mentors and friends who have given generously of their time and wisdom over the years. It is a privilege to be able to thank them publicly. As my first mentor in Japanese literature, the late Professor Terashima Shōichi of Kōnan University set me on a path I might not have taken without the inspiration of his example. In later years, his gift for engaging fully as a reader, as a teacher, and as a human being brought scholarship to life for me in a way I could never otherwise have imagined. Not only at the dissertation stage but also well before that, Professors Edwin Cranston, Stephen Owen, and Richard Sieburth challenged and encouraged me when I was a graduate student at Harvard. Professor Cranston has continued to give freely of his support and his expertise over the years since then. At Gakushūin, Professor Kimura Masanori guided my initial forays into the world of *kokubungaku* scholarship and introduced me to a stimulating circle of scholars. At a later date, I had the pleasure and benefit of frequent, lively talks with Professor Takahashi Tōru of Nagoya University, who brought his creativity and expertise to Bloomington as a Japan Foundation Visiting Professor in 1995.

I owe a great debt to my Bloomington colleague Richard Rubinger, who tried everything, from bribery to badgering, to keep me on some sort of a reasonable timetable. The fact that he did not entirely succeed is no reflection on the intensity of his efforts. He also read and generously commented on the manuscript at a number of crucial stages. The book benefited immensely from the comments of Jurgis Elisonas, an impeccable scholar and stylist whose marginalia were worth—in sheer entertainment value alone—any twinges of pain they may have also caused this writer. Kenneth Wells kindly commented on Chapters 3 and 4, and Bernard Levinson provided well-timed feedback on Chapter 1. In addition to her collegiality in other contexts over a period of several years, Laurel Rodd read the entire manuscript for Stanford University Press and gave me much useful advice. I wish to thank my editors, John Ziemer and Helen Tartar, for their patience and labor. All errors and omissions are of course my own. Funding was provided by two Summer Faculty Fellowships from the College of Arts and Sciences at Indiana University, the Indiana University East Asian Studies Center, a Fulbright-Hays Faculty Research Abroad Fellowship, and a grant from the Joint Committee for Japanese Studies of the Social Science Research Council and the American Council of Learned Societies with funds provided by the Ford Foundation and the National Endowment for the Humanities.

I delivered early versions of almost all the chapters at various conferences and symposia. The list of colleagues from whom I received intellectual stimulation at these venues could be extended, but I would especially like to remember Margaret Childs, H. Mack Horton, Yoshio Iwamoto, Sumie Jones, Elizabeth Lillehoj, Lynne Miyake, Joshua Mostow, Chieko Mulhern, Joseph Parker, Esperanza Ramirez-Christensen, Atsuko Sakaki, and Eiji Sekine. Robert Easley and Oda Hiromi gave their time and technical expertise when hardware, software, and formatting problems threatened to derail me. I am grateful to Robert for many years of kindness and support, only a small part of which had to do with computers. The companionship and good humor of friends saw me through on a daily basis: in Japan, Kiyoshi and Mieko Kobayashi, Shimono Kenji, and Tanaka Masaaki and family; in Bloomington, Colleen Berry, James Capshew, Kyeong Hee Choi, Michael Hynes, Michael Robinson, and last, but far from least, Gregory Evon, who always has been at least virtually present during the more trying passages in the last several years. Closest to home, my neighbor Rod Wampler has provided me what no one else I know could offer: confidence that I will get through the crazy projects I have taken on, as well as the tractor (plus man power) for keeping the front five acres of one of them under control while I coped with this one.

E.S.

Concord Road, Owen County, Indiana

☞ Contents

☞ Abbreviations

HJAS	*Harvard Journal of Asiatic Studies*
KKS	*Kokinwakashū* (first imperially commissioned anthology of Japanese poetry)
M	*The Pillow Book of Sei Shōnagon.* 2 vols. Trans. Ivan Morris. Oxford: Oxford University Press, 1967.
MN	*Monumenta Nipponica*
MSK	*Makura no sōshi kōza.* 4 vols. plus supplement. Yūseidō, 1975–76.
NKBT	*Nihon koten bungaku taikei.* 102 vols. Iwanami Shoten, 1956–68.
NKBZ	*Nihon koten bungaku zenshū.* 51 vols. Shōgakkan, 1970–76.
NKBZ 12–17	Abe Akio et al., eds. *Genji monogatari.* 6 vols. Shōgakkan, 1970–76.
NKBZ 18	Fujioka Tadaharu et al., eds., *Izumi Shikibu nikki, Murasaki Shikibu nikki, Sarashina nikki, Sanuki no suke nikki.* Shōgakkan, 1971.
NKBZ 9	Kimura Masanori, ed. *Kagerō nikki.* Shōgakkan, 1973.
S	*The Tale of Genji.* Trans. Edward Seidensticker. New York: Knopf, 1976.
SKT	*Shinpen kokka taikan.* 10 vols. plus indexes. Kadokawa Shoten, 1983–92.
SNKBT	*Shin Nihon koten bungaku taikei.* 100+ volumes to date. Iwanami Shoten, 1989– .

SNKBT 25   Watanabe Minoru, ed. *Makura no sōshi*. Iwanami
               Shoten, 1991.

SNKS   *Shinchō Nihon koten shūsei*. 48 vols. Shinchōsha,
               1976–89.

SNKS 7   Kuwabara Hiroshi, ed. *Mumyōzōshi*. Shinchōsha,
               1976.

SNKS 39   Akiyama Ken, ed. *Sarashina nikki*. Shinchōsha, 1980.

All translations from the Japanese are mine unless otherwise indicated. Wherever possible, cross-references to complete English translations will also be provided in the notes.

Fictions of Femininity

↷ Introduction

Works that were considered marginal at the time they were written sometimes rise to become exemplars, in later ages, of the most significant literary achievements of the very age that brought them forth and benightedly relegated them to the cultural background. Japanese court women's memoirs (*nikki*) of the Heian period (794–1185) have followed just such a trajectory. Most of the texts now termed *nikki bungaku* (memoir literature) were written between the tenth and the late twelfth centuries by middle-ranking aristocratic women—wives and daughters of minor courtiers, women of the provincial governor class (*zuryō*), and those who served as ladies-in-waiting to members of the imperial house or to other prominent aristocratic families. Along with fictional narratives in Japanese (*monogatari*), of which the early-eleventh-century *Tale of Genji* is the best-known example, Heian women's memoirs represent the first flowering of prose literature in Japanese. The original marginality of this tradition is attributable in part to the gender of its primary audience and many of its practitioners, and also to the fact that women's memoirs were written in Japanese rather than Chinese. With the compilation in 905 of the first imperially commissioned anthology of poetry in Japanese (*waka*), lyric poems in the vernacular began to be recognized as serious literature. But until the latter part of the Heian period, prose in Japanese remained a lesser medium, written largely for and by women. Chinese was the literary language of the male bureaucracy at the Heian court.

The term and the genre *nikki* or *niki* (literally "daily records") are themselves Chinese in origin. In Japan, they originally designated daily records in Chinese prose (*kanbun*) kept by male courtiers in both private and official capacities.[1] Diaries in Chinese prose (*kanbun nikki*) were written exclusively by men, using Chinese characters, or *mana*, an orthography that was therefore marked as a masculine medium. The native *kana* orthography, used to transcribe Japanese, was referred to as *onnade* or *onna no te*, "the woman's hand." In fact, it was used by both men and women in the composition of Japanese poetry, men being thus graced with a kind of cultural and gender ambidexterity if they wished to write poetry. Prose, however, was another story. In the mid-Heian period, if a man wished to write serious *literary* prose, he wrote in Chinese, not Japanese, and he wrote nonfiction. The native language and the woman's hand were not considered appropriate media for serious prose writing.

Education in Chinese was generally restricted to men of the aristocracy. Aristocratic women were carefully educated to read and write Japanese poetry, or *waka*, because this genre formed an important part of their written correspondence with the world outside their own rooms, and in particular, with the men in their lives. Native prose remained an art more or less ancillary to *waka*, and fictional prose narratives in Japanese (*monogatari*) were considered a trifling diversion, fit only for women and children although, significantly, the earliest examples of this genre are thought to have been written by men in imitation of Chinese tales.

Unlike *nikki* or *niki*, the term *nikki bungaku* (diary, or memoir literature) is an academic coinage from this century, designating a tradition of personal records written in Japanese prose (*wabun*), using the native syllabary and the *kana* script. Most histories of *nikki bungaku* begin with Ki no Tsurayuki's the *Tosa nikki* (the *Tosa Memoir*, ca. 935), a memoir written by a man who used the "woman's hand" and a female persona for his narrative. The *Kagerō nikki* (the *Kagerō Memoir*, after 974), by the mother of Fujiwara Michitsuna, is traditionally cited as the next major exemplar of the genre; like the *Tosa nikki*, it conveniently refers to itself as a *nikki* in its opening lines. Although traditional histories usually place the male-authored *Tosa nikki* at the origin of the genre, most of the texts subsumed in the contemporary category of *nikki bungaku* are works by women writing after the middle of the tenth century. Evidence that women were writing *nikki* before that is scanty, though not unheard of. It seems possible that those texts have been traditionally downplayed in the interest of telling a good story: how much more provocative to portray *nikki bungaku* as a genre invented by a man who was pretending to be a woman.

The concern in this study is not with the overlooked traces of earlier feminine forms of memoir writing, but rather with specific, well-known memoirs by women of the mid-Heian period. Three of the four texts analyzed at length in this volume occupy prominent places in the standard histories, but I did not single them out because I wish to endorse or further prove the usefulness of *nikki bungaku* as a generic category (in fact, I find the category questionable on a number of points). The idea for this book arose from my sense that a dialogue was taking place among individual female memoirists of the period. It appeared to me that certain memoirists were writing with an awareness of themselves and of other female memoirists *as* writers grappling with perennial problems touching on their identities as women and as writers. Problems having to do with notions of feminine identity and the meaning of writing a memoir recur as principal themes in a number of *nikki*. What seemed significant to me, and worthy of pursuit, was what these highly self-reflective texts have to teach us about what it meant to be a woman and a writer in the upper levels of Heian court culture.

Because Heian *kana nikki* can be characterized by their fluidity of form—encompassing narrative as well as lyric structures—and because many seem to oscillate between what Western readers would term the autobiographical and the biographical modes, I have deliberately avoided using the words *diary* or *journal* to describe them. In addition to gender-related differences in style and orthography, women's memoirs of the late tenth century and after reveal far greater latitude both in content and format than do the daily records in Chinese kept by Heian aristocratic men. The dated-entry structure peculiar to the masculine *kanbun nikki* genre, which fits the Western categories "diary" or "journal" so well, is not found in *kana nikki* of the mid-Heian period. A possible exception among the texts examined in this book is the first volume of the *Sanuki no suke nikki* (the *Memoir of the Sanuki Assistant Handmaid*, after 1108), in which the writer, an assistant handmaid to Emperor Horikawa, follows a loose daily format for describing the final weeks of the emperor's life. But even here, we have to pause a moment. How many diaries are written about the doings of someone other than the diarist herself? To my mind, the term *memoir* better conveys an idea of the versatility of form and impulse typical of Heian women's *nikki*. For similar reasons, I have also avoided the terms *nikki bungaku* and "memoir literature" in order to discourage a too-ready appropriation of Heian *nikki* as "literature." Like the memoir, the discourse of Heian women's *nikki* occupies a border zone between what might otherwise be unquestioningly domesticated by the reader as "purely literary" texts (that is, poetry collections in Chinese or Japanese) and those that claim to present what is more or less "factual" (diaries in Chinese).

This book is not intended as a further contribution to genre studies, nor am I concerned with challenging the polarization of "literary" and "factual" discourse frequently invoked by Japanese literary historians.[2] My interest in Heian women's memoirs is motivated by my desire to show how gender norms—and attempts to challenge, redefine, or elaborate them—figure in the writings produced by the highly educated women of the Heian aristocracy. My readings have been informed by, and seek to inform the reader about, issues of interest to feminists and students of women's writing as well as to the student of classical Japanese literature. Consequently, my analyses combine a lexicon that will be familiar to scholars of comparative literature and literary criticism (*trope, topos, metaphor, metonymy*) with another common to specialists familiar with figural language and literary motifs in classical Japanese texts (*utamakura, meisho, kaimami, yukari*). Wherever possible, I have tried to gloss these latter terms in paraphrases within the discussion. The chapters themselves pursue a dual interest, asking how the memoirs work as rhetorical constructs and how they might be understood as a medium through which writers tried to come to terms with culturally available fictions about what it was to be an upper-class woman in Heian society. I have therefore been especially concerned with the rhetorical level of the texts and with the intertextual dialogue among them and other less peripheral Heian prose texts (like *The Tale of Genji*) that deal with women's lives and women's writings.

I am particularly interested in the ideologically charged image of the Heian aristocratic woman as the passive yet compelling object of (masculine) desire. I argue that this cultural ideal presents special narratological problems in the context of works that, like Heian women's memoirs, have been traditionally read as the personally authored accounts of actual women about themselves. I use the term *heroine* as shorthand for the various rhetorical strategies by which Heian memoirs and tales represent women as passive, yet powerfully magnetic, figures. As a literary-critical term, *heroine* has roots in an Anglo-American feminist tradition that includes the work of scholars such as Rachel M. Brownstein, Nancy K. Miller, Patricia Meyer Spacks, and in Western-language scholarship on the *The Tale of Genji*, Norma Field. I understand this term to designate culturally specific sets of fictions that revolve around women's negotiations with patriarchal agendas, negotiations largely undertaken by female writers in the Heian context. I do not wish to convey a belief in an essential commonality between the representation of heroines in Western novelistic or autobiographical discourse and the discourse of Heian women's prose. On the contrary, I wish to call attention to intertextual relations between *kana nikki* and fictional tales in Japanese (*monogatari*) and between *kana nikki* and Japanese court poetry (*waka*). I understand these connections between neighboring texts to operate in ways analogous to intertextual relations between the novel and women's autobiographical writings in the West. My authority for this perception of intertextuality in Heian women's memoirs derives from the procedures used in some of the memoirs themselves.[3] I assume that Heian women wrote about themselves in terms of the texts they had already read. They used the language and ready-made themes of fiction and poetry to think through and compose their own texts. *Waka* and *monogatari*, the two genres that were the basic reading material of Heian aristocratic women, provided them with a rich "image-repertoire of poses" (both masculine and feminine) when they came to write their memoirs.[4] One of the intents of this book is to explore what happens to these poses in the context of individual memoirs.

I do not claim that the texts under examination here are in any recognizable sense feminist or even protofeminist—that is, that their authors sought, either consciously or unconsciously, to undo the conditions of patriarchy or to offer in its stead a vision of society based on egalitarianism or even simply greater reciprocity between the sexes. I do not believe that a memoir that openly challenged the very bases of society would have garnered even the small and sporadic audience that Heian women's memoirs have enjoyed in the last ten centuries in Japan, and more recently, in the West. This is not to say that radical challenges to the Heian sex/gender system do not surface in the texts that have been preserved from that era, only to suggest that those that do challenge dominant systems tend to do so in forms that mask or neutralize their own subversive aspects.

And yet, as a reader alert to women's issues, I have long been struck by the extent to which being female constitutes a source for narrative in the native prose genres of the Heian period. On the one hand, the idea that writing and other forms of cultural production by court women provided them with a means of political or social empowerment has gained currency in recent scholarship on premodern Japan. On the other hand, the question of women's collusion with the status quo, that is, whether and in what ways women's writings worked to ameliorate their integration into oppressive systems of marriage, literary expression, religious belief, and so on, has not been directly addressed. In an effort to attend to both these issues, I have tried to highlight the different and sometimes conflicting ideological implications at work within specific texts. I have not found that the shared gender identity of the Heian memoirists has lent their works ideological or thematic coherence. Thus, the reader who hopes to find in these pages generalizations about what characterizes women's writing in the Heian period—or even what might characterize Heian women's memoirs—will come away hungry. My goal has been neither to write a history of Heian women as memoirists nor to highlight links between Heian women writers and the more recognizably political areas of Heian culture, traditionally understood as male-dominated, that have recently been shown to have included women in ways hitherto unacknowledged.

I have instead tried to probe the problem of Heian women's construction of the feminine through an examination of different moments in a history that still remains unclear. I have assumed that the more marginal the genre, the more likely it is to provide the writer with a space for critical reflection on herself and her world. There is evidence to suggest that Heian women's memoirs were—even more so than fictional tales by women—written with a very limited, primarily female or familial, audience in view and that they were given a more discreet circulation than tale literature. These conditions in and of themselves cannot guarantee the emergence of critical self-consciousness, but I believe in some cases that they did provide a breeding ground for it.

I have no wish to participate in essentialist fictions about a separate sphere or discourse that might be identified as peculiarly "feminine." Indeed, I argue throughout for a more complicated understanding of the inscription of femininity in Heian women's writing. At the same time, I am concerned that the important and necessary revision of the portrayal of Heian political life as an exclusive men's club, wherein women brought forth native cultural products in quarantine from things political and Chinese, has obscured the extent to which Heian women were in significant ways limited to and nourished by a cultural milieu that was predominantly female, feminine, and vernacular. I have therefore chosen memoirs in which women appear to speak for, or to respond to, other women or other women's texts. Despite the more or less canonic status of the memoirs I have selected for study, the intertextual dialogue they inscribe provides relatively unexplored ground for scholars of classical Japanese literature.

Texts from traditions remote in time provide the very basis on which we reconstruct social and political contexts. But texts do not simply and passively reflect their lost milieux. In its intertextual dimension, the text acts as a place where cultural fictions circulate according to the exigencies of desire—whether we locate that desire in the author herself or in the language and structure of the texts that now provide the basis for our reconstructions of her intentionality. Desire may also be located in the written traces of a text's classical and modern-day readership. By the same token, I cannot avoid implicating here my own desiderata as a scholarly reader distanced from the Heian writers by a millennium as well as by major differences in race, culture, and language. It has often been remarked that the literature of the Heian court, in which the achievements of women figure both largely and brilliantly, represents an unprecedented moment in world literary history, comparable perhaps only to the salons of seventeenth- and eighteenth-century France, where, as in the city of Heian a thousand years ago, the art of vernacular prose narrative came into being under the auspices of aristocratic—and primarily female—literary enclaves.[5] In this century, scholars with feminist sympathies, as well as novelists, poets, and translators on both sides of the Pacific, have been quick to recognize in the Heian women's tradition an inviting if tangled garden, one of the few places where we might, to borrow the words of Virginia Woolf, whose 1925 review of Arthur Waley's translation of *The Tale of Genji* brought the name Lady Murasaki into the purview of Anglo-American feminism, "think back through our mothers."[6]

Seven decades later, although Murasaki Shikibu remains the dominant "mother" that nonspecialist readers of Japanese literature remember from the Heian period, the image of *The Tale of Genji* as an anomalous masterpiece by an exceptional female has far less currency. The plot (and the reading list) has thickened. But the difficulties contemporary readers continue to have with assimilating the writings of Heian women replicate the difficulties feminist readers have long had in finding more than just something usable in the fragmented, partial history of women as creators of culture. At this level, the study of the Heian women's tradition offers something that is not so unique and therefore perhaps more relevant to modern students of women's writing. My hope for these chapters is that they will map for the reader an itinerary that allows for discoveries of all kinds, including findings that fly in the face of preconceived notions of how relations between gender and literature, gender and literary history, and oppression and subversion work. What I have sought to discover is how members of a fragmented community of writers inscribe spaces for themselves, textual grounds from which to enter into and sometimes to question the dominant culture in spite of the rhetorical, ideological, and political systems in which their own writings participate.

BEGINNING AROUND the early tenth century, key figures at the imperial court began making claims for the vernacular as a medium for serious writing. The most important achievement in this regard was the compilation of the *Kokinwakashū* (a collection of Japanese poems ancient and modern) in 905, and with it, the institution of imperially commissioned anthologies of poetry in Japanese (*waka*). Tsurayuki's the *Tosa nikki* (935) arguably represents another such achievement. My introductory chapter considers the *Tosa nikki* and a few other texts central to these early efforts at legitimizing Japanese as a literary language. Letting the texts themselves provide the terms for my thinking about gender fictions and the relation between women and writing, my analysis attempts to tease out some of the underlying assumptions and expectations that impinged on mid-Heian women as memoirists. Who did they think they were writing for, and what did the writer's gender as a memoirist have to do with the content and the style in which she composed her memoir? What traces may we still find of these assumptions in texts that appeared at the outset of the tradition in the early to mid-tenth century?

For the subsequent chapters I chose memoirs that wrestle with various problems associated with both rhetoricity and the construction of ideals of femininity. I was particularly concerned with texts that call attention to differences between "real" women and idealized images of feminine roles as they are represented in the rich contemporary genres of fictional tales (*monogatari*) and poetry (*waka*) in Japanese. What I have found within and between these texts are traces of a dialogue that asks questions about feminine disclosure and concealment and the significance of reading and writing as means of empowerment, oppression, knowledge of self and other, and the expression of desire. Chapters 2 through 6 trace these issues through four memoirs representing a period of almost a century and a half, from the mid-tenth-century *Kagerō nikki* to the early-twelfth-century *Sanuki no suke nikki*. Each chapter concerns a different set of conceptual issues, since the awareness of the problems with being an aristocratic lady manifests itself in different ways in each memoir. A loose, shifting body of Heian cultural fictions about upper-class women, their writing, and feminine desire function in these memoirs as figures to be resisted, embraced, or modified. These fictions provide underlying links between the individual memoirs and among the chapters in this book.

In both the *Kagerō nikki* and the *Sarashina nikki*,[7] the subjects of Chapters 2, 3, and 4, the memoirist's basic impulse toward commemoration (whether of self or of patron) is complicated by a critical perspective on herself or on the world as she has seen it. An important theme in both memoirs is a disappointment with the unfulfilled promises of fictional literature (implicit in the plots of *monogatari* and/or the "plot" of the courtly love affair as embodied in the books of love poetry in the *Kokinwakashū*). Both narrators explicitly connect the suffering they experienced in their earlier years with their own misguided reading of fictions about romantic relations between men and women and with their subsequent disillusionment with the promises those discourses make about life. For these writers, the narrative problem of presenting how one becomes who one "is" involves both constructing and critiquing the image of a naive or willfully myopic female reader of received "texts"—*monogatari*, *waka*, dreams and omens, and other culturally inscribed versions of ideal relationships between women and men, women and literature, and women and religion. Because I find the intertextual dimensions of the *Sarashina nikki* so intricately realized, my study of it is split into two chapters.

Both the *Kagerō* and *Sarashina* memoirs are basically linear narratives, written at least in part using the device of a retrospective narrating standpoint from which is surveyed a long expanse of years in the life histories of the narrator-heroines. But not all, indeed probably relatively few, Heian women's memoirs employ this type of linear narrative mode. Likewise, there are few *nikki* that limn so self-reflexively the theme of an individual woman's destiny—whether secular and familial (*Kagerō*) or spiritual (*Sarashina*). The *Sanuki no suke nikki*,[8] with which I am concerned in Chapter 5, pursues a more fragmentary narrative mode that borrows loosely from the kinds of cyclical paradigms informing Heian poetic anthologies (though it is, insofar as it contains very few of the memoirist's own poems, one of the least "poetic" *nikki* in the tradition). Rather than reconstructing the past as a sequential, forward-moving course of days and events, the *Sanuki no suke nikki* succeeds in presenting the past *as* fragment, depicting remembered events in a disjointed series of episodic flashbacks embedded within an account of events that are presented as more or less contemporaneous with the moment of narration. The memoir is as much "about" its narrator-heroine's entrapment in the repetitive paradigms of memory as it is "about" the dead Emperor Horikawa (1079–1107), whom it ostensibly commemorates. The narrating persona is that of a lady-in-waiting who represents herself as a "relic" (*mukashi nagara*) left behind from a former reign but still conversant with a world that has become hidden from others with the passage of time. My chapter on this memoir elucidates how metaphors of spirit possession and spirit mediumship are brought into play in the structure of the memoir itself (as well as in the critical commentary surrounding it) as a rhetorical means of negotiating problems of feminine self-disclosure, authorial agency, and patronage.

In Chapter 6, the relation between voyeurism and the memoir takes center stage. Sei Shōnagon's *The Pillow Book* (*Makura no sōshi*, after 990),[9] constructs the image of a writer who enjoys nothing more than "looking" and—within certain self-inscribed bounds—"being looked at" in return. Explicitly questioning the taboos surrounding the convention of woman as passive, erotic spectacle, the memoir sections of *The Pillow Book* deconstruct the polarized gender and class arrangements typically highlighted by the topoi of voyeurism that Sei Shōnagon's work shares with other Heian tales and memoirs. I argue that what emerges is not so much a "feminine" variant of voyeuristic desire as it is an exploration of different possible triangulations of desire and the gaze. These include the possibility of a reciprocal, nonappropriative gaze that is met and returned in ways that challenge normative representations of gender and desire.

The sequence of the first five chapters reflects the sequence in which the memoirs historically appeared. The discussion of *The Pillow Book* in Chapter 6, however, represents a chronological leap backward. *The Pillow Book* was written after the *Kagerō nikki* but before *The Tale of Genji*, the *Sarashina nikki*, and the *Sanuki no suke nikki*. The chapter on it found its place at the end of my book because I wanted to honor the historical identity of *The Pillow Book* as a kind of countertext to *The Tale of Genji*, one that exhibits crucial contrasts to the mood, the themes, and the structures of the well-known tale attributed to Murasaki Shikibu. As my study of *The Pillow Book* took shape, I began to realize that it has been the destiny of Sei Shōnagon's text to occupy a richly ambiguous position in literary history regarding issues of gender, genre, and fictions about femininity.

In terms of genre, *The Pillow Book* is a liminal work; it is clearly not a *nikki*, although scholars classify certain of its passages as being "*nikki*-like." Its relation to *waka* is equally ambivalent. Unlike other memoirists, Sei took a perverse pride in establishing an image of herself in *The Pillow Book* as a lame *waka* poet. *The Pillow Book* is marked by the near absence of *waka*, a quirk that distinguishes it from most mid-Heian tales as well. Its inclusion of passages that consist of what are essentially lists of things and words (*ruisanteki shōdan*) are unique to it among Heian court women's writings. Sei's book is usually (and anachronistically) classified as a *zuihitsu* or as the female ancestor of *zuihitsu*, a nonnarrative genre of miscellaneous reflections and reminiscences in Japanese prose by male authors of the Kamakura period and later. Thus, the communally calculated ironies of literary history come full circle with *The Pillow Book*. We have moved from Ki no Tsurayuki, whose textual transvestite narrator in the *Tosa nikki* imitates a woman appropriating a genre she has heard that men employ, to Sei Shōnagon, who wrote as no one but herself, though engaged by men and the masculine at the level of both medium and message (her woman's hand is peppered with Chinese characters, the mark of the man's hand), to Yoshida Kenkō, whose famous *zuihitsu*, *Tsurezuregusa* (Essays in idleness, ca. 1330), is written in Japanese in the woman's hand, consciously echoing the great Heian court women writers in general and Sei Shōnagon in particular: "As I go on I realize that these sights have long since been enumerated in *The Tale of Genji* and *The Pillow Book*, but I make no pretense of trying to avoid saying the same things again."[10]

The Pillow Book thus occupies a position that is more or less symmetrical with the strange position Tsurayuki's the *Tosa nikki* occupies vis-à-vis the tradition of Heian women's memoirs: it has been portrayed by literary historians as the female progenitor of what later developed as a decidedly masculine genre.

If Heian men could write as women, Heian women were expected to write like women, and nothing else. What a Heian woman was, how she wrote, and what she wanted, have historically not been matters that women decided for themselves. Others have always gotten into the act too, as writers and scholars beginning with the author of the *Tosa nikki* to the present day (and the present book) remind us. In some important ways *The Pillow Book* self-consciously tries the boundaries of Heian fictions of the feminine. In doing so, it throws into relief not only a profile of Sei Shōnagon, but also the limits and achievements of the other Heian court women who labored to write themselves as women.

1 ⎝ The Staging of Feminine Self-Disclosure

Less than a hundred years before *The Tale of Genji* appeared, at a moment that has become identified with the origins of memoir literature in Japanese, Ki no Tsurayuki wrote the *Tosa nikki* (the *Tosa Memoir*, ca. 935), a fictionalized diary detailing his journey back to the Heian capital after a stint as governor of the Tosa province. The work might never have engendered the kind of interest it still draws had it not been for its play with feminine orthography, genre, and language. In composing this memoir, Tsurayuki assumed the persona of a woman in the Tosa governor's entourage, a lady-in-waiting or a nurse who self-consciously adapts a traditionally masculine mode of expression—the writing of nonfictional prose in diary format. The traces of Tsurayuki's feminine narrating persona emerge in both his diction and his orthography. The text was written in Japanese prose, using *kana*, the woman's hand. The *Tosa nikki* is a fiction whose essential fictionality resides in its paradoxical claim that it is not a fiction (it is a memoir) and that it is not a man (it is a woman) who wrote it. Its famous opening line sets the stage for what has been termed "a not-entirely-male, not-entirely-female, gender- and genre-bending text":[1] "I hear that diaries [*niki*] are things that men make, but let's see what a woman can do."[2]

So began the genre of memoirs in Japanese that, despite its ambiguous start, court women, rather than textually cross-dressing male courtiers, later came to dominate. Or such is the story literary historians have told for generations about the origins of this genre.[3] As a story, it parallels the one they have also told about the history of gender arrangements in the production of Heian tale literature: male courtiers, donning the woman's hand and writing for a largely female audience, invented *monogatari*, fictional narratives in Japanese, a genre that only came to full flower a century later at the hands of actual female writers.

The scholarly consensus is that the major fictional tales antedating the eleventh century (the *Taketori monogatari*, the *Utsuho monogatari*, the *Ochikubo monogatari*) were all written by men. Women, the primary audience for this literature, did not become its primary producers until the early eleventh century, the time of Murasaki Shikibu and *The Tale of Genji*, by which point they had also begun to produce a rich body of memoirs in Japanese.

What role does the *Tosa nikki* play in the history of our understanding of actual Heian women as writers of Japanese prose? And more important, what did this memoir represent for the female writers themselves? The first question is the more answerable of the two. While the striking gender play of the *Tosa nikki* has never gone unremarked among scholars of Heian literature, historically the trend has been to explain it away in either strictly formalist or extratextual terms. Rhetorical, philological, and biographical issues have been marshaled to account for it as an anomaly that sheds more light on questions about Tsurayuki's life or his psychology as a poet (or as a poet-courtier bereaved by the death of his imperial patron, Emperor Daigo) than on the connection between Heian notions of gender and the development of the arts of fictional narrative and memoir in Japanese. One of the most prolific strains of commentary on the *Tosa nikki* (and one that is indirectly related to gender issues) concerns itself with the interplay of fictionality and autobiography in the memoir. According to these interpretations, Tsurayuki's feminine mask freed him to write about a range of emotional experiences not otherwise easily expressible for male writers, who normally only wrote nonfictional prose in Chinese, not Japanese. In particular, the various kinds of grief generated by partings stand out. The memoir is organized around the poetic itinerary of a journey that occasions poetic responses to encounters, partings, and the ongoing mourning for the governor's daughter who died in Tosa.[4]

More recently, the issue of gender in the *Tosa nikki* has received extended treatment by Lynne Miyake. Inspired by feminist philosopher Judith Butler's model of gender as a performative act, Miyake offers the view that with the *Tosa nikki*, the Heian tradition produces a text that radically exposes gender as a matter of linguistic performance rather than of the sexual identity of the writer.[5] My own understanding of gender and textuality also owes much to Butler. But the question I wish to raise in regard to the preoccupations with fictionality, memoir writing, and gender in the *Tosa nikki* concerns the work in its intertextual dimension. To put it simply, what implications does Tsurayuki's play with gender hold for the tradition of women's memoirs that emerged toward the end of the tenth century?

Of course, the question may well be ultimately unanswerable. We could say that there is nothing really new here. Male writers everywhere have always invented women as characters and crafted women's voices in fictional prose. It has been well argued that such projects have often enough had little to do with real women. With Tsurayuki, one is prompted to ask whether there is not at work an overtly programmatic construction of what women (or women's writing) could or should be. In at least one other text, Tsurayuki implicitly prescribed norms for the "poetry of women" (*onna no uta*). Consider his remarks on Ono no Komachi, the only female poet to make it onto his list of the "Six Immortals of [Japanese] Poetry" (*Rokkasen*) in the Japanese prose preface (*Kanajo*) to the first imperially commissioned *waka* anthology, the *Kokinwakashū* (905): "Ono no Komachi [composes] in the tradition of the ancient Princess Sotōri. Her manner is moving and without strength. One might say it is like a high-born woman who is troubled by illness. The reason for the lack of strength must be that *hers is the poetry of a woman*."[6]

Regardless of whether "lack of strength" (*tsuyokarazu*) and "a moving manner" (*aware no yō*) might be viewed as positive attributes of the art of Japanese poetry in the Heian context, the *Kanajo* contains no comparable normative dicta regarding the poetry of a man (*otoko no uta*). In fact, the sheer overrepresentation of male poets compared to female poets—not only in the list of the "Six Immortals" but, more significant, in the ratio of male-authored to female-authored *waka* in the *Kokinshū* itself—argues for a plurality of exemplars suitable for the male poet. Implicitly, the *Kokinshū*, which Tsurayuki helped to compile, demonstrates that the range of styles and voices available to the male poet was wider than those recommended for women and was not marked in terms of gender. The short treatment female poets receive in both the *Kanajo* and the anthology itself reinforces the argument that the *Kokinshū* represents a conscious attempt to appropriate *waka* as a legitimate art form by underplaying its association with female poets, while showcasing the virtuosity and variety of Japanese poetry by men.[7]

So if, as some have argued, Tsurayuki's preface to the *Kokinshū* embodies an attempt to set standards of literary taste and style in *waka* while simultaneously placing limits on women's participation in the genre, might it not be that his *Tosa nikki* registers an attempt to do the same for women and Japanese prose? Gender-ambiguous though it may be, the *Tosa nikki* does offer a model for prose in the "woman's hand" for both male and female writers. Thus, Richard Bowring suggests that this memoir represents Tsurayuki's failed attempt to reappropriate prose in Japanese for men. Similarly, Richard Okada suggests that the *Tosa nikki* attempts a "legitimization of *hiragana* over *kambun* diaries." In effect, the *Tosa nikki* attempts to do for prose in Japanese what the *Kokinshū* did for native poetry—instate it as a serious literary medium by rescuing it, not from "the woman's hand," but from languishing in the hands of real women. Bowring's view in particular overstates the gender polarizations that characterize the current understanding of literary history in the early tenth century. In his words, the production of prose in Japanese before and during Tsurayuki's time was so "marked as 'female' and 'private'" that men were "condemned to work in a foreign classical medium."[8] In fact, the situation seems to have been not quite so dire. As already noted, the scholarly consensus has been that men wrote the early fictional Japanese prose narratives, albeit surreptitiously, with the results not considered fit reading for anything other than a female or juvenile audience; the suitability of the tales to women and children had less to do with artistic merit than with the fact that they were overtly fictional and therefore ethically suspect, by Confucian—and to some extent by Buddhist—standards.

More pertinent to my question is the metafiction the *Tosa nikki* relates about a "feminine" transgression of gender and genre boundaries: a "woman" adapts a traditionally male-dominated genre (nonfictional prose) in order to write a text that pretends to be literary and emotional reportage (while calling attention, stylistically, to its play with gender categories). I agree with Miyake that regardless of how it may have been originally intended, the *Tosa nikki* embodies the idea that gender is a fictional construct, a matter of textuality rather than of the physiology of a writer. But I would further argue that the notion of "woman" as a rhetorical construction becomes one of the central themes of Heian prose literature in Japanese partly because of its embodiment in the *Tosa nikki*. I would also venture that this subtext about the fictionality of femininity (and the femininity of fictional literature) had special significance for subsequent female writers, particularly memoirists.

As though in compensation for the equivocal beginnings voiced in the *Tosa nikki*, issues of veracity, as well as anxieties about an actual woman engaging in a mode of writing that promises the reader intimate glimpses of her life and thoughts, surface again and again in women's memoirs of the mid-Heian period. While it may have been liberating for a male courtier like Tsurayuki to use the woman's hand to express his emotions in his native language, the pose of femininity must have been at times less than cathartic for actual female memoirists. Unlike her male contemporaries, the female writer was in very real ways stuck with the necessity of playing the woman's role and writing like a woman— however that may have been conceived. If we take the dictum of the *Kanajo* as a point of departure, women's writing—at least in the form of "women's poetry" (*onna no uta*)—is formulated negatively and tautologically, as a lack of strength and a nod at what generates the lack, the writer's identity as a woman. And there is little or no recognition of individual differences among women writers. Ono no Komachi writes "in the tradition of Princess Sotōri" not simply because both write in a manner that "lacks strength," but rather because both are women and therefore produce women's poems.

Social and literary practice in the mid-Heian period bears out this theme of negativity. A Heian lady could not engage in a reverse version of the textual cross-dressing Tsurayuki pioneered for his fellow male courtiers. In most cases, she could not take up the "man's hand" and write herself in Chinese prose, either because she lacked education in Chinese or because she confronted social taboos that strongly discouraged displays of education in Chinese by women. Furthermore, even simple allusion to knowledge of the Chinese classics was not so easily excused in a female writer, despite the fact that possession of such knowledge might still be something devoutly to be wished for, as long as one managed to wear it lightly and display it only to the right person. Murasaki Shikibu's censure of Sei Shōnagon's flaunting of her allegedly superficial knowledge of Chinese is notorious. So are the mock-humble confidences Murasaki also divulged regarding her own particular gift for Chinese. Readers of her memoir will recall that she outdid her brother at his lessons, much to her father's dismay, and was subsequently "secretly" taken on by Fujiwara Michinaga to tutor his own daughter Empress Shōshi in the poetry of Po Chü-i.[9]

Whether one sees this enforced fidelity to her native script and tongue as a blessing in disguise (had their male colleagues been similarly confined perhaps it would have been their writings that we now regard as the masterpieces of the era), the Heian lady inherited a stigmatized, limited relationship to the range of literary expression available in her day. Outside of *waka*—the only fully legitimate form of literature written in the woman's hand (though, significantly, by both men and women)—women expressed themselves in genres that were not recognized as worthy of serious readers, and this was in large part because these genres bore the double burden of association with the fictional and with a readership that was almost exclusively female.

In representing the feminine as a clever fiction (and by the same token identifying fiction with a female—or cross-dressing male—attempting to write nonfiction), the *Tosa nikki* helped set the stage for one of the central problems facing female memoirists. Artful and ludic gaps there may well be between the memoirist and her memoir, but they are not so easily or so lightly flaunted in a real woman's memoir. For female memoirists, the problem posed by memoirs was not simply that the memoir must legitimize itself by presenting a record of the real, as opposed to the lies (*itsuwari*) and empty words (*soragoto*) of fiction. Because of the class and gender conventions imposed on her (or embraced by her) as an aristocratic woman, the female memoirist was equally compelled to refrain from being too real, from showing too much of herself. A woman's memoir was capable of being all too intimately identified with the writer as woman: her hand, her poetry, her heart or mind (*kokoro*), as well as her social position (*mi*), and by implication, her body (*mi*), however carefully draped with layer upon layer of silk.

The Mid-Heian Eroticization of Women's Writing

"Genji was more secretive with the ladies' manuscripts and especially Princess Asagao's."[10]

The Heian female memoirists were writers who, as upper-class women, not only inhabited but also helped, through their writings, to construct and maintain a discursive world obsessed with concealment and with the arts of minimal revelation, with the perils and possibilities (erotic, political, and literary) of overturned screens and gaps in hedges, and with a society that delighted in multiple layers of clothing and in the length and fullness of the nubile woman's abundant, unbound hair. For the most part, "the highborn women of the day" as Hayashida Takakazu reminds us, "hated being looked at directly in the face ... particularly in her meetings with members of the opposite sex."[11] More so than for her male counterparts, the power a woman wielded in her exchanges with men of her own class or of a higher class often depended on her skill in the exacting arts of self-presentation and self-fictionalization. It was in her interest, and in the interests of her family, to control the conditions under which she would be seen by others. Sur-

rounded at all times by watchful relatives or by a coterie of female attendants trained to ensure that she be seen only under controlled circumstances, the aristocratic woman was assiduously educated in a variety of visual, literary, and musical arts that would allow her to do just
that.

The mentions of women's memoirs in mid-Heian tales idealize these
texts as a peculiarly intimate form of writing. The *Utsuho monogatari*
(the *Tale of the Hollow Tree*, late tenth century) features a set of three
chapters entitled "The Opening of the Storehouse" (*Kurabiraki*), which
concern the discovery of a forgotten library of Chinese books and family papers locked within a magically sealed storehouse by the hero
Nakatada's grandfather Kiyohara Toshikage. The second of these chapters includes a series of notable scenes at the imperial palace in which
the emperor commands Nakatada to read out loud for three consecutive
days and nights from the hoard of poetry collections and family memoirs he has unearthed in the old storehouse on the site of Toshikage's
mansion.[12] The first day and night are completely taken up with readings from Toshikage's magnificent anthology of poems in Chinese.
These readings are continued on the second day and into the second
night, until the emperor asks Nakatada to read from the Japanese poetry collection of Toshikage's father, "[who] had," in the opinion of the
emperor, "the greater literary talent" of the two (*NKBT* 11: 360). On
the third and final night, they at last open the box that contains four
booklets or notebooks (*sōshi*), each written in a different style. From
these four, the emperor chooses first a "lovely" one, in the "usual feminine hand" (*rei no onna no te*), written by the hero's grandmother. Of
this text, the narrator comments: "Things that had happened were simply recorded, as in a *monogatari*, along with the poems of those times.
There were amusing parts here and there, and sad ones," and at length
the emperor, who remembers the woman's reputation as a talented poet
and calligrapher, urges Nakatada to show the booklet to the First Princess, who is Nakatada's wife, and the emperor's daughter (*NKBT* 11:
368–70).

The performance closes with Nakatada reading passages from another collection by Toshikage, this last a marvelous *nikki* recording the
latter's travels from the Heian capital to Tsukushi and on to the T'ang
capital in China. Plans are made for further readings from this rare account at a later date, after Nakatada has had time to recover his voice.
But the grandmother's booklet is laid aside, to be passed on to the First
Princess, perhaps, but not to the readers of the *Utsuho monogatari*. It is

a marginal text, the sort of thing a princess might read for her edification (or as a model for her own efforts in the memoir genre), but nothing to stir more than a passing interest among the imperial audience within the tale or, presumably, the intended readers of the tale itself. It is interesting to note, however, that Nakatada's reading of his grandmother's text is interrupted by the complaints of the empress, who is in attendance on the third night, though separated from the men by bamboo blinds. Aware of her presence, the emperor signals to Nakatada that he should lower his voice. Though she tries to catch Nakatada's words, the empress is thus prevented from overhearing the reading, a state of affairs which she (and I am inclined to join her in these sentiments) "deeply resents" (*imijiu nikumi tamau*) (*NKBT* 11: 369).

Memoirs written by both men and women figure in these scenes as texts whose dissemination men control. The situation resembles what it conventionally was for decisions about the exchange of upper-class daughters as brides and concubines between fathers and potential sons-in-law. Women themselves have little or no say about who sees them (or their texts), while men circulate freely, to see and to be seen, and even their *kana* writings are capable of compelling public attention. These images, though drawn from the pages of an overtly fictional tale, corroborate the scant references to women's *nikki* as a recognizable genre in other documents and nonfictional writings from the Heian period. Granted, there are exceptions. References to the *Kagerō nikki* appear in other works of the Heian period (most notably in *Ōkagami*), beginning relatively soon after its probable completion in the late tenth century.[13] But the *Kagerō nikki* is unusual in that respect, its relative visibility as a text probably having much to do with the political prominence of the memoirist's husband, Fujiwara Kaneie. Sei Shōnagon's writings also seem to have enjoyed something of a circulation, at least among other female writers at the time, though whether in anything like the form now known as *The Pillow Book*, it is impossible to say. Murasaki Shikibu, in her own memoir, does not refer to *The Pillow Book* as such, only to its author's deplorable tendency to litter her writings (*fumi*) with Chinese characters (*mana*, as opposed to Japanese *kana*, the syllabary script marked as both native and feminine), a remark that may only indicate that she had seen samples of letters that Sei Shōnagon wrote to others. Murasaki makes similar nonspecific references to the writings (*fumi*) of Izumi Shikibu and those of Akazome Emon, among other female writers.[14]

Generally speaking, contemporary references to actual women's *nikki* are rare, with little mention of other specific *nikki* or memoirists to be found until the time of the great poet and scholar Fujiwara Teika (1162–1241), whose holograph of the *Sarashina nikki* provides the basis for all modern annotated editions of that work.[15] It is indicative of the relative invisibility of the memoir as a genre during the Heian period that *Mumyōzōshi* (the *Nameless Book*, ca. 1196–1202), a fictional dialogue on women and women's writings, devotes detailed attention to the categories of *monogatari* and poetry collections (*shū*) written or compiled by women, but says nothing about *nikki*, though one of its speakers singles out *The Pillow Book* for comment.[16] It appears that, with a few exceptions, women's memoirs, unlike their tales, were less available as models to the writers themselves. Thus, the relation of *nikki* to other *nikki* appears less relevant than the relation of *nikki* to *waka* and tale literature when it comes to assessing the sort of intertextual dialogue Heian women's memoirs carry on with other works of the time.

The primacy given to *kana nikki* written by men in the passage from the *Utsuho monogatari* is also striking. Vernacular memoirs written by men steal the show, not only in the *Utsuho* scenes just described, but also in the "Picture Contest" (*Eawase*) chapter of *The Tale of Genji*. It is Genji's "illustrated memoir" (*e nikki*), composed during the anxious months of his exile at Suma (a text never before revealed to *her*, the Murasaki lady muses with some pique), that wins the day for Akikonomu's faction in the climactic scene of that chapter's elaborate competition.[17] Contrast the relatively public aesthetic triumphs won by men's *kana* memoirs with the intensely intimate and private impact produced by female memoirists in Heian fiction. Fictional female characters who compile full-fledged memoirs or who leave behind fragments jotted down "as though practicing the hand" (*tenarai no yō ni*) under circumstances of personal deprivation or anxiety appear here and there in eleventh-century tales. However, both the fictional female memoirists and the narrators who describe them characteristically treat these writings with a good deal more discretion (or censorship) than either Toshikage's or Genji's memoirs receive.

In mid-Heian tales, women's memoirs are frequently referred to as *katami*, keepsakes or relics. The word embeds the idea of a form (*kata*) that provides something to look at (*mi*). A *katami* is a means of remembering a dead or otherwise absent person. Usually such texts emerge only after the memoirist herself has died or disappeared, at least from her lover's view. The *Genji* heroine Ukifune, in her initial nunlike existence at Ono, where everyone who used to know her has given her up for dead, is much given to "writing practice" (*tenarai*) as she becomes, during her new life in the final two chapters of the tale, the most prolific poet of all the *Genji* women.[18] Another memorable, though characteristically secretive, fictional memoirist is Asukai no Onnagimi, the fleeting early love of the hero of the *Sagoromo monogatari*, who leaves behind an illustrated memoir as a memento (*katami*) of herself—one that the hero discovers and reads long after her suicide.[19] Upon reading it, he enters a season of deep, sorrowing nostalgia, because the memoir ("these traces from the past") revives the memory of its dead writer with an intensity that recalls all too clearly everything that has passed, just as memoirs that figure in fictional tales conventionally do (*NKBT* 79: 459). The Murasaki lady also sketches and writes about her own circumstances "as if writing a memoir" (*nikki no yō ni kakitamaeri*) during Genji's exile (*NKBZ* 13: 250–51; S, 264), though no mention is ever made of her efforts in the same genre when his illustrated memoir comes to light and triumphs in "The Picture Contest." Yet it is just such written fragments as these—a bundle of kept letters Murasaki sent to Genji at Suma during the same anxious season in their marriage—that resurface hauntingly after her death in "The Wizard" (*Maboroshi*), the final chapter in the narrative of Genji's life (*NKBZ* 15: 532–34; S, 733–34). Following his tearful rereading of them, he consigns the letters to flames, like Murasaki's body itself. In the fictional worlds of Heian tales, a heroine's writing a memoir or leaving behind autobiographical fragments is often associated with her desire for some means of controlling, if not the uncontrollable course of her own destiny, then at least the *terms* by which her fate and her person will be remembered by others. The "others" envisaged as her readership comprise a very small and select circle of female intimates, patrons, and male lovers. The woman's memoir, like the woman's body, is deployed in a manner calculated both to entice readerly desire and to resist disclosure.

Feminine Narration: Looking, Telling, and Showing

The following anecdote appears in a little-noted passage of the *Murasaki Shikibu nikki* (the *Memoir of Murasaki Shikibu*, first decade, eleventh century). It seems at first glance an unproblematic cautionary against an inappropriate or too-intense preoccupation with the things of the past:

"I remember," said Chikuzen no Myōbu, "when the Empress Dowager was alive there were so many imperial visits to the mansion. Ah, such times we had!" and she broke into reminiscences. Fearing this was hardly a propitious way to behave in the circumstances, the others avoided making any response and removed themselves to the other side of the dais. She did look as though, given the slightest encouragement, she would have burst into tears.[20]

Chikuzen no Myōbu's transgression involves a reference to the dead that is highly inauspicious under the circumstances (an imperial visit with a newborn prince). But what Murasaki's anecdote highlights is the subtle ostracism the woman incurs. Her fellow ladies-in-waiting avoid verbal response and simply "remove themselves to the other side of the dais." Here, as in several other passages of the memoir, the narrating voice touches on the peculiar unpleasantnesses that life as a lady-in-waiting at court entailed, among them the frequent and vexing exposure to the eyes of others, and, more specifically, the possibility of being caught unaware in a moment of unselfconscious self-display. If there is something unseemly to the Heian lady about being seen, there is something positively disturbing, even inauspicious, about women who artlessly engage in self-display.

An implicit analogy between Chikuzen no Myōbu's behavior and that of the memoirist-as-narrator hovers just beneath the surface. It is a risky business to leave behind or to set into circulation a memoir. The desire to be read (not as a *waka* poet or a composer of overtly fictional tales but as memoirist) carries with it a cachet of impropriety, because it borders upon expressing the more active desire to show oneself, to make oneself intimately known and remembered. At some level, the Heian female memoirist confronts not only the possibility that her text will fall into the wrong hands, that it will be subjected to the gaze of the wrong reader, but also that even in proper hands she will be seen as violating the boundaries of the private world and the mask of passivity that ordinarily circumscribes her.

These themes are most insistently voiced at the edges of the memoir, in the prefaces, epilogues, and narratorial asides that frame and occasionally punctuate Heian memoirs, passages in which a narrating voice stands back from the matter of the narrative to comment on the motives or process of composition. Whether we read them as the discourse of an author or as the interpolations of a later reader, we are struck less by the individual circumstances that may have occasioned them than by the apparent need to rehearse them. These themes point, in short, to the anxieties associated with the dissemination of women's memoirs. To dismiss them as conventional expressions of writerly humility (or a humility foisted upon the text by another hand such as a later commentator or owner of the memoir, a relative of the memoirist, or a scholar-redactor) does little to clarify the underlying assumptions that gave rise to the convention in the first place. What is at issue here is not whether the memoirist was truly modest or only apparently so. Rather, these themes suggest how the desire to be read conflicts with the idea that the well-bred woman should shun the gaze of others—not only the gazes directed at her body, but also the gazes that would light upon her text.[21]

At the same time it seems necessary to emphasize that the textual dynamics of voyeurism in Heian women's memoirs need not be posited simply in terms of the classic paradigm of active male reader as voyeur versus female writer or text as passive, erotic spectacle. As the *Utsuho* passage summarized above suggests, the appeal of women's prose in Japanese to female readers is very strongly marked in Heian literature. The empress would like nothing more than to get her hands on Nakata-da's grandmother's memoir. As memoirist, Murasaki Shikibu expends a good deal of ink naming and critiquing the writings of female members of her own and competing salons. And the fictional women of mid-Heian tales are forever losing themselves in reading and copying out other fictional women's tales, much to the exasperation of fictional men like the middle-aged Genji of "The Fireflies" (*Hotaru*) or the officious guards' officer of "The Broom Tree" (*Hahakigi*) chapter.

For the actual, historical Heian reader, regardless of his or her gender, it seems possible that the appeal of certain women's memoirs would have been enhanced by the implicit promise of a peculiarly direct mode of readerly voyeurism, since these texts conventionally proffered glimpses of the self-representations of real women of good breeding. Whether we choose to read them as primarily first- or third-person texts, the discourse of women's memoirs, particularly those that foreground a feminine narrator and the image of a female protagonist, intensifies interest in the "to-be-looked-at-ness" of the woman who is the central figure. It does this by eliminating what is arguably one of the distinguishing structural features of fictional tales: the mediating figure of the male character as voyeur.[22] And if we read the Heian woman's memoir as it has traditionally been read, that is, as the personally authored account of an historical woman, the double nature of its narrator-heroine emerges in proportion to the degree to which she overtly commemorates herself. She becomes a figure constituted as both the memoirist/narrator—the one who sees and reveals herself—and as the heroine in the story, the woman who is seen and revealed. Such memoirs implicitly replace the reticence of the passive, fictional *monogatari* heroine with the dramatized self-articulation of a "real" woman (the implied author of the memoir) and her positive desire not merely to be seen, but to present herself.

Intensely aware of her own vulnerability to the potentially censorious gaze of the other, such a memoirist attempts to manipulate the situation to her own advantage. The narration of the woman's memoir is mediated by feminine figures who—both as narrators and as fictionalized characters within the narrative—look at others and show themselves in the act of looking, who practice to one degree or another a conscious manipulation of the readerly gaze toward themselves, and who, more boldly, look about them to construct and to present a world (including the men in that world) in their recorded acts of looking and telling.

In literary studies, no less than in literature and in life, the issue of who looks at whom is intimately linked to questions of desire and power. The chapters that follow attempt to complicate an ongoing critical discussion of voyeurism in Heian literature that has so far been articulated primarily within the context of *The Tale of Genji*, and more specifically, within voyeuristic scenes in which the play of power and desire is accounted for in terms of the gaze of a male character as voyeur. The situation in the critical literature resembles what feminist film critic Judith Mayne has noted in reference to debates on the mechanism of the gaze in contemporary cinema studies: "When we imagine a 'woman' and a 'keyhole,' it is usually a woman on the *other* side of the keyhole."[23] The paradigmatic scenario of Heian literary voyeurism remains the *kaimami* scene, in which a man "steals a glimpse" (*nozokimi*) of an unsuspecting woman (or of a group or pair of women), classically by looking through the interstices (*kaima*) of a hedge or fence. Though the architectural details differ (peepholes in fences replacing keyholes in doors), the trajectory of the critic's gaze shows a remarkable continuity across cultures and genres. Critical interest in both English-language and Japanese *kokubungaku* scholarship on classical *monogatari* typically focuses on the way the *kaimami* topos solicits and inscribes masculine desire.

This focus creates problems for the way we have understood Heian women—not only as figures in texts, but, more pertinently, as writers. Richard Bowring's discussion of the "grammar of sexual relations" in Heian women's literature illustrates one consequence of this understanding of the mechanisms of voyeurism in Heian women's writings: a tendency to conflate the female figure in the *kaimami* scene with the authoress(es) on the one hand and the voyeuristic male character with a masculine reader-critic on the other. A critical blindness to the woman on "this side" of the keyhole—the overlooking of her triple position as writer, reader, and textual figure—is apparent in Bowring's description of Heian women's writing as a tradition in which the power of the male gaze both instigates female writing and then appropriates it as its primary reader: "In the frustration of waiting [for the male], she first begins to read and then writes herself. And as she exists to generate male interest, she can have no power of her own until she is in turn 'read.' Indoors, forever waiting, she can become a force only when seen and opened, for without the male reader the female text is barren."[24]

This polarized view of the dynamics of (female) authorship and (male) readership can be challenged on at least two fundamental points, both of which concern the tendency to conceptualize Heian women's writing primarily in terms of erotic scenarios of courtly love in which the "literary persona of the female is defined in terms of waiting, pining for the male, existing as the object of desire whose thoughts are constantly on the next visit."[25] Such descriptions blur distinctions between female writers and the feminine poses they manipulate within the fictions they themselves author. What is erased from view is the significance of female writing as a means of constructing not only images of the feminine but also a fictionalized masculine gaze (and masculine desire). How do we account critically for the fact that the gaze of the hero in the *kaimami* scene frequently depends on the mediation of feminine narrators and female authors? Who is looking at whom in these scenes? Once we recognize that the masculine perspective in the *kaimami* scene may itself be framed by the ironic perspective of a feminine narrator whose discourse is directed toward a primary audience of female readers, how do we assimilate these more complicated gender arrangements into our conceptualization of the circuitry of desire in Heian women's prose?[26]

Another problem that has particular relevance for the student of Heian women's memoirs concerns the question of the various kinds of "female texts" and their respective audiences. In general, a critical focus on themes of courtly love and its intricate, gender-sensitive codes of etiquette has led to a scanting of texts that do not privilege these themes. This situation exacerbates the tendency by scholars to overlook formal differences among different genres that Heian women employed. Bowring, for example, does not differentiate among the various genres of women's writing in part because his real interest is not women's writing per se, but rather the "grammar of sexual relations" he finds embedded within many of these works. "One can in fact extract from these works a set of rules that governs the literary expression of sexual relations, a sexual grammar that remains *remarkably constant throughout the period*, and that lies at the heart of the *Genji* and many of its presuppositions."[27] It is clear from this quote that more than just *The Tale of Genji* is at issue for Bowring; his description aspires to a validity for texts "throughout the period." In fact, as I have tried to suggest, *monogatari* frequently contextualize both women and women's writings (particularly *nikki*) in ways that eroticize them. On this level, I find Bowring's descriptions compelling. What is questionable about his argument is its overgeneral nature, especially the implication that a simple active male/passive female model of eroticism can account for what are, in fact, far more complex configurations of erotic and literary exchange, especially in works other than *Genji*. I agree with the implications of Bowring's remarks—that *The Tale of Genji* emphasizes heroines who represent a passive relation to the gaze and to desire. However, I think he errs in extrapolating from *Genji* to works in other genres and also in underplaying the extent to which *Genji* subverts its own norms with heroines like Tamakazura, Oigimi, and Ukifune.

In the case of *monogatari* written by women, the idea of a male reader as *primary* addressee has long been understood as problematic. Given what we can see of tale readership from the tales themselves, the gender arrangements associated with the scene of reading are far more complexly constructed than the simple scenario of male reader/addressee and a self-exegetical female scribe who waits and finally writes herself for him. The confessions of the guards' officer in "The Broom Tree" chapter of *Genji* provide a particularly rich example. The officer remembers being included as a child in the immediate circle of women and children who listened and responded empathetically to the old tales. Now, as a man, the guards' officer stands outside that circle both literally and figuratively. The adult male in Heian fiction is typically an eavesdropper on the scene of *monogatari* reading. Whatever his relationship to the tales in private, in public he usually admits only to an outsider's curiosity and skepticism about the fictions that so move the women of the household. Or he plays the role of arbiter and patron. Genji's remarks to his wife Murasaki regarding the selection of appropriate tales for the Akashi princess hint at this latter role and suggest the subtle ways in which authoritative (and frequently male) "readers" peripheral to the circle of female taletellers influence female authors and readers.[28] Presumably not all these patrons (and potential censors) were male, but they are figured as male in *The Tale of Genji* and the *Murasaki Shikibu nikki*.[29]

What about the gender arrangements among the shadowy readership of women's memoirs? Although distinctions between women's *nikki* and *monogatari* in most cases seem to have been rather vague, there is reason to believe that historically there were differences in the degree of dissemination and the kind of readership accorded many of the *kana* texts now designated *nikki* (memoir), *sōshi* (notebook or booklet), and *shū* (collection or anthology). Even if, as I have tried to suggest in my reading of the mentions of *nikki* in *Utsuho*, *Genji*, and *Sagoromo*, women's memoirs traditionally received a narrower circulation than fictional tales or memoirs by men, they almost certainly were not limited to a solely female audience. However, as the proprietary roles of the emperor and Nakatada in *Utsuho* and of Genji in the *Genji monogatari* imply, women's memoirs are portrayed as circulating in a manner similar to the way marriageable daughters circulate between fathers and sons-in-law: like precious objects of exchange whose value hinges in part on their bodies' (and their texts') remaining unseen (unread) by others. Although the historical audience of *monogatari* and *nikki* was primarily female, it is likely that these genres required, for their own survival, approval from an audience of fathers and other authoritative guardians anxious to mold their daughters into suitable marriage candidates. In short, the social and political contexts in which women's tales and memoirs were written and read suggest a wider, more complexly mediated network of implied readers of both genders than can be accounted for by the *kaimami* topos as it has been traditionally understood in the critical literature.

It is easy to see how a critical overattention to the gazes of characters within fictional scenarios concerned with courtly love could result in blindness to the feminine gaze. If one begins with a special interest in the *kaimami* topos, it will readily appear that there are many male, but few female, characters who engage in desirous acts of looking in Heian court literature. The interest in men who look encourages the tendency to assume there is a privileging of a masculine gaze (and masculine desire) in Heian women's writings. What about the feminine figures who "look" and "tell"? What about the narrators whose discourse (and thus perspective) mediates even the most conventional *kaimami* scenes—not only the image of the desired, passive heroine in the fiction, but also the gaze of the amorous male who looks at her or sneaks a peek at her text? A further complication to the scene of looking in Heian women's prose, as yet little explored in the critical literature, is that the narrating voice itself is often linguistically marked as feminine. To borrow another observation from feminist film criticism, "the question is not only who or what is on either side of the keyhole, but also what lies between them, what constitutes the threshold that makes representation possible."[30]

The memoir tradition is capable of accommodating mediations that become, as I have already argued, a bit less complex, more direct, and more intensely focused on the experience of a woman who is at once the focus of readerly voyeurism, and, at the level of narration, the mediator of it, a figure who acts as the very medium through which woman is presented as both the viewed object and the self-disclosing subject. In addition, a number of the memoirs currently considered the most important representatives of the genre construct configurations of gender and desire that in fact challenge the norm of an active male subject and a passive female object by minimizing the gaze of the male character. The *Kagerō nikki*, for example, marginalizes its heroine's husband by presenting him from a critical, always externalized perspective. In *The Pillow Book*, the *Sarashina nikki*, and the *Sanuki no suke nikki*, significant male characters are represented as absent objects of feminine desire or reminiscence.

Finally, if we understand the scenes of looking as narratives about desire, what do we make of the scenes of looking not encompassed by the *kaimami* topos? What of the *Kagerō* heroine's intense scrutiny of her husband's handwriting, the *Sarashina* heroine's guilty, autoerotic absorption in reading about heroines from *The Tale of Genji*, the *Sanuki* narrator's fantasies about the ideal (female) reader for her memoir, or Sei Shōnagon's intricate orchestration of *kaimami* scenes within *kaimami* scenes? In short, the diverse topoi of looking in women's memoirs embody sites and stories that call attention to a chain of mediations among female authors, feminine narrators, other feminine figures within the text, and readers, both historical and implied, male and female. Heian women's memoirs exemplify a tradition in which "women are situated on both sides of the keyhole." Their position as both authors and readers of their own texts challenges us to look more carefully at the interplay of gendered voices and eroticized perspectives in the various scenes of "looking" in Heian women's prose.

2 ☞ The Engendering of the Heroine in the *Kagerō nikki*

As one of the earliest—perhaps the earliest—self-designated *nikki* by a female writer, the *Kagerō nikki* features a remarkably tortured textual history as well as an even more formidable thematic afterlife, traces of which continue to resurface in the I-novels and fiction of twentieth-century Japan.[1] The vigor of the memoirist's posthumous reputation derives largely from her vivid portrait of herself as a woman who spent a disproportionate amount of her life waiting for her man (and writing about waiting). The *matsu onna* (the woman who waits) was already a stock figure in Heian *waka* in the mid-tenth century, and as one of the most potent fictions about feminine behavior and destiny, this figure continued to linger in the tradition long after the Heian period ended. Likewise the shadows of prior readings and rewritings of the *Kagerō nikki* and its apparently frustrated central figure are long, thick, and surprisingly perdurable. It would be difficult if not impossible to disentangle the *Kagerō* memoirist/heroine from them, and this chapter will not attempt it. I will begin instead by examining one of the earliest and a few of the latest of these rereadings, moving after that to a reading of the *Kagerō nikki* that is as self-consciously intertextual as I have been able to make it. The goal of this chapter is to explore how and where the *Kagerō nikki* raises and pursues questions about the connections between writing a memoir and writing as a woman.

At the outset of her account of the notorious "Judgments of a Rainy Night," the narrator of "The Broom Tree" (*Hahakigi*) chapter of *The Tale of Genji* remarks provocatively that the evening had turned up "many things that will be quite unpleasant to hear" (*ito kikinuki koto ō kari*).[2] Addressed to the implied readers of *The Tale of Genji,* her remark hints at her own reactions to the talk of that legendary evening as well as the probable responses of her audience. Invoking the lure of the unlovely, the scandalous, she invites her readers' interest, assured in the knowledge that court society being what it is, they will be especially eager for their eavesdropping narrator's gossip if it should concern things "unpleasant to hear."

It is an idle evening during the rainy season in the fifth month, and the court is in retreat.[3] A conversation takes place among four young men: Genji and his friend and brother-in-law Tō no Chūjō and two men of lesser rank and prospects, a guards' officer and an official in the ministry of rites. Their talk concerns women, or more precisely, erotic adventures among women of different social classes, speculations about how best to manage love affairs with various types of women, and theories about the personality and talents that might qualify a woman as an ideal wife. The passage quoted below, made in the course of that (in)famous conversation, concerns a particular type of troublemaking female—those who, unable to repress their sexual jealousy, abandon romance or marriage and run off to become nuns. The lines are part of an unusually long speech delivered by the guards' officer. Seven years Genji's senior, the officer is the most garrulous and amusing of the four speakers and also perhaps the most offensive. Certainly his stories constitute some of the more scandalous of the "many unpleasant things" the narrator reports from that evening:

When I was a boy, I used to listen to the women reading *monogatari*, and I even shed tears with them, thinking it was all so moving and sad, so full of deep feeling. But now I think it really rather rash and affected [*ito karugarushiku*]. Suppose the woman has a man of deep sensibilities, even though there may have been some painful incidents between them—to run off and hide as though she knew nothing of his feelings [*kokoro*], throwing him into a turmoil, and all for the sake of trying to test his heart [*kokoro o min to suru*], it is really such a shame, and something that will stay with her for the rest of her life. She is praised by her women for her "depth of spirit," and with her sensitivities thus heightened, before long she ends up a nun. While she is in the process of carrying out her resolves, she seems very pure of heart indeed, and it never occurs to her that she might look back again longingly on the world she is renouncing. Acquaintances come to visit her and exclaim, "How sad that your feelings have brought you to this." Or else when the man, who has not given up his feelings for her, is saddened by the news he hears and weeps, her servants and her older attendants tell her, "Your husband has been deeply affected by the sorrow of all this. How regrettable that it turned out thus." She gropes at the tresses she cut away from her own brow herself, and, discouraged and desolate, finds herself on the verge of tears. Though she tries to hide them, when once her tears begin to well up, time and again she finds she is unable to bear it, so many are the regrets she has; and the Buddha is sure to see that she is impure of heart. More so than when she was immured in the dirt of this world, I suspect that in her nun's guise, she is drifting down a path even more sinful than ours. The unending fate that binds a man and a woman is deep. Even if the man comes after her and takes her back before she makes her final vows, do you suppose that there will not be times when they remember and resent the incident? For better or for worse, she stays wedded to her man, and it is because she overlooks the bad times and the untoward incidents that the bonds between them become deep and tender; as for the pair that does otherwise—both the woman and the man will harbor resentment in their hearts.   (*NKBZ* 12: 142–43)

The reader should bear in mind the context of these remarks, the way they are mediated by the multiple ironies of the storytelling situation. A still-youngish man comments on tales about women who are unhappy with their husbands, tales he remembers hearing women repeat and weep over when he was only a boy. He had wept with them at the time, but the version he tells now, although based on the (literary) memories of childhood, contains cynical judgments he has formed only after becoming himself (at least in his own eyes) a man of the world, with his own opinions about what might constitute correct or desirable female behavior. This is a lecture about the intersections between tales and life, then; explicitly framed and commented on by the remarks of one of the elusive, ostensibly female *Genji* narrators, it is further qualified by the responses of the man's fictional listeners. Tō no Chūjō attends the officer's expositions with something approaching rapt credulity (*Chūjō imijiku shinjite*) (*NKBZ* 12: 147). Meanwhile, Genji sleeps (or feigns sleep) through most of it. Finally, the guards' officer goes on to undermine the reliability of his own judgments by capping his lecture with anecdotes from his personal experiences. (Genji wakes up for these, or is awoken by the officer, who sidles closer to him at this point.) His reminiscences reveal him to have been quite the fool in his own dealings with female jealousy and no stranger himself to the self-dramatizing displays of piety for which he berates the jealous woman in the old story. Once, in the middle of a particularly upsetting altercation with a jealous woman of his acquaintance, the lady had seized and bitten his finger. The guards' officer recalls responding (and his apparent lack of self-irony at this point borders on the incredible) by histrionically imagining he will be seen (scarred as he is) as having no other choice but to leave the world and enter holy orders (*NKBZ* 12: 150).

But to bite her lover's finger? Now, here is something unpleasant to hear about. What sort of a woman might she be, and what could have prompted so unorthodox a response? (Perhaps he was shaking it at her pedantically? But these finer details are left to the reader's imagination.) The point is that a woman's emotions—particularly hostile ones—must be repressed, and there is something freakish about women who do not repress them. What happens when these emotions are ignored or left to go underground? The question is not explicitly addressed by the guards' officer, but the end of his anecdote about the jealous woman has its own tale to tell. Without really intending to part with her, he neglects her for a time, sends no messages, and occupies himself with visits to other women, only to discover that the one who bit his finger has continued to await his return, preparing for him on the chance that he might call every night during the long months of his silence. His confidence in her restored, he begins sending messages again and finds her replies judiciously worded, their writer at pains to avoid saying anything that might cause offense. And yet she remains foolishly proud. She continues to demand that he settle down. He decides to press the lesson further. Never admitting that he will change his ways as she wishes, he makes a show of his own strength. In the midst of this "tug of war" (*tsunabikite*, literally, "rope pulling"), the woman, he hears, becomes very sad and finally dies—from what cause he need neither ask about nor tell. The reader will easily solve it on her own (*NKBZ* 12: 150–52). The finger-biting woman thus joins, by her death, the considerable ranks of fictional Heian females who pine to death when their lovers' passions wane.

A Record of Many Unpleasant Things

Let us return momentarily to the passage quoted above and to the old story the guards' officer's remarks outline. It has been suggested that these remarks, particularly the evocation of the woman's ignominious return to her unhappy marriage at her husband's insistence, might well have recalled for Heian readers the events of the second volume of the *Kagerō nikki* (after 974)[4] and the image of its author-heroine, who, after weathering more than sixteen years of competition with her husband's multiple wives and mistresses, rushed off in the summer of Tenroku 2 (971) to Hannyaji, a temple at Narutaki in the hills west of the Heian capital.[5] Though initially followed there by her irate husband, she manages to send him back to the capital without her and ends up staying on for about a month, on the verge, it seems, of taking Buddhist vows and becoming a nun. With her are her only son (Fujiwara Michi-tsuna, 955–1020) and three female attendants, and she is visited by, among others, an aunt, a sister, and someone from her husband's "house," possibly his eldest son (Fujiwara Michitaka, 953–95) by his principal wife (Tokihime, d. 980). The gossip in the capital is that she has already taken the tonsure, but she is still only contemplating the possibility when her husband appears a second time to insist upon her immediate return. A profound passivity engulfs her (masking what strange mixture of relief and resentment?), and she finally allows herself to be bundled into a carriage and driven back to her old house in the capital.

The retreat to Narutaki is one of the central crises in the *Kagerō nikki* and its twenty-year inventory of crises in the memoirist's marriage to Fujiwara Kaneie (929–90), one of the chief architects of the system of marriage politics by which the northern branch of the Fujiwara clan dominated appointments at court during the mid-Heian period. Like his father, Morosuke (908–960), before him, and his son Michinaga (966–1027) after him, Kaneie established his own political prominence by his marriages and by the strategic placement of his own children in marriages that linked his family to that of the imperial house. Kaneie himself had nine known wives and mistresses, among whom the author of the *Kagerō nikki* ranked as a secondary wife who was, to judge from the memoir, acutely aware of her secondary status and often anxious about slipping farther down the loosely defined hierarchy of Kaneie's favorites. Marriage arrangements in the late tenth century were rather fluid. In general, a woman's backing—the wealth and/or prestige of her family—determined her status among her husband's wives. Other determining factors included the number and sex of the children she bore him. In the case of Kaneie, it was the issue of children that, in the long run, made the greatest difference among his wives. Tokihime (the mother of five of Kaneie's children and thus de facto his principal wife) was roughly equal to the *Kagerō* memoirist in terms of family connections. Both women were the daughters of minor provincial governors.[6]

Aside from Tokihime, the *Kagerō nikki* touches on only three of Kaneie's other eight women, each of whom—at least according to the memoir—bore him children.[7] The sex of the children a woman bore contributed greatly to her political importance as a wife, and for wives of aspiring Fujiwara ministers, beautiful and carefully educated daughters were prime assets. Among the threatening events lying in the immediate background of the heroine's flight to Narutaki is news of her hus-

band's marriage to "the Ōmi woman," whose daughter by Kaneie, Suishi, eventually rose to become consort to a crown prince (*NKBZ* 9:
251). The memoir dates reports of their marriage as coming to her after
the tenth day of the second month of 971. She departs for Narutaki four
months later. The *Kagerō* memoirist herself bore Kaneie only one child,
a boy, though a year after her flight to Narutaki she also apparently
adopted one of Kaneie's daughters by a minor mistress.[8]

Readers have long recognized the account of the retreat to Narutaki
as a kind of abortive climax to the work as a whole. In this century,
biographical critics argued for decades that the flight to Narutaki coincided with the memoirist's beginning the project of the *nikki* as a
whole.[9] Even scholars who do not associate the events of volume two
with the inception of the memoir have been inclined to grant it a kind of
generic primacy among the other volumes. Oka Kazuo's highly influential book *Michitsuna no haha* (1942) characterized the second volume
as the most "memoiristic" (*nikki teki*) of the three volumes.[10] In this second volume, the spare prose and quoted *waka* exchanges that dominate
the first volume give way to *dokuei* (*waka* composed in solitude or
without a specific addressee in mind). There are also more extensive
prose passages, often interlaced with poetic allusions and single lines of
old poems (*hikiuta*) quoted as part of a predominantly prose narrative.

If the sheer quantity of detail lavished on the description of events is
any indicator of importance, the passage certainly singles itself out from
others in the memoir as a whole. The account of the seclusion at Narutaki occupies an unusually large percentage of the second volume, an
expenditure of twenty-seven out of ninety-seven pages in the *NKBZ* edition to describe a period of less than a month's time.[11] Setting aside the
question of whether the retreat or its immediate aftermath precipitated
the writing of the memoir, it does seem reasonable to assume that the
flight to Narutaki was an act that won the memoirist both criticism and
praise and that must have seemed to her, in the final analysis, like something that needed explaining to others, perhaps even to herself. It is
clear that the passage plays a pivotal role in the thematic structure of
the tale the memoir tells about a secondary wife's attempts to come to
terms with the limits of her destiny as a wife and as a female.

The Narutaki sequence comprises a far more complexly realized
study of Heian female behavior than the reductive reading such incidents come in for at the hands of the guards' officer in *The Tale of
Genji*. And, of course, the *Genji* author(s) appear well aware of this, as
the elaborate ironies that undercut *The Tale of Genji*'s reprise of the old

story clearly demonstrate. One has only to recall the monstrous depre-
dations of Lady Rokujō's vengeful "living spirit" (ikisudama) among
Genji's other loves to realize that one of the issues explored in Genji is
the precarious balance between a culturally inscribed imperative for the
suppression of female jealousy (and male guilt) and the bizarre forms
that such suppression generates. Thus, it is worth pausing a moment
longer over the guards' officer's rendition of this type of marital crisis.
Despite its unpromising reincarnation in the Genji as the pontifications
of a dubious minor character, the guards' officer's retelling of the old
story furnishes a number of useful clues about the sort of criticism jealous women—and tales about them—were likely to arouse among un-
sympathetic readers of the day. The guards' officer's account is, after
all, an interpretation that aspires to move beyond the apparently simpleminded sympathy the weepy women of his boyhood indulged in,
though presumably few of that older generation of female readers (including no doubt the Kagerō memoirist herself) would have applauded
his understanding.

From the perspective of a certain kind of young (and, in the eyes of
the Genji narrator, unselfconsciously pretentious) male reader, the jealous woman's actions appear karugarushi, or something too lightly
rushed into, affected, even offhand (NKBZ 12: 142). Her decision to
renounce the world has little to do with the depth of spirit for which her
women praise her and may be unfavorably compared to the real depth
of feeling that governs (and, to the guards' officer's way of thinking,
victimizes) her errant husband. As a Heian aristocrat, he aspires to be a
man of deep sensibilities. Indeed, it is these very sensibilities that have
rendered him vulnerable to the attractions of other women in the first
place. But his openly jealous wife has allowed herself, in an outburst of
emotion, to forget this all-important code of sensibility. She unthinkingly trivializes religion for the sake of making a scene and for the sake
of making an ultimately futile and self-sabotaging attempt at seizing
control of her own erotic destiny. The guards' officer's remarks suggest
that what he finds most unpleasant about this type of wife is the excessiveness of her abandonment to hostile emotions. Her real motives, he
assumes, have little to do with religion and stem rather from an ill-
conceived plan to punish the man for acting the hero and dallying with
other women. But the guards' officer is not seriously offended by either
religious hypocrisy or the wife's desire to manipulate her husband. Indeed, he goes on to recommend that she rechannel her impulses into a
medium that would put a more docile face on feminine desire. It is only

natural, he is generous enough to admit, that a woman feel threatened by her husband's other romantic pursuits, and natural too, he seems to imply, that she should desire (and be allowed) a modicum of influence on his erotic strayings. But this desire for control must be played out within the limits of acceptable feminine behavior. And because these limits define what is feminine, they can encompass the abandonment of society and sexuality that Buddhist nunhood implies only as a final recourse.

The limits of proper wifely behavior are to be legislated by the codes of life in this world, by the norms of Heian marriages, and by, one almost wants to say, the same principles of decorum, the same delicate balance between *kokoro* and *kotoba*, interiority and its external mode of expression in highly rhetorical poetic language that theoretically governs the mechanism of *Yamato uta* (Japanese poetry, or *waka*). For good or ill, human emotions (*hito no kokoro*) lie at the base of human relationships, just as they provide the basis for *Yamato uta*, whose poetics, as outlined in the prefaces to the *Kokinshū*, arguably present it as a poetry of interiority and emotion. But such emotions are illegible in raw form. Above all, "a woman must not show her resentment openly," and running off to take vows is a scandalously unacceptable token of social or romantic exchange, because unlike *waka*, it is too direct, too unrhetorical. Indeed, it constitutes a denial of those channels of exchange since nunhood is, in more than a symbolic sense, tantamount to ending one's life as a sexually available female. To make such an open show of resentment is to test the limits of the feminine. The logical extreme of this impulse is, of course, self-annihilation, which the *Kagerō* narrator also contemplates at several different junctures before her flight to Narutaki. The motif of female suicide motivated by erotic complications is not uncommon in early Japanese literature, but it is usually associated with a differently balanced kind of love triangle—a woman caught between two competing men.[12]

Of course, the reader might object, the guards' officer has good reason to suspect the depth of such a woman's piety. Her actions may have little indeed to do with religious motives, and more to do, as Sei Shōnagon for one seems to hint, with the desire to manipulate her husband. Sei's *The Pillow Book* tellingly includes the wife whose self-seclusion does not precipitate her husband's pursuit of her among those "things which lack power" (*mutoku naru mono*) (*SNKBT* 25: 163). In that light the *Kagerō* heroine's seclusion at Narutaki would have to be understood simply as a demonstration of her power over her husband. The fact that

Kaneie pursues her testifies to her continued importance to him as a wife. But despite the "success" of her attempted withdrawal, the strategy of flight (whether aborted or not) exposes the meagerness of feminine power in marriage.

The excerpts from *The Pillow Book* and *The Tale of Genji* adumbrate the different kinds of risks such wives run. But the officer is missing the point by assuming that the woman who attempts to rush into holy orders is unaware of the implications of her act. He fails to take into account, as the heroes in Heian *monogatari* often do, the inverted shapes feminine desire may be forced to take within a system that depends upon its repression. The woman who moves to abandon the world is stating, in the most certain terms available to her, a longing either to deny or to defy the world in which she has been defined and constrained by her relationships with men. Cutting her hair and donning the robes of a nun, she turns her back on that world by relinquishing her identity as a woman. For some upper-class Heian women it was the ultimate (perhaps the only) act of self-determination available. And the guards' officer is correct in underlining its limited use as a means of manipulating the husband. It is a step that cannot be repeated, and once undertaken, cannot be retracted without incurring loss of face or committing a sin (though it is not clear which would have been the greater threat to a Heian lady). The bonds of husband and wife were believed to transcend the cycles of karma. If a married woman headed for the nunnery with hopes of being dissuaded at the last minute, hers was a desperate, perhaps even a grave, religious transgression. And if the act itself may be considered downright sinful, serious flirtation with the possibility of taking such a step carries with it the hint of scandal. Thus, when contemplating nunhood comes as the climax of a tale of thwarted desire, and when this last, scandalously motivated desire (for the extinction of all desire) is, like all her other dreams, ultimately thwarted, then perhaps her readers—especially the women among them—will have an occasion to shed tears of both relief and frustration.

As the *Genji* narrator's opening disclaimer hints, if one reads the guards' officer's speech as a critique of women like the narrator-heroine of the *Kagerō nikki*, it must be seen as very flawed and very "unpleasant to hear," because it fails to address the fundamental problems that arise when a woman's desires exceed the excessively constricted boundaries of her role in society. And the *Kagerō nikki* has long been read as a story about the extremes to which a woman may be driven by her own unsatisfied desires.

The Memoir as Palimpsest: Readings
of Michitsuna's Mother

Like a number of other highly talented and socially well-connected female writers of the Heian period, Michitsuna's mother has long had a
place in the canon of Japanese literature. This means, among other
things, that our image of her and her work comes down to us through
the filter of a long history of other images of her. Our image of her also
takes on different contours depending on whether we consider her reputation as a *waka* poet or her life and talents as they are depicted in the
pages of the *Kagerō nikki*. Despite her ostensible disappointment with
the eventual outcome of her marriage to Kaneie, the match brought her
the right sort of connections for a woman of literary accomplishment.
The memoir records instances of her poetic correspondence with some
of the most elegant and politically important figures of the day, most
notably, Tōshi (d. 975), a sister of both Kaneie and Empress Anshi
(927–64), whose late marriage to Emperor Murakami (926–67; r. 946–
67) was something of a court scandal. But we have to look beyond the
pages of the memoir, to the *waka* anthologies and to the records of poetry contests in the latter half of the tenth century and beyond, to get a
clearer sense of the presence of Michitsuna's mother as a recognized poet
both in her own day and posthumously. The memoir itself—though it
showcases the memoirist's own poetry—makes little or no explicit mention of that aspect of her life and her literary output.

It does, however, record an invitation received in 969 to compose
byōbu uta (screen poems) for the fiftieth birthday celebration held for
Fujiwara Moromasa (920–69), Kaneie's uncle, who was then the Minister of the Left (*NKBZ* 9: 217). Especially in her later years, she seems to
have made her voice heard among the best poetic circles, participating
in poetry contests sponsored by former Emperor Kazan (968–1008; r.
984–86) (*Kazan'in no on'toki no utaawase*, 986), and the future Emperor Sanjō (*Tōgū Okisada Shinnō tachihaki no jin no utaawase*, 993).
The winning *uta* on the *hototogisu* (cuckoo), which she composed for
the former event, was regularly anthologized afterward. *Fukuro zōshi*
(ca. 1157–59) lists it as one of the five greatest poems on the topic.
Within twenty years of her death, Fujiwara Kintō (966–1041), the great
arbiter of poetic taste in Murasaki's day, included her poems in his
imaginary poetry contest (*Saki no jūgoban utaawase*, 1007). The contest included one verse each from twenty-eight poets, mostly from the

mid-Heian period, beginning with Tsurayuki but also encompassing verses by the Man'yō poets Hitomaro and Akahito.[13] Poems by Michitsuna's mother appear in three of Kintō's other personal collections (the *Shū-ishō*, the *Kingyokushū*, and *Shinsō hisshō*), as they do in priest Nōin's (988?–1058) *Gengenshū* (ca. 1046–52). And *waka* by Michitsuna's mother continued to reappear in imaginary poetry contests and *kashū* long after her brother, her husband, and her son had vanished from the literary scene.14 Over thirty-seven of her *waka* were included in twelve different imperially commissioned anthologies (*chokusenshū*), beginning with the *Shūishū* (between 1005 and 1011) and continuing to the *Shinsenzaishū* (1359), including eight in the stylistically innovative *Gyokuyōshū* (1311–12).[15] Until the late seventeenth century, when the nativist scholar Keichū's (1640–1701) annotated edition of the *nikki* began to spark further textual study of the memoir itself, Michitsuna's mother's identity as the author of a memoir was always incidental to her long-established name in the canon of *waka* poets. The mentions of the memoir in classical Japanese prose sources suggest that the text was read chiefly as a sourcebook for her poetry, though even that is ancillary to her identity as wife of Kaneie and mother of Michitsuna:

The second son [of Kaneie], Michitsuna, was the offspring of a daughter of Tomoyasu, the governor of Mutsu. He rose to the office of Major Counselor with the added title of Major Captain of the Right. His mother, an accomplished poet, set down an account of the things that happened while Kaneie was visiting her, together with some poems from the same period. She named the work [*Kagerō no nikki*], and allowed it to be made public.[16]

Taking our cue from the guards' officer in *The Tale of Genji*, however, we might note that the life portrayed in the *Kagerō nikki* has historically provoked a very different caliber of response to Michitsuna's mother, both as a writer and as a woman, with judgments about her character as a woman generally taking precedence over any analysis of the art that produced the memoir's image of her. Of course, the subsuming of rhetorical and intertextual issues to biographical ones typifies criticism of autobiographical works in general and Heian women's memoir literature in particular. What is striking about commentary on the *Kagerō nikki* in this regard is the extreme degree to which passionate responses to Michitsuna's mother as a woman have overshadowed recognition of the constructedness of her memoir. Historically, the memoir has been read as a glass through which can be seen the figure of its poet-author. Readers in the twentieth century have responded to her memoir as the guards' officer did to the finger-biting woman: what is seen is taken for the woman herself, and she is seen first and foremost as a difficult character.

The authority for this mode of reading is sought (and for the most part discovered) in the memoir itself. Indeed, it almost seems as if the narrator of the *Kagerō nikki* is at pains to present herself as a difficult character. Anxious about the political fortunes of her only son, poetically gifted and proud of the recognition her literary merits win her, yet ultimately relegated to a secondary position among her husband's numerous wives and lovers, she seems always to be teetering on the brink of doing something rash, of doing anything to stop her obsession with her own disappointments. And yet, shut up in her house, straining her ears in the darkness for the sound of her husband's outrunners and ox-cart at the gates, there seems very little she can do. If an air of scandal hangs about her memory, it is not the attractive combination of daring personal style and literary accomplishment that makes a figure like Izumi Shikibu so appealing. When the *Kagerō* heroine gloats openly and unabashedly over the death of the only child of one of her low-ranking rivals (*NKBZ* 9: 149–50) or over the fact that another rival's house ("that place that I hate," *NKBZ* 9: 319) has caught fire, one may be inclined to admit, borrowing the restraint of the *Genji* narrator, that the memoir contains many things that are unpleasant to hear. Readings tend to polarize at points like these. Either she is praised for her astonishing candor[17] or her apparently courageous self-knowledge is deconstructed as the unrestrained excesses of pride and personal (or family) ambition, or more compellingly, as a relentless self-loathing.

While scholarly commentators are given to note the "austerity" and "fastidiousness" of her poetic style,[18] many readers both general and specialist come away from the memoir with the distinct impression that not very far beneath the veneer of the memoirist's restrained poetic style there is something radically uncivilized about her, something not at all in keeping with the lovely but pale epitomizations of the Heian period as an age when a "rule of taste" dominated.[19] A reputation for unruliness has been an important feature in the reinvention of Michitsuna's mother as a literary ancestor by twentieth-century Japanese women writers in particular. The late novelist and translator Enchi Fumiko identified the *Kagerō* memoirist's personal style extravagantly (and with more than a hint of the self-loathing the *Kagerō* narrator herself seems to embody for her modern readers) with the "raw, female odor of blood," characterizing the memoir as "decidedly not a work in which only beautiful things are recorded." Though Enchi singled it out as the fountainhead of the long tradition of autobiographical literature by Japanese women, "it is not," she confessed, "a work I can read with pleasure. I do not feel that I could make another novel out of it, nor yet is it the sort of work I want to read over and over again."[20]

The combination of power and repulsiveness that Enchi found so unpleasant in the *Kagerō nikki* becomes a positive object of veneration for the contemporary novelist–turned Buddhist nun, Setouchi Harumi. Highlighting the sharp contrasts between the *Kagerō* memoirist's characterizations of herself and of Kaneie, Setouchi's intensely personal reflections on the memoir artfully mirror the ambivalences she finds in the discourse of the *Kagerō* narrator:

The passages [on Kaneie] . . . bring to mind the image of a charming man, full of masculine vitality, and vividly imbued with liveliness, lust, and humor. Yet when, on the other hand, she receives the man, the hateful visage of an uncompromising, pouting, and obstinate woman appears. And when this happens, am I the only reader who finds it impossible to avoid disliking her? On the whole, the woman [whose image] emerges in this *nikki* is an impassive one, not at all endearing. . . . And yet, though I myself, like the *Kagerō* author, dislike a hesitating, sulking, obstinate temperament, I must list her among the classical women I admire because I revere the coolness of that self-contemplating gaze which portrays, with straightforward detachment, the personality of the self whom she herself so abhors.[21]

Among all the important works by women that have survived from the Heian period, the *Kagerō nikki* has drawn more than the usual share of misogynistic readings.[22] What I find especially striking among contemporary evaluations of the memoir and its author are those (and they seem particularly frequent among female readers) that suggest readers who are both fascinated and repelled by what they read. The *Kagerō nikki* seems to elicit the misogyny that women themselves internalize. We shall have occasion to return later to the question of why this might be so.

Like the heroines of tenth- and eleventh-century *monogatari*, the central figure of the *Kagerō nikki* is a woman who lives out most of her days occupying one of several still points in a web of static, but powerfully attractive, female rivals. Her husband traverses this web at will (all too willfully for her peace of mind), but she is embittered not so much by the system itself as by her position in it. While this memoir does seem to presage the *Genji*'s profound concern with the complex ramifications of Heian marriage systems and the various fates women were subject to in the upper echelons of court society, it does so by means of the intensity, not the extensivity, of its vision. The *Kagerō nikki* concentrates on developing the stark, uncluttered plot of one aristocratic woman's personal circumstances, a narrative strategy that marks it as generically (auto)biographical even as it engages a set of narrative conventions that link it uneasily to the genre of prose fictions (*monogatari*) about romantic relations between women and men.

The memoir dramatizes a perspective on Heian marriage as a system designed to contain and limit feminine desire, a system that labels transgressions of those limits as scandal, proofs of the blind disorder that women will run to if not constrained by marriage ties and familial order. As one of the texts that did the most to bring these issues into the forum of literary prose in Japanese prior to *The Tale of Genji*, the *Kagerō nikki* commands a special quality of attention from students of Heian literature and of writing by and about women in general. Its minute interrogations of episodes from a marriage, particularly those that revolve around extreme gestures like the seclusion at Narutaki, shed light on the limits defining feminine self-representation.

The Woman Who Writes and the Problem of Feminine Destiny

If our image of the *Kagerō* memoirist is overlaid by the images of her that have come down to us through the centuries, chief among these must be the one drawn in the preface to the memoir. The woman described there is a very specific sort of Heian female—one who, hoping, but ultimately failing, to recognize herself in the romantic fictions of her day, sits down to write a record of her own life and leaves it behind for others to read:

The times when things were thus have passed, but there was in those days a person who grew old drifting this way and that, aimless and unsure of her ties to the world. Thinking it natural that it should come to this—her appearance was not beyond the ordinary, nor did she possess great sensibility—she spent her days simply rising and going to bed, and when she dipped into all the old tales, she found them just so many empty words and wondered—might it not be more interesting simply to write down my own worthless affairs in the form of a memoir?—something that would serve perhaps as an example for those who might ask after the life of the well-born? And though, in all the years that had gone by, and even in the last few months, so much had passed that could not be clearly recalled, perhaps this would do; after all, there were so many things she could remember. (*NKBZ* 9: 125)

The memoir opens, as would a personal poetry collection (*shikashū*), with a short prefatory passage written in the third person.[23] The first sentence is brief and declarative, its "there was a person" (*hito arikeri*) reminiscent of opening lines found in earlier works of fiction and poetic biography.[24] The initial phrases of the subsequent sentence continue the biographical trope with a conventional remark on the heroine's appearance and talents, but they devolve quickly at the level of syntax into something rich and strange. The second sentence unwinds itself slowly and sinuously, moving from its initial dismissive glance at her external features into a kind of indirect mimicry of her thoughts as she reads, through the long hours between waking and sleep, parts of the "many old tales" circulating in her time.[25]

The picture presented seems conventional enough at first glance: the classic *monogatari* image of a desultory female reader beguiling the idleness of her days by glancing through (what else?) old *monogatari*; or perhaps she merely reviews them now, in her middle age, as she contemplates the literary education of an adopted daughter.[26] But she seems at second glance more irritated than idle. She has come away from the old tales convinced of their mendacity, and the rhetoric that describes her response aims to convince the reader as well. Her active response to the tales belies the professed listlessness of her reading—she sets them aside with the determination to write her own. We are not to think that *she* would stoop to writing anything like *monogatari*. Those are for a softer, sillier breed of woman than she, and she expects that her readers will rise to her standards in their desire for believable and usable reading matter.

The preface to the *Kagerō nikki* reasserts the traditional Confucian valorization of the historical over the fictional. The old tales are full of "empty words" (*soragoto*) and as such must be firmly denounced. Syntactic parallelism, and the repetition of the word *ōkari* (numerous), reinforce the association between the "many old tales" (*yo no naka ni ōkaru furumonogatari*) and the "many empty words" (*yo ni ōkaru soragoto*) the world contains. Against these, it proposes the matter of the woman's own personal circumstances (*mi no ue*)—stronger medicine than fiction, more useful—something that can stand as an exemplar (*tameshi*) for those who might seek precedents for their own lives in the examples left behind by one of the wellborn. The word *tameshi*, meaning "precedent," "example," or "model," can also mean "topic of gossip." Both meanings of the word are activated here. What is a "personal history" (*mi no ue*) if not gossip? The woman takes up her brush to present what really happened to her, and her story, written in the form of a *nikki*, will be devoid of fiction, except for the fictions that creep in through the vagaries of memory. As the final lines slyly admit, "the things that must have been so" (*sate mo arinubeki koto*), the things she can remember, like the "empty words" that constitute *monogatari*, are also "numerous."

As with all prefaces to memoirs, there is something inherently equivocal about this one. Apparently written after at least part of the body of the text was already completed,[27] yet placed at its head, as though the beginning of the memoir did indeed coincide with the moments of self-definition the memoirist may have realized only as she was in the process of writing, the preface denies a consistency of writerly motives and themes even as it proffers it. Prefaces depend on certain temporal and epistemological pretenses, and these pretenses complicate the narrating voice. In the *Kagerō nikki*, the shift from third to first person that occurs between the preface and the initial lines of the memoir proper suggests a marked distinction between the voice that narrates the preface and the figure that the voice describes. In this sense, there are two narrating voices constituted by the juxtaposition of preface and memoir, though they have traditionally been read as the "voice" of the same woman "speaking" at different moments in time.

The preface suggests the image of a woman older (or other) than the one described there and in subsequent parts of the memoir. She stands at a certain remove from the woman who scorned the empty words in the old tales, and as she describes the moment that prompted the younger woman to take up her brush, she recalls that woman's bitterness as if it were not simply her own. The *Kagerō nikki* begins then, as do many *shikashū*, with a subtly insistent evocation of both the memoirist's difference from her earlier self and her similarity to others ("her appearance was not beyond the ordinary"). To complicate matters still further, the narrator of the preface describes the heroine of the memoir as a woman who began writing in response to an experience of estrangement, specifically the self-estrangement she felt upon reading the old tales and not finding a recognizable image of her own situation. This is a common response among the female readers of tales represented in Heian fiction and memoirs (compare Tamakazura and the *Sarashina* heroine), which also suggests the common expectation of finding in fiction the answer to, or an image of, the problems one faces in life.

Given the scarcity of extant *monogatari* that predate the *Kagerō nikki,* scholars have been hesitant to make strong claims about just what sort of old tales the memoirist may have had in mind, though most would probably agree that, whatever their content, they are likely to have been written by men.[28] Imai Takuji early identified them with frankly fantastic narratives represented by tales like the *Taketori monogatari.*[29] Masuda Shigeo has stressed the rather more interesting possibility of "stories of female success" (*josei no shusse dan*) centering on women of modest social background who found happiness and material security in upwardly mobile marriages.[30] And though *The Tale of Genji* postdates the *Kagerō nikki* by almost forty years, it contains at least one scene that may well illustrate the sort of old tales that so offended the *Kagerō* narrator. The scene takes place in the second "Young Herbs" chapter (*Wakana ge*), when Genji late in life marries the Third Princess, a woman whose social status reminds Genji's wife Murasaki all too painfully of the secondary status she must always occupy, despite Genji's affections. The passage has been preceded by a conversation in which Genji reassures Murasaki that she really has less cause for complaint than most women since she has led a very sheltered life, hidden away from the bitter sexual rivalries to which higher-ranking women and those who live at court are constantly subject. (The *Kagerō* author also lived her whole life in private, as it were. She is the only one of the four memoirists treated in this book who never took court service.) Genji's discussion contains "a number of rather unconvincing points," made all the more dubious by his subsequent departure to spend the night with the Third Princess. But if her husband's smooth talk has done little to reassure her, the "talk" Murasaki turns to next, "the old tales" (*mukashigatari*), is just as disturbing:

In her quarters, as was her habit on evenings when he was not there, Murasaki stayed up late and had her women read *monogatari* to her. It was thus, too, in the old tales that bring together examples of the kinds of things that happen in the world: there were faithless men and women who became entangled with these duplicitous ones and their taste for love. But in these same tales it seemed the hero had one lady by whose side he finally came to rest—how strange it was that she should go on drifting uncertainly. Indeed it had been as he had said: her fate was quite different from most women's, but was she to end her days brooding over the unsatisfied needs anyone would find hard to bear? (*NKBZ* 15: 203)

Given the vehemence of her later disillusionment with tale literature, it is conceivable that the *Kagerō* memoirist remembered beginning life as a would-be believer in her own destiny as the "one lady" with whom her man would settle down. However the old tales may have actually struck her as a girl, the preface to the memoir presents her as a reader who wound up outraged by what her readings and her experience uncovered. Scandalized by the discrepancies between the old tales and her personal affairs, she will become a maker of *tameshi*, not simply a reader or seeker of them.[31] The voice that emerges in the preface suggests a woman who was deeply concerned with problems of self-control and the manipulation of her image. What embitters her now as she reviews the old tales is not so much that her husband played the hero by taking many wives (such was the norm in Heian aristocratic circles), but that in the end he failed to treat her as the central figure of their tale. Faced with these circumstances, she does the only thing a proper Heian lady can do under the circumstances, short of drowning herself or taking the tonsure. She writes a "record of her days" (*nikki*). If her attempts to change her social and erotic destiny have been for the most part abortive, she nonetheless wrests some measure of control for herself as the recorder of these abortive struggles: she provides the terms by which her life will be remembered. Her *nikki* may be read as both the record and the result of an attempt to salvage her status as "the one lady" (*tsui ni yoru kata*) upon which the tale (if not the man) "ultimately depends."

The *Kagerō nikki* shares with many Heian *monogatari* a thematic preoccupation with the fate of its female protagonist. Its "plot" is about a woman's social and erotic destiny. But what makes it different from and memorable among other such tales (including those in *The Tale of Genji*) is the fact that this destiny is one over which the woman herself actively and more or less openly seeks some means of control. And because the *Kagerō* narrator presents herself as the central figure in her own tale, there is a conflict that persists at the heart of the memoir, a tension between the ideal of the compelling, indirectly powerful, and passively attractive lady and the poetically empowered woman who competes fiercely with her rivals and strains the limits of the feminine repertoire in her efforts to design her own fate. The preface to the memoir gives us fair warning of the unstable gap the *Kagerō* memoirist must straddle between passivity and activity, the desire for control that in part motivates the writing itself and the aspiration toward acceptance that characterizes heroines of *monogatari*. More than most, her images of herself display, from the outset of the memoir and from the outset of the tale of her marriage, the earmarks of both the would-be acquiescent wife and her freakish double: the troublemaking, finger-biting, jealous one who will run off, if not constrained, to the very edges of Heian society and sensibility.

If the *Kagerō* memoirist found it impossible, finally, to present herself in the acquiescent role recommended by fools like the guards' officer in "Judgments of a Rainy Night," it was apparently not for want of trying to do otherwise. Part, though not all, of the difficulty may be blamed on the autobiographical mode itself. There are obvious narratological problems associated with actively portraying oneself as the passive heroine of one's own tale. As narrator of her own life story, she lays herself open, as autobiographers necessarily do, to suspicions of disingenuousness. Yet even in her most self-effacing moments, the heroine the *Kagerō nikki* portrays would win no prizes for docility. In fact, her performances in the acquiescent mode seem always to border upon parody, sarcasm, and defiance: "Why do you say nothing?" her husband asks, in a fragment of quoted conversation that appears very late in the memoir, very late in the tale of the marriage. "What shall I say?" she asks, and waits. "You could ask me why I do not come, why I don't inquire after you, say that you hate it, that it hurts you; you might hit me, or pinch me." And she replies, "What else is there to say, when you have said all that should be said?" (*NKBZ* 9: 336). More often her frustrations seek less indirect outlets. Before the marriage, Kaneie is always portrayed as the instigator of poetic exchanges. But of the twenty-one poetic exchanges she records between them during the first twelve years of their marriage, she initiates fourteen, with those initiated by her husband concentrated in the early years. The famous *Nagekitsutsu hitori nuru* poem, anthologized in Teika's *Hyakunin isshu* and elsewhere, and thus emblematic of her identity for later classical readers, is the fruit of one of these self-initiated exchanges, precipitated by her jealousy over her husband's affair with the Machi no kōji woman.[32]

The *Kagerō* narrative inscribes its heroine as an excessive woman, one whose responses frequently exceed the register of culturally sanctioned images of the ideal wife or at least of the uncertain glimpses of that ideal we discern here and there in works like *The Tale of Genji* and within the *Kagerō nikki* itself (in the ascribed comments and reactions of the heroine's female attendants, for example). Would she have struck a contemporary the same way? We know much less about social norms and ideals in the last half of the tenth century than we know about those in even the fifty years that follow it. Is her excessiveness simply an illusion born of our ignorance about the standards of her time? I cannot claim to answer this question with anything more than my own speculations and those of other readers, but I am inclined to imagine, following Enchi's hunches, that the *Kagerō* memoirist does paint herself as a woman who tended toward extremes.[33] Given this point of departure, we can turn to a more readily answerable question. The narrating voice in the *Kagerō nikki* conjures up both a figure in a story and an image of the writer of that story. How do her excesses—the rhetorical means she uses to get what she wants from other figures in the story and from her reader—work for her, as the heroine in the narrative and as a narrating persona?

Narrative forms, by their very nature, draw attention to problems of order; they suggest a special concern with metonymic structures, with questions about sequence and contiguity, and may even hint that the order of certain events in time provides leading clues to an understanding of the events themselves. Thus, the writing of a life story in narrative prose is apt to concern itself with questions about the course of the central figure's life, and the *Kagerō nikki* is no exception. I will be concentrating, in the discussion that follows, on the Narutaki sequence as both a climactic crisis in the memoir's marriage tale and as the heroine's most excessive (and ambivalent) bid to create a unique and memorable image of herself and her dilemmas. I assume that the seclusion at Narutaki was probably seen by contemporaries and later readers (like the author[s] and readers of *The Tale of Genji*), as a rash and desperate step. But in the *Kagerō nikki* it is described, with consummate writerly control, as the almost inevitable result of circumstances over which the heroine repeatedly tries and fails to assert control. It is, in other words, an overdetermined episode, elaborately prepared for by the course of events preceding it in the narrative, but implicitly designed to argue for the heroine's loss of control. Before we turn to the crisis itself, it will be useful to consider some of the main points of the narrative preceding it.

Fictions About *Waka*, Fictions About Women

Unlike the narrator of the *Sarashina nikki*, who, by her own account, came to recognize the fictionality of *monogatari* and its misleading versions of the world only rather late in life, the *Kagerō* narrator describes facing bitter evidences of this falseness from the outset of her marriage. Disillusionment is a daily reality, endlessly repeated in all the many bad signs she is so quick to discover in the domestic world she inhabits. Her grim but lucid readings of her husband's behavior begin with the begin-

ning of the memoir itself, preceding even her oblique reference to the
formal consummation of their marriage. They coincide, in fact, with her
account of the inception of their courtship.

It has been noted that the narrator's remarks concerning the courtship imply that there was a proper and an improper way to go about
initiating things and that her future husband behaved with disturbing
impropriety. Nothing he does conforms to the usual expectations. A
correspondence that begins lightly, as "superficial love notes" (*aena-
karishi sukigoto*), turns into something unexpectedly and oddly insistent.[34] But rather than pursuing the affair through the more conventional channels of a lady-in-waiting or one of the memoirist's intimates,
he instead approaches her father directly in a half-serious, half-joking
manner that renders his intentions supremely difficult to read. Ignoring
the hesitations the memoirist seems to have voiced through her father,
he sends a mounted messenger to pound on her gate. Now she holds in
her hands the note that embodies his first direct indication of serious
courtship and sees that her difficulties reading him have only just begun.
The paper and the calligraphy are so poor as to make her suspect that
they are not his at all. The letter is, in effect, a shocking document, the
testimony it bears to the man's sensibilities appalling. After all the rumors she has heard of his accomplishment in these things, this is at best
strange (*ito zo ayashiki*) and at worst an insulting harbinger of bad
things to come: either the rumors are false and he is not the impeccable
man (*itaranu tokoro nashi*) they have made him out to be or the man
himself, out of lack of esteem for her and her family, is not performing
at his best. Neither case augurs well, but of course her women, and especially her mother ("an old-fashioned person") insist the letter must
not go unanswered (*NKBZ* 9: 126–27). So begins her account of the
conventional poetic correspondence that results in their marriage, some
three or four months later, and the birth of a son in the eighth month of
the following year. The first volume of the memoir is built largely upon
a record of the poems she exchanges with her husband during the first
sixteen years or so of their marriage.

If the *Kagerō* narrator presents her playing of the woman's part during the early years of her marriage as somewhat more than ordinarily
assertive and poetically articulate, her narrative also suggests that she
was frequently rewarded for her excesses. To this extent, the first volume reinforces cultural myths of the efficacy of poetry as a means of
getting what one wants. Despite the several serious crises she recalls
facing during these years (most notably, her anxiety over her husband's

liaison with the Machi no kōji woman), the figure that emerges from the first volume is a relatively buoyant and powerful one. This was, on the whole, a promising period in her life. While she may be mortified or enraged by numerous instances of her husband's bad faith and bad taste, the knowledge she gains from her early recognition of his nature also empowers her. The forms her empowerment take concern her ability to see (to suspect and to read correctly the signs of his behavior) and to use her critical vision to articulate and manipulate her own situation through speech, written correspondence with him, and the organizing discourse of her memoir. *Waka,* of course, play a central role in this narrative. Before moving to consider that role in detail, let us consider some of the cultural fictions surrounding that art in the late tenth century.[35]

Having heard that Hōshi knew [the *Kokinshū*] by heart, the Emperor made up his mind to test her memory. He hid the book from sight, read off "The poetry of Japan" and continued with the first seventeen syllables of each poem, calling on her to supply the remainder; and she recited everything without making a mistake—both the forewords and the poems. When [her father] Morotada found out what was happening, he put on formal attire, cleansed his hands, ordered sutra readings at temples, and offered fervent prayers for his daughter's success.[36]

While it is a commonplace of contemporary English-language scholarship on Heian culture to remark that most members of court society participated in the almost daily composition of *waka,* a powerful, pervasive tradition of occasional poetry, that perception is also perhaps one of the greatest stumbling blocks in our enjoyment of Heian literature. For we have forgotten (if indeed we ever knew it) the art of reading occasional verse. If we read it at all, it is through the lenses of a very different set of aesthetic ideals, a poetics that is inclined to stress the psychic and social isolation of the poet and the privacy of his utterance. Writing at mid-century, literary critic Northrop Frye was able to define the lyric as "the genre in which the poet, like the ironic writer, turns his back on his audience."[37] Great poetry, in the post-Romantic Anglo-European tradition, is ultimately great private poetry, though we would never call it that, for the idea of a "private poetry" sounds curiously redundant to us. The modes of reading that the notion of private poetry generates remain peculiarly ill-suited to the task of appreciating one of the most crucial dimensions of occasional verse: its sociability.

Given the ill-defined position occasional poetry occupies in contemporary literature, it is not surprising to find that much of the commentary written in English on the subject of Heian *waka* poetics often polarizes around the kinds of issues related to the one outlined above, namely, the implicit opposition our own history inscribes between expressive lyric utterances and those of an occasional nature. My own thinking about the subject of *waka* poetics begins with the assumption that the perceived opposition between highly rhetorical occasional poetry and more "private," essentially expressive, lyric modes is itself a critical fiction, historically grounded in their oppositional relationship in Anglo-European literary criticism since at least the nineteenth century.

But the fiction of the power of *waka* as an expressive mode of discourse is not solely the product of post-Romantic, old New Critical assumptions about the nature of lyric. It has sources in Heian literature and culture, and specifically, for the tenth century, in borrowed traditions of classical Chinese poetics. Steeped in allusions to classical Chinese statements about the nature of *shih* poetry, Tsurayuki's Japanese preface (*Kanajo*) to the *Kokinshū* (905) comprises one of the most succinct and historically influential statements on the nature of Heian *waka*, its social and cosmological impact, and the myth of its origin as the expressive utterance of a poet's interiority.[38] The opening passage of the *Kanajo*, which Morotada's daughter Hōshi reputedly memorized along with the eleven hundred *waka* that follow it in the anthology, reads something like this:

The poetry of Japan has taken seed in the human heart, and burst forth in a myriad leaves of words. It is what people in this world, creatures entangled in events, say of the feelings in their hearts, alluding to things they see and hear. Listening to the warbler who cries among the flowers, and the voice of the frog who lives in the water we ask, can there be any creature among all those that breathe, who does not compose poetry? Indeed it is poetry which, without effort moves the heavens and the earth, incites to pity the unseen gods and demons, softens the bonds between men and women, and soothes the spirits of fierce warriors.[39]

This is, before all else, a lovely fiction, in which all creatures, warblers and frogs, gods and demons, men and women, avail themselves naturally and without effort of the verbal or musical power that will allow them to have a desirable effect on their world. The poetic impulse takes root in the mind of the poet in response to things seen and heard. And the process thus set in motion suggests an art that claims to be no art at all but a bringing forth (to use the metaphors of the preface itself)

as "leaves of words" the feelings that stir within the heart when someone confronts the things of this world. Here there is no gap between
signifier and signified and no prodigious poetic genius necessary to
bridge perceived gaps between a lost abundance of original impulse or
vision and the reductions of writing.

Yet despite the expressive/affective fictions the *Kanajo* enshrines,
there is the apparent fact, usually perceived as a paradoxical one, that
the *Kanajo* and the poetry canonized in the *Kokinshū* heralded a tradition of poetic practice that was highly rhetorical and strictly bound by
rigid conventions of social and literary occasions. Commentators writing in English are particularly fond of grappling with this as a paradox
and of taking sides about it. On the one hand, some argue that Tsurayuki describes *waka* as a fundamentally expressive art: "In sum, one can
say there is no new critical theory in the *Kokinshū* prefaces; it is all
based on Chinese models, but with an emphasis that highlights the expressive function of literature."[40] On the other hand, others emphasize
that the whole lyric vision the preface invokes is really primarily "concerned with the rhetorical uses of poetry and [is] itself an eminently
pragmatic document. An enduring cultural solipsism reads this preface
as an incitement to lyric expressivity. It is no such thing."[41]

Even if one limited oneself to the debate as it continues to unfold in
Anglo-American academic circles, the task of sorting out its various implications could easily occupy a small book.[42] I wish merely to fasten
onto the notion that the *Kanajo* set in circulation a few very powerful
fictions regarding the nature of *waka*. In turn, these fictions set the stage
for a kind of intellectual play that involved a loose set of expectations
among readers and writers of both Heian *waka* and the various forms
of prose narrative that embedded *waka*. Because of the promises they
make about the nature of poetry and its function in society—its power
to move the listener, its origin in the poet's heart—the critical fictions
established by the *Kanajo* generate tensions that inform the stories and
memoirs written around this poetry.

If a poetic canon is internalized, literally made one's own through a
lifelong process of memorization and daily use (on the model, say, of an
ambitious imperial concubine like Hōshi), then the possibility of its
functioning as a framework for expressive literature remains a live issue,
despite the procrustean nature of the code itself. Strictures of poetic diction and rhetoricity come to inform how and what one is most apt to
write (and think) about—in this case, canonically defined categories
such as courtly love and the seasons and within those categories a range

of conventional topics and sentiments. The phenomenon is not unlike the one that the nineteenth-century French poet Rimbaud, in a totally different context, epitomized as a process of "being thought by" the language one has internalized.[43] A limited poetic vocabulary and a strictly defined repertoire of conventional tropes and themes need not preclude what one might elsewhere more readily recognize as "expressivity," nor does it prevent the reader from reading the poem as autobiographical utterance. It merely makes explicit its prescription of the ways in which the self may express itself and limit what will be revealed to the reader. Because it functioned in the Heian context as an art of responding to occasions, the *waka* may be read as a token, the coin of social interaction, a gesture one makes in a given situation. And if one starts with the assumption that poetic language will provide certain things—a glimpse of the poet's heart, or, on the poet's end, a specific effect upon the reader—then poetic situations themselves may provide a rich source for the stuff of narrative complications.

For the Heian writer of fiction or memoir (narratives that frequently include not only poems but also some version of what happens to people before and after the moment of poetic composition), there is a particular set of problems, a range of themes that take on weight and importance by virtue of their association with the tradition of occasional verse. The narrative texts written within this tradition implicitly anticipate readers who will bring a certain quality of attentiveness to the task of reading and appreciating crises that hinge on an internalization of codes, especially poetic codes. Figures within the fiction may rise or fall according to their knowledge and mastery of poetic codes. There are the poetically skilled and unskilled and a complicated array of types in between: lovers who manipulate poetic language with devastating skill or with a ludicrous lack of it and readers who respond to the poems they receive with so acute an ear that the smallest quirk stands out and becomes a telling sign. The hyperscrutiny of revealing signs of a writer's otherwise hidden interiority extends not only to the message but to the medium as well. The *Kagerō* heroine is understandably dismayed when she gets her first glimpse of her future husband's handwriting. The reader who interprets her reaction in light of the conventions of a literature preoccupied with the significance of written exchanges will immediately recognize the lineaments of her situation, the probable course of her past, and the likely turns of her destiny. She is a woman of taste and education, carefully raised by Fujiwara relatives who expect much from the verbal and aesthetic accomplishments that distinguish her. And for

her, given her dependence on her future marital affiliation and her limited sources of information about the outside world, *waka*—and tales
that revolve around the exchange of them—constitute a crucial means
of evaluating the suitor.

The feminine figures that people Heian women's writings, perhaps
even more so than their masculine counterparts, appear deeply involved
in the tradition of occasional *waka*. Reading through this literature, we
are asked to believe that the composition and reception of *waka* was,
especially for the women who spent their lives on the other, inner side
of screens and hanging blinds, one of the chief means of knowing the
world (knowing the suitor) on the outside of the blinds; we are also
asked to believe that it was, according to the logic of this same spatial
imagery of inside and outside, one of the chief means of attracting and
sustaining the interest of the right people—especially the right man or
men. In short, the tradition of Heian court women's writings is itself
largely responsible for portraying literary and other artistic skills as a
powerful means (one of the only potentially efficacious ones outside of
proper family connections and fecundity) for a woman to make a success of herself or her family in society. The anecdote concerning Hōshi's
amazing poetic memory is legendary, appearing also in *The Pillow Book*
and in the *Eiga monogatari*,[44] among other works. It is followed, in the
Ōkagami version, by an account of Emperor Murakami's powerful infatuation with her and a brief history of her career as one of his favorites. What is important to establish is not whether these are accurate
depictions of real circumstances, but the fact that we are being asked to
see things in a certain way. A woman who knows the code, who might
manipulate it with just the right balance of rhetorical skill and personal
expressivity, might find a place for herself and her children in the lives
of the powerful. She might—and this destiny is rarer still for a Heian
woman—make a name for herself.

Perhaps because it was one of the very few media through which they
could present a public image of themselves or judge the images of others, *waka* seems to have come in for particularly critical scrutiny by its
female practitioners, at least in the fictions Heian women wrote about
themselves. As I have already suggested, the mid-tenth century saw the
rise of personal poetry collections compiled and authored by women
and an increasing tendency to supplement the poems with long prose
headnotes, radicalized in texts such as books two and three of the
Kagerō nikki to the point that prose becomes the dominant medium of
the text. Could this subordination of poetry to prose have been an im-

pulse to which women writers were especially prone? There was less of a stigma attached to women who wrote prose in Japanese than to men. Might it not also be that women felt more intensely the inadequacies of *waka* as a medium than their male counterparts did because the greater limitations placed on their mobility resulted in a greater reliance on *waka* as a means of social expression?

The Poetically Empowered Heroine

According to the lovely theoretical fictions of Tsurayuki's *Kanajo, waka* is a form of expression that claims for itself the power of making something good or useful happen within a relationship: "Indeed it is poetry which without effort moves the heavens and the earth, incites to pity the unseen gods and demons, softens the bonds between men and women, and soothes the spirits of fierce warriors."[45]

To a great extent, the *Kagerō nikki* affirms the claims the *Kanajo* makes regarding the power of *waka*. The first volume in particular is scattered throughout with episodes testifying to the woman's power to modify her husband's behavior or her own situation via verbal, and particularly poetic, communication. Despite the long and largely unhappy marital history the memoir records, its early passages are crisscrossed by upbeat illustrations of the heroine's empowerment as an astute reader, a skilled poet, and a headstrong and verbally articulate woman. One of the foremost *Kagerō* scholars, Uemura Etsuko, goes so far as to suggest that without the monitory preface and the famous closing passage of volume one in which the narrator describes herself as someone who laments that her position has not turned out the way she had hoped it would (*omou yō ni mo aranu mi o shi nagekeba*) (NKBZ 9: 202), the events recounted in the first volume might convey the impression of a relatively happy and successful marriage by Heian standards.[46]

The *Kagerō* heroine discovers, within a month of her son's birth, the first material evidence of her husband's wandering affections: in her own writing box (forgotten or deliberately planted?) she finds a letter in his hand, intended for another woman. She writes immediately to let him know what she has seen and what she anxiously foresees—his footsteps/letters (*fumi*) leading to another's door, not hers. The assertiveness of her response may be seen in the medium as well as its message. The content of the *waka* questions him about the future of his visits and correspondence with her. The *waka* itself is written directly on the letter her husband had intended for another (*NKBZ* 9: 135). When her husband reappears, acting as though "nothing had happened" (*tsurenōte*) after an absence of three consecutive nights, she actively pursues and confirms her own suspicions, having him trailed (*hito o tsukete misureba*) to the vicinity of Machi no kōji, where this new dalliance has taken him (*NKBZ* 9: 135–36). The number of nights here is significant because it suggests the heroine feared her husband had formalized his liaison with the Machi no kōji woman by passing the ritual three consecutive nights with her.

The *Kagerō* heroine's poetic exchanges with her husband succeed, if only sporadically and temporarily. His interest in the Machi no kōji woman wanes of its own accord, and as it wanes, the heroine wins him back poetically. More than once her *waka* figure as primary catalysts in his decisions to spend a night with her (*NKBZ* 9: 147–48)[47] or to give up, during a period of particularly suspicious wanderings, another night "at court" (*NKBZ* 9: 164).[48] And when he lies ill during the third month of 966, her writing implicitly reaps her considerable erotic rewards. The narrator confesses, "I sent him letters twice, sometimes three times a day. There will be those who find me loathsome [for it], but how could I refrain?" (*NKBZ* 9: 177). Not only does she find it impossible to refrain from acts that, she is careful to remind us, are bound to draw others' criticism, but also she makes it clear that she was well compensated for these risky written displays of passion: her husband asks her twice to visit him before he is well enough to go about on his own. The pages describing her nocturnal visit to his house (a daringly romantic reversal of contemporary social and literary norms of husband-wife visitation) depict what is arguably the most passionate episode recounted in the memoir (*NKBZ* 9: 178–80).

Perhaps the most excessive of all her rhetorical efforts to sway her husband is the *chōka* she composes and leaves for him to read during a visit when she refuses to receive him personally.[49] The poem recapitulates in miniature the history of their relationship and lyrically inventories the sources of the heroine's marital anxieties through allusions to episodes and poems that appear earlier in the memoir. The exchange is preceded in the narrative by a report that the Machi no kōji woman had fallen from favor since the birth of her child and followed by the even more consoling news that the woman is in a frenzy now that she has been abandoned. Of the immediate outcome of the *chōka*, the narrator remarks: "Perhaps he realized it was but natural of me [to feel as I did]—he seemed a bit more attentive, and so the months passed"

(*NKBZ* 9: 156). A happier period ensues, promoted, as the narrator herself recognizes, by a lull in the man's political fortunes.[50] But even when his fortunes begin to show signs of climbing (as they do for a few years after 968 when he has his daughter Chōshi made junior consort to former Emperor Reizei),[51] the heroine continues to assert her hold on his movements and affections. She insists on making her pilgrimage to Hase as scheduled, even if (or probably precisely because) the trip coincides with preparations for Chōshi's participation in the *Daijō'e* festival at court. Both her husband and Tokihime's households are busy with plans for the festival. But in spite of his offer to make the excursion with her if she will delay her own plans to accommodate his, the heroine wants no part of these preparations: "Since all of this was none of my affair, I thought I might slip off quietly on my own" (*NKBZ* 9: 194).

The journey nets her, as writer, the first, and one of the loveliest sustained *kikō* passages (travel accounts) in the memoir. And there are romantic dividends as well: her husband unexpectedly comes out to meet her at Uji. They spend an idyllic few days feasting, visiting a neighboring villa, and enjoying the scenery before returning to the capital together, where this time—as though rewarding him for his attentiveness to her (and his snubbing of his principal wife)—she obliges him by busying herself with "the list of things to do" that he sends her household in preparation for the *Daijō'e* (*NKBZ* 9: 201–2). At this point in her life, however, the differences between the *Kagerō* memoirist's status as a wife and Tokihime's were becoming rather marked. And, as one commentator notes, this is the last episode in the memoir that touches directly upon Tokihime.[52] As the mother of five of Kaneie's most important children, Tokihime has by this date achieved a degree of security and stability in her relationship to Kaneie that the *Kagerō* memoirist was never to know.

Increasingly as the years go by and volume one draws to its close, the heroine grows more and more inclined to meet disappointment or competition by turning her active powers of vision and rhetorical eloquence inward. When she no longer sees her husband, or hears from him only indirectly through messengers or the gossip of her attendants, she turns her gaze upon herself and the things that circumscribe her existence. At these moments her most characteristic tactics are those of silence and refusal. She sends back his robes unsewn, answers his messages only when pressed by her women. Such impulses are with her from the beginning. When, as a young wife, she finds his letter to the Machi no kōji woman in her own writing box, her first move is to confront him openly with her knowledge, complaining of the slight directly. But her closing comments on the episode suggest different, conflicting impulses and desires: "At that time he still, to a degree I found painfully odd, acted as though there was nothing wrong; but I thought really, for the time being, he ought at least to have tried to hide the affair, tell me he was busy at court or something—was there no end to his callousness?" (NKBZ 9: 137).

She wishes her husband had the courtesy to hide his affairs, a desire that springs from shame and from fear of the inevitable gossip about his waning affections for her and that also perhaps betrays an ambivalence about the powerful and power-seeking strategies his indifference elicits in her. Her comments suggest that illusion would be a happier state than lucidity for a woman, if only because her socially defined role as a wife leaves her with so very little she can do to act on her knowledge. She gives in, at these junctures, to a cynical awareness that because she is a secondary wife, and therefore always relatively powerless, knowledge and vision will only gain her suffering in the end. Her knowledge (and overwhelming compulsion to react openly to it) thwarts her own conflicting desire to appear unmoved, accepting, the heroine.

Throughout the first volume, but especially at moments when the heroine's own self-confidence wavers, her husband will appear much the same figure he was in the opening lines of the memoir. He is consistently portrayed as being both provocatively flagrant and yet somehow coolly indifferent to the effects of his behavior on her. But what really bothers his wife is his apparent belief that he has done nothing that can reasonably give cause for offense. His manner is *tsurenashi*, an adjective that means "cool," "impassive," "showing no emotion." The word is frequently used in the *Kagerō nikki* to describe the husband's nonchalance after intervals of absence that are, at least for the heroine, fraught with anxiety. He returns with an indifferent air that bespeaks his obliviousness to the connections between his absences and her rage. His manner incenses her because it suggests all too clearly that she has no right to resent him, that her disappointment and anger are groundless. He refuses to conceal his affairs from her because to do so would be to admit his own guilt, his own sense of wrongdoing.

The memoirist seems to say that power, or the desire for it, can deform one and can exercise its greatest deforming influence when the desire is deferred or denied, as it was to the *Kagerō* heroine and memoirist. Like her, her husband was impelled by the desire for power and the determination of his own destiny, but he found outlets, as a man could, in an erotic and political world that was closed to his wife. Within the pages of the memoir his face remains the same, though his entourage, and the robes he wears, get grander with the passage of years and the accumulation of power and prestige. What happens to his wife is a very different story. While her husband and the women surrounding her remain more or less constant—he in his inconstancy, they in their predictable advocacy of practicality and conciliatory behavior—she changes, or at least struggles to change. The latent conflict between her aspirations as a poetically empowered woman and her inclination to surrender, as the ideal wife should, to a disappointing fate, and to turn her considerable powers inward on an increasingly embattled sense of her own identity, reaches crisis proportions in volume two.

The comments of the woman's household attendants, sometimes sympathetic to, but more often in conflict with, their mistress's unspoken broodings, play an essential role in the emerging conflict between *kokoro* (heart/mind) and *wagami* (body/social position), between interiority and external pressures, between private emotions and public appearances. Their uncomprehending, tactless, or foolishly well-intentioned comments contribute to her characterization as a woman surrounded by insensitive people who do not recognize the extremity of her emotional situation (or who, even if they do see it, have, like her husband, other priorities).[53] Against the background noise of their remarks (at different times sympathetic, critical, comic, or simply banal), the heroine begins to seem a more and more passive figure, a woman who listens more than she looks and who endures the comments of the people around her while she herself maintains silence. At such moments it is as though her formidable rhetorical powers can fasten only on thoughts that remain unvoiced, and poems that, unsent, will never become the coin of romantic exchange. Her response to the early, infamous scene her husband makes by flagrantly parading the Machi no kōji woman past her gates in his carriage is paradigmatic in this respect. She portrays herself as having been shocked into silence by this affront and lets the quoted remarks of her servants speak for her. Here her servants assume an empathetic viewpoint that, she seems to suggest, the reader would do well to imitate:

At his latest mistress's place [*kono toki no tokoro ni*], it was about time for the child to be born. Choosing an auspicious direction, he packed her into his carriage and they drove off together, raising an awful racket that echoed all over the capital—and even went so far as to parade before my gates! I was beside myself, utterly speechless. Those who saw it, from the servants on up, all started clamoring, "A shameful insult! Of all the streets in this city!" Listening to their noise, I wished only that I might die. (*NKBZ* 9: 144)

As the years go by and the narrative proceeds, the silent, brooding figure of the passive, neglected wife starts to dominate the stage. If she now begins to appear less assertive than she had been in the early years of her marriage, she also seems more keenly attuned to the tiny fluctuations in her own fortunes. Take, for example, the minute sensitivity to the idiosyncratic rhythm of her husband's visits and absences, a series of unpredictable comings and goings the description of which is paralleled, more and more insistently beginning with the second volume, by the small changes and subtle disasters the narrator notes unfolding in her garden. The relation of garden to mistress in these passages is essentially synecdochic, a relation of the container to the contained. Looking at the proliferating weeds or shriveled rice sprouts, she sees evidences of her deteriorating marriage. Her references to it are steeped in the rhetoric of Heian fiction: a weedy garden is part of a conventional *monogatari* vocabulary for an erotically abandoned woman; the neglected wife, like the well-tended one, sees herself as a creature of her surroundings.[54] When she looks about her and finds her surroundings unworthy, unkempt, not in keeping with the image of an erotically and materially successful wife, her feelings seek outlet in supremely witty, supremely literary responses. Words are her chief defense against banality and experiencing herself as powerless; with them, she may at least appear to control her situation by describing it masterfully:

With no one about to see to keeping things up, the place was getting more and more run-down. My worries grew as tangled as weeds [*chigusa ni omoimidaru*], while he came and went indifferently, not even seeming to notice how very neglected I felt. He said he was busy—well, maybe he had more things to do than I had weeds about my ruinous house. (*NKBZ* 9: 182–83)

The passage employs a sarcastic play on the half-pun between *koto* [*shigeshi*], "busy," and *aretaru yado no yomogi yori mo* [*shigege*] *nari*, "shaggier than the weeds around my ruinous house." Her husband is busy: *kotoshigeshi* means, literally, shaggy, overgrown with, or beset by *koto*—events, matters, things to do. And though the proliferation of his duties bodes well for the man's political career, it is an ill omen for his wife's relation to him. While he busies himself (at court or elsewhere), leaving her place empty of people who might help her keep up appearances, the real weeds about her run-down house—and the figurative ones inside her head (*chigusa ni omoimidaru*)—proliferate.[55] If the state of the garden measures the material and emotional neglect she and her household suffer, it also becomes an occasion for the mistress's display of her ever-active rhetorical powers.

But there is a retreat here from poetic exchange to soliloquy (*dokuei*), from doing things with words to simply using them to describe things to herself and the less immediate audience of the memoir. The pattern is repeated in the passages immediately following this one when "a string of idle remarks" (*hakanaki koto ii ii no hate ni*) made during an otherwise relaxed day together leads to "nasty words on both our parts" (*ware mo hito mo ashū ii narite*), and her husband storms off in a fit of rage after pointedly telling their boy that he "intends never to come again" (*ware wa ima wa koji to su*) (*NKBZ* 9: 183). The lines bitterly echo the toddler's mimicry of his father's habitual parting words— quoted earlier in the memoir—"I'll come again soon" (*Ima komu yo*) (*NKBZ* 9: 150). The incident sets the heroine to brooding about the instability of their marriage. As with earlier crises, she meets this one by turning to the primeval powers of poetry. This time, however, she addresses her *waka* not to her husband but to the gods. She offers them as prayers in the course of her first serious pilgrimage, "undertaken in great secrecy, in order to tell my trivial affairs to the gods" (*NKBZ* 9: 184), one of several she will take before embarking on the critical one to Narutaki in the summer of 971. There is a logical progression inscribed here, perhaps, from the stately form and diction of *chōka* (with its archaic ties to Shinto *norito*) to *waka* as prayers, but the sequence also implies that the heroine has rounded the first bend in what will become a spiral of mounting desperation and shrinking options. She has begun to despair of the ordinary channels of marital communication. Poetic correspondence has given way to prayer, secular appeals to supplications directed at the gods.

Beginning with volume two, the focus of attention is not so much on the course of events themselves as it is on the woman's attitude toward them. More and more, she struggles to accept her husband's unreliability, to blame her unhappiness on her own fate (*waga sukuse*), to resign herself to her own bad karma. She actively endeavors to be passive, but passivity itself generates suffering. Her infrequent spells of professed resignation (though followed, she almost invariably reports, by brief periods of calm and happiness) bring her only a very dubious sort of relief that is also short-lived (*NKBZ* 9: 156). "I thought it would be a relief," she confesses one year before her flight to Narutaki, "to die" (*NKBZ* 9: 234). Her husband may refuse to oblige her in her demands for attention, his blatant interest in other wives may force her to accept her own secondary status, but he cannot force her to endure it. Death would be for her, as it was for the heroines of many Victorian novels, "peculiarly and significantly feminine, a dramatization of passivity which declares the woman's perfect virtue and perfect acceptance in the very act of defiance."[56]

But suicide is too scandalous a plot, even for her.[57] And pining away is not in the cards for a woman of her energy and ambitions. She is bound to the world, she continually tells us, by her worries for her son's future, and these concerns check and modify the shape her death wishes take. On a pilgrimage to Ishiyama in the seventh month of 970, she overhears two of her men talking about Sakunadani and the dangerous currents there: "People had been swept away." The news prompts her to fantasize about death by accidental drowning. To be swept away, without willing it oneself: this would be the ideal answer to the dilemma her conflicting desires create (NKBZ 9: 241). Into the impasse between her desire for self-extinction and her ambitions for her son's worldly success, the thought of nunhood inserts itself as a logical compromise and a practical alternative to dying.

As I have already suggested, the woman who took religious vows in her youth or in middle age might compensate for the self-determination she was unable to achieve in the erotic realm by removing herself from all erotic relationships. Like death by pining, religious renunciation might conceal (most effectively and importantly, perhaps, from the woman herself) an act of defiance under the cloak of ultimate resignation. The thought of it occurs to the heroine long before Narutaki, and she uses the threat of it in one of the earliest crises of her marriage (in the highly rhetorical context of her chōka to her husband). But as one crisis follows another in the account of the years 970–71, the idea of renunciation begins to take on the proportions of an obsession.

The second volume of the Kagerō nikki begins with the account of a gesture of unprecedented boldness that the heroine ends up regretting, her New Year's wish for 969, written in the form of a charm, but sent (at the urging of her women and her sister, she coyly assures us) to her husband as a New Year's greeting: "That he may be with me thirty days and thirty nights [a month]" (NKBZ 9: 203). By the sixth month of 970, his long absences have made a mockery of those desires: "When I counted them up, I realized it had been more than thirty days since I had seen him in the evenings, and more than forty since I had seen him during the day" (NKBZ 9: 225). This is the longest period of neglect she has suffered so far in her marriage, and she responds as any well-bred Heian lady would at such a juncture by staring at the garden, weeping face-down on the floor, and going on a pilgrimage with another "woman in the same situation as myself" (*waga onaji yō naru hito*) (NKBZ 9: 226). Finally, in the summer of 971, there comes a period when the struggle to change (which is primarily, as is so often the case for literary heroines, a struggle to accept the changes in her man's behavior) almost wins her the self-determination she has been constantly seeking with her poems and her less extended pilgrimages. The heroine's decision to seclude herself at Narutaki is carefully embedded in a tale of her arduous and uncertain process of coming to terms with the limits of her own destiny. And certainly, on the surface of things, it seems clear that she initiated the retreat as an attempt to alter the course of her life before time and the final attenuations of her husband's erotic interest changed things for her. But part of the fascination the sequence continues to exert on its readers derives from the complex network of paradoxical motives and impulses that underlie its readable surface. It is of the essence of her image as would-be passive heroine that the narrator does not recall her stay at Narutaki as one she wholeheartedly wished to make.

The following passage, a prelude to the events immediately preceding the flight to Narutaki, rhymes with prior and subsequent passages describing the heroine's garden as a synecdochic emblem of the woman and her marriage. Here, the heroine's disinterest in her garden suggests her flagging confidence in herself and in more active means of maintaining her husband's interest. Like the death wishes that precede and underlie it, it heralds the ascendance of a desperate mode of heroinism, a radically self-effacing one that might sustain a drastic, last-ditch effort to seize control of her destiny while appearing merely to relinquish it:

For the most part I now found the things of this world meaningless, and so when they said they would send me the black bamboo I had asked for in the spring of the year before when I had been thinking of planting, I told them: "In this world where I have come to feel that even the things I have will not sustain me, do you suppose I would try to do something to console myself?"

"What a narrow-minded thing to say," they rejoined. "It was precisely for those who were to survive him in the distant future that Gyōgi Bosatsu planted fruit-bearing gardens and trees."[58] When they sent it over, I wept as I planted it, thinking maybe someone might see it some day and be moved to remember this place where I once was. After only two days there came a heavy rain and a wind blowing fiercely from the east. One or two of the stalks were beaten down

and as I pondered them, hoping for a break in the rain when I might try to prop
them back up, I thought to myself:

Nabiku kana	Wavering in
omowanu kata ni	an unforeseen direction
kuretake no	even so were the tips—
ukiyo no sue wa	the end of a sad world—
kaku koso arikere	of my black bamboo

Today it is the twenty-fourth, with the rain streaming down so gently it is
quite moving. Toward evening there is a strange letter from him. It says, among
other things, "It is because you have frightened me off with your fearsome behavior that I have let the days go by." I made no reply. On the twenty-fifth, the
rain still did not clear off, and like the day when I spoke listlessly of those
"unforeseen mountains" it came to me that the only inexhaustible thing I have
is my tears.   (NKBZ 9: 252–53)

The narrator explicitly frames the planting of the bamboo as something she did in the hope of soliciting some future reader's nostalgia for
her; by the same metonymic token, she also implicitly figures the writing
of the memoir—an attempt to leave behind something that would cause
others to remember "this place where I was." But like all her other desires, the desire to be remembered seems in danger of coming to nothing. The rain beating down on the bamboo confirms her anxiety about
the erasure of her text and herself. Her garden (her text!) appears to
promise the opposite of Gyōgi Bosatsu's garden, with its fruit- and
truth-bearing trees that outlast their propagator to sustain future generations (the passage exploits the conventional pun on *mi* as both fruit
and truth). Neither the bamboo in the garden nor the text seem capable
of fulfilling her far more modest hopes: wavering in the face of mere
rain and wind, they will not outlast even her ephemeral existence.

But the bamboo also paradoxically points her a way out of this scenario of anxious passivity. The wind that comes with the rain blows
from the east, so that the newly planted stalks lean toward the west, literally the direction of the mountain temple she has been thinking of and
symbolically the direction of the Pure Land's Western Paradise. *Omowanu kata*, the "unforeseen direction" in the poem, seems to be something of a cliché for paradise (see also NKBZ 9: 210, n. 7). But *omowanu* suggests other things as well, something undesired or unwished for,
such as her husband's faithlessness and the dramatic renunciation she
both does and does not wish to make in response to his wavering affections. There is a famous *Kokinshū* (708) poem that revolves around the

image of fishers at Suma tending a salt fire. The poem, according to the prose headnote that precedes it in the *Ise monogatari* 112, may also be read as a complaint against a lover who proves faithless, whose affections drift off in an unforeseen direction:

> Suma no ama no   the smoke of the salt fires
> shio yaku keburi   of the fishers at Suma
>   kaze o itami   swirls in the wind,
> omowanu kata ni   wavers and wafts away
> tanabikinikeri   in an unforeseen direction
>   (NKBZ 7: 281)

In the prose passage immediately following the poem in the memoir the "unforeseen direction" is explicitly identified with "unforeseen mountains" (*omowanu yama*), the undesired option of Buddhist renunciation. From this point on and throughout most of the second volume, the heroine preoccupies herself with the religious alternative she has entertained before only at odd, isolated moments.

One of the more urgent questions that the Narutaki sequence poses and then explores is explicitly raised a few lines after the passage quoted above, as the heroine recalls her youthful view of religiously inclined women. She has come to see herself as somehow different from the woman she once was, and this difference bothers her. What she wants to know, and what the story of her actions implicitly tries to disclose, is how she has become the woman she is, the one who longs to abandon her marriage, the one who finds the old tales full of lies. This same question is asked in the preface to the memoir; it rises to the surface of the text again just before the account of her departure for Narutaki. While staying at her father's house in the fourth month of 971, she initiates a preliminary regime of devotions to prepare herself for the possibility of an even longer retreat. But even as she makes these first tentative gropings in the new, unexpected, and unwished-for direction, she is tormented by the memory of how she had once unthinkingly disparaged religious women and the futures she assumed they were unwittingly preparing for themselves:

Once, when I heard someone going on about how these days there isn't a single woman around who doesn't end up telling over beads and reading sutras I retorted that it is just that sort of wretched woman who winds up without a man. Where had those feelings gone? Night and day, restlessly and without a break I was at it—maybe a little desultory about it perhaps, but—oh, how amused they would be to see me now, those who had heard me talking like that. When I think of how unsure my relations with him have been, I wonder how I could ever have said those things, and I go on praying after my own fashion, but there isn't a single moment when my eyes are not brimming with tears. Ashamed at just how wretched I look now in the eyes of others, I spend my days holding back my tears. (NKBZ 9: 255–56)

More so even than her reading of the old tales, the serious contemplation of nunhood involves a consciously felt and fully articulated experience of seeing herself, her situation, her very words and deeds as the acts of another—someone she had no intention of becoming when she first entertained the idea of such behavior.

At the end of her retreat, she returns to her own house and falls prey once more to the insult of her husband's indifference. "There came a day when that awful man passed by my gate, sweeping all before him, with the usual show of dazzling glitter" (NKBZ 9: 257). Her people get ready to receive him, but his outrunners pass by without so much as a nod in their direction. The heroine is shocked into speechlessness for hours. This time even her women, usually so ready to present her husband in the best possible light, are upset:

Someone said, "How strange! What can he mean by this?" and some even wept. I struggled to contain myself for a moment, and then spoke. "I really resent this; I've been held back so far by others' advice, and continued to live on in this house until now, but here I am, facing the same kind of hateful scene again." That was all I said, but the things that charred away in my heart were beyond words. (NKBZ 9: 257–58)

She receives, on the first of the sixth month, a letter from her husband either feigning or unwittingly betraying his ignorance that she has returned from her father's house. Feigned or not, to her the message can only signify his utter lack of concern for her whereabouts. This is the last straw, and she makes her plans now, in a kind of controlled frenzy, to leave for her long, momentous sojourn at Narutaki. The words that keep appearing in this passage are *kokoro awatatashi*. Meaning something like feverish, frantic, or frenzied, they are used twice to describe the quality of the heroine's actions and once to evoke the attitude of a messenger sent after her by the women of her household once she is en route to Narutaki.[59]

Faced with crises in her marriage before, she had responded rhetorically, with poetic appeals and supplications. Or, should her husband appear, she would punish him (and herself) with silence (and probably sexual refusal), "behaving all night like a rock or a tree."[60] But her flight to Narutaki takes the mode of silence and denial to its logical extreme. Far more so than letting her husband's letters go unanswered or dismissing a messenger without a reply, it is a radically nonverbal, almost incomprehensible act, affording very little room for ambiguous response from her husband; he must either attempt to dissuade her or let her go for good. Unlike her earlier poetic responses, her flight involves serious risks to her marriage and to her personal and family reputation, while offering only very limited potential as a means of communicating with or manipulating her husband. And so she sets out, in one hectic, impulsive burst of activity, dashing off a hasty note to her husband in which she labels her words and her flight (outguessing, and thereby upstaging, his labeling of them) as a "weird, unasked-for tale" or "outburst" (*aya-shiki towazugatari*): "I go today, assuming there is a world where you cannot drive past my gate. But this too, you see, has ended up another weird, unasked-for tale" (*NKBZ* 9: 259).

She has seized this particular day, she tells us, because her husband is still himself secluded, observing the last day of a penance. To wait a day longer (when he would be mobile again) might have brought him to her gates to stop her before she could even leave the house. One can easily imagine the vicarious thrill a contemporary female reader in particular might have felt at this scenario of physical escape. The passage combines all the exhilarating independence of the heroine's earlier excursion to Hase—a momentary triumph over an increasingly banal and claustral routine—with the added intoxication of a reckless indifference to the fate of her oppressive marriage. Her husband's response to her note signals that he immediately recognizes her move for what it signifies according to social and literary convention: a threat to their marriage.[61] To the narrator, however, it is all this and more. As we shall see, her own account of events presents her stay at Narutaki as something bordering on the illegible, especially to herself, a profound (and profoundly desired) relinquishing of self-control and of others' images of her that unfolds, as these things so often do in Heian women's writing, in a mountain temple, a space that lies outside the realm of normal social and sexual exchange. It is within this space that she will stage some of her most momentous writerly discoveries.

A Weird, Unasked-for Tale:
Seclusion and Self-estrangement

And there, in the midst of a mass of flowers I did not recognize, was a clump of peonies. They seemed so pathetic, with their petals completely scattered. Sad and distracted, my thoughts revolved around some verse about how "this flower, too, blooms only once." (NKBZ 9: 261)

Pausing at the priests' quarters upon her arrival at Hannyaji, the woman notices a stand of peonies that brings to mind a line from a *waka* by the *Kokinshū* poet, bishop Henjō (*KKS* 1016):

aki no no ni	flirtatiously they
namameki tateru	sway in the fields of autumn
ominaeshi	fair maiden flowers
ana kashigamashi	competing loudly for my gaze
hana mo hito toki	your blossoms too are short-lived[62]

Her association of the scene and the old poem implicitly traces connections between her personal drama and the problem of woman's fate in general. Henjō's flowers are *ominaeshi*, "maiden flowers," and they comprise a gaudy field of women, all equally attractive, all equally desirous of the speaker's gaze. In fact, one could argue that the real focus of Henjō's poem is not women or flowers at all, but the speaker himself, striking the familiar pose of the Heian hero enchanted by a plurality of feminine charms and charmers. And how like the *Kagerō* memoirist to recontextualize such a line to highlight her narrator-heroine's situation. For *she* would never liken herself to just any "maiden flower." She singles out a stand of peonies, and her allusion to the old poem corrects an indiscriminate male perspective on woman as a lovely mass of unindividuated flowers and substitutes for it a version that is proudly (even snobbishly) discriminating: the image of one rather splendid variety of flower, majestic even in desuetude, surrounded by a bevy of lesser ones "whose names I do not know" (*nani to mo shiranu kusa domo*). Her description of the peonies both is and is not a reflection on the fate of women in general,[63] because the context in which she embeds the allusion implicitly frames the flower as a metaphor for the fate of a very special, well-born woman, an aging *heroine*, who stands out, nameable, among a crowd of other, unknown sisters. The gesture has much to do with her crystallizing preoccupation with questions of gender and identity and the tensions between these two issues. She confronts herself with this sign just within the gates to the temple compound—on the threshold of that strange borderland between society and nature that troubled—or troublemaking—women seek in Buddhist nunhood. Other women have sought the same refuge, but should she? Is it, this peculiarly feminine, peculiarly upper-class destiny she is on the verge of choosing, an authentic one for her? Such questions haunt the narrative of her stay at Narutaki.

Within hours of her arrival, her husband is at the gates of the temple, ordering her to return to the capital. His response to her is immediate and dramatic (he comes before the end of his own period of ritual abstinence), and must be seen as gratifying to her after the months of indifference and neglect. An epistolary feud ensues, during which their son serves as overwrought letter-bearer, tearing up and down the lengthy flight of stone steps between his father's carriage and his mother's hermitage. During earlier marital disputes, the boy has often figured as a pawn or a prize, shamelessly made use of by both husband and wife. But he is older now (sixteen, by the Heian count),[64] and as if to register some transitional phase in his mother's perception of him, the narrator equivocates here, slipping rapidly from references to him as simply "the child" (*osanaki hito*) to "the person walking [back and forth between us]" (*ariku hito*) to other locutions that reflect changes in his relationship to her. When her husband, exasperated, prepares to depart without her and the son announces that he is going to return to the capital with his father, "the child" becomes "the person I relied on" (*tanomoshi hito*). When his father then refuses him and sends him weeping back to his mother, the narrator adopts a more intimate, sympathetic tone, and the boy becomes simply "this one" (*kono hito*). Finally, in the morning, when the son leaves for the capital to ask after his father's safe return, she gives a nod to his court title and his new status as adult male by referring to him as "the Master" (*Taifu*) (NKBZ 9: 262–64).

Whether this sequence "expresses the author's sympathy for Michitsuna's objective existence as an individual apart from herself,"[65] it certainly foreshadows the problematic role the son will play in his mother's attempts to come to a decision about religious vows. At the end of her stay at Narutaki, it is as "the Master" that her son will frantically gather up his mother's belongings and lead her by the hand into his father's waiting carriage, thus putting an end to the question that propels the narrative of her seclusion: Will she or won't she return to the capital and her unhappy marriage? But there is much ground to cover before we witness Michitsuna's mother finding herself being driven back to the capital.

Alone at Narutaki she enters a strange, liminal state. While she hesitates between wifehood and nunhood (or is left—by her husband—to cool her heels), the mountains surround her like an ambiguous borderland, a wild zone between renunciation and society.[66] The sound of temple bells replaces the erratic noise of her husband's carriage passing her gates and marks the passage of her days apart from the world. The rich descriptions of the locale, which pick out, here and there, a peculiarly feminine perspective (the narration notes, for example, that the woman spends the first few days after her arrival waiting out her menstrual period at a house somewhere outside the precincts of the temple), are, like some of the earlier travel accounts in the memoir, beautiful and elaborately wrought. They are also a bit eerie. The woman's aunt, for example, finds the place "a rather novel dwelling" (ito mezurakanaru sumai), but "somewhat unsettling" (shizugokoro mo nakute namu):[67]

Some five or six days after my arrival the moon of the sixth month was at the full. It flooded through the trees, while over in the shadow of the mountain great swarms of fireflies wheeled about. . . . In the evening came the booming of the great sunset bells, and the hum of cicadas, and the choruses of small bells from the temples in the hills around us, chiming in one after another as though afraid to be left out, and the chanting of sutras from the shrine on the hill in front of us. (NKBZ 9: 266–67)[68]

Seventeen years of mounting uneasiness about the outcome of her relations with her husband have brought her to this pass, and it is a dire one, by the standards of the day, but one that differs little, at least in her view, from the effective celibacy and seclusion she has been sporadically forced to endure as a neglected wife. And yet there is a difference, although the narrative never quite explicitly acknowledges it. While the move may not have begun as an entirely volitional one, by threatening to abandon the marriage bed herself, she preempts her husband's erotic abandonment of her and appropriates for herself the active role in what threatens to be the last act of their marriage. For one last time, she will force his hand; he must either taste acquiescence himself or rise to the occasion and alter the course of events. Either way she will win, as long as she can bear the consequences of his acquiescence and/or refrain from returning home on her own.

And yet, in cutting herself off from the world—if only tentatively and geographically at this point—she is also somehow curiously cut off from herself. She continues for some days to nurse the illusion that the choice to leave the world (or even to return to the capital) is hers alone, but almost from the moment of her arrival, the reports of gossip in the city affect and limit her movements. She will not even return to the city to wait out her menses because rumors that she has taken religious vows have already spread. While she hesitates during the long summer hours at Narutaki, she measures the distance between herself and the image of the lady she aspires to be. The difficulty of acting on either of her conflicting impulses (to return to the capital on her own or to go "deeper into the mountains" and become a nun) seems, like her musings on the peonies at the threshold of the temple, to concern the conflict between personal authenticity and the choice of what might prove ultimately to be a merely generic sort of feminine destiny. If the gossips in the capital have already made her out to be a nun, should she follow through on a plot others have already foreseen? Or worse, would her taking of vows fulfill a plot of someone else's devising? Paranoid in her isolation, she wonders about the real motives of a party of visitors who claim to have come at her husband's request to dissuade her from taking vows. The advice of their pretentious spokesman, half-scolding, half-challenging, seems calculated to goad her into making the final, irrevocable step: "Perhaps there is someone who hopes I will decide not to return [to the capital]" (*NKBZ* 9: 271).[69]

And there are other more problematic motives for her ambivalence. Her concern over her son's diet and physical well-being mingles with, and is perhaps meant to mask, a less-than-nunlike anxiety about his future political fortunes as the son of a wife who incurred public ridicule (*hitowarare*) and her husband's disfavor. Perhaps she never really wanted the chance to take the final step toward renunciation; perhaps she brought her son with her as an excuse to hesitate. But her anxieties about her son veil still other, less obvious but possibly more compelling, reasons to hesitate. Motherly concern for Michitsuna devolves quickly, in the following passage, into a shocked recognition of the appalling fact of her sisterhood with all the religious women she had so thoughtlessly disparaged in her younger days:

In the gathering twilight, as I lie listening intently to the drone of voices chanting invocations to the Buddha, I recall how, long ago, it had never occurred to me even in dreams that I would come to this. They had all seemed so pathetic to me then: sometimes I had boldly sketched pictures of them, and too full of my own thoughts to keep them to myself, had spoken out freely on just how awful I thought them. And now here I am, no different from what I had imagined them to be. Maybe it had been an omen of what I would become. (*NKBZ* 9: 268–69)

As she faces the ugly lesson of her unwitting acquiescence to the common female lot, her anger finds a target, not in the familial relationships that confine and torment her, but in the image of her former self, the scornful, proud, verbally adept woman who "had spoken out freely" and fancied herself exempt from a nun's destiny. Whatever the real motives behind her seclusion as it unfolded in her life, her account of its abortive end yields a strikingly alienated image of herself as a woman entrapped in the stereotypically feminine paradigms she herself so detests (and is furtively fascinated by). Like the nuns she used to pity and abhor, she sees herself as an essentially powerless object, manipulated and constrained first by her own misguided expectations and finally, and most decisively, by the men in her family.

In the last moments of her stay at Narutaki, the three relationships that define the sequence of a woman's life according to Confucian societal ideals (that of obedience to one's father, husband, and son) close in on her and determine the course of events. Glimmering just on the surface of her description of these final moments is a self-conscious critique of Heian marriage as a romanticized exchange of women among fathers, sons-in-law, and sons. And yet the narrator of this vision remains—and this comes close to the heart of what readers like Enchi and Setouchi find both fascinating and repulsive in the memoir—more than a little complicitous with the paradigms that so oppress her. The passage is laced with superbly controlled images of helpless entanglement, the overdetermination of the event in the narrative compensating for the frustrating lack of control (which is also of course, paradoxically fulfilling) that the narrator-heroine will continue, throughout the rest of the memoir, to experience in her relations with the three significant men in her story. In the final pages of the Narutaki sequence, the actions of all three of these men conspire to render her deliberations utterly—even ludicrously—futile.

Her father ("the one person whose opinion I cannot ignore") arrives on the scene the very day of his return from the provinces. In the capital, his daughter's scandalous seclusion is the talk of the town. Confronted with the prospect of public humiliation (*hitowarae*), the specter of "what people will say" (*tenge no koto*), and Michitsuna's "despondence" (*kono kimi ito kuchioshū nari tamainikeri*) (NKBZ 9: 282), he orders her to return to the capital:

"You must come away quickly. Come today, if the directional taboos permit, and we can return together. But whether it is to be today or tomorrow, I will come for you."

I was being told that there would be no protests, and I felt powerless and confused. Without thinking I responded, "If that's how it must be, then let it be tomorrow." Tossed about like a fisherman's float, my mind was completely at sea, and then there was a clamor—someone had arrived. It seemed to be him—and now I was completely frantic. (NKBZ 9: 282)

"Fisherman" (ama) doubles homophonously with ama as nun. The fisherman's float (tsuri suru ama no uke), an image of restless movement within a limited compass, figures the heroine's inability to decide as a futile wavering, a series of movements that is doomed to get her nowhere. The metaphor is spelled out by the explicit allusion to Kokinshū 509:

ise no umi ni	restlessly drifts my
tsuri suru ama no	heart as unsettled as the
uke nare ya	bobbing buoys of the
kokoro hitotsu o	fisherfolk who cast their nets
sadamekanetsuru	into the sea at Ise[70]

In a now-classic essay on Heian women's literature, Akiyama Ken cites the passage quoted above as an illustration of the Kagerō memoirist's skillful use of poetic allusions (hikiuta) to establish a kind of "magnetic field" that foreshadows and motivates subsequent events in the narrative.[71] In other words (though Akiyama does not develop the argument this far), the allusion suggests that because the heroine cannot or will not leave the mountain of her own volition, the next scene, in which her husband arrives to take her back to the capital himself, accords perfectly with both the heroine's utter lack of will and the narrator's masterful rhetorical control. The helpless motions of her own desires, ambivalently tied to both self and other, nun and fishermen, captive and captor, are part of a role of her own devising, and her father and husband oblige her by playing fishermen. The narrator dictates the terms of their actions (and her own restless inaction) in more ways than one. The scene that unfolds elaborates this figure of the self as an ambivalently passive object, stunned into silence and utter indecision by the words and actions of the men around her:

Since he just came right in, I was put at a loss. I could only pull up a screen and try to half hide myself behind it, but it was no good. Looking around at the still-smoking incense, the rosary I had in my hands, the sutras I'd left open, he said, "Frightful indeed. I had no idea it had gone this far. Aren't we the unapproachable one now! I came here on the chance that you would be ready to come back, but now it looks like returning would be a sin." And to Michitsuna, "How about it Master, what do you think of her staying on like this?"

"I feel terrible about it, but what is to be done?" Since he just stared at the floor, his father sighed,

"Pitiful," and then, "well, if that's how it's to be, you settle it one way or the other. If you decide she should come back, have a carriage brought around."

Before he had even finished speaking the other was up and bustling about, grabbing up the things that lay scattered around, stuffing what he could into bundles and bags, and having it all loaded into the carriage. He yanked down the hanging screens all around, and swept off with the standing ones, leaving me stunned and confused. Casting glances my way from time to time, my husband surveyed the scene wreathed in smiles.

"Well, it's done now. Looks like you will have to come out with us after all. Inform the Buddha of it. It's only proper, you know."

There seemed to be lots of jokes told in loud voices, but I was as speechless as one in a dream. Tears came to my eyes, but as I sat, repeating invocations to the Buddha, the carriages were pulled up, and time passed. Though he had arrived around four in the afternoon, it had now gotten dark enough to light the torches. I still did not appear ready to move, so he got up.

"Well, I'll be going now." And to the boy, "I leave the rest to you."

After his father went out, he took me by the hand. "Hurry up," he said, and since he was in tears, I knew there was nothing else for it but to leave, yet it was as though I was no longer myself.   (*NKBZ* 9: 282–84)

Of Rain Frogs and Returned Nuns

The denouement of the *Kagerō* heroine's seclusion has to be one of the most relentlessly self-deflating episodes in Heian women's memoir literature. It is also one of the wittiest. The reader will recall that it was the heroine's melodramatic musings on the horticultural disasters in her own garden that had triggered her flight in the first place. Now the lurking banality of those beginnings comes back to her with a vengeance. She is delivered to her own house late in the evening, after a trying carriage ride down from the mountains that she passed in rigid silence, while her husband chatted and joked with her sister. What caps the evening is the reception her women give her—a report on the garden that parodically recalls the mental landscape she had inhabited in the dreary weeks before Narutaki:

Feeling quite worn out, I pulled up a screen to separate myself from him, and had just lain down behind it when suddenly one of my women popped in and said: "I thought I should try to harvest seeds from the carnations, but they shriveled up and now even the roots are dead. And then your black bamboo— one of the stalks fell over, but I had that set back up again."

Surely this is something she could have kept to herself for now, I thought. I didn't respond, but he—whom I'd taken to be asleep—was listening carefully, and raising his voice to be heard through the screens separating us from my sister, said: "Did you hear that? Here's some news. She turned her back on the world and left her home to seek enlightenment, but to hear her women tell it, 'the pinks are in the pink,'[72] and the bamboo has been set straight." His listeners laughed out loud. It really was quite amusing, but I showed not even the trace of a smile.   (NKBZ 9: 285)

As one commentator notes, the entire Narutaki episode had little or no apparent effect on the heroine's relationship with her husband, though one may perhaps detect here the emergence of a new self-irony in her outlook as the heroine of her own memoir.[73] The rhythm of domestic life goes on much as it did before. He invents a witty sobriquet for her post-Narutaki persona: *ama gaeru*, meaning "rain frog" and/or "the nun returns," a name that trivializes her arduous struggle with destiny by reducing it to garden-variety flightiness (NKBZ 9: 300). Her adoption of the nickname, in a poem that appears toward the end of the volume, is in itself quite powerful, if we attune ourselves to the small-scale heroics of those who go on controlling the text of their lives, despite their double awareness of their victimization by others and their own self-betrayals. But the bitterness of these witticisms finally undercuts their humor and self-irony. There is something about the whole sequence that is not really funny at all. What it suggests, and rather strongly, is that the woman who insists on either having things her own way or trying to escape will be belittled for her efforts—particularly should her struggles result in an unseemly display, a dramatic exit worthy of (and perhaps only truly available to) the heroines of the old tales.

Many biographical commentators assume (and I am not inclined to dismiss their arguments) that in real life the author could not but have been relieved that Kaneie appeared at Narutaki a second time to reclaim her. The gossip in the capital had made it impossible by that time to act on either of her other options (taking Buddhist vows or returning of her own volition) without considerable loss of face. But what of Kaneie's side of the story? Why should he have troubled himself so if things were as bad between them as they seem to have been? One might imagine a number of possible reasons. Kaneie genuinely did not wish to give her up just yet—for implicit but unmentioned political, erotic, or social reasons, for the sake of his own pride or social standing, because of the fear, on both his part and her father's, of incurring public ridicule. Certainly the memoir seems to imply that he did not suffer from their marriage as she did. Or does it? Are we meant to read his maddeningly consistent air of guilelessness as a mask for a deeply repressed guilt (of which the memoirist as narrator is aware)? Are we expected to see his retrieval of her as an attempt to assuage his own unacknowledged sense of wrongdoing? The memoir does not give a direct answer to these questions, particularly those concerning Kaneie's state of mind. The text (by the narrator's own account "a memoir in which I record only my own personal affairs" [NKBZ 9: 207]) does not, or perhaps will not, out of deference to generic constraints (the specter of soragoto—the empty words of which monogatari are spun), inquire deeply into Kaneie's motives. Perhaps there was no need to, perhaps the answers would have been obvious to a Heian reader.

In the final volume of the memoir, the narrative becomes preoccupied again with the old rhythms of courtship, this time not the heroine's own, but those of her son and her adopted daughter. Waka exchanges reassert themselves as the dominant medium of the narrative, but this time it is no longer simply her waka that occupy center stage, but those of her son and the suitor who comes for her adopted daughter. The political significance of her adoption of the girl cannot be overlooked. Like Genji's childless wife Murasaki adopting his daughter by the provincial Akashi lady, the Kagerō memoirist may well have acted in an attempt to bolster her own importance to Kaneie by raising and grooming the girl as a potentially valuable political pawn.[74]

Volume three of the Kagerō nikki opens with a description of the dawning of the first day of Tenroku 3 (972), the only passage in the memoir that is specifically dated to year. It is during this year that, still casting about for some means of changing her destiny and emboldened now by a series of prophetic dreams about her family's political success, she hits upon the plan of adopting a former rival's daughter as her own. While the adoption provides her with a socially acceptable and at least temporarily effective means of recouping her husband's attentions, it also prefigures her final submission to the reality of the end of her childbearing years and her own waning personal influence on her husband.[75] She rewards herself for this rare triumph in the feminine art of acceptance with the sunny depiction of a kind of Indian summer in her relations with him. Intrigued by the sudden appearance of this forgotten daughter, stirred by the plans for her education in the literary arts, her husband comes calling more frequently now than he has for many months. His esteem for the heroine and her efforts on behalf of the adopted daughter take public form as well when he proposes that the girl be given her coming-of-age ceremony in conjunction with that of Senshi, the younger daughter of his principal wife, Tokihime (*NKBZ* 9: 320). The heroine responds accordingly, and the change may be read in the new eyes she turns on her weedy garden:

These days the skies were clear, and the weather turned mild and tranquil. A breeze that was neither too warm nor too cool wafted through the flowering plums, enticing the warblers with its fragrance. The voices of the dooryard fowl blended together amiably, and when I gazed up toward the roof, there were swallows at nest building, darting in and out beneath the tiles. The grasses in the garden wore the look of something freed from ice. (*NKBZ* 9: 320)

The account of the year 973 in particular features a number of scenes in which the narrator explicitly compares the heroine's external appearance to her husband's, and it seems as if her resentment of her husband softens as she delineates the emotional and physical signs of aging—his as well as her own. She recalls having an unexpected number of visits from him during the first month. In the second month, no one came to enjoy the red plums with her, though the blossoms were brighter than in other years. When he appears at noon on the third she confesses, "Feeling old and ashamed of my appearance, it was quite painful to see him, but what could I do?" (*NKBZ* 9: 341). She describes the way he looks in a set of cherry-colored robes she had herself seen to dyeing for him, and after he leaves she broods upon the poor figure she must have cut next to him: "As I listened to his men sweeping the way clear before him on his return to his own residence, I was painfully aware of how very run-down I must have looked. I took a good look at my robes and found them all shabby and worn, peered into the mirror and found the image there quite despicable. I was sure this time he would end up completely disgusted with me" (*NKBZ* 9: 341–42).

Perhaps because he has been portrayed throughout most of the memoir as doing so little to conceal his affairs or to mollify her outrage, her husband has always come off as a figure strangely lacking in interiority. It is not until the last volume, when the narrator contrasts his splendid outward appearance with suggestions of an interior difference, that we begin to see a more human side. Notably, it is a gesture of self-concealment (of shame or unexpected coyness on his part, a sign of either weakness or conscious flirtation) that captures her imagination. She remembers watching his carriage during the procession at the Yahata festival in the third month and being surprised to catch him ducking suddenly behind his fan as his carriage passes hers. She teases him about it in a letter sent the next day, and he admits that he had hidden his face out of shame for his wrinkles (*NKBZ* 9: 343).

Time has done its work, it seems. And yet, after all the fire and ice of their early years, and the brief, tentative reconciliations brought about by her adoption of the girl, within three years of her return to the capital she leaves the marriage bed again. This time she goes unopposed, and apparently for good, no doubt because she goes quietly now, and not to a nunnery. In the eighth month of 973, she lets out her own house and moves to the smaller one her father owns at Nakagawa— acquiescing quietly and without unseemly show to the reality of age and the end of her husband's erotic interest in her. The move puts a stop to her husband's visits because of the modesty of the house itself—it is too small and insignificant to receive a man of his rank and entourage.

DRAMATIZING THE difficulty of one woman's efforts to come to terms with the social structures and cultural categories that enclose and define her, the *Kagerō nikki* paints a picture of Heian marriage that flatters neither party in its polarized world of victims and victimizers. Aside from a certain amount of rakish charm and humor, the husband is boorish, his social and erotic dominance of his wife (particularly as it is exposed in the Narutaki sequence) little more than insensitive bullying. It is no wonder, lively and gifted as she was, that in seeking the option of an exit she would strive to make it a dramatic one. She only had one child, and the dwindling of her husband's interest in her over the years had left her with little to do. However, if she was understandably frustrated by the narrowness of her destiny as a woman, she also presents herself as having been made mean by it—the most obvious targets of this meanness being other women. As noted before, commentators have been quick to fasten on her vengefulness toward her female rivals—especially those who were, for reasons of wealth or social status, her inferiors or her equals (the Machi no kōji woman and the Ōmi woman, for example), while Tokihime figures as someone with whom she occasionally initiates a correspondence (until the latter's rise in social status presumably rendered it presumptuous). Although her anger at her husband and at the societal structures that constrain her and women in general seems to be subsumed by the passion of raw jealousy, nonetheless that passion continues to resist reduction to a simpleminded hatred of other women and the self-hatred such rivalries thinly veil. The self-portrait she creates is a profoundly ambivalent one, both proud and punishing in its commemoration of a woman whose liveliness, independence of mind, and spirited powers of articulation made her, at least for a time, the empowered heroine of her own tale. It is as the author of the *Kagerō nikki* that Michitsuna's mother manages to construct herself as a memorable woman, to rescue herself from the relative insignificance to which her role as one of Kaneie's several wives would otherwise have consigned her.

Obviously, that story, the story of her insignificance, remains outside the frame of the narrative. Instead, the memoir fulfills the bravura retort, in the form of a question, its heroine once made to her husband when he questioned her about her silence: "What else is there to say, after everything that *should* be said has been said?" In answering its heroine's own question, the *Kagerō nikki* extended the boundaries that define what a woman might say about herself after everything that should be said about her has already been told. In doing so, the memoir opened the way for the more lovely, but no less challenging, indictments of Heian marriage orchestrated so magnificently and at such length in *The Tale of Genji*.

3 ☞ Fictions of Desire in the *Sarashina nikki*

The provincial governor's daughter commemorated in the *Sarashina nikki* is best remembered as an avid reader of fiction.[1] The memoir has been mined repeatedly by generations of scholars for its vivid depictions of what reading *monogatari* meant to the sheltered, carefully educated aristocratic ladies of mid-Heian court society. Its status as a minor classic owes much to its portrait of the heroine as a young woman lying down alone with her beloved volumes behind a screen. As Saigō Nobutsuna has pointed out, descriptions of the *Sarashina* heroine reading provide a suggestive counterpoint in ongoing scholarly debates over the historical circumstances of Heian *monogatari* dissemination.[2] Unlike the oral group readings by ladies-in-waiting depicted in *Genji monogatari* and illustrated in surviving fragments of the twelfth-century *Genji monogatari emaki*, the *Sarashina nikki* portrays a girl reading silently and in solitude.

At last I had them!—the fifty-odd volumes of *The Tale of Genji* in a coffer, along with *Zai chūjō, Togimi, Serikawa, Shirara, Asauzu,* and other tales!— What joy I felt, returning home with them all together in one sack. Here was the *Genji*—of which I had had only scattered, tantalizing glimpses before, and for which I had yearned so restlessly. To read it from the first volume on, lying down alone behind my screens, and taking out the volumes to look at one by one, what could the rank of an empress be to the way I felt? From daylight until nightfall, and in the evenings as long as I could keep my eyes open, I would draw the lamp close to me, and since I did nothing else but read these books, in no time images and lines from the tales would come to my mind of their own accord, something I thought wonderful indeed. (*NKBZ* 18: 302)

The *Sarashina nikki* has traditionally been read as the memoir of a woman who started out as a provincial girl driven by an overwhelming desire to travel to the center, where she might read all the tales there were to be had in that romantic city of tales, the Heian capital. The initial two thirds of the memoir revolve around the story of her desire for *monogatari*, the genre of fictional tales in Japanese prose that was regarded in the early eleventh century as a notoriously, even reprehensibly, feminine type of literature. Scholarly attention in this century has focused on the heroine who emerges at the beginning of the memoir, partly because that figure elaborates on one of the great character types of Heian fiction: a girl from a slightly less-than-impeccable family who beguiles the tedium of her premarital existence by immersing herself in tale literature. But while much of the *Sarashina nikki* evokes the image of an almost incredibly naive reader, it is no naif who narrates the account, but an adept, polished narrating persona preoccupied with questions about relations between fiction and religious truth. And the narration is not merely concerned with chronicling and debunking a history of childish delusions. The *Sarashina nikki* tracks its heroine's movement from childhood to old age, locating her finally in a place that could not be farther from that of the *Kagerō* narrator, who cynically and eloquently begins by relegating all fictional tales to the province of mere "empty words."

The seriousness of the memoir's entertainment of ideas about fiction, desire, and religious salvation has been obscured by the same girlish charms that have secured its place in literary history. Commentators who take at face value the naif persona in the opening passages of the memoir frequently conflate the memoirist herself with the narrator on the one hand (the image of the memoirist that appears in the text) and with the image of the girl the narrator recalls on the other. The result is that Sugawara Takasue's daughter has been sentimentalized as a girlish writer and her memoir trivialized as a more or less juvenile production, despite the rhetorical intricacy of the text and the advanced age at which she is believed to have composed it.[3] Stylistically, the *Sarashina nikki* is remarkable for its elegant lucidity, a feature that stems in part from its relatively uncomplicated textual history.[4] At the same time, however, its clarity has been too easily regarded not as a deliberate choice, but as a symptom of simplemindedness. In a number of crucial passages, rapid, almost breathless syntax and significant ellipses contribute enormously to the evocation of a more or less silly girl's perspective. The very success of this ingenuous voice has skewed the way the text as a whole has been perceived. Part of the discussion in this chapter will be devoted to recovering the stylistic richness of voice and perspective in the *Sarashina nikki*.

Because of the complexity of the memoir's treatment of both its heroine and the theme of reading, I have devoted two chapters to the *Sarashina nikki*. In each, the aim has been to clarify how the desire to read—whether fiction, dreams, or the numerous other signs of the memoirist's life—organizes the narrative presented in the memoir. This pursuit will involve us in an examination of thematic and rhetorical relationships, the contours of which change and develop as the memoir and its heroine progress. Crucial to the analyses in both chapters is a re-reading of the *Sarashina nikki* that recognizes the constructedness, not only of the figure of the heroine as a passionate reader, but also of the stylistic and epistemological differences between the voices of the heroine and the narrator-memoirist. Thus, the present chapter begins with a section surveying previous commentary on the theme of the heroine's "addiction" to fictional tales, laying the groundwork for an alternative account of the role that desire plays in this memoir. The second section moves, via a close reading of the memoir's opening passages, toward an analysis that takes fuller account of the emergence of multiple voices and images of author, narrating voice, and heroine throughout the memoir. The two sections that follow examine the geographical and spiritual itineraries presented in the *Sarashina nikki* as fictions about desire. In the first of these we will consider the heroine's trip from the eastern provinces to the capital; in the second, we will move on to her passionate reading of *The Tale of Genji* and her concurrent misreadings and dismissals of the holy icons and dreams that trouble her readerly euphoria. In each, we will attend to the memoir's use of Buddhist pilgrimage paradigms as a framework for coming to terms with the problem of religious salvation for women and the belief that fictional literature might serve as a vehicle for religious teaching.

The analysis in Chapter 4 centers on the memoir's appropriation of specific figures from *The Tale of Genji* and other texts both fictional and religious, concluding with an extended meditation on the memoirist's attempt to reconcile secular fictions with the sacred figures that dominate the final pages of her narrative.

Readerly Vices

It has become a kind of critical commonplace among Japanese scholars to caution that *reading* is too mild a term to describe the *Sarashina* heroine's relationship to fiction. "Addiction" (*tandeki*) is the metaphor

that continues to surface in contemporary Japanese critical readings of
the memoir in reference to the memoirist/heroine's unbridled consumption of fictional literature. Although it is easy to concur, at least with
the recognition of appetite implicit in that metaphor, one can take issue
with it on at least two counts. Addiction implies a problem of agency, a
compulsive activity in which the subject exercises little or no control,
acting only to repeat the addictive behavior. While such a characterization certainly warrants further pursuit, particularly in the context of a
memoir that seems so spectacularly to commemorate compulsive, repetitive behavior, the assumptions underlying it have not been seriously in-
vestigated. Because the image of the *Sarashina* heroine as an addict implies a weakness of authorial agency, the metaphor has become a stumbling block to more serious reexaminations of rhetorical aspects of the
memoir. The assessment of the *Sarashina* heroine (and by extension, the
Sarashina memoirist) as simply an addicted reader denies both the tro-
pological nature of the way reading is portrayed in the memoir and the
richness of the concept of reading in the Heian context.

The word for reading in Heian Japanese (the verb *yomu*) involves a
wider field of reference than *yomu* ("to read") does in modern usage. It
connotes something more active than contemporary usage allows, over-
lapping significantly with notions of composition and formal utterance—the oral composition and recitation of *waka*, the oral readings of
monogatari that took place in the women's quarters of the palace and
other literary salons, and the scribal copying out and reproduction by
hand, with resulting textual variations (inadvertent or interpretive), in
the texts so "read."[5] As already noted, the scenes of reading idealized in
the *Sarashina nikki* involve images of a girl reading silently and in an
almost sensuous solitude that suggests autoerotic pleasure. But it is not
at all clear that these passages describing the heroine's involvement with
what the narration will later deplore as "frivolous tales and poems" (*yoshi naki monogatari uta*) do not also imply active writing, the copying
out or even composition of the texts with which the reader secludes herself. As we will see in Chapter 4, the more active image of reading is
implicit in some of the intertextual moves of the memoir itself.

But let us return to the metaphor of the *Sarashina* heroine as a more
or less passive reader addicted to fictional tales. Previous commentators
have generally approached the problem from a slightly different angle,
asking not what was reading, but rather, what did the tales mean to the
writer, Sugawara Takasue's daughter, or to the image of her that appears in her memoir. Akiyama Ken's introductory essay to the *Shinchō*

Nihon koten shūsei edition of the text synthesizes recent mainstream views on the nature of readerly addiction in the *Sarashina nikki*. Here we find the argument that the *Sarashina* heroine's tenacious fascination with *monogatari* signifies not an unusual perdurance of illusions about "the world" (*yo no naka*, that is, relations between men and women), but rather a response to the shattering of those illusions. Akiyama's argument revises the earlier scholarly consensus on the memoirist's use of *monogatari* as a means of escapist fantasy.[6] It also elaborates on the views of yet other commentators who see her interest in *monogatari* as a means of textualizing the pain of the several deaths and partings that punctuate the account of her early years in the capital. As Akiyama notes, the accounts of these partings organize the narrative of the early years in the capital like individual *dan*, or segments, in an *uta monogatari*. In his view, absorption in tale literature provided her with a means of coming to terms with the harsh realities of life and death.[7]

To shore up his argument that *monogatari* signify a negotiation of the complexities of "life" rather than simply a "barrier of fantasy," Akiyama recalls Inukai Kiyoshi's remarks that the *Genji* heroines the memoir explicitly mentions (Ukifune and Yūgao) suggest a clearheaded class consciousness. The memoirist didn't, for example, identify herself with figures from notably higher-ranking family backgrounds (the Akashi lady, Murasaki no ue) presumably because she would have seen in these figures no plausible precedent for her own prospects and destiny.[8] I would add that the appeal of figures like Ukifune and Yūgao to a provincial governor's daughter concerns not just their comparable social status but also, more compellingly, the fact that these figures become significant to *The Tale of Genji* (and in Ukifune's case absolutely central to its final chapters) *despite* their own relatively insignificant social status and obscurity. What operates behind the young reader's fascination with figures like Ukifune is the fantasy of becoming a central and important figure in spite of one's marginality as a female, as a reader/writer of *monogatari*, as the daughter of a not very prominent provincial governor.

Inukai has also pointed out that the period of the memoirist's first, most intensive immersion in talereading coincided with what must also have been firsthand observation of her elder sister's domestic arrangements. In other words, her obsessive interest in fiction was further fueled by her first glimpse (a preview of her own probable future) of the texture of life for a woman of the middle ranks who remains in her own house after marriage and receives her husband there. In Inukai's understanding, "*monogatari* represented reality to a young, inexperienced girl's mind, and her immersion in them signals curiosity about the world, not escapism."[9] One is tempted to marshal the conceptual vocabulary of Lacanian psychoanalysis to fill out Inukai's suggestions. Looking at *monogatari*, the girl learns to recognize and to identify herself with the figures in a representational structure that proffers the illusion of order and meaning. The pleasure of self-recognition that her reading of fiction affords her derives from the fact that her reading allows her to make sense of the chaos surrounding her, to understand and to predict (to master, in a sense) her own place in it. In Lacanian terms, what Inukai touches on here is a description of reading as an enactment of the mirror stage.

In all the readings outlined above, Takasue's daughter appears little different from other Heian female readers who read *monogatari* avidly because they offered potentially usable precedents (*tameshi*) for the course of their own lives. Such readers, pursuing precisely such modes of reading, frequently figure in Heian tales and memoirs. It was for this reason, the *Kagerō* narrator implies in the prologue to that memoir, that she read tales—and found them to be sadly lacking (then going on to offer her own memoir as a more reliable *tameshi*). And it is in the vain hope of finding some precedent to clarify the peculiarities of her own predicament that Tamakazura, Genji's foster daughter, pores over her tales so intently in "The Fireflies" (*Hotaru*) chapter of *The Tale of Genji*. To dismiss this mode of reading as escapist is to ignore the complex way in which romantic fictions spoke to the realities of Heian female readers' daily lives and probable destinies as mistresses and wives. Tale literature is likely to have appealed to feminine—and more broadly human—desires, especially the desire to be and/or to exert agency as the central figure in a meaningful "story," a sequence of events over which, if only through the agency of reading as interpretation, she might understand herself as a central figure within her own world.

Tamakazura's absorption in tales suggests the double-edged nature of the discourse of *monogatari*. Tales both oppress and fascinate the young female reader, and they are what she turns to, faute de mieux, not simply for the pleasure and pain of losing herself in lovely, sad stories, but also, in a hermeneutical spirit, to seek in them some clearer sense of the place she occupies in the world that surrounds her. For such a reader, *monogatari* cannot be reduced to either "truth" or "lies."

The middle position that *monogatari* occupies (somewhere between the conventional oppositions of truth and falsehood) parallels the limi-

nal position of the reader herself, who, because she is a sheltered, aristocratic female and therefore lives in a peculiarly heightened relation to
the literary, is neither simply "inside" nor "outside" the fictional world
of *monogatari*. Norma Field's reading of Tamakazura's rejoinders to
Genji in their discussion of the art of *monogatari* from "The Fireflies"
throws into relief this gendered conflict between different modes of understanding fiction.[10] As Field points out, "for the women who were the
intended consumers of fiction, the vicarious life in duplicitous words
was the true life."[11] Genji, of course, being the adept talker that he is
("someone accustomed to lying," as Tamakazura astutely puts it), is
quick to take advantage of this feature of fiction's power over female
readers. In conversation with Tamakazura, he cynically appropriates the
young woman's point of view on *monogatari*, dignifying the genre by
his ironic and playful, but also serious, defense of its complicated relation to "truth" (*makoto*). His purpose, however, has nothing to do with
defending the truth value of *monogatari*. His actual aim is to awaken
Tamakazura's desire for him. Championing fiction, Genji attempts to
manipulate Tamakazura's desire for fiction for the purpose of seducing
her.

   While Genji's "defense" of *monogatari* takes as its point of departure
the conventional (and, in the Heian context, the conventionally masculine) view of the genre as morally suspect, a tissue of fabrications
(*itsuwari*) that only fallible feminine minds could regard as truth, his
anxiety over the kinds of *monogatari* Murasaki selects for his daughter's
consumption signals his equal awareness of the power of *monogatari* to
awaken (feminine) desire. Feminine desire here is refracted through the
lens of masculine anxiety: if not carefully trained, daughters might dis-
rupt or confound paternal agendas. Underlying Genji's censorious conversation with Murasaki is an acknowledgment of the potential threat
posed by *monogatari* to his own plans for his daughter's future, a tacit
recognition of the way in which tales exercise power over the young female reader—with the implication that the peril the genre embodies is
that of female empowerment. The nature of the threat Genji fears as a
father is clear. Tales potentially confer on young women the power of
imagining alternatives, models of feminine behavior that may be inappropriate from a paternal perspective. Murasaki, for her part, exhibits
the perfection with which she embodies the ideal wife and mother-sur-
rogate Genji has groomed her to be by playing mouthpiece for patriarchal models of appropriate feminine behavior. Recognizing the power of
monogatari heroines as problematic models of femininity, what she

tellingly criticizes in them are two possible extremes: wanton women (*kokoroasahigenaru hito*) and overly disciplined heroines like Fujiwara no kimi in the *Utsuho monogatari,* who, though she doesn't make mistakes, lacks womanliness because of her straightforward speech and manner (*NKBZ* 14: 207; S, 438–39). As Okada points out, the "feminine," which is valorized in Murasaki's explicitly didactic view of *monogatari,* is "not only the feminine that men desire, but one that women (learn to) desire as well."[12]

Field's arguments echo those of Rachel M. Brownstein, who, working in a rather different context, observes that for the female reader, whose options in life were a priori severely limited by her class and gender, novels offered an exciting glimpse of multiple worlds, many of them focusing on or constantly returning to the reflective consciousness of a woman who waits at the center of a complex web of men and relationships.[13] Recent essays by *kokubungaku* scholars like Akiyama Ken and Tada Kazuomi construct a similar frame of reference for understanding the leisure class of female readers of court fiction in mid Heian. Their arguments stop short of recognizing the authority of feminine perspectives on fiction in the Heian context, however, downplaying the extent to which Heian women, in both their writing and their "reading" of fiction, themselves constructed in *monogatari* and *nikki* challenging or subversive views of the world.

I would contend that the increased rhetorical and intellectual sophistication of tale literature in the eleventh century enhanced the genre's capacity to provide a space for imagining creative negotiations with the world as it actually was. Perhaps one of the greatest differences between the world the *Kagerō* memoirist faced and that confronted by the author of the *Sarashina nikki* can be traced in the altered field of reference invoked by the term *monogatari* in the mid-eleventh century. To judge from the *Kagerō* narrator's terms, the word *monogatari* seems to have stood for everything she implicitly wished to avoid in leaving a record, in the form of a *nikki,* as an "example [*tameshi*] for those who might ask after the well-born."[14] She professes an especial wariness of the deceptive promises, the empty words (*soragoto*) of fictional tales. Similarly disgruntled female readers may well have reflected, as Imai Takuji suggested earlier in this century, that the early-tenth-century tale the *Taketori monogatari* featured a heroine from the moon.[15] Perhaps more disappointing still, because of their greater capacity to deceive the hopes of young female readers, were the romantic accounts of successful matches and enduring passion between beautiful, low-ranking human females and tenderhearted noblemen.[16] Minamoto Tamenori (941?–1011), the author of the preface to *Sanbōe* (984), offered his collection of Buddhist tales as a healthy substitute for the kind of lascivious fiction assumed to both delight and deceive the women of his day. His remarks suggest a slightly more moralistic basis for critiquing *monogatari*: "These *monogatari* all depict the affairs of men and women as though they were possessed of all the loveliness of the flowers and butterflies. They are in fact the very root of sin."[17]

But though the depiction of improbable events such as the success of romantic alliances across class boundaries persisted as staples of the *monogatari* repertoire throughout its history, by the year 1020, when Sugawara Takasue and his family began their return journey to the capital from the eastern provinces, the form had realized much of its potential as a medium for subtler critiques of social realities, particularly the kinds of risks and pressures women (and especially women of the Heian "middle ranks," orphaned or unrecognized daughters of the nobility, provincial governors' daughters, and so on) encountered in their relations with politically powerful men in court society. This was a mode of writing and a vision of the world to which the *Kagerō nikki* had itself made a substantial contribution. But the great and still-unparalleled progenitor of this new meaning of the word *monogatari* was, of course, the *Genji monogatari*, which Takasue's daughter avidly read and deeply admired. We will postpone until Chapter 4 a fuller exploration of what intertextual complexities, whether *Genji*-inspired or not, inform the story told in the *Sarashina nikki*. For the moment I simply wish to hold on to the position that it was a reader very much alive to complexity who held the brush from which the memoir initially took shape, and that she is not to be confused with (though not entirely dissociated from) the girlish reader she commemorates.

Let us spell out the implications of Akiyama's understanding of the meaning of *monogatari* in the *Sarashina nikki*. As with other young women of her class, life offered Takasue's daughter only a very limited range of possibilities, chief among these (at least by fiction's standards) romantic and erotic alliance with a handsome and sensitive man. To these young women (not so different from young women of the leisure classes in other highly literate societies—the daughters of the bourgeoisie in eighteenth- and nineteenth-century England, for example) *monogatari* held up for their admiration one path in particular: to please their fathers and to bear the right child to the right man. But to attract the right man and to win his interest—one needed an education in this art (for indeed

it was art in the court society of the eleventh-century Heian capital). It
was *monogatari*, inlaid with *waka*, the lovely coin of romantic senti-
ment, that provided this schooling. Mitsuno Yōichi, using mostly literary sources like the *Genji monogatari* (particularly the young Murasaki,
Suetsumuhana, and Tamakazura episodes), the *Utsuho monogatari*, and
Sanbōe, goes so far as to postulate three distinct stages in the education
of young Heian ladies, all of which involved varying degrees of *monogatari* reading and composition practice, in training for the adult
business of *waka* composition and poetic correspondence with men and
other people beyond the confines of their own households.[18] *Monogatari*
provided both solace for the vacancy of the female reader's sedentary
existence and training, at once practical and ideological, for the court-
ships that would shape her married life as well as (if she was the daughter of an ambitious man) the political career of her father.

Akiyama would have us read the *Sarashina* heroine thus: immersing
herself in *monogatari* day and night, she learns the art of poetic correspondence and additionally preoccupies herself with fantasies about the
lives of other women like herself, court ambitions, the hope for romantic love—all realizable possibilities for a woman of her position, as
many of the middle-ranking female figures of *monogatari* (themselves
also often depicted as avid readers of *monogatari*) clearly demonstrated.
But this argument, insofar as it understands the *Sarashina* heroine's obsession with reading simply as a passive consumption of fictional tales,
illuminates only part of the question of readerly appetites, while ne-
glecting the overt preoccupation with figures of reading that is sustained
throughout the memoir, including the sections that detail the heroine's
life after her professed disillusionment with the charms of *monogatari*.

If we follow through on the implications of Akiyama's vision of tale
literature as a window on the world of the capital, then tales should figure in the beginning of this memoir only as a means of access to things
the girl has not experienced for herself.[19] Yet signs that the appetite for
fiction portends something more complicated than a spectator's interest
in the extraliterary, secular world portrayed by the tales are evident
from the outset. As Akiyama himself notes, the girl's initial "addiction"
to tales signifies the awakening of desire. Active desire, then, but what is
the nature and what is the object of this desire?

In mid Heian, the noun *yukashisa* (related to the adjective *yukashi*)
signifies an intense longing to hear, see, meet, or know something for
oneself, the state of being intrigued by something. It appears in the
opening lines of the *Sarashina nikki* and elsewhere to characterize the

girl's desire for tales. The metaphor of desire as movement, a longing literally to "go to that place where good things are expected to be,"[20] underlies the term *yukashisa*, which is etymologically related to the verb *yuku*, "to go." The events recounted in the opening lines of the *Sarashina nikki* activate the metaphor of desire as movement by giving it literal form. Desire, *yukashisa*, precipitates a journey to the city where the girl expects good things (tales) to be. The first conscious thoughts the narrator recalls concern not so much the world itself, but more specifically, the marvelous "things called tales" that the world was said to contain. The girl's first desire, the one that catalyzes her initial wanderings, is the longing to see and read these tales for herself. But way out in Azuma, at the outset of her readerly pilgrimages, actual tales are impossible to procure in written form. The girl is as yet only a would-be reader of the fabulous stories she has heard in bits and pieces from older women in the household, and thus it is the tales themselves, not the world they are supposed to shed light on, that constitutes the object of her desire. The initial lines of the memoir are energized by the headlong desire to run off and see for herself not the world, but the stories written about the world. The nature of her desire for tales resembles what the nature of her reading of them will be; it is not passive, but rather an interpretive activity that—at least in the pages of her memoir—is understood to have made things happen not only in the mind of the girl who sat reading the stories over and over again, but also in real life. The idea of reading as interpretation, and beyond that, as a means of seizing and designing, of "authoring," rather than simply foreshadowing or elucidating her own destiny, comes to the fore from the very beginning of the memoir. Consider the tale that the opening passage of the memoir tells us about how the *Sarashina* heroine began her pursuit of fiction.

The Girl from the Provinces and the Old Woman of Sarashina

Part of the difficulty involved in answering questions about authorial agency (or agency run amok as obsession) and readerly appetite (desire run amok as addiction) in the *Sarashina nikki* stems from the fact that even the most familiar sort of narratological distinctions among author, narrator, and character are blurred in Japanese scholarly usage, just as they are to a great extent, though for different reasons, in the discourse of mid-Heian narrative in general. As pointed out by Konishi Jin'ichi,

Amanda Mayer Stinchecum, and Richard Okada, to name three scholars of Heian *monogatari* whose essays are available in English, one of the cardinal features of Heian prose is its "obfuscation of the distinction between the speaker *of* the text and the speaker *in* the text, between first and third person narration."[21] To recognize that these distinctions are often blurred or shifting, however, is not to say that we can afford to proceed as if they do not exist or play an important role in how we understand Heian narratives.

The fluidity of narrative voice becomes particularly problematic in a text like the *Sarashina nikki* because it is precisely evolutions in the consciousness of the main character, shifts in the presentation of her understanding of herself and her world, that periodically occupy the focus of narratorial attention. As it traces the pilgrimage of its own heroine from girlhood to old age, the *Sarashina nikki* moves back and forth between a narrating voice that may be characterized as sounding older and wiser and that of a younger woman—the narrator's earlier self, if one reads the memoir as autobiography. The narrating voice brings to life and comments on the appetites and experiences of the earlier self, at times empathetically, as though mimicking her, at times standing back to criticize her. And of course—to continue here with the autobiographical reading—the distance between narrating voice and the increasingly disillusioned perspective of the heroine in the narrative narrows to the vanishing point as the memoir moves toward its final passages. Add to these complications the venerable *kokubungaku* reading tradition in which little or no distinction is drawn between historical author (Takasue's daughter) and narrating persona,[22] and one begins to sense the difficulty of disentangling the figures of "author," "narrator," and "character" in Heian prose genres, to say nothing of negotiating the differences of agency and desire signified by those interrelated figures in a work like the *Sarashina nikki*, preoccupied as it is with questions about spiritual blindness and enlightenment.

The woman portrayed in the *Sarashina nikki* is possessed of desires that seem to launch her from, and ultimately return her to, a place beyond the margins of the courtly world. As we shall see at the end of Chapter 4, the poem on the topos of Mount Obasute that appears toward the end of the memoir situates the heroine figuratively near Sarashina, in the mountains of Shinano, the province where the memoirist's husband had his last governorship and also the place where, in a more literary vein, storybook aunts were abandoned to die. Appearing as it does near the close of the memoir, the poem conjures up a doubly submarginal world: the provincial village of Sarashina and the outlandish space of old age. It creates a strikingly histrionic image of limits and liminality, but it is no more hyperbolic than the gesture with which the memoir opens, lines that locate the girl's origins in a place even further beyond the pale of Heian civilization than was Mount Obasute: "A person raised in a province even more remote than the one at the end of the Eastern Road—how utterly outlandish I must have been!" (*NKBZ* 18: 283).

The eastern provinces (referred to collectively as Azuma) comprised the frontiers of Heian society. They were also, as readers of the *Ise monogatari* and *The Tale of Genji* would have known, the space of *monogatari*, the land in which its archetypical hero Narihira wandered in exile and the childhood home of the *Genji* heroine Ukifune.[23] Thus, from the very first word of the *Sarashina nikki* (*Azumaji*, the Eastern Road), the narrator identifies girlhood with a place beyond even the already remote limits of the world of *monogatari*.

Of course the eastern provinces were not, as Akiyama reminds us, the point from which the memoirist's real life began, nor were they even, in all probability, the place to which her earliest memories would have referred.[24] Takasue's daughter was born in the capital and was already nine years old when her father moved the family to the province of Kazusa, where he had been appointed assistant governor.[25] Kazusa was closer to the capital as the crow flies than Ukifune's Hitachi but farther away if one followed the roads. Hitachi lay north of Kazusa; Kazusa itself lay to the east of the Eastern Road in present-day Chiba prefecture, between the Pacific Ocean and what is now Tokyo. Neither province is explicitly named in the opening passage, but it is Hitachi, not Kazusa, that provides the crucial point of departure here. The opening line of the memoir, "a person who grew up in a place more remote than the end of the Eastern Road" (*Azumaji no michi no hate yori mo, nao okutsukata ni oiidetaru hito*), alludes to a *waka* in which Hitachi is described as the place "at the end of the Eastern Road" (*Azumaji no michi no hate naru Hitachi*).[26] The initial allusion to Hitachi is a memorable one, aimed at the common literary memories of other *monogatari* readers. Opening the story of the girl's life by referring to an unnamed province even more remote than Ukifune's Hitachi, the memoirist locates her beginnings in a place farther out on the periphery than even that of her favorite *Genji* heroine. In terms of her physical and social marginality, she is as provincial as they come, and the memoirist wants her readers to know it.[27]

A person raised in a province even more remote than the one at the end of the
Eastern Road—how utterly outlandish I must have been. What started me
thinking about them, I don't recall, but hearing there were in the world these
things called tales, I fell to wondering how I might see them for myself. On idle
afternoons and evenings I would listen to my sister and my stepmother and the
others telling snatches from this or that tale—the kind of things that were written in the one about the Shining Genji—but their talk just made me long to find
out more. With only memory to rely on, how could they tell the tales in a way
that would satisfy me? In my restlessness, I made a Yakushi Buddha to match
my own size. Cleansing my hands, when no one was around I would go to it in
secret and kneel down, touching my head to the ground to pray, "Grant that I
may soon go to the capital where there are so many tales, and there let me read
all the tales there are." The year I turned twelve we left our house in preparation for the journey up to the capital. It was the third day of the ninth month:
we moved to a place called Imatachi.   (*NKBZ* 18: 283)

The above excerpt reads as two long sentences in the original, and although they are not as long as some of the sentences in *The Tale of
Genji*, they make a lengthy passage, starting with a place beyond the
farthest reaches of the Eastern Road at one end and ending with the beginnings of a trajectory away from there.[28] Momentum builds rapidly.
The first phrases shift equivocally from third to first person, to give way
with "how did I begin thinking of them" (*ika ni omoihajimekeru ka*) to
the breathless syntax of the subsequent phrases, where desire leads to
prayer (the momentum has not climaxed yet and won't until the party
sets out) to prayers getting answered by the family's imminent departure
for the capital. They arrive first at Imatachi (a place-name that translates literally as "Imminent Departure"). The passage that begins so
evasively, first deftly raising and then sidestepping the enigmatic origin
of desire, devolves into what may seem at first glance a charmingly
guileless narrative of the girl's unstinting pursuit of her questionable desires. Snatches of stories she overhears only increase her initial restlessness (*itodo yukashisa masaredo*). She "makes" (*tsukurite*) a Yakushi
Buddha, a claim that may well have been meant to strike the Heian
reader as a fabrication, a hyperbolic evocation of the extremes to which
her desire for tales impelled her.[29]

Whatever its genesis, this ambiguous Yakushi icon initiates the complex subnarrative that the use of figures of Buddhist authority creates in
the weave of the text. To this image the narrator goes in secret (because
she is sensitive to the impropriety of her desires?) to pray that she be
allowed to journey to the capital and there read all the tales there are.
The biographical circumstances behind the timing of this journey (the

end of her father's term of appointment in Kazusa) do not enter explicitly into the narrative. In the economy of the passage it is only the girl's fierce longing and prayers that precede and thus appear to motivate the family's return to the capital.[30] The implication that there is a causal relation between her secretive prayers and the journey is there, but in a move characteristic of the *Sarashina* narrative, the connection remains only implicitly made.

The girl's voice is not the only one speaking here. The opening phrases in particular bear all the traces of the accomplished writer. The vestigial remnant of third-person narration (the use of the word *hito*, "person," in the first phrase) overlays the girl's voice with a more sophisticated, self-consciously fictionalizing one, drawing the well-versed reader's attention to the poetic allusion that links the figure of the girl to the *Genji* heroine Ukifune. The technique also recalls the opening passage of the *Kagerō nikki*, which similarly begins by commemorating its narrator-heroine's early interest in old tales using third-person discourse.

The entanglement of the narrating perspective with the girl's perspective alerts the reader to a complicated dance of sympathies. The narration is highly attuned to the courtly view of young women from the provinces, as well it should be, given their prominence in court fiction. Provincial heroines are *ayashi*—rustic, countrified, "strange," even—but the idiom of the memoir subtly resists the strength of that cliché, refusing to embrace fully the courtly perspective. In the language of the *Sarashina* narrator, the girl is *ayashikarikemu*, only surmised to have been "outlandish" (*-kemu* being a perfective auxiliary that connotes speculation: "how outlandish I/she must have appeared"). Yet the narrating voice speaks as much for the perspective of the girl as it does for an older, more sophisticated one, conveying, for example, the girl's first encounter with the idea of tales in a kind of indirect free style that unmistakably mimics the speech of a girl still unfamiliar with even the word *monogatari*: "hearing there are in the world *these things called tales*" (*yo no naka ni monogatari to iu mono annaru o*). Furthermore, despite the obvious rhetorical accomplishment in the opening lines, the rapid sequence of events in this passage gives the fleeting impression that the narrator (and thus, some assume, the memoirist) recounts memories she does not deeply reflect on. Though the technique is, I would argue, a highly deliberate syntactic manipulation, it is an unobtrusive one, showcasing neither the skill of the memoirist nor the sophistication of the narrating voice, but rather the dismissive offhandedness with which the girl portrayed treats the portentous events of her life.

Evidence that stylization of the voice as juvenile and ingenuous was a deliberate rhetorical strategy is at best only implicit in the wording, the syntax, and especially the elliptical sequencing of events in the *Sarashina nikki*. Certainly if contiguity in this memoir implies more than simple sequentiality or chronology, the *Sarashina* narrator does not comment on it. But the absence of self-reflexive commentary need not be taken as evidence that the memoirist herself was unaware of the suggestiveness of her juxtapositions. On the contrary, highly suggestive juxtapositions recorded without narratorial comment are one of the outstanding features of the prose style of the *Sarashina nikki* (particularly in the early passages), and this will not be the last time the reader is prodded into speculation about the implicit relation between contiguous events in the memoir. Although few Heian court women's memoirs can be read as linear narratives, the *Sarashina nikki* appears to play with conventions of linearity, tracing an itinerary of changes over time and composing a story around the significance of sequences. Unlike many other texts designated as *nikki*, it characteristically gives the reader not a paratactic series of "segments" (*fushi bushi*, to borrow Genji's idiom for *monogatari*),[31] but a sustained tale of changes and developments in a sensibility that still seems to be evolving even as the memoir itself draws to a close.

Consider the juxtaposition of incidents that occurs within the sequence preceding the account of her sister's death. The girl and her sister are sitting together on the veranda enjoying the moonlight late one night when her sister muses, "How would you feel if I were to fly off and disappear just now without saying where I'd gone?" (*NKBZ* 18: 307). The girl responds immediately with a look of naked fear but is soon cajoled out of it. Her sister changes the subject, and after that both women are distracted by the elegant sounds of a male visitor at a neighboring residence. For the reader as well, any sense of foreboding the passage may generate is temporarily deflected by the subsequent account of the flute-playing nocturnal visitor, only to reemerge with more force in the next section, where we read of the sister's early and unexpected death in childbirth.[32] The relation between these two passages is an extremely elliptical one. In it one might read not only the radical contingencies of life and the utter absence of cause and effect but also the blindness of innocence, the apparent randomness of events to eyes that habitually misread or ignore the signs they are given. The narrator makes no explicit attempt to interpret these contiguities. Perhaps we should assume that the Heian reader would not have needed to have them spelled out for her or perhaps that the juxtaposition is designed to reflect a heedless quality in the narrator's voice, a voice sometimes in sympathy with and therefore not consistently distinguishable from that of the girl she evokes. Like the girl portrayed in these passages, the narrating voice at this point also sounds artless, uncalculating, impatient to get through the whole story from beginning to end.

What is provocative about the *Sarashina nikki* in this regard is the way in which the text calls attention to its own procedure of shifting back and forth between narratorial distance and empathy. The narrator's unwillingness to draw attention to the links between some events, coupled with the tendency to draw explicitly problematic, perhaps even intentionally misleading links elsewhere, should alert the attentive reader to the questions of interpretive agency and blindness (and, paradoxically, blindness as a mode of agency) that riddle the memoir. The memoir's fictions about desire (disguised as the simple tale of a girl's desire for fiction) begins, as we have just seen, in the rhetoric of the opening lines and in its half-hidden grammar of consequence—desire leading to the utterance of desire in prayer and prayer leading to its own answer in the beginning of the girl's journey. The opening passage inscribes a little fiction about desire, and it is a fiction that will meet its first crises long before the girl reaches the capital in the travel account to which we now turn.

The Traveler as Reader

The account of the journey to the capital repeatedly brings the memoir's implicit questioning of relations among fiction, desire, reality, and the problem of feminine destinies to the brink of crisis. It shares with other classical Japanese travel writings (*kikōbun*), and with the toponymic poetry that is often a prominent feature of those texts, a thematic concern with the relationship between poetic language and reality. In its own highly individualized way, the travel account carries forward these generic preoccupations, questioning how conventional poetic fictions condition the way one sees the world and whether life (or implicitly, the writing of a life) is doomed to fail in its attempt to repeat the literary fantasies it admires and imitates. Read within the memoir's larger story about the relation between reading and desire, the account also commemorates an early stage in the girl's understanding of literary fictions. In it, structures borrowed from earlier classics of the *uta monogatari* genre organize and valorize her journey, situating the undistinguished girl from the provinces at the center of an elegant plot that retraces the footsteps and verses of great poets of the past. Her path reverses that of her most illustrious predecessor, "the man" (*otoko*, traditionally identified as Ariwara Narihira) in the *Ise monogatari*, both geographically and symbolically. The man goes east into exile, away from the world of the court, and she goes west toward the capital and her own eventual debut in court society. Their paths cover some of the same ground, but the girl, and the account in which she figures, repeatedly uncovers differences and disappointments precisely at those places where one would expect recapitulation of her predecessors.

The Eastern Road's itinerary of poetic toponyms (*utamakura*) plays a central role in the girl's initial deflating lessons in reading.[33] But who or what is being deflated in this travel account? The conventions of *uta monogatari*? The figure of the young traveler as reader/writer, a girl so green she can only lament that topography does not live up to the standards of toponymic poetry (laments made largely, and significantly, in prose, not *waka*, the lyric medium in which her predecessor Narihira so excelled)? Delicately, intricately, both of these impulses are at work in the story of her momentous journey.

At almost every juncture along the route to the capital, the traveler and the reader of the memoir are presented with striking evidence of the unreliability of names and poetic reputations, and the inadequate, arbitrary, and frequently unfaithful nature of language in its relationship to physical phenomena. What we witness in this narrative both is and is not "a use of language that is anything but representational."[34] For to read with the expectation that what one reads might serve as a model for encounters outside the pages of a tale is in the nature of the naive female reader in Heian fiction. It calls for something akin to a suspension of disbelief that figural language might function as a means of representation. The narrator frequently notes that the places visited do not appear in reality as they do in poetic fiction, contrasting their actual appearance with the expectations aroused by their names, a technique that underscores the authority of the girl's experience even as it highlights the writer's skill in manipulating the rhetorical razzle-dazzle of poetic toponyms. Unlike the account of the journey to the east (*Azuma kudari*) in section 9 of the *Ise monogatari*, where, as Okada points out, "the 'journey' . . . turns out to be a series of toponyms . . . and instead of recounting events or describing scenery, the narrating offers an etymology, a focus . . . on the linguistic event itself,"[35] the *Sarashina* narrative keeps an eye on both topography and toponym. Language and landscape compete for the traveler's attention, with narrative interest balancing precariously on the tension between these two poles. The account of the journey to the capital seesaws between a fascination with rhetoric and the impulse to make note of the topographical realities that give the lie to the rhetorical.

On the whole, the perspective that apprehends this play of discrepancies delights in it. The account is polished, sophisticated, thoroughly in command of the tropes of travel writing, but like the opening passage of the memoir, it celebrates the neophyte's fresh viewpoint, in this case the girl's newfound pride as a participant in the old literary game of places and poetic place-names. The mood, particularly in the early stages of the journey, is light and amused, commemorating the surprised responses and unexpected discoveries of the traveler as naive reader. At Kuroto no hama ("Black Sand Beach"), white dunes stretch into the distance (*NKBZ* 18: 285). Since it is autumn when they reach the plains of Musashi, famed in poetry for their purple *murasaki* flowers, she finds the plains buried in tall reeds (*NKBZ* 18: 287). At Morokoshi Plain ("the Plain of China"), known for its "brocade" of *Yamato nadeshiko* (Japanese carnations), an irony that the party is well versed enough to find amusing, she uncovers only a scattering of "pathetic-looking blossoms" (*NKBZ* 18: 291).

Here and there, however, the sprightly mood flags. This constant unmasking of difference between reality and rhetoric is no fun. Sumidagawa is traversed in haste, with only a perfunctory aside on the famous poem that makes it memorable (*NKBZ* 18: 290). Then the traveler falls ill and misses the passage across Saya no Nakayama entirely (*NKBZ* 18: 295). And Yatsuhashi, "Eight Bridges in name only," turns out to be uninteresting, lacking all trace of the bridges that the hero of the *Ise monogatari* found so enchanting (*NKBZ* 18: 295). In the young traveler's eyes, the discrepancies between topography and toponymic poetry—conventionally masked or formulaically lamented in the discourse of *kikōbun*—are strange enough to be worthy of note. And yet like Don Quixote,[36] this traveler romantically reverses the usual order of words and things, literature and life, by subordinating topography to toponym. The actual landscape itself, not the lovely fictions woven around it in poetry, must take the blame for all unsatisfactory revelations. It is not the misrepresentational aspect of toponymic poetry that disappoints the girl so much as it is the topography itself and the difficulties of moving through it, confronting difference at every turn. Landscape, not literature, presents an unaccountably perverse and deviating face. If poetic

fictions in this account can be said to embody the object of desire, then
it is clear that the girl's desires are repeatedly thrown into question by
reality. And what is her response? Her allegiance will be to the literary,
to the rhetorical falsehoods (*itsuwari*) that speak the truth(s) of desire,
not to the desire for reality or conventional truths. The experience
chronicled in the travel account motivates not a rejection of poetic fiction, but a minimizing, within the economy of the narrative, of all that
does not partake of the poetic.

From the girl's perspective, "life," the landscape of the "real," continues to give signs that the safest course is one of minimalization. There
is a moment very early in the journey when even the moon, the loveliest
of traveler's friends, becomes a figure for the equivocal relation of literature to "the world" (*yo no naka*, affairs between men and women) and
the dangers of reading (and leading) life in terms of the elegant fictions
of poem-tales. At Kuroto Beach, inspired by the brilliance of the full
moon, the girl is determined to stay up all night composing poetry and
enjoying the charm of the scene. And so she does; the passage records
one of the few *waka* included in the travel account as a whole. The total
comes to only three, a striking fact, not only in the context of the *Sarashina nikki* itself, which includes elsewhere in its brief compass a total
of eighty-eight *waka*, but even more strikingly in the context of classical
travel writings in general, which characteristically feature a high concentration of *waka*.

Yet the moonlight that produced such sophisticated pleasures at
Kuroto presides over a very different scene the next night at the ford of
Matsusato (Pine Village). Here life and its reality overwhelm the barri-
cade of desirable fictions to impinge painfully upon the girl. Her nurse
gives birth to a child and is thus forced to remain behind, pining among
the pines. The pun activated here is on the word *matsu*, which as a
nominal indicates "pine tree" in the place-name Matsusato but is also
homophonous with the verb *matsu*, "to wait," or more specifically, by
virtue of its frequency in the lexicon of Heian *waka*, "to wait longingly," "to pine." One can't help remarking that here, as at Imatachi ("Imminent Departure"), the name of the place—though not noteworthy as
a toponym from earlier usage in the *waka* or *uta monogatari* tradition—
nonetheless resonates with almost allegorical force with the events that
take place there in the narrative. It is as though the narration is bent on
inventing its own poetic toponyms, both of which, it should be noted,
correspond more faithfully than ordinary *utamakura* to the events that
take place under their sign in the narrative. The girl has her brother

gather her in his arms to carry her off to the nurse's hut for a farewell visit. Moonbeams pierce every gap in the rough thatch that roofs the woman's makeshift lodgings, lighting up her prostrate form, her anxious face, and her skin, preternaturally white against her red robes. The closing comments on the visit highlight the fact that the passage is the antithesis of the preceding account of moon-viewing and vaguely presage the figure of the abandoned aunt that waits far in the future of the girl's story: "As she stroked my hair, surprised and moved to see me, she burst into tears; it was so hard to leave her like that, but I knew my brother felt we should hurry back. It was difficult to tear myself away. The image of her face haunted and saddened me so that I lost all interest in the moon and finally lay down full of heavy cares" (*NKBZ* 18: 286).

The suspicion that poetic fictions may provide neither a lovely nor even a reliable blueprint for a young woman's destiny hovers just beneath the surface here. Especially striking is the fact (mentioned twice in the space of four sentences) that the nurse suffered in part because she had no man to take care of her: "Her man, having died . . . her man not being by her side" (*otoko nado mo naku nashite . . . otoko nado mo sowaneba*) (*NKBZ* 18: 286). The motif of piercing moonbeams also calls attention to itself, casting a bad light on the prospect of sexual relations with men and on maternity, light that also incisively alludes to the symbolism of Buddhist enlightenment, as it illuminates so vividly in this passage the sufferings caused by attachment to the world. We will see the moonlight again in the even more traumatic nocturnal scene of the girl's sister's death in childbirth several years later.

When the travelers finally reach the capital, they settle into a place that to the girl differs little from the rustic surroundings she has left behind: "Spacious and wild, overgrown with trees as big and fearsome as those in the mountains we had crossed, it was a place that didn't even look like it belonged in the capital" (*NKBZ* 18: 298). By the end of the travel account it is clear to the reader that almost nothing the traveler has seen resembles the wonderful tales her sister and stepmother told her back in Azuma. Yet none of these bad signs has been sufficient to dampen the girl's eagerness for fiction. If anything, disillusion with the world heightens desire for the tales that world is said to contain. In the next sentence we learn that her first act upon arrival in these disappointing precincts is begging her mother to find some *monogatari* for her.

This portion of the memoir is indeed, as others have pointed out,[37] a transitional passage, linking the narrator's nostalgic evocation of girlhood in Azuma, with all its still unexamined assumptions about *mono-gatari*, to the later years in the capital, the place where the girl will come gradually and painfully to recognize the trickier side of relations be-tween literature and life—not so much the mendacity of *monogatari* as its poeticizing of the very real scenarios of abandonment and suffering that lie in store for women who cross over from fantasies about the world and relations with men to actual relations. The narrator is for the most part a silent mediator throughout the travel account. Asides to the reader on the folly of the girl's behavior will not crop up until later in the narrative. Withholding the wiser judgment that the narrating voice offers at other points, the narration re-creates from a youthful point of view the girl's earliest encounters with the curious gaps between litera-ture and reality and the even more disturbing consequences of their in-terpenetration. Recuperating the young traveler's myopic perspective, the travel account inscribes the girl's first inklings of the interpretive cri-ses that lie in store for her as misread or deliberately unheeded signs. By this means, the naive reader might also read innocently, only coming gradually via her own pilgrimage as reader to realize what the narrator voices a bit later: that one had been "quite crazy" (*ana monoguruhoshi*) (*NKBZ* 18: 332) to hope that tales might hold in abeyance the world beyond the margins of the tale.

But what is the reader who is not naive to make of the ambiguous signs the traveler encounters? In his thoughtful essay on this section of the memoir, Moriya Shōgo argues that the travel account is governed by a very specific kind of nostalgia, the memoirist's yearning (*akogare*) for the eastern provinces. He posits a period in the life of Takasue's daugh-ter that predates her actual reading of *monogatari*: an idyllic, untutored state of mind that he believes she later comes to associate with her girl-hood home in Azuma.[38] But if we bracket as perhaps ultimately unre-coverable the original object of the memoirist's nostalgia and confine our attention instead to the image of the traveler and the nature of the nostalgia inscribed in the narration itself, a somewhat different picture emerges. The narrating voice tells us only that the girl's earliest thoughts revolved around *monogatari* and the problem of getting them, that self-consciousness began with the very aspirations that seemed to propel her away from Azuma ("What started me thinking about them I don't re-call, but hearing there were in the world these things called tales, I fell to wondering how I might see them for myself" [*NKBZ* 18: 283]). The object of nostalgic desire the text inscribes is not, as Moriya suggests, a time of innocence before the girl fell prey to the delusive fantasies of *monogatari*, but rather the season of her earliest interest in tales and the girlish belief that simply finding and reading tales might make one the central figure in a tale of one's own devising.

Certainly a fascination with girls who act on their curiosity about the relation between poetic fictions and their own destinies underlies the inclusion and retelling of the Takeshiba legend in the midst of the travel account. But it is not merely a nostalgic interest in tales that informs the retelling of this legend. Incorporated into the travel narrative ostensibly as an explanation for the place-name Takeshiba, the legend in fact ends up conveying far more than the origins of a toponym. With its story about a young princess who responds too intensely to the charms of a strange man's song, the legend comments on the mysterious (even scandalous) interpenetration of poetic fiction and human destiny:

Now we are finally in Musashi Province. It doesn't appear to be an especially interesting place. There is no beach of white sand, it is like mud, and even the fields I'd heard about, where the *murasaki* grow, are grown tall with only reeds and rushes. Riding on horseback, you can't see the end of a hanging bow held upright from the saddle, so high and overgrown it is. Parting the grasses as we go we come to a temple called Takeshiba. There are foundation stones and such, the remains of a place that was known long ago as the Haha estate. When I asked what kind of place it was, I was told the following story:

> In past generations, this was a manor called Takeshiba. There was a man of this province who was sent up as a guard to keep the fires lit in the imperial fire-hut. One day as he was sweeping the palace gardens he muttered to himself:
> "Why have I met with such miserable luck?
> Back home I set out wine jars in sevens and in threes,
> And on those jars gourd ladles I did hang:
> they point to the north when the south wind blows,
> they point to the south when the north wind blows,
> if it blows from the west, they point to the east,
> if it blows from the east, they point to the west,
> I used to watch them then, but now here I sit."

It was just then that the emperor's pampered daughter came out alone and stood near the outer blinds of her quarters; leaning against a pillar, she gazed out at this man, feeling quite moved by his murmuring thus to himself. And since she was so intrigued by those gourd ladles, and how they floated about in the wind, she pulled up the blinds and called out:

"Come over here, boy." Though taken aback by her command, the man approached the edge of the veranda.

"That song you were just singing, let me hear you sing it again," she said, and when he had repeated the part about the wine jars, she told him "Take me to see them. I have reason to speak thus."

The man was overwhelmed, but perhaps because it was fated to be, he took her up on his back and headed for the provinces.   (*NKBZ* 18: 287–89)

At the center of the Takeshiba legend as it is recounted in the *Sarashina nikki*, the mysterious charms of a poetic song catalyze an encounter between an imperial princess and a fire-hut guard. Tsumoto, following up on the observations of earlier scholars, notes connections with an actual historical figure named Musashi no Takeshiba who appears in *Shōmonki*, as well as with the quasi-historical origin of the legend in accounts of an actual abduction that took place in the twelfth month of 767 (a version of which is recorded in the *Shoku Nihongi*).[39] He also cites tales from the *Yamato monogatari* and the *Konjaku monogatarishū*, which are thought to derive from the same or similar incidents.[40] Both the latter stories recount the kidnapping of an aristocratic woman and her removal from the capital. But it will be readily noted that the *Sarashina* version of the legend, whether or not it derives from similar sources, is *not* the story of a conventional abduction. The princess in this account is firmly in charge of the vacillating guard whom she recruits as her abductor, and it is she who initiates their flight to the east.

What unfolds is a striking fantasy of feminine mastery that abrogates class divisions and reverses gender hierarchies. What moves the princess? Alone, poised on the threshold of her childhood home, she is intrigued by the curious imagery of the guard's song and moved to sympathy for him in his yearning for the home he can no longer see. The term in question here is again *yukashisa*: desire figured as movement, a yearning to go and see something for oneself. First the girl peers out from behind her blinds to spy on him, then she translates her desirous gaze into action by commanding him to carry her off to the provinces. In this movement, the ground shifts from desire to action, from poetic fiction to life. Hearing his song, she pities the homesick guard and, just as urgently, longs to see those gourd ladles for herself. Calling the man over to the veranda, she seizes her own destiny, uttering a command that might render her, were the man a bit more imposing (like Genji, say) and their destination a little less down-home (something more along the lines of the abandoned mansion where Genji sequestered himself with Yūgao), the heroine of one of the most conventionally romantic plots of the *monogatari* tradition: a woman stolen away by a man to a hideaway beyond the ken of the stifling public world of the capital.

But the Takeshiba princess's choices have powerfully subversive ideological implications. To thrill to the cadences of a folk song rather than to a courtly *waka*, to choose, as her hero, a fire-hut guard rather than a prince (and that she should choose at all)—here is a real threat to order and subordination and evidence of the perverse moves women might be prone to if left unattended. The pair make their escape to Musashi and the princess finds it, as she explains to the imperial messengers when they reach her a belated three months later, "a very good place to be" (*NKBZ* 18: 289). The man is not only spared punishment for his transgression, he is granted the province "for as long as he shall live" and exempted from taxation. To the princess, the emperor grants domain over the province unconditionally, and the children she bears to the former fire-hut guard are given the surname Musashi.

One can agree with Tsumoto and Moriya (both of whom also qualify and question the adequacy of their own readings)[41] that the conclusion of the tale realizes a happily ending feminine variant of the classic noble-in-exile tale (*kishū ryūri tan*)—an archaic plot basic to a number of major works of Heian fiction, and, some would argue, crucial to the development of *monogatari* in general: a young man (usually of noble or divine origin) commits a transgression that results in his expulsion from the community and a period of wandering or exile, during which time he atones for his sins and is transformed into a heroic figure.[42] Of course, there is more to this tale than that, even if we approach it simply in terms of its significance as an elaborate figure of desire. The interpolation of a tale about a woman who escapes the complications of life in the capital to pursue a monogamous future as the wife of a commoner in the provinces may symbolize, as Moriya suggests, the memoirist's aggressive denial of courtly culture (*miyabi*) and her nostalgic desire to return to the innocence, freedom, and rusticity (*hinabi*) of her childhood in Azuma.[43] But how are we meant to evaluate the *destiny* of the Takeshiba princess (or for that matter the woman commemorated in the *Sarashina nikki*)? One could argue that the ultimate worth of both heroines' desires is deliberately called into question by the destination at which each woman arrives and by the process by which both figures and both tales move toward closure.

As a variant of the noble-in-exile plot, the Takeshiba legend inverts gender roles and the pattern of socioeconomic relations between men and women idealized in *Genji* and other mid-Heian *monogatari*, and to that extent at least, it weaves a fantasy of feminine mastery. The initial encounter between the princess and the guard unfolds as a quirky rever-

sal of the classic *kaimami* scene. Here it is a female subject who is overcome with desire, not upon glimpsing the unsuspecting male, but upon
overhearing his song. But unlike the *Genji*'s romantically and aesthetically, if not always politically plausible, pairings of noble men with
women of the middle ranks, the erotic destiny of the princess traces a
downwardly mobile slide that lands her out in the provinces, the wife
(almost always a banal fate in *monogatari*) of a man who seems to lack
even a surname. Like the ambiguous conflicts between poetry and topography presented elsewhere in the travel account, the Takeshiba legend emerges as a cautionary tale with an ambivalent message to impart
about the strange connections between literature and life. The writer
who included it in the story of a girlhood pilgrimage to the Heian capital may well be hinting at the hidden complications lurking in the naive
reader's dreams of becoming a woman like the heroines of court fiction.
For such a reader, literature forecasts the script of one's own life, and in
that script, the girl who reads and dreams, thrilling to the charms of poetic song within the cozy, private spaces behind the screens of her father's house, is actually no more protected from the perils of life than
are the heroines she dreams of imitating. Poetry reaches her from outside as well as inside her house, and her response to it may involve her
in more than just a quiet evening lying down alone with her books.

The idea that literary fictions interact with and interpenetrate feminine
destinies in strange and perilous ways surfaces repeatedly in the first third
of the *Sarashina nikki*. One of the first gifts the young reader receives upon
her arrival in the capital—and it is a logical and practical one, given her
need to get on with the business of learning to read and write *waka*—is a
copybook of poems in the hand of the daughter of the famous calligrapher
Fujiwara Yukinari (972–1027), which she is told to "use as a model"
(*tehon*), presumably for her own efforts in poetic composition (*NKBZ* 18:
300). But when, a year later, the copybook's author dies at a young age in
the smallpox epidemic that swept the city in 1021, the girl who has so intensely "read"—copied, and no doubt tried to imitate, not only the calli-
graphic but also the poetic style of the work—is plunged into grief. Nor
does the strong "connection" between the two girls embodied by the
copybook end with the death of the copybook's author. (The Buddhist
terminology that the memoir employs to describe this connection is striking. The term is *en*, or karmic link.) The tale of Yukinari's daughter's rebirth as a cat who takes up residence with the young reader and her sister
(whose karma and true identity are revealed to the latter in a dream) will
figure in subsequent pages of the memoir.

The most heavy-handed use of the image of the literary text as exerting a mysterious force both to influence and karmically to connect "authors," "readers," and "texts" appears in the account of the heroine's sister's death. In this instance, the interpenetration of fiction, desire, and destiny appears to have had fatal results. The narrator notes, not long after recounting the sister's death, that the tale the sister had been searching for just prior to her death has now turned up, sent by another woman, who also recognizes the frightening ironies of the situation: the sister who had sought *The Tale of the Princess Who Sought a Corpse* has herself become a corpse (NKBZ 18: 309).

To return then to the Takeshiba legend, with its forging of uncanny links among literature, life, and women's destinies, are we to read it as a simple cautionary about the risks a woman runs when she ventures beyond the blinds of her father's house? Or does it not also, on the other hand, hold up something to be carefully considered, and even, perhaps, covertly admired? As an imperial princess, the Takeshiba heroine capitalizes on her class superiority over the fire-hut guard to reverse standard gender roles. She chooses to choose (rather than be chosen by some more suitable man). She embraces her future without hesitation and gains, in the long run, imperial sanction. If she is rash, her rashness also marks her, if not simply as the active agent of her own unusual karma, at least as a sensitive "reader," alive to the mysterious energies beckoning just beneath the surface of the everyday.

And there are subtler analogies operating between the figure of the princess in the legend and the situation of the girl commemorated in the *Sarashina nikki*. The princess speculates that she must have been moved by a kind of predestined yearning for the province of Musashi. She tells the imperial messengers that she suspects her rashness may have been the result of her destiny (*sukuse*), the deeds of a former life that impelled her to leave her traces in the province (*kore mo saki no yo ni, kono kuni ni ato o tarubeki sukuse koso arikeme*) (NKBZ 18: 289). Are we to take this simply as a retrospective motivation for the unusual "plot" of her destiny? Or is it an excuse for disobedience, calculated to placate her imperial family? At the crucial moment of soliciting the fire-hut guard, the princess is shown to act out of a desire to cross over from poetic fiction into life, as though one might move unproblematically between the two spheres. For what are the eastern provinces to the sheltered daughter of an emperor but the space of literature—a place she hears about in the guard's song? Like the girl in the *Sarashina nikki*, whose journey to the capital originates with her restless yearning to go and see "all the tales there are," the princess is impelled by *yukashisa*, her own desire to go and see things for herself. And that desire is aroused, like the desire figured in the opening lines of the memoir, by a literary fiction—the song she overhears the guard singing.

In the end, the desires of both women are realized: the princess settles in Musashi with the guard and is even granted the title to the province. The young traveler in the *Sarashina nikki* reaches the capital and in time obtains the answer to her most fervent prayers: her own copy of *Genji* (a luxury before which all other aspirations pale, including "the rank of an empress" [NKBZ 18: 302]). Although the memoir ultimately indicates that there comes a point at which the heroine abandons her obsessive solitary reading, her *monogatari*-inspired dreams and the discourse out of which such fictions are spun are not so easily relinquished. At the close of the memoir the voice of the young reader has given way to that of one of the most pathetically marginalized figures of the *monogatari* tradition, the abandoned aunt of the Obasute legend. In the end, the memoir inscribes its central figure on the margins, in the space of *monogatari* once more, despite its narrator-heroine's disavowal of them. But is this not also perhaps exactly where she had wanted to arrive all along? Is it not, as Musashi was for the Takeshiba princess, "a very good place to be"? In key ways, the Takeshiba legend recapitulates the travel account in which it is embedded like a *mise en abîme*; it is a retelling in little of the would-be reader's headlong journey to the capital. Does it not also, like the travel account itself, flirt with the dream of a self-authored destiny? Whether one interprets these narratives as cautionary or celebratory depends in large part on how one evaluates their central figures' final destinations. And the *Sarashina* traveler's destination will be no less ambiguously portrayed than that of the Takeshiba princess.

At once both biographical and rhetorical, the travel account in the *Sarashina nikki* probes not only figural language itself but also, more precisely, a particular feminine figure's relationship to figural language. The would-be bibliophile turns traveler and embarks on her first interrogations of rhetoricity to discover that topography and toponymic poetry seldom correspond to each other. At the journey's end, she is still naive enough to hold on to the hope that the topography of the capital, at least, will pass muster. And though the landscape of the capital may ultimately prove no more faithful to its literary precedents than that of the provinces, it is in the capital that her relationship to literature takes, at least initially, a wonderful turn. She approaches it as she approached each poetic site along the Eastern Road, with a name and a set of expectations conjured by that name. The difference this time is in the origin of the name—a name generated by the force of her own desire: "[That capital] where they say there are so many tales" (*NKBZ* 18: 283).

Calling attention to the traveler's naive expectation of a faithful correspondence between figural language and reality, the travel account lays bare the limits of figurality, the seams and gaps, the articulations between words (*kotonoha*) and things/events (*koto*). But when at the end of the journey the girl finally arrives in the capital, receives the long-hoped-for tales, and lies down alone to read them behind her screens, she dwells for a time in the one place (the site of the passionate reader's immersion in fiction) where faithful correspondence reigns, a space and an activity that sutures the gaps between words and events. Her prayers to go to the capital and there to see for herself "all the tales there are" have apparently made things happen. Now her name for the capital appears to be true. The relationship between figure and ground shifts again. What we are given, in the initial blissful passages describing the girl's first residence in the capital, is a topos of euphoria, a locus of textual pleasure. The girl's new residence in the capital is described as idyllic, the space of her first adventures in getting and reading her own books: a first batch from her imperial neighbor Princess Shūshi, the *Genji* and others from a generous provincial aunt, "the Chinese poem, *The Tale of Everlasting Sorrow* written as a *monogatari*" (*NKBZ* 18: 306), the copybook she learns to read and write from and that brings Fujiwara Yukinari's daughter, reborn as a cat, into her life.

It is a charmed space, though in a move that should by now seem familiar to the reader of the memoir, its charms are undercut by untoward events. Signs that even the girl herself harbors doubt about her own bliss perforate the euphoria periodically, most notably in the intermittent reports of her guilty dreams. And then her stepmother, presumably because of marital difficulties with the girl's father, leaves the house, the old nurse dies, and though the cat was once a Major Counselor's daughter, one fears for the latter's soul, reborn in the realm of beasts and fated to perish again when the house burns down, bringing to a bad end (with suitably Buddhist symbolic overtones)[44] the house, the space, and the period of the girl's initial dwelling in the city of tales. The house she next inhabits will become the site of much greater sorrows (her sister's death and her father's disappointment at court) and the point of departure for a life that will become, in the manner of her desire itself, increasingly peripatetic.

Good Reads and Bad Signs

Some of the most circuitous plots about fiction and desire in the *Sarashina nikki* evolve in the passages depicting the young reader's ambivalent perception of the relation between figures of Buddhist authority and her own passion for fiction. As we have already noted, the opening sequence of the memoir implicates the Yakushi Buddha as the benefactor in the tale of the girl's journey to the capital, and Buddhist icons continue to haunt the narrative like signs that the narration, much less the girl it constructs, fails to decipher explicitly.

Buddhist images preside over the account of the journey to the capital, punctuating the narrative at both the beginning and the end of the travel section. The girl's tearful parting from the Yakushi Buddha in the eastern provinces is echoed at the journey's end by the description of a Buddha statue at the eastern gates of the capital that catches her eye upon entrance to the city. Like the Yakushi Buddha, which corresponds to her own height, the tall, unfinished Miroku Buddha[45] at Sekidera, "as yet only roughed out" (*imada arazukuri ni owasuru*), corresponds, if not to her height, at least to her youth and to her no doubt travel-worn demeanor after three and a half months on the road (*NKBZ* 18: 297–98). Later in the memoir, some twenty-five years after her initial return to the capital from Azuma, she has a second encounter with the same statue while on a pilgrimage to Ishiyama. At this juncture too, the statue, which now appears "so splendidly accomplished" (*ikameshū tsukuraretaru*) (*NKBZ* 18: 343) is made to rhyme with her own materially improved lot (*NKBZ* 18: 342). And finally, toward the close of the memoir, Amida Buddha appears in the last and most compelling of the eleven short dream accounts embedded in the *Sarashina nikki* (*NKBZ* 18: 359–60). The dreamer has a vision of him standing in her own garden just beyond the eaves of her house, beckoning to her and promising to return for her later.

In between these momentous partings and encounters with specifically identified Buddhist icons—often on borderlines (geographical, metaphorical, and textual, liminal places in a narrative of spatial and spiritual wanderings)—a bewildering array of holy figures traverses the text, perplexing and tantalizing heroine and reader alike. Colorfully attired but stern Buddhist priests dominate three of the earliest dreams recounted in the memoir (*NKBZ* 18: 302, 304, and 322–23), only to give way in the dreams of the heroine's middle years to the smiling goddesses and court ladies who evoke either the bodhisattva Kannon or the principal Shinto goddess, Amateru onkami (hereafter Amaterasu)—or both simultaneously (*NKBZ* 18: 304, 323–24, and 347–48).[46]

As Kondō Hajime notes, the variety of holy figures either explicitly named or evoked by reference to specific temples in the *Sarashina nikki* is not so unusual; similarly random groupings may be found in the *Kagerō nikki* and *The Pillow Book*.[47] What he doesn't note, though his essay reflects this concern, is that commentators on the *Sarashina nikki* have been haunted for decades by the suspicion that the sacred figures mentioned in the *Sarashina nikki* signify in a more complex way than they do in other Heian court women's memoirs. Despite Kondō's conclusion that the *Sarashina nikki* evinces no "depth of religious consciousness," his essay has been followed by a rich array of studies that grapple with the religious symbolism everywhere apparent in the memoir.

Underlying many of these discussions is the assumption of an irreconcilable opposition between the "religious" and the "literary" impulses discernible in the language and symbolism of the *Sarashina nikki*. The memoir is seen as performing a kind of discursive balancing act that slides finally (and unhappily) toward the literary and the secular, the "world" (*sekai*) or "discourse" (*hyōgen*) of *monogatari*. Its closural gestures are generally understood to represent the memoirist's inability to extricate herself either from her lifelong addiction to *monogatari*[48] or from her nostalgia for the courtly world of *miyabi*,[49] despite the religious and renunciatory impulses that emerge so strongly in the final pages of the text. To oversimplify matters only a bit, the *Sarashina nikki* has been read as the tale of a lifelong spiritual pilgrimage in which the pilgrim simply fails to uncover the proper path toward enlightenment.

The seriousness of the *Sarashina nikki* as a text concerned with the process of its narrator-heroine's metaphysical destiny, the extent to which—to borrow Kondō's terms—it evinces "depth of religious consciousness," is masked not only by its heroine's professed obsession with fictional tales, but also by the writer's use of a *monogatari*-like narrative medium for her memoir. Not all Heian court women's memoirs were written as linear autobiographical narratives; in fact, it might be argued that most were not, depending on how one defines "*nikki*" and "autobiographical narrative." Many Heian works now labeled *nikki* tend toward the more or less disjointed, paratactic structures of personal poetry collections (*kashū*). As already noted, the *Sarashina nikki* appears in contrast much more concerned with developing narrative sequences that include implicit narrative relationships among events recounted. It is a tale haunted by questions about its own heroine's destiny—in the sense of both her literal destinations in time or space (*yuku-saki*) and her metaphysical destiny (*sukuse*)—and these questions impart form, and a kind of suspense, to the account of the heroine's spatial and spiritual wanderings from girlhood to old age.

Part of the tale the *Sarashina nikki* attempts to tell is that of a gradual movement toward truth, a movement that is made problematic both because it is rendered by a woman and because it is impelled by desire—the very impulse that Buddhist teachings enjoin the seeker to relinquish. The use of memoiristic narrative as the medium for such a tale creates further obfuscation. The heroine does not, indeed cannot, since the tale the *Sarashina nikki* tells is essentially autobiographical, arrive at her desired destination, though the memoir evokes that destination via the language and imagery of Buddhist beliefs, particularly those associated with the Pure Land (Jōdo) of Amida devotion, then being promoted by leaders of the Tendai sect such as the famous priest Genshin (942–1017). At the same time, like the *Genji monogatari* and some later Heian tales (most conspicuously the *Hamamatsu Chūnagon monogatari*), the memoir moves toward legitimizing the fictional discourse of *monogatari* (and its own *monogatari*-inspired narrative processes) by integrating figures drawn from more conventionally religious discourses. In the discussion that follows I will consider both the *Sarashina* heroine's narrative "destiny" and the way in which the memoir dramatizes, through the medium of a tale about a woman's destiny, tensions between the claims of *monogatari* and contemporary Heian Buddhist beliefs regarding fictional literature and salvation for women (*nyonin ōjō*).

Mid-eleventh-century Buddhist teachings were equivocal about the moral status of fictional literature. On the one hand, it was generally believed that both writers and readers of secular literature (particularly *monogatari*) risked committing one or more of the four "sins of language" (*kugō*) proscribed by the sutras, namely, falsehood (*mōgo*), equivocation (*ryōzetsu*), slander (*akku*), and frivolous or specious talk (*kigo*); any of these sins could, according to the *Kegon Sutra*, condemn one to rebirth in one of the three subhuman realms of existence: hell, the realm of hungry ghosts, or the realm of beasts[50] (one still worries about the feline fate of Yukinari's daughter). The belief that readers as well as writers of *monogatari* were risking their future salvation by involving themselves in the propagation and consumption of literary fictions is borne out by texts like the preface to *Sanbōe*.[51]

On the other hand, there is also evidence of a more conciliatory view of fictional literature available in eleventh-century Buddhist thought, the most obvious example being the allusion, via Genji's reference in "The Fireflies" chapter of *The Tale of Genji,* to the Buddhist defense of fiction on the grounds of its potential efficacy as *hōben* (literally, an "expedient means," a compassionately motivated modification of the truth for the sake of reaching those who might not even begin to understand it otherwise and thus a means of gradually leading the nonenlightened to a saving apprehension of the danger of attachment to the passions of this world).[52] This idea did not, of course, originate with the *Genji.* It reflects an older argument devised in part to account for the fact that the historical Buddha himself had used fictional parables to preach the Dharma. The concept of *hōben* is expounded by such enormously influential Buddhist scriptures as the *Lotus Sutra.*

The equivocality of popular Heian Buddhist beliefs regarding this issue is also played out in the variety of *setsuwa* concerning the fate of Murasaki Shikibu in the afterworld, a number of which depict her burning in hell for the sins she incurred by writing the *Genji monogatari.* Others, holding that so masterful a work as *Genji* could not possibly have been the work of a mortal, much less a woman, claim that Murasaki was in fact an incarnation of the bodhisattva Kannon.[53] The author of *Mumyōzōshi* (ca. 1196–1202) implicitly argued against both these extremes. One of the fictional ladies in that work describes Murasaki Shikibu as both pious and fully mortal and female, while the narrator, a nun whose chance visit to the decaying mansion full of reclusive ladies occasions the dialogue on tales and women, wins herself an invitation onto the veranda of the mansion when she begins intoning verses from the first fascicle of the *Lotus Sutra,* significantly, the chapter "Expedient Means."[54]

It has also been suggested that the *Sarashina* memoirist's preoccupation with both the spiritual dangers of secular fiction and poetry and their possible efficacy as vehicles of religious truth may have been fed in part by the professional concerns of the men in her traditionally literary family, the heads of which had, for four generations going back to their illustrious, if politically disgraced, ancestor Sugawara Michizane (845–903), held official scholarly posts such as *daigaku no kami* (head of the university) and *monjō hakase* (professor of literature).[55] During the later years of the Chōgen era (1028–36), the memoirist's brother Sadayoshi, having regained the scholarly post his family had lost during his father's day, seems to have been much involved with the Society for the Advancement of Learning (*Kangaku'e*), handling Buddhist ceremonies for the absolution of literary scholars from the sin of kyōgen kigo ("wild words and fancy phrases" in Po Chü-i's famous poetic formulation), that is, composing or indulging in the readership of nonreligious literature—informal poetry and fiction in Chinese and Japanese.[56] The Kangaku'e rites themselves underscore the conflicts in mid-Heian beliefs regarding the spiritual value of literary fictions. On the one hand, they testify that indulgence in kyōgen kigo was considered enough of a sin to warrant the performance of special prayers and rites. Yet on the other hand, the particulars of the rites, especially the use of Po Chü-i's poems (which legitimate the possibility that "even the basest writings are a hymn of praise to the Buddha"), simultaneously affirm the religious significance of the most secular literature.[57]

If mid-Heian Buddhist teachings were intellectually penetrated by the seductive discourse of secular literature, the seduction worked both ways. Court literature in mid Heian bears traces of a profound fascination with Buddhist doctrinal debate. The creation of a new category of poetry in the imperial anthologies that could incorporate Buddhist lexical items and imagery attests to attempts at deliberate assimilation of Buddhist themes into the court literary canon.[58] Somewhat earlier, Hosshin wakashū, a collection of waka on Buddhist themes by the Kamo High Priestess Senshi (964–1035), had overtly addressed the issue of nyonin ōjō (rebirth in paradise for women).[59] It should also be clear from the above that the issue of monogatari as "expedient means" played an important part in controversies over the boundaries between sacred and secular literature in the mid- to late-Heian period, with the Genji monogatari and its female author(s) and predominantly female readers providing an important focus for debate.[60] The Sarashina nikki also participates in and gives voice to the mid-Heian atmosphere of anxiety concerning the relationship between the production and consumption of fictional literature (especially by women) and religious ideology and practice (especially the issue of salvation for women). For our purposes, asking why the memoirist was thus preoccupied is of less interest than asking how the memoir manifests that preoccupation, by what rhetorical means it participates in that dialogue, and what contribution it makes.

As I have already noted in my reading of the topographical and toponymical games in the travel account, the Sarashina nikki delights in playing with fictions about the interpenetration of worlds that are otherwise commonly depicted as mutually antagonistic or exclusive. Of interest here is the rhetorical means by which the memoir toys with the idea of the permeability of boundaries and oppositions, especially be-tween the discourse of *monogatari* and what I will provisionally call the discourse of religious "truth." In this toying with different, sometimes conflicting attitudes, the metaphor of the dream (*yume*) plays a crucial role—as well it might, given its rootedness in the discourse of both Bud-dhist tradition and secular poetry. In the language of *waka*, the dream is the very image of fictional delusion, benighted, blind sleep, entangle-ment in the confusion of erotic passions, enlightenment's opposite. And yet dreams might also be sought and understood as messages from the gods and Buddhas, portents from the other world. Dreams spoke impor-tant truths to those who knew how to listen. To the extent that *mo-nogatari* appropriate the status of *hōben*, religious parable, while re-taining their link to the seductive pleasures of worldly fictions, they pos-sess the same double valence that invests the figure of the dream with so much fascination.

The image of Takasue's daughter as a breathless, passionate, but rather unreflective reader of dreams and *monogatari* is one of the clichés of critical commentary on the *Sarashina nikki*. Takasue's daughter has been charged (indeed she charges herself) with the error of confusing *monogatari* with reality and of misinterpreting and ignoring her own dreams, while the story of her eventual recognition of these errors be-comes an important part of the tale the *Sarashina nikki* tells. One of the subnarratives less frequently remarked on, however, is that of the sub-tle, positive connections the memoir makes among secular literature, holy figures, and religious truth. Later in her life, around the time of her marriage, the heroine emphatically discards *monogatari* as indicators of what life in the city of tales is like. But the possibility of their relation to holy figures and the discourse of truth is one she never completely dis-misses, though she only hints at the religious dimensions of tale litera-ture in the story of her own life.

A dream reported approximately midway through the *Sarashina nikki* strongly implies the didactic value of writing a memoir loaded with Buddhist figures, of integrating religious visions into the tale of a provincial governor's daughter's life. The woman is informed in the dream by a priest of Kiyomizu temple that she had been in a prior exis-tence a *busshi*, a maker of Buddhist icons. The priest indicates an unfin-ished Buddha statue on the premises that she had been working on at the time of her death and explains that though she had not been able to complete the statue in her lifetime, a disciple had finished the job for her, and the merit she had accumulated as a maker of many Buddhist icons had enabled her to be reborn into a good family in her present life (*NKBZ* 18: 330). While *monogatari* can only be controversial candidates for the status of *hōben*, Buddhist icons were legitimate art with a higher purpose, despite the humble social status of the craftspeople who made them. The dream (recapitulating in little the project of the memoir itself) dignifies the fantasy of the self as a maker of fictions by translating it into a sacred idiom.

In this dream account, as elsewhere, the memoir obliquely addresses the possibility of its own discourse as a heuristic means of indicating religious truth, perhaps the only means appropriate to the brush of a female pilgrim. But because this possibility is raised within the context of autobiographical narrative, the question about which voice makes this address complicates our reading and renders ambiguous the ultimate "position" of the memoir on the different viewpoints it entertains. Whom do we identify as the source of the memoir's disavowals and creative appropriations of Buddhist figures? With whose "voice" do we associate the distinctions and preferences hinted at by the play with different holy figures in this text? When and where is the heroine's heedless or wishfully idealized understanding of the relationship between tales and Buddhas distinguishable from the implicit viewpoints of the narrator/memoirist, whose perspectives also encompass a later life punctuated by more conventional pilgrimages and visions?

In the account of the girl's early years, holy figures are clearly caught up in the question of her guilty or blind desire for tales and the benighted dreams of a self-authored destiny that her reading of them nurtures. The Yakushi Buddha is presented as having had a hand both in granting her desires and in admonishing her to renounce them, an ambiguous role that plays out the equivocalities inherent in eleventh-century Buddhist views regarding the sinfulness of secular literature. We have already noted the suggestive role of the Yakushi icon in seeing the girl off on the road to the capital; if a timely journey home to the city of tales might be something one gained by addressing prayers to a Buddhist icon, then maybe the reading of them need not be seen as an irredeemably worthless pursuit. But when, at the age of fourteen (also apparently thanks in part to a Yakushi icon enshrined at Kōryūji in Uzumasa), the girl realizes her dream of possessing the *Genji*, she launches upon a season of intense reading that seems unalloyed by any conscious awareness that the gift bringing her so much pleasure might be connected to the prayers she offered up during her retreat at Uzumasa. Neither she, nor the narrator in her asides, explicitly seeks for any deeper, more occult origin of the gift; and neither acknowledges the possibility that her acceptance of it should have occasioned a burst of religious insight or warranted some act of gratitude. On the contrary, the girl's guilty dreams about overbearing yet handsome priests suggest she fails to recognize (or fears to trust) the signs she has had elsewhere that the Buddha has looked with favor on her prayers for procuring *monogatari*. But the apparent blindness of the heroine and the ambiguous silence of the narrator should not be simply dismissed as authorial confusion about the relationship of Buddhist figures to secular literature.

Between the lines of her life story (emphatically a story about wanting, pursuing, procuring, reading, and finally ostensibly renouncing secular fictions), a subplot about religious fantasies and granted prayers (that go unacknowledged) and sacred signs and texts (that go unread) recurs and persists, even beyond the point at which the narrating voice overtly comments on the folly of youthful immersion in *monogatari* and *monogatari*-inspired fantasies about an Ukifune-like destiny. Intimately linked to the young woman's willful, transgressive nature as a reader of tales, her readerly blindness will also not be confined to the interpretation of written texts. A kind of willful heedlessness, akin to the blind interpretations that initially govern her understanding of topography and toponymic poetry, operates in her dream life, especially when those dreams comment in a negative way on her passion for fiction.

Similarly, the larger tale of readerly blindness (reading as blindness, blindness as a sign of desire) persists well beyond the account of the young woman's period of interest in fictional literature. The woman's dreams themselves are treated as signs that may be willfully misread, dismissed, or reread. Late in the memoir, we read about her husband's (first and last) departure for the Shinano province and the ominous report the woman receives at the time of a *hitodama* (literally, a human spirit taking the form of a fiery shape) that is seen fleeing toward the capital along the road her husband's party had taken (*NKBZ* 18: 358). A *hitodama* is a bad omen, usually portending someone's death. Her initial response to the report (she unthinkingly assumes it portends the fate of someone else in the party) is characteristic of her lifelong habit of suppressing the negative signs she has seen in favor of others, more specifically, the dreams and signs that speak to the destiny she prefers imagining. Here again, the observation that the *Sarashina* memoirist simultaneously valorizes and distrusts "signs" (*shirushi*) is wonderfully suggestive of the way in which the memoir dramatizes the role desire plays in acts of reading and interpretation.[61]

Let us return for a moment to the debate summarized above concerning the ultimate position of this memoir (and the memoirist) regarding the relationship between secular literature and the discourse of religious truth. If we read the *Sarashina nikki* as the memoir of a spiritual pilgrimage, it becomes clear that both the girlish heroine and the older, somewhat wiser narrating persona fail to uncover a proper path to enlightenment. But this is not to suggest that the author herself was no further along than her literary (self-)creations or that the narrative bears no trace of an even wiser third hand implicit in its overall orchestration—especially its carefully plotted symbolic itineraries—a number of whose sequences we have already examined (the journey to the capital and the heroine's readings and misreadings of her own dreams). Let us consider another of these sets of symbolic structures. Commentators have often noted the neat, structural balance between the Yakushi Buddha figure in the opening passage of the *Sarashina nikki* and the Amida Buddha that appears toward the end.[62] In a fascinating essay on this topic, Kubo Tomotaka brings research on Pure Land iconography and temple design to bear on the prominent positioning of the Yakushi and Amida figures in the organization of the memoir.[63] Kubo identifies a typical Pure Land temple layout in which the hall housing images of the Yakushi Buddha occupies the east side of a central garden with icons facing west, while the Amida hall stands on the west side with icons facing east. The architectural arrangement defines a pilgrimage route for the worshiper by which the path through the temple compound symbolically replicates the journey of the soul from birth in the eastern Pure Land of Lapis Lazuli (*Jōruri*) presided over by Yakushi through the sufferings and passions of this world represented by the central garden itself, often divided by a stream or pond, which the pilgrim crosses midway in his path from "this shore" (*shigan*) to reach the "Other Shore" (*higan*), and culminating finally in an approach to the brink of rebirth (*ōjō*) in the Pure Land of Amida's Western Paradise, at the edge of which Amida waits to welcome the faithful. The significance of Yakushi's positioning in an eastern hall (and thus at the beginning of the worshiper's route through the compound) relates to that bodhisattva's identity as the Buddha of the Past. As such he oversees the beginning and the early stages of the pilgrim's spiritual journey. Along with Shaka (who may occupy a central hall on the north side of the compound), Yakushi is a figure to whom people commonly prayed for worldly benefits: good health, long life, safe childbirth, and so on.

Despite the scarcity of documentation on Heian temple layouts,

Kubo's main point is suggestive.[64] The topographical layouts of Pure Land–influenced temples in mid Heian embody a specific spatial and symbolic itinerary that corresponds broadly to a topographical and iconographic macrostructure discernible in the memoir: the girl's departure from her childhood home (with its Yakushi image) in the eastern provinces on a journey that takes her west to the capital and ultimately to a late, visionary encounter with Amida near the end of her life and of the memoir.[65]

Regardless of whether the finer points of Kubo's argument can be worked out satisfactorily against details in the memoir, his main argument—that the memoir incorporates a clearly articulated Pure Land itinerary within its own symbolic structure—goes a long way toward rescuing the *Sarashina nikki* and its author from charges of superficiality and vagueness on religious matters. The thematic structure of pilgrimage toward the Western Paradise points to a very specific religious aspiration: *ōjō* (crossing over, or rebirth in Paradise), as opposed to *jōbutsu* (direct attainment of Buddhahood), the former being a much more modest goal, appropriate especially to a female pilgrim in the "Latter Days of the Law."[66] What this structure suggests is a far more precise appropriation of Buddhist symbolism in the *Sarashina nikki* than has been generally thought. It also returns us to the question of how the text rhetorically engages the problematic status of women (not to mention *monogatari*, that nefariously fictional genre women so loved to read) in mid-Heian Buddhist thought.

Like *Hosshin wakashū*, the *Sarashina nikki* is preoccupied not simply with the question of religious salvation, but more specifically with the issue of salvation for women. The problem was apparently a nagging one for upper-class Heian women. For if woman is, as she was according to some Heian Buddhist beliefs, always reducible to an object of desire, she is in her very essence as female something that must be transcended. One cannot be both female and a Buddha, as the tale of the Dragon King's daughter affirms (see discussion below, pp. 123–24), even as it establishes grounds for the possibility that women might aspire to a transcendence of their gender. And yet, the *Sarashina nikki* seems at some pains to draw connections between spiritual progress toward rebirth in Paradise and those feminine agents and fictional media conventionally considered at odds with religious enlightenment and the transcendence of desire. In other words, the *Sarashina nikki* also portrays feminine figures and *monogatari* as bearers of signs that can potentially lead the reader toward enlightenment. This is a bold move, and tell-

ingly, the memoir downplays its own polemic by underscoring the eccentricity of its heroine and her deviance from the common lot of other
Heian ladies, both fictional and historical.

In the opening passage of the memoir, the girl performs her ablutions
and prays to Yakushi in a kind of guilty secrecy that suggests awareness
of the sinful impropriety of addressing a holy figure with requests for
fictional tales. During her first retreat to worship Yakushi at Uzumasa,
she similarly defies convention and prays to see the entire *Tale of Genji*
from beginning to end (*NKBZ* 18: 301). Pilgrimages were, in principle,
to be performed for the purpose of accumulating religious merit or
worldly gain. One prayed for the repose of souls in the afterworld, for a
loved one's health, or for the advancement at court of a father or husband, but nothing so vain as procuring a pack of silly tales. Strictly
speaking, such literature was inherently sinful because it was false, par-
taking in lies. Regardless of the possible efficacy of fiction as an "expedient means," both the narrator and the heroine she evokes appear well
aware that infatuation with tales has not drawn her in the direction
most people seem properly bent on traveling: "I sometimes make pilgrimages but I am never able to pray sincerely that I might become like
others. These days, it seems that people begin reading sutras and engaging in religious services from the age of seventeen or eighteen, but
such things interest me not at all" (*NKBZ* 18: 317).

The contrast made here between the willfully unconventional behavior of the girl and that of those around her who conform docilely to
the norms of Buddhist practice places her in the company of other literary women. The reader will recall the protagonist of the *Kagerō nikki*
who also rebels, though in a significantly more strident, outspoken
manner, against women who go around "telling over beads and reading
sutras" (*NKBZ* 9: 255). In both these examples, the topoi of conventional religious practices become occasions for bringing into focus issues
of gender and identity. The disinclination to fulfill the norms of lay
Buddhist practice becomes a sign of the individual woman's difference
from other women, a posture that indicates her unique identity among
other women.

Whatever the girl, or the memoirist as a girl, might have gleaned
from tales regarding life and love in court circles, the memoir's portrayal of her abiding interest in fiction also concerns the way these fictions call into question mid-Heian religious practices and gender ideologies. In this respect, the early sections of the memoir can be read as a
sustained attempt to recuperate and dignify, by means of an intricate

appropriation of Buddhist themes and figures, the role of *monogatari* in young women's lives. We have already noted how the portrait of a provincial girl who spends most of her teens and twenties shut up behind her screens reading whatever fiction she can get her hands on extends and exaggerates the figure of certain socially marginalized heroines of *monogatari* (Tamakazura, Suetsumuhana, and Ukifune, to name only three from *The Tale of Genji* alone). What is especially interesting about the reinscription of that feminine figure in the *Sarashina nikki*, however, is the way the memoir involves it in the dramatization of a broader ambivalence about desire (as manifest in the girl's appetite for fiction) and the religious truths and practices that the girl at first evades and then gradually comes to embrace more and more eagerly as the venues and objects of her desire shift from literature to more conventional worldly gains such as a successful career at court for herself and securing her children's futures.

Anxieties about the relation of fiction and the feminine to Buddhist belief surface elsewhere in Heian court literature and were perhaps most memorably staged in the famous dialogue on *monogatari* that takes place between Genji and Tamakazura in "The Fireflies" chapter of *The Tale of Genji*. In the *Sarashina nikki*, as in the discussion of *monogatari* in *Genji*, the issue of gender differences complicates the thematic treatment of the relationship between fictional literature and religious truth. If Genji, on the one hand, and Tamakazura, on the other, can be said to voice conventionally masculine and feminine perspectives in an argument about the nature and value of fictional tales, then the *Sarashina nikki* portrays its heroine's entire life as an arena for the playing out of dialectic tensions between masculine authority and feminine resistance and religious dogma and literary fictions.

Gender-specific attitudes toward fiction and religious truth crisscross the *Sarashina nikki*, becoming most vividly apparent in the accounts of the girl's search for books and the guilty dreams and prayers her search inspires. In this quest, as in many of the dreams that punctuate the early pages of the memoir, masculine and feminine figures embody conspicuously opposing viewpoints. While the girl's misgivings about the spiritual evils of fiction find form and voice in censorious male authority figures (the admonitory Buddhist priests who figure in her first three dreams), her female relatives and acquaintances license her illicit desires for fiction and directly abet her in her passionate acquisition of them. The narrative frames the arrival of the girl's first bundle of books as the result of a series of cross-class and cross-generational exchanges among

different female intercessors. The girl begs tales from her mother, who
in turn begs them by letter on her behalf from a certain Emon no myōbu, a female relative in service at the neighboring Sanjō Palace, the residence of Princess Shūshi. The texts finally sent her had themselves been
a gift from the Princess to Emon no myōbu, who in turn gives them to
the girl (NKBZ 18: 298–99). In this exchange, female figures stand
clearly and conventionally on the side of fantasy and indulgence in fictional literature. Fiction and religious truth, however, appear problem-
atically linked, at least at this phase in the narrative.

On the surface, the same pattern seems to govern the portrayal of her
acquisition of The Tale of Genji from an "aunt." Biographical scholars,
whose readings indicate yet another involved chain of female intercessors, date the episode to 1021 and speculate that this copy of Genji may
ultimately have come into the memoirist's hands through family connections with Murasaki Shikibu's daughter, Daini no Sanmi (999–after
1078), to whom the memoirist's stepmother was related by marriage.[67]
But true to the girl's persona as an outsider to capital society, the memoir frames the transaction as far more unprepossessing. The tales come
as a gift from an otherwise unidentified aunt (oba naru hito) who has
just returned from the provinces. And yet more is implied. The sequence
of events leading up to the visit suggests that the ultimate provenance of
the tales was a bit more miraculous than books from an aunt in the
provinces. In the passage immediately preceding the account of the visit
with the aunt, the narrator describes the first of three religious retreats
made to Uzumasa, where, obsessed with her desire for more tales, the
one thing the girl prays for is that she may be "shown the entire Tale of
Genji from the first chapter on" (NKBZ 18: 301). The narrating voice,
merging empathetically at this point with the perspective of the girl, implies disappointment when she sees no evidence that her prayer finds an
immediate answer upon emergence from the retreat, but this remark is
something of a red herring, since the next event related is the momentous visit soon thereafter with the aunt who hands over, as though in
belated answer to the girl's prayer, "the fifty-odd chapters of The Tale
of Genji" (NKBZ 18: 301–2).

As in the opening passage of the memoir, the sequence of events in
the narrative here implicates Yakushi as the ultimate patron of the girl's
acquisition of presumably bad books, while at the same time underscoring the importance of female agency, for example, the mother's retreat to Uzumasa with her daughter in tow, the girl's feverish prayers
themselves, and the kindly aunt from the provinces. But despite the im-

plicit positive links suggested here and elsewhere between ostensibly
genderless figures of Buddhist authority like Yakushi and Amida and
emphatically female purveyors of secular literature, the early sections of
the *Sarashina nikki* express profound anxiety about the conventional
terms by which Heian women were expected to accommodate themselves to existing standards of religious behavior and belief. Although
the narrator's later denunciation of *monogatari* brings her and the memoir into apparent conformity with more conservative views on fiction as
morally perilous *kyōgen kigo* ("wild words and fancy phrases"), the
memoir subtly but repeatedly suggests that the alternatives to the pleasures of fiction—in both the secular world of court society and the alternative world of Buddhist renunciation—were supremely unattractive
and just as unlikely as fiction to offer a realizable (or morally acceptable) model for a woman's destiny. And the undesirable (because they
are excessively difficult to realize) models afforded by the Buddhist
teachings explicitly identified in the early sections of the memoir are
also strikingly associated with masculine or masculinized figures.

Consider the first dream in the memoir, which the girl has during the
height of her initial immersion in *The Tale of Genji*. A handsome priest
in a yellow surplice who disapproves of her preferred reading material
appears before her and tersely orders her to "learn the fifth fascicle
[*kan*] of the *Lotus Sutra* immediately" (*NKBZ* 18: 302). Though neither
he nor the narrating voice expands on its contents, the book the dream-
priest recommends contains the tale of the Dragon King's daughter and
her miraculous transformation at the age of eight into a Buddha
(overcoming instantaneously the "Five Obstacles" [*itsutsu no sawari*]
that prevent women from attaining enlightenment, according to some
doctrines).[68] The text was important to revisionist developments in mid-
Heian and later in medieval Buddhist thought because it provided a
scriptural basis for the argument that even women might be capable of
attaining Buddhahood (*jōbutsu*)—though significantly not without first
transcending their female bodies.[69] Assuming that the memoirist, recounting the dream as part of the memoir she carefully crafts in her
later years, was aware of the content of the fifth fascicle of the *Lotus
Sutra*, I read the passage as yet another symbolic juncture in the subnarrative of the young reader's half-blind pilgrimage through the range of
social and metaphysical options offered mid-Heian females. The path of
jōbutsu for women indicated in the *Lotus Sutra* would have been a narrow one indeed, significantly not taken, to be superseded instead in the
symbolic topography hinted at in the itineraries of the *Sarashina nikki*

by the broader one offered through devotion to Amida. In other words, the memoir ultimately seems to advocate ōjō, or rebirth in the Pure Land of Amida's Western Paradise, where, encouraged by the happy environment in that higher realm of existence, the pilgrim might have a better start at approaching the more difficult goal of Buddhahood in a subsequent rebirth.

But at this stage in the memoir, these matters are not spelled out. What is commemorated instead is the apparent blindness and passion of the young reader. What is the girl's response to the dream? This sign—both the man in the dream and the sacred text he recommends—will go unheeded and unread. She will continue to read only what she wishes to read. Displaced before it can fully emerge, the fifth fascicle of the *Lotus Sutra*, with its story about the Dragon King's wise but ultimately masculine daughter, pales before the erotic, exaggeratedly feminine figures the girl prefers aspiring to. She confesses:

I told no one of the dream, and I had no intention of learning the sutra. I cared only for tales. I may not be much to look at these days, but when I come into full flower, I will be as lovely as any, and my hair will grow so long. In my heart I imagined that I would become a lady like Shining Genji's Yūgao, or the Uji Captain's Ukifune—and now, before all else, it is this that I find so very vain and appalling. (*NKBZ* 18: 302–3)

The final line in this passage comprises one of the first of the several asides in which a distinctly distanced narrating voice emerges to deplore the folly of the young reader and her heedless heart ("before all else it is this"). But one suspects that the regret expressed here is somewhat disingenuous, that the voice is not fully convinced of the spiritual worthlessness of the girl's chosen reading matter (or indeed of the unworthiness of her gender). Nostalgically evoking her euphoric youthful immersion in readerly pleasures, the early sections of the memoir implicitly protest the exacting and joyless alternatives that await the Heian lady in other spheres, such as a peripheral position in court service or an arranged, polygynous marriage. Or, if she is spiritually inclined, she can contemplate the unsatisfactory subtext in the tale of the Dragon King's daughter, that the only woman worth imitating is a woman who, heeding the priestly men who denounce her for her foolishness, relinquishes womanhood entirely and becomes more like what the dream-priests would have her become (neither male nor female, but a gender-transcendent Buddha).

The critical consensus on the *Sarashina* heroine (and memoirist) as a

naive reader whose passion for fiction was an addiction and whose religious consciousness remains undeveloped fails to take into account the
considerable energy and creative activity that inform the acts of reading,
dreaming, and interpretation portrayed in this memoir. In particular, it
has failed to address the extent to which the sequence of these acts
comprises a narrative of spiritual seeking, a movement that seeks to me-
diate between the oppositions (religion and literature, truth and falsehood, masculinity and femininity) that inform the text. It is the force of
desire that motivates the heroine to resist or ignore the agendas others
seek to impose on her, and she attempts to exert power, to "author" her
own destiny and define its significance by the way she reads and mis-
reads her experiences. And her resistance is not simply and clearly a
matter of resisting the agendas of authoritative figures like Buddhist
priests and their teachings or the normative plots of aristocratic courtship and marriage. As I have already suggested in my reading of the
travel account, the tales themselves, like the girl's dreams, proffer their
own ambiguous scripts and signs for female readers. And not even they
are safe from the *Sarashina* memoirist's willful readings. It is there, in
the memoir's appropriations of the figures of *monogatari,* that the
shapes of desire emerge most clearly.

4 ⌒ The Desire for Fiction in the *Sarashina nikki*

In this chapter I argue that the last word on fiction in the *Sarashina nikki* is not disillusionment but rather an effort to establish a meaningful place for the desire for fiction in the story of a woman's movement toward religious enlightenment. My argument revolves around readings of the new tales the memoir creates out of the stories its heroine so avidly reads; thus, each section of the chapter involves intertextual readings of specific figures the memoir appropriates from other "texts," both literary and religious. The first section profiles the three *Genji* heroines named or alluded to in the *Sarashina nikki*: Yūgao, Ukifune, and Suetsumuhana, analyzing the unique composite the memoir creates with its reprise of these heroines.[1] The second section explores the way biographical and contextual details surrounding the *Sarashina* memoirist's career at court reinforce and supplement the significance of the heroine's preferred *Genji* intertexts. The third section focuses on the role that figures of a different sort—bodhisattvas and Shinto deities—play in the dreams and pilgrimages of the heroine's middle and later years. The chapter closes with a meditation on the final passages of the memoir and its closural reconfiguring of the desire to read as the desire for a reader. The aim of these analyses is twofold. First, this chapter carries through the work begun in Chapter 3; it delineates the memoir's thematics of reading as they are dramatized in the plot of the heroine's pilgrimage as a reader. Second, it suggests the way the thematic strategies of the *Sarashina nikki*—particularly its engagement of religious issues and its preference for certain types of fictional heroes and heroines—link the work both to ideas latent in the final third of *The Tale of Genji* and to major thematic preoccupations discernible in late Heian *monogatari*.

We begin, however, with a few remarks on a *Genji* heroine the memoir does not mention, though she clearly embodies the type of *monoga-tari* heroine who characteristically reads tales naively as source books of plausible precedents for her own destiny. We have already mentioned the *Genji* heroine Tamakazura and her feverish quest for precedents to her own bizarre situation vis-à-vis Genji (*NKBZ* 14: 202; S, 436–37), but it is worth pausing a moment longer over the notion of her as precedent, as *tameshi*, if only because it suggests so vividly a range of attributes and possibilities that the *Sarashina* memoirist may have actively preferred to exclude from her tale.

Like both Takasue's daughter and the fictional character Ukifune, Tamakazura hails from the provincial borderlands of Heian civilization, and her beginnings, like theirs, are extremely unpromising. And yet, as one of the nameless ladies in *Mumyōzōshi* notes, "proud and clever, Tamakazura was no *yukari* ["link" or "surrogate"] for [her] ephemeral [mother] Yūgao."[2] Her case differs remarkably from most fictional females of the middle ranks (and especially her mother's), in that life turns out comparatively well for her as far as her material well-being is concerned, thanks in part to her own practicality. This point marks a crucial difference between Tamakazura and her less tenacious fictional kin. Her story turns in part on her discovery that the situations one faces in life may in fact have no precedent in fiction (itself a ruse, which the *Genji* narration is at some pains to ensure that the reader will see through—Tamakazura's tale is one of the more self-consciously intertextual in the *Genji* narrative). Her sweaty search through the tales as she sojourns uneasily at Genji's Rokujō mansion during the rainy season one year yields her little that sheds light on the uncomfortably complex dynamics of her relationship to Genji, who, while masquerading as her father and patron in the business of finding her a proper husband, also presses her with his own suit as lover.

The manner in which she is finally coupled with a husband involves a similar negation of the *tameshi* trope, of precedents and models, of the already written, if only because that segment of her story goes untold. The account of Tamakazura's sudden marriage to Higekuro comprises one of the significant ellipses in *The Tale of Genji*. It is not actually recounted; we are simply presented with the results at the opening of "The Cypress Pillar" (*Makibashira*): Genji admonishing Higekuro to keep the marriage quiet for a while, Tamakazura's continued unhappiness, and Genji's own disappointment. But although Higekuro has none of the seductive allure of which heroes like Genji are made, he is the third most powerful man in the regime. With him as her husband, Tamakazura finally emerges from the protracted romantic plots Genji seeks to weave around her, and yet she maintains Genji's interest and respect despite the strange difficulties of her past life as his "unfilial daughter." We might also note in passing that the *Sarashina* heroine's marriage is similarly passed over in silence, though apparently the silence on her account masks the banality rather than the scandal of her coupling. Takasue's daughter was no orphan, prey to the libidinous attentions of a foster father or the preemptive intrusions of the politically powerful. In her memoir both parents are present and actively, even obtrusively, involved in deliberations about her future, both her marriage and her career at court. As for the narrator's attitude toward the marriage, we are offered only one oblique remark, an expression of disillusionment with a reality that compares unfavorably to literary fantasy: "Is there, in this world, any man like the Shining Genji? Or a woman like the one Captain Kaoru hid away at Uji?—this is a world where she could never be. I had been quite crazy to think otherwise" (*NKBZ* 18: 332).

Of course, Tamakazura—and here one assumes that her story rhymes with that of Takasue's daughter—also does not, in all this, make the match she would herself have preferred. Previously there had been plans for installing her as *naishi no kami* (principal handmaid)—and thus as possible concubine or consort—to Emperor Reizei, Genji's handsome illegitimate son by Fujitsubo, whom Tamakazura had been allowed to see and to compare with her other suitors in the striking scene of female spectatorship and male self-display occasioned by the royal procession to Oharano in "The Royal Outing" (*Miyuki, NKBZ* 14: 282–83; S, 468–69). Higekuro, also part of the procession that Tamakazura watches so attentively, fares poorly in comparison to the other men on the scene. Tamakazura's judicious, discriminating, and desirous gazing is worth remarking on because it further elaborates the trope of the unprecedented (and therefore, perhaps, unrepeatable) tale.

It borders on the unprecedented simply that Tamakazura should be represented as a woman who conceives her own desire for a man (and that man an emperor, no less), though her viewing of him, her vision, is manipulated.[3] Although Tamakazura is ultimately denied fulfillment of her desire for Emperor Reizei,[4] the orphan who grew up in the wilds of Tsukushi ends by becoming fully integrated into the world of court society (a development that again negates the precedent of other provincial heroines in court fiction, who usually remain dispossessed and marginalized—though often beautifully and movingly so). We see Tamakazura last in "The Bamboo River" (*Takegawa*) as a widowed matron preoccupied not with romance but with the material success of her numerous and healthy brood. As an exemplar of the kind of socioeconomic success that might be open to obscure yet quick-witted and adaptable provincial heroines, Tamakazura's story stands, on a number of counts, in direct opposition to the tale of her mother, Yūgao, and that of Ukifune (not to mention the story of the Takeshiba princess as retold in the *Sarashina nikki*, who, though royal by birth, actively embraces the destiny of obscurity and monogamy in the provinces). Tamakazura's itinerary also resonates in a number of ways with the practical aspects of the *Sarashina* memoirist's "real" life, aspects that do not figure prominently in her memoir, perhaps because they all relate to stories she has not authored herself and therefore does not wish to claim—her late marriage and maternity (both events elided in the *Sarashina nikki*), the raising of her dead sister's children, her management of her father's household after her older sister's death and her mother's taking of lay religious orders—in short, the tale of her active participation in the ordinary run of Heian family life. What the memoirist excludes or minimizes is as much a comment on her aspirations as the things she expressly names.[5]

A Lady Like Shining Genji's Yūgao, or the Uji Captain's Ukifune

What do we make of the three rather more ephemeral *Genji* women named as analogues for the heroine in the *Sarashina nikki*? What scenarios of desire and destiny do they imply? And what do they suggest about the rhetorical strategies at work in the story of her life? The memoir alludes explicitly to two different *Genji* heroines (Yūgao and Ukifune) and implicitly, in its final passages, to a third (Suetsumuhana). The first two represent heroines the girl wishes to emulate. Steeped in the blissful space of her first readings of *The Tale of Genji*, the girl actively wants to become a "lady like Shining Genji's Yūgao, or the Uji Captain's Ukifune," whereas the allusion to Suetsumuhana appears only very late in the memoir, indicating what in fact the older woman becomes, despite her youthful desires. This is not to say, however, that the figure of Suetsumuhana signifies only disillusionment with the dream of becoming a *Genji*-type heroine. Like the memoir's late reprise of the Obasute legend, the allusion to Suetsumuhana, if less ingenuous in tone than the earlier references to Yūgao and Ukifune, suggests equally complex fictions of desire.

But let us turn our attention first to the inter- and intratextual resonances among these three *Genji* heroines. All of them are figures whose stories hinge on an initial geographical and symbolic peripherality to, and eventual exclusion from, the world of the court. Of no one is this more tragically true than Yūgao, whose name crops up only once in the *Sarashina nikki*. Having been admonished to read the fifth fascicle of the *Lotus Sutra*, the *Sarashina* heroine continues to read *Genji* and to fantasize instead about growing up to look like Yūgao, an aspiration that itself could only belong to a girl young enough to see the childlike Yūgao as a plausible role model. *Genji* readers would of course recall that Yūgao's brief affair with Genji reaches its unexpected climax in an abandoned estate on the edge of the capital where the heroine winds up dead, the victim of an unidentified vengeful spirit who appears to be that of Lady Rokujō, one of Genji's high-ranking women.

Given this gothic outcome, it seems likely that the singling out of Yūgao by the girl in the *Sarashina nikki* would have struck a contemporary reader as an ill-omened choice, as yet another detail to add to the image of the heroine's persistent benightedness. And indeed, although no explicit reference to Yūgao reoccurs, some ghost of her memory breathes on in the dark closing pages of the memoir, with its evocation of the aged *Sarashina* heroine's lonely, unvisited house—buried in wormwood, like both Suetsumuhana's Hitachi mansion and the ramshackle villa where Yūgao met her end. This same allusion to the overgrown setting of the Hitachi mansion, the scene of Suetsumuhana's neglected state after her father's death and before Genji's rediscovery of her, subtly links all three *Genji* heroines, since Ukifune came to the capital originally from the Hitachi province, where her stepfather was vice-governor. And though Suetsumuhana was not of the provincial governor's class and had never been tainted by residence in the provinces, her late father was the Hitachi Prince—Hitachi being a province nominally governed by a prince of the blood. The young reader in the *Sarashina nikki* who prefers Yūgao and Ukifune to the Dragon King's daughter, and who imagines she will grow up to be a peerless beauty with long hair, ends up an old woman, composing a poem that alludes to the incorrigibly hopeful Suetsumuhana—the lady who (despite her own extravagantly long and lovely hair) failed to win a sexually active position for herself among Genji's loves and yet nonetheless gained herself a permanent place, by sheer tenacity, on the margins of Genji's world.

All three figures, but especially Suetsumuhana and Ukifune, represent peculiarly exaggerated instances of the figure of the *yukari,* or erotic surrogate, a woman singled out for pursuit by a male admirer longing to find in her some resemblance to a prior love now lost or out of reach. All three fail to fulfill the erotic destinies their would-be admirers project on them. But their failure is more complex and perhaps not as inadvertent on their parts as it may initially appear. Recent rereadings of their stories suggest that they are not simply women barred from entering into sustained romantic involvement because they cannot measure up to the idealized images of other women whom the hero wishes them to replace. Yūgao, who came into Genji's orbit partly as a result of his frustrated pursuit of the ultimately unattainable Fujitsubo, is barred, of course, by her early death. But Doris Bargen's reexamination of the spirit possession episodes in *Genji* suggests that the narrative of Yūgao's strange demise masks a subplot of feminine resistance and will. Highlighting the less obvious triangulations at work in "The Evening Faces" (*Yūgao*), Bargen reads that heroine's spirit possession as "an oblique aggressive strategy" for reversing, if only momentarily, the hierarchies of class and gender between herself and her two high-ranking lovers, Genji and Tō no Chūjō, thereby deliberately absenting herself from a world that offers her no secure options.[6]

Suetsumuhana's relation to Fujitsubo, Genji's original ideal but forbidden love, is even more attenuated than Yūgao's. Genji initiates his affair with her in the hope of discovering a substitute for the dead Yūgao. Suetsumuhana is thus sought merely as a surrogate for a surrogate. She is blighted and disqualified by her unfortunate nose, red and elongated as her sobriquet suggests, but it is not just her nose that disconcerts Genji (and everyone else who comes into contact with her). Suetsumuhana is a willfully self-marginalizing figure, possessed of an excessively timid and reclusive yet stubbornly tenacious temperament. In the arch idiom of Edward Seidensticker's *Genji* narrator, she "in no respect even rises to mediocrity" (*NKBZ* 13: 343; S, 302). Her bloodlines do, of course, work in her favor, but what makes her memorable to Genji (and to *Genji* readers) is her decided oddness. Had she lacked the features marking her as bizarre, Genji might have forgotten her entirely.

Her peculiarities secure her finally—and improbably—a place on the fringes of Genji's erotic and political concerns. After completely renovating Suetsumuhana's dilapidated Hitachi mansion and restoring its overgrown garden, Genji installs her in his Eastern Pavilion rather than in his mansion at Rokujō, the residence of women who were "either ac-

tive sexual partners or actual sources of power."[7] The *Genji* narrator
tentatively suggests that Suetsumuhana feels at times somewhat less
than gratified with the ultimate outcome of her short-lived affair with
Genji and with the peripheral, if enduring, place she gains for herself in
his world (*NKBZ* 14: 146; S, 413). But it is also made clear, given her
ridiculously unfashionable and unerotic identity, that her destiny is, like
that of the Takeshiba Princess, a "very good place to be," if not clearly
so in her own eyes, then at least from the perspective of many around
her. Certainly it is far beyond anything for which Suetsumuhana, a fa-
therless Heian woman with a combination of stubbornness, pride, and
physical deformities, could have reasonably hoped. She gets more, at
least by the standards of the world of *Genji*, than she merits, though
what she gets also testifies to her comic oddness.

But whereas Yūgao and Suetsumuhana only make cameo appearances in the memoir, Ukifune is explicitly named four times in the
Sarashina nikki, and there are several allusions implicitly recalling her as
well.[8] Critics who downplay the self-consciously rhetorical aspects of
figures of reading in this memoir have also been inclined to regard the
girl's infatuation with Ukifune as simply inappropriate, as an uncomprehending admiration based on a simplistic reading (by the memoirist
herself) of Ukifune's destiny. For the most part, the woman portrayed in
the *Sarashina nikki* is no *yukari*, no surrogate for Ukifune, if for no
other reason than that her life story lacks the very elements that have
made Ukifune's so interesting to readers in the last decades of the twentieth century. The tale of Ukifune's destiny plays itself out in the arena
of her two blighted love affairs, and subplots revolving around bedroom
politics and class consciousness in the mid-Heian court play large roles
in the development of her story. Comparisons of the two life stories invariably highlight the *Sarashina* heroine's extreme reclusiveness, especially when it comes to her relations with men and to her career at
court. And yet, as I shall argue below, the several references to Ukifune
in the *Sarashina nikki* are quite discriminating, illuminating elements of
the appeal this heroine bore for later readers in the Heian court tradition.[9] Rather than dismissing the heroine's affinity for Ukifune as inappropriate, we might ask instead who Ukifune is in the context of the
Sarashina nikki.

Once one begins to recognize the marginal, the "readerly," and the
autoerotic as sites of positive textual pleasure and creativity in the
Sarashina nikki, a new understanding of the fictions about desire (and
the desire for fiction) becomes not only possible, but central to further

pursuit of the question: How does feminine desire inscribe itself in a literary tradition where such desire must at least appear to remain contained by patriarchal limits? In Chapters 5 and 6, I will explore the mechanism of the gaze and its role in inscribing desire in the memoirs of women who spent significant parts of their lives immersed in service at court, where everyone, male and female, spent much of their time looking and being looked at in return. But we need not be bound by the assumption that the Heian heroines and female writers who appropriated the gaze did so merely to mimic or to deconstruct masculinized patterns of looking. *The Pillow Book* and the *Sanuki no suke nikki* raise the possibility that feminine desire may "express itself voyeuristically, through a gaze that is mediated . . . in ways that are not recognizable on the basis of male-oriented discussions of the triangulation of desire."[10]

The *Sarashina nikki* also bears closer examination in this regard. Its heroine embodies a figure who actively prefers looking at representations of love affairs to love affairs themselves, the space of solitary reading to the exposed conditions of a career as a lady-in-waiting, where, she explains, her own gaze lacks focus, while she herself can only submit to becoming the object of someone else's apprising eye and ear: "I could do nothing but stare into thin air and brood [*sora ni nagamekurasaru*]. Then too, it seemed there was always someone standing and listening, or peeking in on me, and this made me very ill at ease" (*NKBZ* 18: 328–29). The readerly vices the *Sarashina* narrator confesses to throughout the memoir center not just on a blind obsession with fiction, but also, and more to the point, on a willful preference for looking at fiction rather than at other kinds of "texts." She actively uses reading fiction as something she can interpose between herself and the passively sexual scenarios of "normal" feminine destiny, scenarios in which, as the above quotation suggests, the woman, unable to pursue her own desires, is rendered merely the unwilling object of the desirous male gaze.

The marginal and the autoerotic as sites of textual pleasure become most conspicuous in the account of the *Sarashina* heroine's efforts in the arena of courtly love. The slight, inconsequential affair she almost has with a courtier who enters her life briefly in the context of two chance conversations, to be textualized as poignant, extended passages in the memoir (six pages in the *NKBZ* edition), underlines the extremity of her outsider status at court.[11] Read against the precedent of Ukifune's performances in the realm of courtly romance and even compared to the brief comic and tragic roles of Suetsumuhana and Yūgao, the account of the *Sarashina* heroine's exchanges with the courtier, whom later readers identified as Minamoto Sukemichi (1005–60), inscribes new lows in the history of the provincial heroine's erotic potential. But need we see this simply as a failure?

The reasons for the failure of this affair have been variously interpreted, usually with Takasue's daughter coming off as simply a rather pale and timid thing. Again, commentators typically conflate memoirist and heroine and resort to biography to account for trope, though arguably the relation here may be working in the opposite direction, with trope giving rise to biography. Whether they understand her as an actual historical personage or as a textual construct based on the memoir, critics compare Takasue's daughter unfavorably to wittily acerbic figures like Sei Shōnagon and the "sexually enterprising" Izumi Shikibu. One translator-commentator even speculates that the fault might be laid on Takasue's daughter's lack of sex appeal.[12] All these interpretations assume an underlying desire on the part of the memoirist-*cum*-heroine to enter into a sexual liaison with Sukemichi. I would argue, however, that regardless of what Takasue's daughter may have desired of Minamoto Sukemichi, the heroine evoked in the *Sarashina nikki* is portrayed as actively preferring to stay out of sexual entanglements; furthermore, what is appealing about Sukemichi, as he is depicted in the memoir, is precisely his distance and elegant reserve. Sukemichi, to play with the lines of the anonymous lady reader in *Mumyōzōshi*, is no *yukari* for Genji (or even for the more ambivalent, though ultimately, perhaps, no less libidinous Kaoru). The elegant reserve that signifies his difference from the great *Genji* heroes suggests more than an ambiguous (because it is merely negative) sign of the *Sarashina* memoirist's ambivalent desire. It also foreshadows a new breed of *monogatari* hero, anticipating some of the developments characteristic of late Heian *monogatari*.

The positive eroticizing of sexual reserve or even abstinence in the construction of central masculine figures becomes a key theme in both the *Hamamatsu Chūnagon monogatari* and the *Torikaebaya monogatari*.[13] In the former tale, the hero returns from his long sojourn in China to find that his first love has become a Buddhist nun. Descriptions of their chaste yet idyllic cohabitation punctuate the narrative of that tale; the hero's eroticized restraint with his former lover now turned nun recalls, but reworks Kaoru's treatment of Ōigimi (and Ōigimi's treatment of Kaoru). Regardless of whether Takasue's daughter actually wrote the *Hamamatsu Chūnagon monogatari*, the thematic linkages between this late Heian tale and the *Sarashina nikki* involve more than just both works' extensive use of dream accounts and Buddhist motifs. What we witness in both is not so much a naive, uncomprehending appropriation of *Genji* figures as, on the contrary, a hyperbolic rewriting that gestures, by its rhetoric of exaggeration, toward elements present but usually undercut in the Uji chapters of the *Genji* narrative.

Remembering that here as elsewhere "reading" also connotes the activity of "writing," it could be argued that the *Sarashina* heroine's interest in *monogatari* implies her fabrication of variant tales. The fantasies she confesses having bear eloquent if subtle testimony to the fact that her preference for literature over "life" (court service, marriage, maternity) is not simply a repetition of the literary stereotype of the neophyte court lady merely anxious to avoid the eyes of others. The young heroine yearns only to grow up to look like Yūgao or Ukifune. But at the peak of her infatuation with the figure of Ukifune, her fantasies take on a curious edge. The memoir hints at a very writerly mode of reading, the beginning of an active, creative appropriation of selected parts of the tales she "reads": "And since I did nothing but read these books, before I knew it I had the lines by heart and their images would float before my eyes of their own accord" (*NKBZ* 18: 302).

The suggestion of a similar movement—from passive readership to a subtle rewriting of remembered texts—occurs again in a subsequent passage in connection with a reference to Ukifune. What is especially telling about this later passage is what it reveals of the literally literary kind of love affair the woman imagines when she stops poring over her books long enough to envision what relations with a really ideal man might be like:

What ultimately possessed me was the idea that a man of peerless looks and noble bearing, someone like the Shining Genji in the tale, would come to visit me just once every year; I would be hidden away in a mountain village like Lady Ukifune, and though it would be terribly lonely there, gazing at the blossoms and the turning leaves, the moon and the snow, I would have his wonderful letters to wait for and to read from time to time. This was all I yearned for, this was the vision I longed to realize. (*NKBZ* 18: 317)

In this reincarnation Ukifune both is and is not the figure readers of *The Tale of Genji* will remember, for the young woman's aspirations have given her a new script. Selecting and reshaping elements of the original story, she creates her own fantasy of romance and deferred sexuality with herself as heroine. Both Kaoru and Niou, the two courtiers who pursue Ukifune in *The Tale of Genji*, are out of the picture, and the Ukifune-like heroine is coupled with a more reliable yet significantly distant hero ("someone like the Shining Genji") in a setting that resembles the Tanabata legend of the Weaver Maiden and the Cowherd more than any of the affairs depicted in *Genji*. The scenario also resembles very closely the fantasy that Ukifune's mother indulges in after catching a glimpse of Niou from behind the blinds at Nakanokimi's residence: "Oh my, what kind of a man is this! How splendid—just to be near him. As an outsider, I always imagined that no matter how wonderful such princes might be, when they made you suffer, they were odious sorts. But now that I see him—such presence, and such a magnificent appearance—even if he visited only once a year—like the Cowherd with the Weaver Maid—what an event it would be" (*NKBZ* 17: 37).

The Tanabata scenario seems to be something of a stereotypical fantasy for women of the provincial governors' class (especially mothers of daughters) in *monogatari*. What stands out in the *Sarashina* memoirist's appropriation of the cliché is a slight but enormously suggestive shift of interest from the man to his writings. The *Sarashina nikki* emphasizes neither the magnificence of the prince himself nor the ecstasy of an annual visit, but rather the sporadic yet significantly repeatable thrill provided by his letters. Though she pays lip service to the ideal of a Genji-like lover, hers is a curiously absent hero. For her, the truly ideal man is the one who is hardly ever around. Even in her fantasies (or perhaps especially in her fantasies) she envisions her relationship to him as a largely readerly affair. What she pines for is not so much his presence as "his wonderful letters." Might this not be because, unlike the man himself—any man given the norms of aristocratic Heian courtship and marriage—his letters are things she may not only receive but also keep and look at from time to time at will.

In the fantasy quoted above, the lover is ideal because he is a source of further texts that the woman will be free to peruse at her leisure. And although the heroine's late marriage brings her willy-nilly into the world of "normal" sexuality, as the memoir also discreetly reveals, the memoir minimizes (thereby idealizing) the role the husband plays in the story of the woman's life. Like the image of Minamoto Sukemichi, the elegantly reserved courtier as conversationalist, a man of words not action, the image of the memoirist's husband stands in striking contrast to *Genji* figures. To put the matter crudely, he wins what small place he has in the pages of the *Sarashina nikki* by virtue of his occasional accommodations to his wife's desire (how far we are here from the world of the

Kagerō nikki). He makes his first appearance in the memoir some five years after their marriage as "the children's parent" (*chigodomo no oya naru hito*) (*NKBZ* 18: 344), impressing her with his empathetic (and permissive) response to her plea to leave the capital to go on a pilgrimage to Hase the very day that crowds of people are flowing into the city to celebrate the accession of Emperor GoReizei. Here his behavior is made to contrast starkly and favorably with the censorious response of the woman's other relatives (*sarubeki hitobito*, "people who could be expected to do that" (*NKBZ* 18: 343) and most notably with the sibling (*hara kara naru hito*), possibly her younger brother, who angrily frets that she is crazy to pick this of all days to leave the capital. His expressed fear, the narration coyly notes, is that her deed will become "a tale" told for generations to come (*nagarete no monogatari to mo narinubeki koto nari*) (*NKBZ* 18: 344). Finally, and most significant, the husband reappears, by virtue of his absence, in the form of brief descriptions of his departure for a post as governor in the Shinano province (*NKBZ* 18: 357) and then his death (*NKBZ* 18: 358).

The real fantasy figure in her tale is not "someone like the Shining Genji" but rather a figure "like Lady Ukifune," and by extension, the dream of readerly engagement, solitary contemplation, religious seeking, and autoerotic creativity that Ukifune represents in her intertextual reincarnation in the *Sarashina nikki*. The skewed lines the girl's fantasies draw between herself and Ukifune are underscored in the passage immediately following the fantasy quoted above by the narrator's remark that "father had just been appointed to the vice-governorship of Hitachi," the province, as the well-versed reader will recall, that was Ukifune's provincial home, her stepfather having also been vice-governor of Hitachi in the fictional world of *Genji*. At this point, the extraliterary aspects of the *Sarashina* heroine's passion for *monogatari* are fully revealed. What she wants (and now appears to believe might actually happen) is nothing short of the realization of a tale of her own devising. The desire that life should follow the paradigms of the girl's preferred fictions seems about to be fulfilled. The direction of her wishes (to go to the capital and to be able to read *The Tale of Genji*) shifts from a passive consumption of tales to actually seeing the tales replicated (with a difference) in her own life. And this activity of replication is, like so many of the other readerly activities recounted in this memoir, largely a hermeneutical one: the girl contextualizes (and poeticizes) her father's disappointing provincial appointment by drawing attention to its resonance with details from the tale whose heroine she most wishes to resemble.

If the *Sarashina nikki* reconjures Ukifune as a reclusive reader, the recipient of occasional splendid letters, we also have to consider what Ukifune (and the *Sarashina* heroine in her desired guise as "a lady like Ukifune") was doing in her reclusion besides reading letters. Ukifune left the provinces at a relatively late age to follow a strange and complicated itinerary—from Hitachi to the capital and back to her father's residence at Uji on the outermost limits of the capital again—and her wanderings draw to a suspended close only in the final chapter of *Genji*, at the very end of the tale itself. Like Hashihime, the mythical lady of the bridge at Uji with whom she is poetically associated, Ukifune ends as a woman whose movements come to an uncertain halt finally at Ono, in the hills west of Mount Hiei, poised between the insistent pressures of her ties to the world and a growing desire for a life of Buddhist renunciation. And it is from this position that she takes up her brush and begins to write.

As Field has pointed out, Ukifune, the unlikely, untutored, and unrecognized daughter of a dispossessed prince and stepdaughter of an especially boorish provincial vice-governor, produces more *waka* than any of the other female figures in *Genji*, all of whom outdo her in social rank.[14] The penultimate chapter of *Genji*, "At Writing Practice" (*Tenarai*), takes its title from the image of Ukifune textualizing herself "as though practicing her hand" (*tenarai no yō ni*) in a medium that, in its ostensibly secret preoccupation with relieving pent-up emotion and desire, sounds very much like memoir writing: "She had never been good at telling people what was on her mind, and now more than ever, she had no intimate companions to turn things over with; all she could do when she felt as if she might burst was to turn to her inkstone and struggle to put her thoughts into writing, just as if she were practicing her hand."[15]

Ukifune's distinction as a writer is more apparent than that of any other female figure in *Genji*, except perhaps the Murasaki lady, who kept a *nikki* during Genji's exile in Suma and who is depicted turning to the ruse of "practicing her hand" (*tenarai*) during the difficult time of Genji's marriage to the Third Princess.[16] Ukifune's post-Uji season of tentative religious seeking and unassuming self-exegesis by means of a *nikki*-like medium resonates strongly with the persona the *Sarashina* memoirist herself projects.

Appropriative, creative, and voyeuristic, the pleasures of reading and rewriting evoked by the memoir's use of *Genji* intertexts suggest anything but a passive whiling away of time before the desired entrance of a real hero. As we have already noted in our discussion of the opening lines in the memoir, the written text is no poor substitute, but rather the tangible object of desire itself. And furthermore, reading (as a mode of desirous envisioning) in some ways empowers the young woman, if only because she uses it to defer her own entrance into the unhappy economy of Heian marriage: while the girl reads and dreams, her sister marries, has children, and dies young in childbirth. Finally, and perhaps most important, the *Sarashina* heroine's reading, parallel in function to the *Sarashina* memoirist's self-commemorative, hermeneutical writing, provides a means for imagining, interpreting, and articulating a preferred destiny. And it is a destiny in which—by the memoirist's own design— men other than her father will play only a peripheral part.

What are we to make of the extreme emphasis on pleasures associated with the marginal, of the self-identification with ladies like Yūgao and Ukifune, of the voyeuristic autoeroticism of solitary reading and self-commemoration in the *Sarashina nikki*? Leaving aside any relationship it may have had to the historical author's actual experience or personality, what is its significance within the rhetorical and thematic structures of the memoir as narrative? In Heian court narratives—both *nikki* and *monogatari*—a kind of passively active sexuality is part of the stereotypic ideal of femininity, where the appealingly feminine is understood as what men desire in women and what women (like the impeccably groomed Murasaki lady) learn to desire in themselves. The plots of *monogatari* perpetuate and accommodate the norms of Heian polygyny by romanticizing them. For both the men and the well-tutored women in Heian fiction, the ideally desirable woman is beautiful, talented, and passionately ready to respond to masculine desire. Such a figure—an Izumi Shikibu or a Fujitsubo, even—although she resists for a time, gives in to the worthy suitor; she cannot but be moved by him, often despite her own fears (as Yūgao), pride and pain (Lady Rokujō, the Akashi lady), or better judgment (Fujitsubo).

The *Sarashina* heroine's apparent lack of passion for "real" men has been regarded as strange and as not at all the ideal woman's part as that ideal had been classically defined, and it is partly because of this that she has been so frequently read as a more or less girlish figure. But it is important to recognize how this figure deviates from the type of the sexually uninitiated juvenile heroines it vaguely recalls. The woman depicted in the *Sarashina nikki* is not a superannuated version of the young Murasaki, but rather a would-be version of Yūgao or Ukifune. A persistent critical blindness to the complexity of those figures (and the twists in their intertextual destinies in later Heian court narratives) has also contributed to the view of the *Sarashina* heroine as merely an Emma Bovary manqué, too timid to venture beyond the pages of her tales and the boundaries of her own tale-inspired fantasies. However, once one begins to recognize in the tales of Yūgao and Ukifune something more complicated than stories of failed love affairs between elusive women and exquisitely sensitive men, the nature of the *Sarashina* heroine's fascination with these figures (and the memoir's deliberate, hyperbolic rewriting of them) is also laid open to new questions.

The manner in which the *Sarashina nikki* reprises the *Genji* heroines calls attention to the resistance of both the heroines and the memoirist, as socially marginalized women, to the more conventional figure of the erotic surrogate and her predetermined entanglement in the plots of courtly romance. In a series of rhetorical moves that should by now seem typical of the *Sarashina nikki*, the preinscribed plots of heterosexual love and romance are happily refined into near nonexistence. What emerges instead is a narrative underlain by a form of textual pleasure that has much to do with the autoerotic. And the "idea of the autoerotic as compensation for social restrictions," as Brownstein puckishly reminds us, "has real interest for feminists."[17] When the autoerotic appears as insistently and as pleasurably as it does in this memoir, what is at issue is not simply the writer's or the heroine's (or the heroine's favorite heroines') deviance from the norm of her literary sisters. The locus of textual pleasure doubles as the site of ideological conflict and challenge. The memoir's preoccupation with limits (embodied in its rhetoric of exaggeration and its fascination with hyperbole and the tropes and themes of travel writing) indirectly calls into question the myths of courtly love, or more precisely, the social and spiritual limits that make those myths so constricting and so unsatisfactory to the women (both fictional heroines and historical writers) who were caught up in them.

What makes a narrative like *Genji* both subversive of and complicit with the Fujiwara-dominated patriarchal elite is its deftly ironic poeticization of the hard facts of Heian aristocratic marriage: the romantic abandonment of women by men, the physical dangers of pregnancy and childbirth, the oppressive censoriousness of male relatives and male clergy, fundamentally misogynist systems of religious belief and social practice, and the lack of sexual satisfaction for upper-class women who must share their men with other women while having recourse to few, if any, socially acceptable means of venting their frustration or of seeking satisfactory compensation.

Given such circumstances, it should come as no surprise that auto-erotic desire emerges in women's writing after *Genji* as a preferred mode of sexuality. What is surprising is that the autoerotic as a pre-ferred mode did not play a more prominent role in earlier Heian works. Strong resistance to dominant ideological pressures is seldom condoned in any society. To excuse herself, the *Sarashina* memoirist must some-how convince her reader that she is extraordinary—if only extraordi-narily ill-equipped to live out the unhappy norms to which her real and her literary sisters succumbed. If the triad of Yūgao, Ukifune, and Sue-tsumuhana can be said to suggest a trinity of peripheral women who further isolate themselves by passively resisting the roles others would have them play, the allusions to them scattered throughout the *Sara-shina nikki* suggest that its heroine is even more disqualified from, and more resistant to, disclosure and self-dissemination. Gesturing at the icons of marginality the girl so admires in the tales she reads, the *Sarashina nikki* claims for its heroine a marginality that exceeds that of even her most exaggeratedly marginalized fictional predecessors. The rhetorical play with limits underscores the shortcomings of that which is central.

A Sporadic Visitor

If allusions to Ukifune's Hitachi and the lonely setting of Suetsumu-hana's obscure years in the Hitachi mansion enrich the images of isola-tion and marginality that dominate the beginning and ending, respec-tively, of the *Sarashina nikki,* then the account of the *Sarashina* hero-ine's transient status at court recalls and revises the figure of Ukifune in the capital. From the moment she leaves the eastern provinces, Ukifune is doomed to a life of wandering. With her mother she journeys to the capital where she plays poor relation to her half-sister Nakanokimi, moves back and forth between the capital and Uji, makes pilgrimages to Hase, and is abducted by first one lover and then the other. To borrow Kaoru's elegant euphemism for her, Ukifune is "the visitor" (*marōto*) par excellence, just as her poetic sobriquet, "floating boat," would lead one to imagine.[18] The motif of wandering (*sasurai*)[19] and the perspective of "a visitor" also govern the *Sarashina* narrative's accounts of its heroine's service at court during her middle years and her later pilgrim-

ages to temples outside the capital. In these accounts, the fiction of desire as *yukashisa*, the yearning to "go to where good things are expected
to be," migrates from the enclosed spaces of the woman's house to the
more thickly peopled setting of Heian court society and to the sacred
spaces beyond the city—Ishiyama, Hase, Kurama, and others. Despite
the *Sarashina* heroine's newfound disillusionment with *monogatari*, the
desire to be the central figure in a tale of one's own devising continues
to inflect the narrative—acted out now on the stage of life at court, and,
increasingly, through the itineraries of religious pilgrimage.

The woman's first attendances at court are sporadic indeed: they
consist of a single night in the tenth month, after which she immediately
returns home, another stint of about ten days early in the twelfth month
of the same year, and one more, on the twenty-fifth day of the same
month, for the *Butsumyō'e* festival. In these earliest attendances, she is
acutely and uncomfortably aware of her own awkwardness; for the
reader, the sense of displacement and the anxiety about being constantly
on display is palpable:

After the beginning of the twelfth month, I went to court again. Having received quarters of my own, this time I stayed on in attendance for several days.
There were a few times when I had to wait upon the princess at night, and then
I lay down among women I did not know and found I could not sleep at all.
Embarrassed and awkward, I would weep quietly to myself until dawn, and return to my chambers before it got light. I spent the days yearning for my father
and worrying about how old and feeble he was getting and how he depended
on me as his daughter and his support. And then there were my nieces, who had
lost their mother and had been with me since their birth, sleeping next to me
every night, one on the right, one on the left. Overcome with these anxious
thoughts, I would do nothing but stare into thin air and brood. Then, too, it
seemed there was always someone standing and listening, or peeking in on me,
and this made me very ill at ease. (*NKBZ* 18: 328–29)

The *Sarashina* author was not, of course, the only memoirist who
complained about the physical exposure one was subjected to by court
service. Similar reminiscences are to be found in the *Murasaki Shikibu
nikki* and even *The Pillow Book*.[20] What is outstanding about the images in the *Sarashina nikki* is the emphasis on the large numbers, the
sheer quantity of faceless, unindividualized women that surrounds the
newcomer. Confronting such crowds, compelled to sit among them and
become one of the many on display for others to behold, her strategy is
first to hide and second to return home:

There was a summons to appear at the princess's court for the *Butsumyō'e* festival on the twenty-fifth of the twelfth month. Reminding myself that it was only for that one night, I went. Everyone wore white underrobes beneath deep crimson silk ones, and I took my place among a retinue of more than forty women. I hid myself behind the lady who had first brought me to court, and among all those others, I was hardly visible at all. I left the following morning. (*NKBZ* 18: 330–31)

The experience initiates her into an appalling vision of her own ordinariness and insignificance. At court she is simply one among many other women (anathema to the sort of woman who aspires to a reclusiveness outdoing that of even the most reclusive *Genji* heroines) and such a long way from the deliciously private spaces in which she enjoyed reading about life at court. Her situation is now the exact opposite of both the content and the context of her maidenly dreams of becoming "a lady like Ukifune," of visions of herself waiting alone in a house in the hills for an ideal lover's annual visit, visions nurtured and savored during long days and nights of uninterrupted reading, huddled close to the lamp behind the curtains and blinds of her father's house. To return home after such knowledge is to return to the illusion of her own specialness, to her dreams of becoming the woman she has imagined herself destined to be. And return she does, repeatedly and at frequent intervals, with the particulars of each return and the lavish attention she receives at home from the appreciative audience of two her parents make carefully noted.

The account of this initial phase of the woman's career at court comes to a close with the description of her attendance at the *Butsumyō'e* festival quoted above. The initial decision to leave court service does not seem to have been entirely her own or to have been merely a matter of retiring to stay close to her father and nieces. Most commentators now agree that this was the point at which Takasue's daughter married Tachibana Toshimichi (1002?–58). The particulars of that episode in her life need not detain the reader of her memoir. They are passed over in relative silence by the *Sarashina nikki*. Her later attendances take place during the four years (1041–45) in which Toshimichi was posted as governor to the Shimotsuke province (*NKBZ* 18: 333, headnote). With characteristic self-deprecation, she insists that this later phase of her service was something she could not escape (*NKBZ* 18: 332), that it was a task she took up principally out of concern for the future of her nieces, who were now old enough to be presented in court circles and whom she had been specifically requested to present, although this insis-

tence may in fact mask a more specific ambition: it later appears that
she had hopes of becoming an imperial wet nurse. The following passage gives one of the most extended descriptions of the continued eccentricity of her position:

I came to court now and then, but since I could no longer pretend to the hopes I
had had when I was there before, I just let myself be drawn into it by my girls
and attended occasionally. The ladies-in-waiting, who are used to life at court,
always look as though they've seen it all no matter what happens, but I belonged with neither the very young ladies nor with those older, more experienced ones. As a kind of sporadic visitor, I was excluded from both groups, and
though mine was a vague position, since I did not have to depend entirely on
my service at court, I never envied even the ladies who were much superior to
me. On the contrary, I felt a certain peace of mind, and I would attend the princess when it was appropriate and talk with the other women who had idle moments. (NKBZ 18: 332–33)

   She is still on the fringes of the court, but she appears more carefree
there than she was during her initial visits, having won a modicum of
composure, or at least enough to allow her to indulge her readerly hab-
its in new kinds of "texts," the most extended of which will be, as we
have already noted, her two chance conversations with Minamoto
Sukemichi: "On special occasions, and when there were amusements or
entertainments at court, I would mingle in this way with the others, and
since I couldn't bear it that I might be noticed and felt that I should stay
out of the way, I just remained as I was and followed the main events"
(NKBZ 18: 333).
   How does the memoir's rendering of the heroine's service at court
correspond to the actual details of the memoirist's career? Does a biographical reading contribute to our understanding of the literary quality
of these accounts? I believe that it does. What follows is an attempt to
draw out the symbolic nature of the biographical details the memoirist
chooses to disclose. The memoir itself does not directly identify whose
service the heroine enters or give specific dates for her attendance. The
more or less elaborate chronology that biographical scholars have
woven out of the sparse details provided by the memoir stems from the
authority of the interlinear commentary in Fujiwara Teika's manuscript.[21] Working from Teika's glosses and a web of other court records
and diaries in Chinese, biographical scholars extrapolate from the
highly elliptical descriptions of court service found in the *Sarashina
nikki* the following "history" of the career of Takasue's daughter at
court.

Beginning in the early winter of 1039 when she was about thirty-two years old—a late age to make one's debut in court circles—Takasue's daughter served a number of brief terms of attendance at Fujiwara Yorimichi's Takakura Detached Palace, then the residence of Princess Yūshi (1038–1105), the young daughter of Emperor GoSuzaku (1009–45; r. 1036–45) and Empress Genshi (1016–39; r. 1037–39). Empress Genshi had died earlier that same year shortly after giving birth to Yūshi's sister, Princess Baishi (1039–96). The current scholarly consensus is that the marriage of Takasue's daughter to Tachibana Toshimichi took place in 1040, interrupting her attendance on Yūshi only temporarily.[22] Toshimichi was, like the memoirist's father, a member of the provincial governor class, and when he was posted as governor to the Shimotsuke province the following year, Takasue's daughter remained in the capital and continued her attendance on the princess off and on during the four years of his absence. Speculating that she bore her son Nakatoshi (b. 1041?) during the first year of her marriage and the early years of the princesses' lives,[23] Tsumoto suggests it was the timely birth of her son that gave rise to the ambitions the memoir implies she harbored at this period in her life: to "be an imperial wet nurse, serve at the palace, and be able to gain the favor of the emperor and the empress" (NKBZ 18: 359). The role of wet nurse (menoto) traditionally involved more status than that accorded ordinary ladies-in-waiting, and it brought with it the possibility of future patronage for those of her own children who became "breast siblings" (menotogo) to her upper-class nursling. Raised with her mother's aristocratic charge, a wet nurse's child might go on to become companion or attendant to its foster sibling for life.[24] Ultimately, however, Takasue's daughter does not seem to have made any great success at court for herself or her children, though it seems likely that she contributed to, and was in turn stimulated by, the literary activities surrounding the princesses she served.

Both Princesses Yūshi and Baishi were the wards of Fujiwara Yorimichi (992–1074), the eldest son and heir of the powerful Fujiwara Michinaga (966–1027), whose political and cultural dominance of the Heian court spanned the decades during which The Tale of Genji came into being. It was Michinaga's daughter (and Yorimichi's sister) Empress Shōshi (988–1074) whose salon nurtured the talents of great writers like Murasaki Shikibu and Izumi Shikibu. Though it cannot claim credit for the patronage of a work like Genji, Yorimichi's long period of regency is also noted for the brilliance of its literary salons. Yorimichi himself seems to have been actively involved in promoting the practice of literature, particularly among the women in service in his household and the households of his various offspring and wards.[25] Beginning with the 1040s, during the first half of which Takasue's daughter made her attendances, the households of Yūshi and Baishi sponsored more than twenty-five poetry competitions (*utaawase*) altogether. Baishi became an especially active patron of *waka* during her tenure as high priestess of the Kamo Shrine (1046–58), sponsoring more than twenty contests herself, including in 1055 a contest matching poems taken from *monogatari* written by Baishi's ladies.[26] One of Baishi's ladies, Rokujō Saiin Baishi Naishinnō no Senji (d. 1092), is generally credited with the authorship of the *Sagoromo monogatari*, an important post-*Genji* tale. Yūshi's household was less active than Baishi's, but it is worth noting that two of the six contests known to have been sponsored there centered on poems involving poetic toponyms (*utamakura*) associated with sites famous in poetic tradition (*meisho*), tropes that deeply interested Takasue's daughter, as even the most cursory glance at her memoir reveals. The first of these *meisho utaawase* took place in 1041, during the memoirist's second period of attendances on Yūshi, but it is impossible to know whether Takasue's daughter participated in this or in any of the other six contests, since a proper text exists for only one of them and the memoir makes no mention of poetry contests at court.

It is not clear how or why Takasue's daughter ended up making her bid for a career in court service in the household of a minor newly orphaned infant princess, but whatever historical circumstances combined to join the fortunes of Takasue's daughter to Yūshi's, the link itself develops the already overdetermined image of the *Sarashina* heroine as a creature on the periphery, a devotee of the obscure pleasures of life on the margins where she is free to be—among other things—willfully obtuse about the meaning of the signs she remembers constantly seeing. Unlike the memoirs of Sei Shōnagon or Murasaki Shikibu, the *Sarashina nikki* is not, and no one would expect it to be, replete with the names and doings of the great women of the Heian court, but the few that do appear create a select and highly suggestive configuration. Most of them are (like the memoirist herself) fleeting figures on the stage of Heian society, notable as a group for the transience of their careers—princesses who lacked strong political backing and imperial consorts who failed to produce sons, because they either died young or they took Buddhist vows early in life: Princess Shūshi, Empress Genshi, Princess Yūshi, and Junior Consort Seishi.

Empress Genshi's family history unfolds in the shadow cast by Michinaga's brilliant house. She was the only offspring of Prince Atsuyasu (999–1018), himself the only son born to Emperor Ichijō (980–1011; r. 986–1011) by Empress Teishi (976–1000), whose political fortunes and whose literary salon—home to Sei Shōnagon—declined as those of her younger rival, Michinaga's daughter and Murasaki Shikibu's patroness, Empress Shōshi ascended. Genshi's natural father, Atsuyasu, was unable to become crown prince due to Michinaga's opposition, and Genshi was adopted at birth by Yorimichi's wife Takahime. Though she was thus able, through Yorimichi's backing, to rise rapidly to the position of consort and empress, her career was brief, intense (two pregnancies in two years), and cut short by her early death. She entered GoSuzaku's court as high consort (nyōgo) in the first month of 1037, was named empress (chūgu) in the third month of the same year, and at her death two years later she left behind two princesses and no sons. Her daughter Yūshi—with whom Takasue's daughter was directly connected—is by far the more obscure of the two orphan princesses, her life undistinguished by the prolific literary activities that continue to make her sister Baishi's salon a matter of interest to scholars of Heian waka.

Genshi was not only already two months dead in the tenth month of 1039 when Takasue's daughter made her first appearance at the Takakura Detached Palace, but she had also long been overshadowed by GoSuzaku's other ladies and was immediately replaced (late in the twelfth month of the same year) in GoSuzaku's boudoir by Fujiwara Norimichi's daughter Seishi (1014–68), a mournful detail that the memoir does not fail to exploit: during an attendance on Yūshi while the latter is making a rare visit to the Imperial Palace (events datable to 1042), the Sarashina heroine overhears a nocturnal procession by the "Umetsubo consort" (Seishi) and her attendants to the emperor's chamber and uses it as an occasion to compose a waka in which she speaks in the persona of the dead Empress Genshi (NKBZ 18: 334). But Seishi's own career, which proceeded so precipitously on the heels of Genshi's, was stymied from the start because she was neither the daughter nor even the ward of the regent. It came to nothing at GoSuzaku's death in 1045. She bore only one child, a daughter who was born only after the emperor's death. Seishi herself became a nun in 1053.

It is possible that Takasue's daughter made her connection with Genshi's daughter Yūshi through ties the Sugawara family already had with Princess Shūshi (997–1050), the same princess whose Sanjō household, the reader might recall, provided the heroine with her first cache of *monogatari* during her early days in the capital (see discussion in Chapter 3, pp. 121-22). Shūshi was future Empress Genshi's paternal aunt, and her fortunes, like those of her niece and her brother Prince Atsuyasu, were eclipsed by the careers of her own cousins, Michinaga's daughters and granddaughters. Though granted *ippon no miya* status (First Princess) in 1007, she was left without her strongest backer when her father, Emperor Ichijō, died in 1011, and so she joined the ranks of the many imperial princesses who became nuns faute de mieux, taking Buddhist vows in 1024. During the twenty-five years after she took the tonsure, she was known as Nyūdō Ippon no Miya and was the center of a small literary salon that included the poetess Sagami (ca. 994–after 1061), as well as the daughter of Sugawara Tamemasa, a cousin of the *Sarashina* memoirist on her father's side who may be the real-life version of Emon no myōbu, the "relative" who acted as go-between for Shūshi's gift of *monogatari* to the *Sarashina* heroine soon after her arrival in the capital.[27]

The one exception to this constellation of dim stars is Imperial Princess Teishi (1013–94), who, as granddaughter to Michinaga and daughter of a Grand Empress Dowager, was destined to become a far more prominent member of GoSuzaku's harem than Shūshi's niece Genshi could ever have dreamed of being. Her name crops up—as if in counterpoint to that of the soon to be tonsured Shūshi—very early in the memoir in the account of the *Sarashina* heroine's second dream. The sequence of the two princesses' names in the memoir (Shūshi's first, then Teishi's) is paralleled by the topographical sequencing of them in relation to the *Sarashina* heroine's Sanjō residence. Shūshi's mansion was located to the east of Sugawara Takasue's first house in the capital, while Teishi's garden,[28] whose cherry trees the heroine gazes on as though "they are my own" (*NKBZ* 18: 304), seems to be in sight just to the west. The dream obliquely suggests that the myopic reader-as-dreamer missed her best chance for a career among the circles of the great during those earliest years in the capital—the years when, thanks to the generosity of benefactors like Princess Shūshi and the Yakushi Buddha, she was able instead to immure herself reading *monogatari* in her father's house, somewhere in between the residences of a future nun and a future empress and in ambiguous communication with both.

There was at the time a recent and possibly useful family connection between the *Sarashina* memoirist and Teishi. Beginning in 1018, Fujiwara

Michitsuna (955–1020), the only son of the *Kagerō* author (and thus the *Sarashina* memoirist's first cousin), held for two years until his death the important post of Master of the Grand Empress Dowager's Household (Kōtaigōgu Daibu). The dowager in question was none other than Teishi's mother, Grand Empress Dowager Kenshi. In a passage recording events around 1023, when Teishi had her coming-of-age ceremony and was granted the rank of *ippon no miya* (First Princess), the *Sarashina* heroine dreams that someone informs her that he has just finished making a stream for the temple garden at Rokkakudō for the sake of the First Princess, daughter of the Grand Empress Dowager. Having delivered this information, he pointedly advises the dreamer to pray to Amaterasu,[29] advice that the girl, then happily lost in the lush recesses of *Genji* and pointedly uninterested in mere matters of court rank ("what could the rank of an empress be to the way I felt?"), pointedly ignores. Had the memoirist managed to link her fortunes to those of her near contemporary Teishi rather than waiting sixteen years to link them instead with those of a dead empress's lackluster infant daughter, her career could well have been more exciting. Four years later, in 1027, Teishi became consort to the crown prince (future Emperor GoSuzaku) and was named empress in 1037, soon after his accession as emperor. Unlike Genshi, Teishi displayed enormous staying power. As mother to a crown prince (who later became Emperor GoSanjō [r. 1068–72]), her position and rise in status were ensured even beyond the death of GoSuzaku himself. She became Grand Empress in 1052, Senior Grand Empress in 1068, and retired as Yōmeimon'in in 1069 after her son acceded to the throne. She lived for another twenty-five years as mother of an emperor.

The way in which Teishi's name appears in the memoir—in connection with her mother the Grand Empress Dowager (and thus obliquely indicating the memoirist's cousin Michitsuna's influential post in that lady's household)—leads Tsumoto to venture that the passage underscores Takasue's daughter's heightened anticipation at the time of her own prospects as a lady-in-waiting.[30] But though she may in later life have harbored such hopes, this is not the image the memoir paints. When the man in the girl's dream informs her that Teishi has just commissioned the construction of a stream at a temple devoted to Kannon and that she herself ought implicitly to emulate the princess by praying to Amaterasu, the patron deity of the imperial family, these suggestive details fall on deaf ears: "I consulted no one [about the dream], and ended by thinking it meant nothing" (*NKBZ* 18: 304).

Beyond the City of Tales

> As to this dream too, I know not whether it portends good or
> evil—but I write it down thus, so that those who might hear
> how my life comes out may judge whether or not to believe
> in dreams and the Buddha.
>   —*Kagerō nikki*[31]

The sun goddess Amaterasu, like Imperial Princess Teishi, is another
powerful feminine figure whose possible influence over her destiny the
girl ignores to her own disadvantage and, later, regret. Predictably, it is
precisely this deity and the unheeded advice to pray to her that will turn
up repeatedly (like the return of the repressed) in the narrative of the
woman's middle years. When the young woman who had read *Genji*
and improvised her own fantasies about life "in the world" finally attempts, at the age of thirty-two, to enact those fantasies by entering
court service, the shift in her desired destiny is heralded by a resurfacing
of the subnarrative of her dreams, but with this very important difference: the dreams reported now no longer conflict with the course of her
desires. And it is only now, when the world of dreams begins to speak
to and for (rather than against) the desires of her waking hours, that its
messages compete successfully with the fantasies inspired by *monogatari*. The figures of Amaterasu and Kannon become central, if somewhat
ambivalent, focal points in the narrative of the heroine's middle years.

Signs of good fortune, auspicious omens, and congenial advice are
everywhere in the dreams and pilgrimages of her middle years, as is a
preponderance of feminine figures. For the dreamer, the world of court
service and the holy figures who abet her interest in that world are
feminine, a pattern that seems to repeat the gender polarizations seen
earlier in the memoir in the passages chronicling her pursuit of tale literature aided by female relatives and acquaintances. But unlike the girl
daily ensconced alone with her tales and subject in her sleep to verbal
chastisements by handsome priests, the older woman spends her days
moving between court and home or pilgrimaging. At night she has
dreams in which admonitory masculine figures no longer intrude; instead, goddesses and beautiful court women smile on her. The bodhisattva Kannon has displaced Yakushi as the guide-figure of choice, both as
patron of her prayers for success at court and as object of her several
pilgrimages. Though Kannon is never explicitly named in the memoir,
four of the twelve temples the memoir mentions were centers of Kannon
worship, and the woman makes multiple pilgrimages to the most impor-

tant of these in her middle years: she goes twice to Ishiyama and twice to Hase (after her mother's dedication of a mirror at that temple). Kiyomizu, also an important center of Kannon worship, figures repeatedly in the memoir, twice as the site of dreams about the woman's future or past.

The woman's first attendances at court are preceded in the narrative and motivated in part by her cheerful but incomplete reading of the dual vision she is granted when her mother dedicates a mirror to the Kannon at Hasedera and asks for a dream about her daughter's future (NKBZ 18: 323–25). The choice of this particular Kannon is a conventional one for the period and for the type of prophecy the women are seeking. Hasedera was renowned in mid-Heian society and literature as a place for the vouchsafing of dreams about the future and the past. The fateful pilgrimages of Ukon and Tamakazura, and their chance meeting there in the Genji monogatari, reflect the widespread belief in Hase Kannon's efficacy in reuniting people. But if Hase Kannon was famous for sponsoring reunions, it was also renowned for its influence on reproduction. As Saigō Nobutsuna has noted, pilgrims also came to Hase Kannon with prayers for fertility and safe childbirth. With its Shinto manifestations, Inari and Ise Amaterasu (and the latter deity's influence on doings in the imperial household), Hase Kannon engages a complex network of feminine archetypes and spaces (motherhood, earth, night, dreams, caves, wombs, tombs, and—through the association with the sun goddess Amaterasu—the Sacred Mirror Room at the Imperial Palace). In short, the Kannon at Hase would have been a highly appropriate choice as patron bodhisattva for a woman who aspires to become an imperial wet nurse.

The first half of the dual vision is a dark one, the image of someone weeping and rolling on the floor, which the narrator will recall and identify later in the narrative as an omen of what her overly optimistic interpretations ultimately won her. But it is only the second, sunny half of the dream that captures her imagination now: a lavish and vividly realized court scene, full of flowers (plum blossoms and cherries anachronistically blooming together), bird song, and a myriad of colored sleeves—all clichés common to descriptions of both Buddhist paradise and the splendor of the imperial court. The fresh content of this dream and particularly its changed personnel (no pedantic priests warning her about the follies of poems and tales, but a splendid female guide figure—a goddess attired like a court lady, or a court lady as beautiful as a goddess) typifies the dreams she recalls from her middle years. And the dreamer herself presents a new face. No longer so intent on tales alone, increasingly attuned to external circumstances like her father's career and what effect it might have on her own future (*NKBZ* 18: 319), she can no longer easily dismiss the dream or the advice of "the person who tells me to pray to Amater[asu]" (*NKBZ* 18: 324).

Changes in both the content of the heroine's dreams and her responses to them make for interesting comparisons with the process of her disillusionment as a reader of tales. Like her reading of tales, her progress as a reader of dreams begins in a kind of reckless desire (the habit of ignoring the warning signs in her dreams) that gradually gives way to growing doubts about her own understanding and results finally in the effort to move from text to life, from reading to action, from deferring desire to its consummation. As she loses interest in *monogatari*, her preoccupation with the increasingly encouraging messages her dreams convey mounts in proportion to the extent that these dreams touch on her ambition for a clearly defined place at court. Because she now likes what she sees in them, dreams come to replace tales as compelling signposts of her destiny.

And yet restlessness persists as the governing metaphor of desire. The sparse, intermittent accounts of attendance at court peter out, and the (secular) figure of the *Sarashina* heroine as a sporadic visitor at Yūshi's court, intruding on less than stellar circles to which she will always remain an outsider, gives way toward the end of the memoir to overtly spiritual preoccupations. The story of the woman's growing seriousness about more appropriate concerns (that is, not simply the worldly success of herself and her family at court but also her own fate in the afterworld) overlaps with and finally overtakes the accounts of her experiences at court. After years of delusive wanderings—at the outset via her girlish absorption in *monogatari* and in her middle years in the account of her peripatetic attempts to win some sort of place for herself or her nieces at court—the now middle-aged woman sets out again and again on the series of pilgrimages that makes the final pages of the memoir (reprising the travel account of the first pages of the memoir) into a narrative of actual spatial wanderings. Like the girl who journeyed to the capital in restless pursuit of *monogatari*, the woman continues to be an eager, aggressive, even willful pilgrim. The same energy that drives the narrative of her early passion for tales fuels the account of her late religious pilgrimages. Yet her final relation to the plots and issues of Buddhist beliefs is ultimately no less ambivalent than her relation to the world of tale literature and her gradually relinquished interest in a career at court. The realm of the sacred remains, as the final lines of the memoir testify, a world that she never fully embraces or enters, and she remains a restless figure commuting between this world and the other.

One of the richest, most sustained treatments of the heroine's relation to the plots of religious seeking is the account of her first pilgrimage to Hasedera late in 1046. The results of this journey suggest that the pilgrim gets exactly what she sets out to find, "a sign" (*shirushi*) from the Buddha in the form of two dreams that address her ambitions at court. In the first dream, which she has while still en route to Hasedera, the dreamer comes to a place where the "wind is blowing fiercely" (a detail that literalizes the term *kamikaze* or "divine wind," a *makurakotoba*, or poetic epithet for the place-name Ise). Here she encounters a beautiful woman who accosts her and advises her to seek the aid of Lady Hakase (Hakase no myōbu) (*NKBZ* 18: 347–48). Once more, the figure of the smiling, beneficent woman—a court lady? a goddess?—conflates both sacred and profane aspects of the dreamer's desires (a conflation that will be repeated again when she actually encounters the aged court lady Hakase no myōbu, who guides her on a "pilgrimage" to the Sacred Mirror Room at the Imperial Palace, where she finally follows through on the advice she has been repeatedly given to "pray to [Amaterasu]" [*NKBZ* 18: 334]). In the dream the pilgrim has at Hasedera, she receives what she had expressly set out to obtain: a sign (*shirushi*), in the form of a sprig of *sugi* from the god Inari.

It is thus not that the other gods and bodhisattvas in the *Sarashina nikki* fail to perform with the efficacy and alacrity of Yakushi or that, as Kubo suggests, the heroine trusts only in Yakushi.[32] Kannon, Amaterasu, and Inari are presented as being as responsive to the pilgrim's prayers as Yakushi was to the fiction-addicted girl long ago, and the memoir continues to imply that the dreamer/pilgrim still fails to recognize the way in which her prayers do in fact get answered. "If only," she laments in a later passage, "I had made a pilgrimage right away to the Inari shrine after I was thrown that branch of *sugi* as a sign from Inari, things might have come out otherwise" (*NKBZ* 18: 359).

The peculiar blend of blindness and vision that marks her as a seer of dreams recalls and parallels her earlier performance as a reader of tales. Even at this late juncture, tales, like dreams, are accorded a rich and suggestive space in the account of her first pilgrimage to Hase. The journey itself unfolds in the context of a change in imperial rule. Emperor GoSuzaku had died in 1045. In the tenth month of 1046, at the accession of the new emperor, the annual harvest festival at court was superseded by the Daijō'e, the enthronement ceremony for Emperor GoReizei (r. 1046–68). The people of Heian, joined by crowds of sight-seers thronging in from the outskirts, converged on the avenues south of the imperial palace to witness the procession associated with this "once in an imperial reign period" event. The *Sarashina nikki* commemorates the occasion with the unforgettable image of its heroine, literally locked in an arduous struggle to extricate herself from the city to which her desires have so long bound her (*NKBZ* 18: 343–46). The imagery of dichotomous modes of vision—vulgar gawking and metaphysical seeking, sight-seers, and supplicants hoping to see signs—runs throughout the entire account, dramatically juxtaposing the otherworldly gaze of the visionary and the profane staring of the crowd. In the middle of this festive confusion and hounded by the jeers of onlookers bent on a holiday of a more secular sort, the heroine's carriage plies its torturously slow route. Her attendants are somberly decked out in pure white for the pilgrimage to Hase and are preceded by reluctant forerunners who would rather be going in the opposite direction to see the festival, the whole spectacle destined to become (through the agency of the memoir itself) matter for the taletellers for generations to come, just as the heroine's irate brother had predicted.

The *Sarashina* heroine's characteristic desire to see rather than be seen backfires with a vengeance from the outset. Having set out confident that going on a pilgrimage at such a time will ensure that she will "see a sign from the Buddha" (*kanarazu Hotoke no onshirushi o mimu*) (*NKBZ* 18: 344), she winds up, at least for the first part of her journey, the painfully self-conscious object of the sight-seers' rude stares. The hordes of people through which her carriage makes its slow progress jostle and leer, their comments audible to her and carefully noted, to be balanced against the sole favorable remark conveniently supplied by a person in front of the residence of Fujiwara Yoshiyori (1002–48), "who speaks with sobriety" (*mameyaka ni iu hito*): "Of what use is it to feast our eyes for one day only . . . this woman is sure to see the favor of the Buddha. We are the foolish ones! Going off only to see a procession" (*NKBZ* 18: 344–45).

The pilgrimage both recalls and reverses the one the girl made twenty-five years earlier from Azuma to the capital, that "place where there are so many tales." Tales are emphatically not her destination this time, though the image of her own eccentric movement against that of everyone else around her aptly elaborates the tale she has always told about her following of desire's itineraries. And yet the account embeds the last explicit references to *The Tale of Genji* in the *Sarashina nikki*, and in it the *Genji* allusions occupy important, if only temporary, stopping places, diverting sights to be seen (one thinks of Narihira going to "see the *utamakura* in Azuma") at significant crossroads on the journey away from "this world" and toward the sacred space of Hase.

Her progress is halted entirely as dawn breaks on the southeast edge of the city, where she pauses to "wait for the mist to clear" at the gate of Hōshōji, a temple just the other side of the Kamo River on the road to Uji, the same juncture at which Kaoru and Ukifune paused on their flight to Uji in "The Eastern Cottage" (*Azumaya*) chapter of *Genji* (*NKBZ* 17: 87; S, 968). For Kaoru's party, too, dawn was just breaking and rendering faces visible. But what the *Sarashina* heroine sees ("the sight-seers coming up from the countryside like a flowing stream of water," *NKBZ* 18: 345) bears little resemblance to the intimate scenes Kaoru's carriage encloses. She halts again further down the road on the east bank (the capital side) of the Uji River, where the crowds and the ferrymen's dawdling force yet another wait, which gives her the chance to look around at this "place where the daughters of the Uji Prince in Murasaki's tale had been made to live," a site she admits she had "once restlessly yearned to see" (*NKBZ* 18: 346). Eventually she crosses the Uji to the western shore, which is to her the Other Shore both symbolically and literally: after this crossing, the road is clear of crowds and lies open to Hase, where she will have her two dreams.

But let us linger for a moment with the myopic pilgrim on the west bank of the Uji River to consider just what she makes of the space of *monogatari* as she pauses in it on her way to a destination beyond. The pause occasions a side trip to visit the villa of Fujiwara Yorimichi, whose ward, Princess Yūshi, had been the memoirist's link to court circles. Though at the time (1046) it would still have been merely an elegant villa, the building was destined to be transformed in 1052–53 into a temple devoted to Amida. Remembering Ukifune, that other heroine from the eastern provinces who was so given to making pilgrimages to Hase, she muses that the hall in which Kaoru installed Ukifune must have looked something like Yorimichi's. Morris comments that the memoirist is simply "glamour[izing] the world of fiction" here, but I would argue that this enigmatic musing on a house destined to become a temple and the *Genji* heroine who was once destined to be enshrined as a holy icon in another house turned temple indicates a much more complex and concrete set of intersections among the world of fiction, the world of the everyday, and the world of the sacred.

In "The Eastern Cottage," Kaoru completes his plans for the renovation and rebuilding of the Uji Prince's former residence on the east bank of the Uji River, plans which, *Genji* readers will recall, realize his expressed wish to create a hall in that mountain village to enshrine Ukifune as a living "statue" (*hitogata*) of his dead love, Ōigimi. As Field has demonstrated at length, the language of erotic substitution, in a move characteristic of the Ukifune tale, slides into the language of Buddhist icons, talismans, and even scapegoats (*katashiro*). Kaoru's metaphors, at once erotic and pious, reify the beloved. In his words, Ukifune becomes more place than person, more thing than woman, albeit a strangely holy sort of thing, an erotic, sacrificial figure who takes on the sins of others for purposes of expiation. Kaoru has the old furnishings and screens of the prince's house removed and donated to a neighboring monastery, and the new hall is so much more splendid than its predecessor that it renders him nostalgic for the faded comfort of the old house, just as Ukifune's actual presence intensifies for him his longing for her dead half-sister, Ōigimi.

In the *Sarashina* memoirist's own day, Yorimichi had inherited his villa on the west bank of the Uji River from his father, Michinaga, who had gotten it in turn ultimately from Minamoto Tōru. When Murasaki Shikibu wrote *The Tale of Genji* a generation earlier, the villa—then still Michinaga's—is thought to have provided the real-life prototype for Genji's son Yūgiri's villa at Uji, but not for the villa that the Eighth Prince passes on to Kaoru. But in 1053, only seven years after Takasue's daughter makes her visit there, Yorimichi (as though playing pious Kaoru to his father Michinaga's secular Genji or Yūgiri) has his villa rebuilt as a temple devoted to Amida.

One of the compelling features of the Ukifune narrative, and one compellingly recalled in the *Sarashina nikki*, is a dramatic polarization of sacred and profane in terms of literal spatial movements between two opposing worlds. The account of the *Sarashina* heroine's first pilgrimage to Hasedera portrays this dialectic by recourse to the metonyms of travel literature, and in doing so, subtly underscores the position of *monogatari* as somewhere in between the two poles of the dialectic: the memory of Ukifune's tale surfaces at a site on a pilgrimage beyond the secular world. Instead of representing her destination ("that place where there are so many tales"), *monogatari* now occupy a lonely threshold space between the world of the capital and the Other World represented by Hase.

The perception that literary and religious discourse are oppositional in their relation to "truth" was, as we have already mentioned, a common Heian view that certain *monogatari* themselves reinforce, signaling the genre's ideological complicity with the myths of courtly love and the polygynous couplings that those myths romanticize. Religion, for the heroines of Heian *monogatari*, is almost always a last resort, and even then, it is usually presented as a thwarted alternative. The woman who chooses to embrace Buddhist teachings fully, who "turns her back on the world," in the idiom of the tales, also necessarily removes herself from the Heian traffic in wives and daughters. In this respect, Suetsumuhana, with her preference for old poems and tales rather than sutras, is typical, though her adherence to a "norm" whose chief raison d'être is ensuring that nubile women make themselves attractive and available until properly wed and impregnated is rendered ludicrous and inappropriate by her abnormal appearance and behavior:

> Every now and then she would open up a musty cabinet and amuse herself by looking through illustrated copies of Karamori, The Mistress of Hakoya, or The Tale of the Shining Princess. . . . She found the sutra chanting and rites that women of her day pursued to be almost shameful, and though there was no one about who might catch her at it, she never went in for rosaries and such. She lived, in this way, a very proper sort of life. (*NKBZ* 13: 321)

In Suetsumuhana's case, sutras and nunhood would have been more in keeping with her real prospects and skills than the fantasies of love and elegant romance propagated by the tales she favored. But Suetsumuhana is essentially a comic figure, and her perverse preference for unsuitable reading matter is part of the web of inappropriate aspirations that makes her (lacking as she is in all other conventional qualifications—compelling beauty, good taste, ready wit) an unlikely candidate for the romantic affairs she prefers reading about. Like Suetsumuhana, the *Sarashina* heroine, retiring and lacking the social skills that might have won her recognition (erotic and otherwise) at court, never speaks of taking vows, for all her energetic pilgrimaging in later life. And this is perhaps why it is not Ukifune (who in fact manages to take the first steps toward nunhood before her tale ends) but the marginalized figures of Suetsumuhana and the deceived aunt of the Obasute legend that surface at the close of the *Sarashina nikki*. As a final analogue for the woman and her late self-delusions, the Suetsumuhana intertext outlines a picture that is both self-disparaging (critical of the woman's lack of moral and religious seriousness) and excessively and implausibly erotic.

It is likely that parable and biography mirror each other here. Takasue's daughter may have been prevented from pursuing religious aspirations any further than her memoir says she did by the usual pressures of family responsibilities (her concerns—supremely appropriate for a widow—for the success at court of her nieces and her own children). But the point remains that the *Sarashina* narrator's insistent deploring of her own inattention to religion also finds a literary source in the conventions of *monogatari*, which themselves both reflect and disseminate biases against people (especially women) who make an ostentatious or histrionic show of their religious aspirations. Certainly the *Genji monogatari* contrasts women who rush into holy vows with little or no real understanding of their significance with those truly thoughtful characters (like the older Murasaki lady and Genji) who are prevented from pursuing their religious aspirations by worldly responsibilities. With the exception of Fujitsubo, the examples of the *Genji* heroines seem to imply that it is not the heroine's part to be too quick to follow through on ascetic impulses. And the *Sarashina* memoirist may have been guided (or entrapped) in this attitude toward religion by her admiration for the various images of ideal women inscribed in *Genji*.

As a figure that deconstructs the polarization of secular and sacred in *monogatari* discourse, Ukifune presents a striking exception to the other *Genji* women. Initially sought out by both her half-sister, Nakanokimi, and her would-be lover, Kaoru, as the living image of her dead half-sister, Ōigimi, a human statue to be enshrined at Uji for Kaoru's strange blend of spiritual and sensual idolatry, Ukifune becomes a creature of the crossroads, positioned between the spiritual and the secular and at rest in neither. The memoirist's fascination with her as a literary precedent for the *Sarashina* heroine augurs the latter's own intermediary positioning between the sacred and the profane, in the middle ground that is the space ultimately occupied by both dreams and *monogatari* in the world of the *Sarashina nikki*. Consider the passage in which the heroine's and the narrator's perspectives first join to recant the girlish preoccupation with tales:

After that, I was distracted by various things, and I completely forgot about the matter of my tales. And as I became more serious and composed, I wondered how I could have spent so many years and months merely rising and going to bed and never practicing devotions or making pilgrimages. And these fantasies, these things I had yearned for so much, could they possibly exist in this world of ours? Is there, in this world, any man like the Shining Genji? And a woman like the one Captain Kaoru hid away at Uji?—this is a world where she could never be. I had been quite crazy! (*NKBZ* 18: 332)

As always, the fascination with tales emerges in opposition to a serious life of religious devotions and pilgrimages. But the passage is less damning than it appears at first glance. The heroine suggests that her real sin was not preferring tales to religious texts and practices, but rather crediting fantasies (*aramashigoto*, "things that might be but aren't") with reality. Though it thoroughly castigates the young woman as reader ("I had been quite crazy!"), it also subtly exonerates *monogatari*; they are not falsehoods (*itsuwari*), but rather improbable or unrealized things/words (*aramashigoto*) that she once desired (*omoishikoto*). Tales are thus not evil in themselves; rather, the danger lies in how one reads them and what one makes of them. The implication that they might well be understood as "expedient means" (*hōben*) hovers just beneath the surface. *Monogatari* are posited here as something intermediate between "truth" and "the world," and the narrator sees herself as wrong to have become absorbed in them—not because they are inherently sinful, but because she allowed them to distract her from both her worldly ties (her family and a successful career at court) and from her hopes for the Other World. Like the metaphor of the dream as it is used in the *waka* tradition, literary fictions are both the very image of human delusion and a discourse that is in communication with truth and the sacred: signposts on the road to truth, a path to lead the reader out of illusion and into enlightenment.

The rich *va-et-vient* between the sacred and the profane so prominent in the accounts of the heroine's late dreams and pilgrimages surfaces once more before the end of the memoir in the splendid dream of Amida she recalls having "on the thirteenth night of the tenth month in the third year of the Tengi era [1055]." In the romantically charged context of the *Sarashina nikki*, where the admonitions and promises of well-dressed priests and court women who look like goddesses compete with fantasies of "a man like the Shining Genji and a lady like Captain Kaoru's Ukifune," the vision reads like a sacralized version of the romantic encounter that all the great ladies of *The Tale of Genji* await:

He did not appear to the others, only to me. I felt both deeply grateful and afraid, and so I didn't move any closer to my blinds to get a better look at him. His voice as he said, "I will be going back this time, but I will return for you later," was audible to my ears alone; the others could not hear him. When I noticed this, I was so surprised that I woke up, and found it was the fourteenth. On this dream alone I hung my hopes for the afterworld. (*NKBZ* 18: 360)

The dream includes elements essential to the initiatory scenes of courtly love: the woman is sitting behind her blinds—unseen yet recognizable and compelling to the visitor on the other side—and the visitor's promise to "return for you later" (the promise Amida made universally to all who call on his name and also one that mimics the vows of a hero bent on romantic abduction) translates into something holy, the secular image of the storied lover whom she dreamed of waiting for as a young woman. And yet this is the *kaimami* motif with a characteristic twist, vaguely reminiscent of the Takeshiba princess's tale in its highlighting of the woman's singularly powerful and appropriative faculties of sight and hearing: "He did not appear to the others, only to me. . . . His voice . . . was audible to me alone; the others could not hear him." The dream is the only one of the eleven dreams recounted in the memoir that is precisely dated, a detail that anchors it in the realm of the historical and the quotidian, differentiating it from the fantasies fiction breeds.

And yet on second glance, the quotidian itself slides into the sacred. The hands of Amida icons usually display one of nine *inzō*, symbolic positionings of the fingers and hands defined in terms of three possible positions for the hand. As Akiyama notes, the memoir gives just enough detail about the position of the Amida figure's hands—one lowered and open, the other with fingers joined to form a sign—to surmise that it displays one of three possible *inzō*, depending on the position of the signing hand. All three of these possibilities, however, signify the same sign (*raigō'in*) and the same vow, Amida's promise to welcome believers into paradise. She fastens tenaciously on the vision as an auspicious omen for her future salvation, and yet even as she does so her gesture discloses the unchanged restlessness of her desire as it circulates around the question that so often bridges the sacred and the profane in Heian *monogatari*. The enigma that worries the tales of all her favorite *Genji* heroines is the same one her own tale holds sacred: the question of the heroine's destiny.

The Destiny of a Reader

The village of Sarashina, in the mountains of central Japan, is a *meisho*, literally, a place with a name, with a reputation. In *waka* tradition, the place-name "Sarashina" is an *utamakura*, a poetic toponym that conjures a locale renowned for the beauty of its moonlight. But Sarashina is also, both geographically and rhetorically, the site of Obasuteyama, the mountain where, according to old legends, natives of the region left their aged parents to die alone and exposed to the elements. To Heian readers, the Sarashina topos would have brought to mind a famous episode (recorded in the *Yamato monogatari* and elsewhere) that conflates courtly and provincial associations into a single story.

A man who had lost his own parents was raised from childhood by a kindly aunt who treated him like a son. When the man married, however, the old woman became the object of his wife's hostility. The wife's ruthless complaints turned the nephew's heart against his aunt, and though he had treated her well in the past he now began to neglect her. One night the nephew finally gave in to his wife's suggestions. He tricked the old woman into thinking he was taking her to witness a special Buddhist service, carried her off on his back far into the hills, and abandoned her there, ignoring her cries as he hurried off. But back at home he passes a sleepless night recalling his aunt's kindness and regretting his deed. Gazing at the bright moon, he utters a poem that expresses his inconsolable grief, and in the end, he gets up and goes back up the mountain to fetch his aunt. The anonymous poem through which the nephew vented his sorrow was also well known as one of the most quoted *Kokinshū* lyrics, passed down as a conventional expression of disconsolate grief:

> Waga kokoro   Alas my heart
> nagusamekanetsu   can find no consolation
>   Sarashina ya   in Sarashina!
> Obasuteyama ni   where I gaze on the moon that
> teru tsuki o mite   shines on Mount Obasute

The poem that the *Sarashina* memoirist composed on this topos appears in one of the closing passages of the memoir, capping the passage that inspired Teika or some earlier reader to formulate the title by which all subsequent readers have known the work. Though Takasue's daughter herself may not have named her memoir the *Sarashina nikki*, it appears that early readers came to see in the abandoned aunt of the Obasute legend a kind of presiding persona for the work. And since the text as a whole is believed to be a product of the memoirist's later years, the persona of the abandoned aunt is one that calls for particular attention. The poem was composed ostensibly some months after the death of the memoirist's husband. In the memoir, it closes a passage describing an unexpected visit from one of the heroine's nephews after he and his siblings had moved away and left her to live alone in the house she had occupied during her marriage:

Living in the same place with my nephews, I saw them morning and night, but after these sad events they went their separate ways and I seldom saw them at all. There was an especially dark night, when one of the younger of them came calling. It seemed such a rare event that I was moved to write:

Tsuki mo idede	No moon emerges
yami ni kuretaru	Where I live on in darkness
Obasute ni	At Obasute
nani tote koyoi	Why then in this night
tazune kitsuramu	Do you come calling?
	(NKBZ 18: 360–61)

Of all the female figures available from the classical repertoire, there is perhaps none so thoroughly silenced and marginalized as the abandoned aunt of Mount Obasute, and many readers will recognize this appropriation of the legend as another of the memoirist's characteristically hyperbolic gestures of self-deprecation. But to dismiss the figure as simply another repetition of the motif of marginality begs the question of the memoirist's rhetorically complex performance of the ceremony of closure. The autobiographical references suggested by the reprise of this topos in the closing pages of the memoir will be obvious to the reader. After the early death of her elder sister, Takasue's daughter, like the aunt in the Obasute legend, took on the task of raising her nephews and nieces as her own children. The complaint that they have moved away from her in her declining years distantly echoes the legend of the nephew's abandonment of his aged aunt. Her husband Toshimichi's last governorship (the one from which he returned home to die) was in Shinano, the mountainous central province east of the capital where the actual Sarashina village and Mount Obasute lie. To "live on in darkness at Obasute," then, is also to dwell on the memory of her late husband. In terms of its place in the economy of the memoir as a whole, the near-closural appearance of the Sarashina topos figuratively (re)situates the heroine on the provincial margins of court society, closing the circle that began in the opening line of the memoir, with its fictionalization of her origins on the outer peripheries of the eastern provinces ("A person raised in a province even more remote than the one at the end of the Eastern Road—how utterly outlandish I must have been") (NKBZ 18.

283). And for the patient reader, the reader who reads through the lenses of old stories and poems, there is even more to discover here.

Oddly, the Mount Obasute of the *Sarashina nikki* is not bathed in moonlight but sunk in a darkness (*yami*) that is both physical and metaphysical; *yami* means both the absence of light and the delusions of ignorance and worldly attachment—spiritual darkness. The moon, doubling here as both symbol of Buddhist enlightenment and as the very secular moon whose beauty draws travelers to Sarashina village (guilty nephews and courtiers come to enjoy moon viewing), fails to emerge on the dark night the woman's nephew chooses to come calling. Comparing this poem to a number of earlier *waka* on the Sarashina topos, Moriya notes not only an unusual emphasis on the Obasuteyama legend in the *Sarashina* poem and its accompanying prose passages, but also a unique insistence in the poem on the absence of moonlight, an absence he reads as a metaphor for the memoirist's rejection in her later years of the tradition and culture of courtly elegance (*miyabi*).

Certainly, the memoir's reinscription of the Sarashina topos emphatically negates the identity of Sarashina village as a place famous for moonlight (*tsuki no meisho*), a destination for courtiers intent on the poetic pleasures of moon viewing. And indeed, if one further considers the poem in the context of other poems in the memoir, the absence of moonlight here is all the more striking. Out of a total of eighty-eight *waka* included in the pages of the *Sarashina nikki*, twelve contain explicit references to the moon or to moonlight, and images of the moon (particularly the dawn moon and the waning moon) figure prominently in a number of important prose passages as well. In short, the *Sarashina nikki* is itself a kind of *tsuki no meisho*, a text famous for its moon imagery. The moon's failure to shine, in a poem on a place renowned for its moonlight, is particularly noticeable at the close of a memoir that makes descriptions of moonlight and poems on the moon into a kind of signature image.

The voice that utters the poem, then, is a voice that calls attention to the condition of blindness, a kind of physical and metaphysical darkness that obscures both the speaker's thoughts and her nephew's errand. Recalling the old tale, she questions why he has come seeking her in her lightless world, and her question lodges, beneath the intricate play of allusion, the half-serious hope that her nephew has called for the purpose of taking her home with him. Because her poem retells the legend from the traditionally unvoiced viewpoint of the abandoned aunt, it also exposes the untold view, the unvoiced perspective latent in the original story, and in doing so underscores the implicit uncertainty of the tale's conclusion: How would the aunt, having once been abandoned to old age and death, receive her contrite nephew?

The subsequent and final passages of the memoir repeat and amplify the image of an old woman whom people have nearly forgotten, while the moonlight, so conspicuous because of its absence in the Obasute poem, becomes a now equally conspicuous presence. In the lines immediately following the passage quoted above, the narrator tells us that she had sent another poem inquiring after a friend from whom she had long had no word (*NKBZ* 18: 361). On the full moon of the tenth month, she records a poem she composed as she gazed alone at the moon (*NKBZ* 18: 361). But the most evocative repetition of the theme of an abandoned crone and the tricky play of moonlight occurs in the last lines of the memoir, a passage that recalls the weed-grown backdrop of another minor figure from the margins of the courtly world—Suetsumuhana, the bookish, tenacious, old-fashioned woman whom nearly everyone had deserted by the time Genji finally remembers to look in on her, half by accident, after long years of neglect. The shadow of her memory moves in gentle self-irony between the lines of the prose headnote, deepening the resonance of the penultimate poem in the *Sarashina nikki*:

The years and months have turned and passed, but whenever that dreamlike season comes back to mind, my thoughts wander and the world grows dark before my eyes; even now I cannot clearly recall the events of that time. My people all went to live elsewhere, and I stayed on alone in the old house, anxious and saddened by the uncertainty of my lot. After a bitter night spent staring sleeplessly until dawn, I sent this to one from whom I had long had no word:

Shigeri yuku	Sodden with dew,
yomogi ga tsuyu ni	the wormwood grows
sobochitsutsu	ever more rank and tangled;
hito ni towarenu	no sound but the weeping of
ne o nomi zo naku	one on whom none comes to call.

(*NKBZ* 18: 361–62)

Suetsumuhana, like the woman commemorated in the *Sarashina nikki*, assiduously avoided Buddhist vows and preferred reading *monogatari* and waiting for Genji's unlikely return to reciting sutras or following the practical advice of the serving women around her, most of whom abandon her household for greener pastures as the lonely years roll by.

But the ghost of Suetsumuhana's presence in the *Sarashina nikki* recalls not only the blind futility but also the unlooked-for good fortune of that *Genji* heroine, for she was a woman whose ridiculously romantic illusions about herself were rewarded, after a fashion, upon Genji's miraculous return. Hers was "a destiny," as one of the ladies in *Mumyōzōshi* irreverently quips, "harder to come by even than that of Buddhahood" (*SNKS* 7: 30).

What indeed might one hope to find, revisiting this passage with Suetsumuhana in mind? Beginning with the sentence that starts "My people all went to live elsewhere," the passage recalls the story of Genji's return to Suetsumuhana on a night when the moon is obscured by clouds. Koremitsu has been sent on ahead to search out signs of life beyond the tangled garden of the old estate. The undergrowth in question in both the *Genji monogatari* and the *Sarashina nikki* is *yomogi* (mugwort, wormwood, or simply weeds—the *Genji* chapter containing the account of Genji's rediscovery of Suetsumuhana is entitled *Yomogiu*, Seidensticker's "Wormwood Patch," after this especially memorable passage). The weed is the same one the *Kagerō* narrator complains of in the first volume of that memoir, and it is a conventional metaphor for the neglect visited upon the gardens (and by metonymic extension, the bodies) of forgotten or abandoned Heian ladies. Koremitsu is just about to give up his scouting among the wet and shaggy ruins of the Hitachi mansion's garden when the moon breaks through. He notices now, in its faint light, signs of recent housecleaning, the result of Suetsumuhana's vaguely premonitory afternoon dream (a dream visitation from her dead father). He hears the voice of a serving woman, cracked with age and punctuated by eerie laughter, and clears a path through the dew-laden weeds so that Genji may pass to find awaiting him in her dilapidated mansion a woman still possessed of "a constant spirit," "the same heart" (*moto no kokoro*).

But there is no Genji to uncover this latter-day Suetsumuhana, unless the reader sees herself as playing Genji's part. The *Sarashina* heroine sends the poem she composes in her own weed-grown house to the weed-buried hut of a Buddhist nun, and the nun's response is the poem with which the memoir concludes, one that also lingers on the image of a lonely dwelling place, the abode of a woman who has renounced even the desire for visitors. Chiding the heroine for clinging to the romantic themes of weed-grown mansions and the hoped-for arrival of some long-lost visitor, the nun's poem sounds again a Buddhist warning against desire and spiritual darkness:

Yo no tsune no
yado no yomogi o
omoiyare
somukihatetaru
niwa no kusamura

Wormwood around the house
of a woman of this world!
—try to imagine mine—
the stands of grass in the garden of one
who turned her back on all

(NKBZ 18: 362)

So ends the *Sarashina nikki*, poised between the secular and the sacred, the imagery of romantic anticipation and the gentle admonitions of a Buddhist nun. And perhaps, after her years of hard-won lessons in the illusory nature of fantasy, *aramashigoto* ("things that might be"), Takasue's daughter intended to let the nun's poetic remonstrance stand as a final metaphor for her belated renunciation of the tradition of courtly elegance. Yet taken as a pair, it seems to me that the two poems recapitulate the competing perspectives that inform the memoir throughout—the opposition between an older woman's disillusionment with the secular world, which *monogatari* both romanticize and comprise a part of, and a tenacious nostalgia for the girlish perspective that endowed that world (because of its tales) with irresistible charm. These tensions are not resolved, but merely left suspended at the end of the memoir. Deeply versed as she is in the powerful discourse of *monogatari*, the memoirist appears intensely aware of the futility (and perhaps the undesirability) of denying either of the two perspectives. At the close of the memoir the figure that ventures forth is that of a woman who is still, like Suetsumuhana, "of the same mind," a "constant spirit" (*moto no kokoro*), which is to say, in the language of the first lines of the memoir, "lacking in a steady mind or fixed intent" (*kokoro moto nashi*). In the darkness of the closing pages speaks a voice still possessed of the profound ambivalence that animates the figure of the restless reader for which this memoir is renowned.

Figures of reading dominate the fictions of desire inscribed in the *Sarashina nikki*, and among these figures, that of readerly wandering—and wandering as reading—recurs with notable frequency. As if to signify that reading and wandering (desire itself, conceived of as movement) have reached their limits, the old woman's yearning for a visitor comes to the fore late in the memoir in conjunction with an exaggerated evocation of limits (at the same time geographical, symbolic, metaphysical, and textual). It is a suggestive image for the mental landscape of a woman who, because of age and the attenuation of desire, can literally go no further. Her longing for a visitor reverses the direction of desire's movement and articulates a more conventionally feminine configuration (the desire to be desired, the woman as a stationary, magnetic center toward which other figures move, first to see and possess, and then to abandon).

The late longing for a visitor is bound up in a complex way with the desire that implicitly underlies the act of writing a memoir: the unspoken (perhaps because it is experienced as unseemly) longing for a reader. And if we are to see the memoir's final figure for "reading" as a scenario of visiting, a coming to call at the site where a writer or the fictional surrogate for the writer promises still to dwell, then the Obasute poem and the repeated entreaties in the final passages of the memoir also beckon to us, the longed-for but unforeseen readers of the *Sarashina nikki*. The subsequent passages of the memoir are also filled with invitational utterances, ambivalent though they may be, which both proffer and withhold the promise of the hostess's presence, the promise of an encounter. The question the old woman puts to her nephew is also at some level addressed to the readers of the memoir. Why have you come calling in the darkness of this night—here, where no moon breaks through? The dwelling you will find is a lightless one, inhabited by an old, abandoned woman. You will discover neither the courtly charms of moonlight nor the illumination of true understanding. Here there is only I. And how can you hope to find me in such darkness? Yet the allusions to unlikely visitors from the old tales such as Amida, who promises to return to take her with him to paradise, the contrite nephew who wants her back at home after all, and Suetsumuhana's Genji—the negligent lover who returns, never quite able to forget the past however unsatisfactory it may have been—anticipate that we too shall, having come, discover her in this darkness.

The *Sarashina nikki* thus ends as it began, in the provincial space of old age, in the double vision of a memoirist who keeps one eye on the future and the other glancing back to the point from which so many Heian literary ladies begin: the eastern provinces and a girl's dreams of what life in the city of tales might be like. What the reader is left to find here, behind the mask of the old woman, in the sudden moonlight that comes flooding back just as we turn to go—is the same heart (*moto no kokoro*) still restlessly yearning (*kokoro moto naku*) of the girl who dreamed long ago in far-off Azuma of all those things she had yet to see for herself. What is the final destination of desire in this memoir? Is it to convince the reader that the heroine (and the memoirist) had been in fact as unwittingly heedless as the narrative implicitly (yet so artfully!) claims she was? Is it to show that the story (her life!) might have ended, or probably did end, differently? Perhaps the memoir hints that the impulse behind both errancy and progress toward paradise is *yukashisa*, desire itself—one that drives the pursuit of many fictions, among them the fantasy of a charming, girlish blindness that veils a serious probing of the discourse of *monogatari* and its liminal position between reality and truth, a flawed blueprint for life in this world and a faulty intimation of the other world. *Monogatari* occupy an invitingly traversable, intermediary space, which intersects in the *Sarashina nikki* with the space of dreams and with Buddhist parables, Buddhist icons, and the figure of the bodhisattva, generously and mercifully poised between this world and the promise of another.

The girl saw *monogatari*, not as a metaphor for the world, but rather as standing in a metonymic relation to it; the capital is "that place where there are so many tales." In her early years she prefers not to see the analogies between *monogatari* and the world on the one hand or the discourse of religious truth on the other. What she dreams instead, as she unravels the mystery of her own destiny, what the text of the memoir maps, are relations of sequence, causality, and contiguity, a meaningful narrative framework for the story of a life. The world of *monogatari*, like the world of dreams, borders on both the profane (the world of the court and of family life) and the sacred (the space of the gods and the buddhas, the belief in an afterworld). The seer of dreams, like the reader of tales, moves between both worlds as she reads and dreams. The girl who yearned to encounter figures like the men and women she had read about in her tales and the holy figures she had dreamed about with guilt or longing becomes an old woman circumscribed by an idiom derived from both worlds. It is not they (Shining Genji and the Uji Captain, lovely Yūgao and poor Ukifune, or even Amida himself) who have burst through the boundaries of the tale into the realm of her quotidian existence, but the old woman herself who constructs the memoir in which she, companioned by those lovely shades, crosses the fascinating boundaries between *monogatari* and Buddhist fictions of transmigration and transcendence. Rewriting herself in terms of the pathetic minor heroines of *monogatari*, the memoirist succeeds in doing more than establishing her own identity on the margins of that world. Straining against the limits of the tales, her memoir indicates some of the directions toward which fiction itself moves in the years following *Genji*.

5 ☙ The Problem of Others in the *Sanuki no suke nikki*

The figure of the Heian woman as memoirist inscribes a dual position with respect to the gaze. On the one hand, she is constituted as its subject, the one who, in the act of narrating, both looks and tells. As narrator, through her discourse she brings into being and disseminates what is seen. But to the extent that what she narrates is herself or her own history, she also occupies the position of the heroine, a feminine figure whose interiority becomes the organizing principle of the text and the object of the reader's voyeuristic gaze. On this point, Heian memoirs distinguish themselves from many *monogatari*, in which the voyeurism of the (ostensibly female) implied reader of the tale is mediated by both a feminine narrating perspective and—at key junctures—the gaze of an amorous hero as voyeur within the tale. With Heian memoirs, as indeed with any text that presents itself as primarily autobiographical discourse, we are asked to believe that the relation between reader and heroine is less mediated than it is in tale literature. The heroine is identified with the narrator, and the narrator is identified with the memoirist herself. The one who speaks is also the one who is spoken about. The fiction of immediacy that characterizes the discourse of the memoir, its collapsing of seer with seen, short-circuits classic paradigms of literary voyeurism like the *kaimami* topos, which is predicated on an eroticized power imbalance that is divided between an active (masculine) beholder and a passive (feminine) beheld, the whole mediated by a mobile, shifting narrating perspective that cannot be simply identified with either the masculine voyeur or the feminine object of his gaze.

If part of the generic pact the Heian memoir makes with its historical reader involves the implicit promise of immediacy, the *Sanuki no suke nikki* further distinguishes itself from other memoirs by its singularly explicit preoccupation with the anxiety of self-disclosure.[1] Its narrating voice oscillates with unusual uneasiness between the positions of seer and seen, repeatedly calling attention to the problem of self-display. As both narrating voice or "source" of the memoir, and as heroine within the memoir-narrative, the figure of the Sanuki handmaid occupies a number of different positions with respect to the topoi of looking and being seen. She takes on different profiles at different moments: the mourner who hides herself from the eyes of others and stares in solitude, the active and voyeuristic lady-in-waiting who looks (or remembers looking), in her capacity as assistant handmaid (*naishi no suke*) to emperors Horikawa and Toba, and finally, the lady-in-waiting whose ubiquitous presence (and on occasion conspicuous absence) renders her vulnerable to the critical gaze of others. This third image of the handmaid has historically played a determining role in the interpretation of the *Sanuki* memoir and its author, and it has done so partly because the memoir itself seems to insist upon it.

The present exploration of the *Sanuki no suke nikki* takes as its point of departure a scandalous story told about its author in later life. According to an account that survives in a contemporary courtier's diary in Chinese, the Sanuki handmaid was dismissed from her position as assistant handmaid (*naishi no suke*) to Emperor Toba because she was possessed by the spirit of Toba's dead father, the former emperor Horikawa. Perhaps because the account of the possession and dismissal is tantalizingly vague, it has long provided a fruitful problem in traditional biographical and formalistic scholarship, coloring the way most commentators have evaluated the memoirist and the literary merit of her memoir. Scholars seldom consider the possibility that the courtier's account of her possession may be manipulative or biased. When the authority of the courtier's diary is questioned, it is questioned on the grounds of prior convictions regarding the Sanuki handmaid's "personality" as revealed in the *Sanuki no suke nikki*. Convinced of the handmaid's ingenuousness, Ikeda Kikan regards the story as a malicious apocryphal tale: "This sort of thing [her possession] is unthinkable, given [Sanuki no] suke's personality."[2] Those who, on the other hand, read the courtier's account as reportage rather than as unkind gossip understand her possession as an episode of mental illness[3] or the result of her "dissociated personality" (*bunretsushitsuteki seikaku*).[4] The resulting thesis that traces of the memoirist's pathology might be discerned in the style of the memoir, gave rise to a new, and in some respects rich, vein of stylistic analysis, although unfortunately, the direction and conclusions of such analyses were foreclosed by the critical consensus that this

memoir does not measure up to the high literary standards of other, bet-
ter-known mid-Heian women's memoirs. Until quite recently, little attention has been given to the idea that the phenomenon of spirit possession might be understood as something other than either a hoax or a
species of madness. My concern is that crucial connections among the
memoirist's gender and position at court, her own and others' political
interests, and the relation of spirit possession to all these issues have not
been addressed. In what follows I will suggest ways of rethinking the
relation among Heian gender norms, court intrigues, and spirit possession. The section that immediately follows reviews the political context
of the memoirist's career at court, the writing of her memoir, and the
later account of her possession by the spirit of Horikawa. In the second,
third, and fourth sections, close examinations of the rhetorical and intertextual moves in the prologue and second volume of the memoir will
allow us to trace the way the topoi of looking and self-display, so prominent a part of this memoir, become sites for the literary (and critical)
invention of the memoirist's identity as a favored imperial handmaid
and as a "shamanistic" personality . My point is not to champion the
literary talents of this memoirist so much as to offer a reading that will
elucidate the way her memoir dramatizes links among gender, political
identity, and rhetorical structures.

The Memoirist as Medium

The title of this section makes a pun on the two different senses of the
term *medium* in English. First, and most obviously, there is the *Sanuki
no suke nikki* itself as the discursive medium by which Emperor Horikawa and Fujiwara Nagako, the lady-in-waiting who presumably wrote
the memoir, are commemorated.[5] The term *medium* also identifies the
memoirist as one who assumes the role of a spirit medium, or, to borrow the Japanese term, a *miko*, a woman who acts as mouthpiece for
the voice of a possessing spirit. In this century, scholars have grappled
with both issues for reasons that will become clear from a review of the
memoirist's family affiliations and unusual career as assistant handmaid
(*naishi no suke*) to two emperors: Horikawa (1079–1107; r. 1086–
1107) and Toba (1103–56; r. 1107–23). But while the details of her biography and the historical reception of the memoir may be briefly outlined, the questions they raise and the problems they still pose for the interpretation of the memoir are not so easily resolved. The perception of

the memoirist as a woman capable of becoming possessed (and her memoir as the discourse of mediumship) is bound up in a striking way with details of political intrigues at Toba's court during the memoirist's middle age. What the commentators have done with these details in their interpretation of the memoir is no less striking and of great relevance to the study of gender as literary invention in Heian women's memoirs.

The memoirist's biography has been pieced together from court records, contemporary courtiers' diaries, and passages from the *Sanuki no suke nikki* itself. For generations scholars confused Fujiwara Nagako (more commonly referred to by her court sobriquet, Sanuki no suke, or the Sanuki assistant handmaid), with her elder sister, Kaneko (1049–1133), who was a wet nurse to Emperor Horikawa. It is now thought that she was, in fact, roughly thirty years Kaneko's junior and more or less an exact contemporary of Horikawa himself.[6] Nagako is thought to have been the youngest daughter of Fujiwara Akitsuna (d. 1107?), the head of a cadet branch of the Fujiwara clan that, though not historically important in the politics of the Heian period, had gained importance to the imperial house in the late eleventh century. Nagako's sobriquet "Sanuki no suke" (the Sanuki assistant) reflects her father's term of appointment as governor of the Sanuki province. Her memoir thus joins the list of distinguished Heian literary works by daughters of the provincial governor class. Hereafter I will refer to her as the Sanuki handmaid.

Despite the sentimentalization of ambitious provincial governors and their alluring daughters in *The Tale of Genji*, the provincial governor class (*zuryō*) represented a group of families in political decline in the early eleventh century. After the time of Fujiwara Kaneie (husband of the *Kagerō* memoirist), Kaneie's line of the Fujiwara family assured its hegemony at court by maintaining a preponderance of its own daughters in the imperial harem. As fathers of empresses and imperial consorts and grandfathers to crown princes and emperors, they cemented their control of the key positions of imperial regent and chancellor (*sesshō* and *kanpaku*).[7] Eventually these positions became more or less hereditary, and Kaneie's line maintained a virtual monopoly on them. The social mobility of a figure like Kaneie's principal wife, Tokihime, herself a provincial governor's daughter, but whose own daughters were named empresses, became a thing of the past during her son Michinaga's day and immediately thereafter.

However, because of shifting alliances within and around the imperial court during the last decades of the eleventh century, families such as the Sanuki handmaid's, long associated with the traditionally less prestigious but historically more lucrative posts of provincial governor, found themselves in positions of upward social mobility unprecedented since the mid-tenth century. Beginning with the reign of Emperor Go-Sanjō in 1068 and continuing through the reigns of emperors Shirakawa, Horikawa, and Toba, the imperial clan found in the provincial governor class a group of families willing and able to cooperate with their efforts to loosen the Fujiwara regents' hold on the imperial succession.

The increased political prominence of these "client families" (*kinshin*) of the imperial house in the late eleventh and early twelfth centuries owed much to imperial efforts to counter encroachments not only in the women's quarters of the palace but also in the provinces, where the Fujiwara regents had been busily amassing tax-free estates (*shōen*) for generations. Because of the frequent inheritance of houses by daughters from their mothers in mid Heian, many of these estates tended to remain in the hands of the Fujiwara regents, who were related matrilineally to the imperial clan.[8] The disproportionate growth of these privately held estates adversely affected the size and income of the imperial clan's provincial holdings. For their part, the provincial governors, whose own wealth depended on their ability to administer the collection and distribution of yearly rice harvests from imperial lands in the provinces, also suffered losses as a result of gains made by the Fujiwara regents and other powerful nonimperial families. As provincial governors, the heads of the client families had their own material interests in mind in making common cause with the imperial family to curb the influence of the Fujiwara regents both outside the capital and in the imperial harem.

At court, the alliances forged between the imperial house and its client families are well illustrated by the number of women from client families appointed to serve in key posts at the imperial palace during this period. Positions in the women's quarters, which had historically gone to daughters of the Fujiwara regents and ministers of state, began to be awarded to daughters of client families instead. The Sanuki handmaid, along with a number of her female relatives at the courts of Horikawa and Toba, was among those who jockeyed for imperial favor and position as assistant handmaids (*naishi no suke*), handmaids (*naishi*), and imperial wet nurses (*menoto*).[9] Although the Fujiwara regents were thus under siege in the early twelfth century, none of the client families was influential enough in its own right to duplicate their formula for success. This too worked to the advantage of the imperial house, which was in this way able for several generations to maintain an unusual degree of independence by colluding with a shifting coalition of client and Murakami Genji families (I will have more to say later concerning this latter group, an influential branch of the Minamoto clan).

The bureaucratic institution associated with this period of relative independence on the part of the imperial house was the *in no chō*, or office of the retired emperor. Historians traditionally characterize the entire period beginning with the early abdication of Emperor GoSanjō in 1072 up to the outbreak of the Genpei wars in 1179 as the "age of rule by the retired emperors" (*inseiki* or *insei jidai*). Emperor GoSanjō (1034–73; r. 1068–72) is often identified as the architect of the imperial clan's renewed authority, and the Sanuki handmaid's father, Fujiwara Akitsuna, was one of the early beneficiaries of the imperial family's political resurgence, having served, as had most heads of client families, as director (*bettō*) of Retired Emperor GoSanjō's *in no chō*. The longest-lived and most vigorous exploiter of the political potential of the office of retired emperor was GoSanjō's son Emperor Shirakawa (1053–1129; r. 1072–86), whose independent-minded maneuverings in time put him at odds with the wishes of his own father, brother, son, and grandson and gained for him the hostility of many of their disgruntled retainers. He easily overshadowed his son, Horikawa (1072–1107; r. 1086–1107), who died young. After Horikawa's death, Shirakawa continued to exert authority behind the scenes during the reign of his grandson Toba (1103–56; r. 1107–23). As the daughter of one of GoSanjō's client families, and handmaid to Shirakawa's son and grandson, the Sanuki handmaid's fortunes were strongly bound to Shirakawa's, a relationship that could not fail to be for her both a source of strength and a liability.

The Sanuki handmaid entered the court of Emperor Horikawa in 1100, an event most likely precipitated by her father's taking the tonsure and retiring from secular life that same year. She was made assistant handmaid in late 1101 and spent the next six and a half years, until the emperor's early death in 1107, attending to his daily needs in that capacity. The position of assistant handmaid was a highly privileged one, indicating the involvement of her family in the political rivalries of the day. Duties varied depending on the degree of imperial favor an assistant handmaid and her family enjoyed. A number of handmaids bore children to the emperors they served, and by the early twelfth century they were considered a sort of concubine. Though the Sanuki handmaid's name does not appear in any list of Horikawa's official consorts, this probably has less to do with her status than with the fact that she bore him no children.[10] It is thus not clear whether she was sexually intimate with Horikawa. Like most court women's memoirs, hers manages to be both suggestive and vague about these matters. Passages from it have been cited in support of both views. But although the exact nature and extent of the Sanuki handmaid's relations with Horikawa are uncertain, the memoir clearly implies that she attended him in morning prayers and religious observances regularly and also helped serve his meals. Their relationship, though not necessarily sexual, was of an intimate, daily nature.

When Emperor Horikawa became terminally ill in the summer of 1107, according to her account, the Sanuki handmaid waited on him constantly, remaining with him until his death. The second phase of her career in court service began only a few months after the emperor's death, when she was called out of mourning by order of Horikawa's father, Retired Emperor Shirakawa, to assist at the accession ceremony of Horikawa's son and successor Toba (1103–56; r. 1107–23). The ceremony took place in the twelfth month of 1107. A month later, she was asked to take up regular service at court again as assistant handmaid to Emperor Toba. The first volume of the *Sanuki no suke nikki* chronicles the last weeks of Horikawa's life in the summer of 1107. The second volume concentrates on the handmaid's life at court during 1108, the first of the eleven years she spent in service to Toba. The text as a whole, including the prologue, whose composition is thought to postdate the rest of the memoir, was probably completed in 1109 or 1110, and was thus possibly in circulation among readers at court while the memoirist herself was still occupying her position as assistant handmaid. Her career at court came to a sudden end in 1119. In the eighth month of that year, when she was about forty-one, her name was the focus of gossip because she was requested to leave court service under mysterious circumstances. According to a brief passage from *Chōshūki*, a *kanbun* diary by the courtier Miamoto Morotoki (1077–1136), there were reports that she had been possessed by the spirit of the late Emperor Horikawa off and on since the autumn of 1118. No record remains of her after her removal from court.

The contents of the passage from *Chōshūki* can be briefly summarized. The handmaid was relieved of court duty, and her elder brother Michitsune, governor of Izumi, was asked to take her into his keeping because since the previous year she had claimed that she was possessed by the spirit of the late Horikawa. In the autumn of 1118, during the pregnancy of Toba's new empress, later known as Taikenmon'in (and hereafter referred to by that name), the Sanuki handmaid, speaking in Horikawa's name, had prophesied the safe birth of an imperial prince to the empress. When the child was born as predicted in 1119, she claimed the authority of the former emperor's spirit again and urged that she be rewarded for her prophecy. Her wishes were that her brother be granted the governorship of Ōmi, while she herself be provided with a new residence, since her own had been destroyed by fire. What made the incident dire was the death threat she leveled at "the descendants of Lady Nii," should her wishes not be granted. Lady Nii had been a wet nurse to Emperor Horikawa and was the widow of Fujiwara Kinzane (1053–1107), the head of one of Retired Emperor Shirakawa's most important client families. She was also the mother of Toba's new empress and thus the grandmother of the newborn infant prince.[11]

As already noted, commentators on the *Sanuki no suke nikki* seldom concern themselves at any length with the possibility that the *Chōshūki* account of the possession may itself be politically motivated. Because the *kanbun* diaries of Heian courtiers are understood primarily as factual rather than as fictionalized accounts, scholars whose main interest is the *Sanuki no suke nikki* have largely read the *Chōshūki* entry at face value, ignoring the extent to which it is situated as a text both in terms of the political interests and intentions of its author, Minamoto Morotoki, and the rhetorical conventions governing courtiers' diaries. Before we can begin to suggest anything about the politics and rhetoric of the *Chōshūki* account of the handmaid's demise, it will be necessary to examine the situation at court during the ten years between Horikawa's death and the handmaid's dismissal.

Consider the circumstances surrounding the memoirist's return to court service after Horikawa's death. The imperial summons that brought the Sanuki handmaid back to court to serve at Toba's accession ceremony is described at the beginning of the second volume of her memoir, and if we can judge from that, the memoirist was worried about the vulnerability of her position at that juncture. Expressions of anxiety about one's lack of "backers" (*ushiromi*, literally, someone who watches over another from behind, usually a male relative with connections at court) are a commonplace in court women's memoirs, but we need not assume that all such claims were merely matters of literary form. It seems clear that her position after Horikawa's death was politically tenuous. She was childless, and though her father had represented the interests of an important client family, not only had he taken Buddhist orders around the time his youngest daughter entered court, but also he had apparently died within a few months of Horikawa.[12] The emperor's death also bereaved the Sanuki handmaid of her elder sister's support since the latter, as one of the late emperor's former wet nurses, had taken the tonsure a month after the emperor's funeral.

The memoir presents the summons to court as both an honor and an imposition on the former handmaid. She responds with dread, while her elder brother insists that she comply with the request, underlining the advantage she is being given by the opportunity to participate in the inauguration of the next emperor's reign. It is likely that her elder brother would have had in mind the advantages that might accrue to his own career as well. Despite the conventional rhetoric, so much in evidence here, of the mourner's disgust with the superficiality of those not in mourning, the memoirist seems to have kept the career of at least one of her elder brothers (Michitsune, fl. 1072–1129) in the forefront of her mind, even during the closing days of her own career, if we are to believe the *Chōshūki* account of her possession.[13]

Ordinarily, the handmaid of a recently dead emperor would not be called on to participate in public events before the end of the year-long mourning period, since she might still be in full mourning dress; indeed, the summons to serve at Toba's accession ceremony specified she was to put off her mourning robes at once (*NKBZ* 18: 411). The memoir explains the irregularity in the following terms. The task of raising the curtains before the imperial dais at the ceremony was to have been given to Toba's wet nurse, Fujiwara Saneko, a daughter of Horikawa's former wet nurse, the influential Lady Nii. Saneko was unavailable because of the recent death of her father, Fujiwara Kinzane. Because the Sanuki handmaid's sister Kaneko had raised the curtains at Horikawa's accession, Kaneko was apparently called on for advice, and it was she who urged her younger sister to accept the summons and attend in Saneko's place. The memoirist carefully couches the description in terms of the Sanuki handmaid's reluctant compliance with the advice of her elder brother and sister, repeated written requests by Lady Nii and by Retired Emperor Shirakawa himself, as well as the chance event of Kinzane's death. She also describes how she had briefly entertained the possibility of taking the tonsure herself, only to explain in conscientious detail her decision against such a move. Ishino Keiko comments that "[the memoirist] recounts the particulars of her return to court service almost as though she were apologizing for it."[14]

My contention is that the memoir *is* an apology, in a sense, and that its apologetic tone has as much to do with pragmatic considerations on the memoirist's part as with the poetics of mourning. On this point, the political and the literary are not easily separable. The memoirist's creative use of the language of mourning displays both the vulnerability and, paradoxically, the strength of her position, balanced, as she was, in the middle of factional conflicts involving Retired Emperor Shirakawa and his politically discontented half-brother Prince Sukehito (1073–1119), Shirakawa's various allies among the imperial client families (particularly that of Kinzane and Lady Nii), and Prince Sukehito's Murakami Genji supporters. A brief excursus on the shifting rivalries and alliances at court during the first two decades of the twelfth century will shed some further light.

The Sanuki handmaid's political association with Horikawa would not necessarily in itself have recommended her to Shirakawa as an appropriate attendant to his grandson Toba. Emperor Horikawa had been a sickly man, politically dominated by Shirakawa. More significant, Horikawa's maternal relatives represented potential threats to Shirakawa's efforts to maintain control over the imperial succession. Therefore, from the handmaid's point of view, her association with Horikawa was a tricky asset, if it was an asset at all. He was Shirakawa's son, certainly, but he was also the son of a Minamoto woman whose relatives were interested in seeing on the throne not Shirakawa's grandson Toba, but Shirakawa's half-brother Prince Sukehito, who had in their view been cheated of the throne when he was passed over in favor of Horikawa and again when Horikawa's son Toba was named crown prince, squeezing out Sukehito's son Arihito.

While the mothers of both Horikawa and his half-uncle Prince Sukehito were daughters of Minamoto courtiers, specifically members of the Murakami Genji family,[15] Toba's mother and maternal relatives linked him firmly to Shirakawa's network of non-Minamoto client families, which explains Shirakawa's eagerness to promote Toba. Toba's mother was Fujiwara Shishi, sister to Kinzane and cousin to Shirakawa.[16] Kinzane had been the head of a client family in competition not only with the Sanuki handmaid's relatives, but also, more significant, with the Murakami Genji. As maternal uncle to Toba, Kinzane, his principal wife, Lady Nii, and their numerous female offspring posed direct challenges to the hopes of Prince Sukehito and his Murakami Genji supporters. Lady Nii was a strong figure in her own right, both physically and politically. She bore Kinzane eight children. She had been wet nurse to Emperor Horikawa, and, despite her advanced age at the time (she was forty-five), she was immediately made wet nurse to Toba upon the early death of his birth mother in 1103. The position was turned over to her daughter Saneko in 1104. Because of the importance of Kinzane and his women to Shirakawa, Lady Nii and her daughters continued to play central roles in Toba's life throughout the period under discussion. In 1117, as we have already seen, her daughter (Taikenmon'in) entered Toba's court, was made his empress, and became the mother of his heir.[17] For the Sanuki handmaid, returning to court at the behest of Shirakawa and Lady Nii was tantamount to turning her back on the potential support of Horikawa's disenfranchised maternal relatives, a potentially grave mistake, should that faction eventually win out in the struggle for the throne, as it seemed capable of doing at several points during Toba's reign.

Volume two of the *Sanuki no suke nikki* opens with the Sanuki handmaid being importuned by a letter from none other than Lady Nii herself, reporting Shirakawa's request that the Sanuki handmaid take up service with Toba, who was then still the crown prince. The handmaid's response to the letter is double-edged. She accepts the summons, but with great reluctance, making it clear that her actions represent compliance with the advice of others, including her elder sister and brother. She seeks authority for her own reluctance in the memory of Horikawa himself, touching subtly on the precedent of how he had ignored, some years before, similar requests by Shirakawa that she be transferred to Toba's service (*NKBZ* 18: 407; Brewster, 81).

Shirakawa's repeated efforts to place the Sanuki handmaid in attendance on Toba rather than Horikawa suggest that he wished to count her among the available pool of female attendants from client families while simultaneously weakening her ties to Horikawa's maternal relatives. To judge from the memoir, it also appears that she thought it best to present her own feelings about the summons as mixed and as still governed by her ties to the dead emperor. To portray oneself as injured, in the throes of grief, by everyone else's concern with worldly affairs is a venerable literary pose. It may also hide a multitude of other concerns that have little to do with mourning for the dead. It is likely that the Sanuki handmaid found it expedient to cloak the issue of her loyalties in the language of bereavement in order to play to both sides of the room. In intricate ways, her memoir functions as a way to identify its author as politically innocuous, a distraught handmaid with her mind on the past and not on the plots of the tricky present. Her position—bereft of Horikawa and with little if any support from her own relatives—in some ways resembles the position of the child emperor Toba himself; he is too dependent on Shirakawa and his allies to resist their agendas, and yet he is in danger of being pulled down with these patrons, should the Murakami Genji find a way to instate Prince Sukehito or his heir as successor.

Given this context, the memoirist's obsessive absorption in memories of Horikawa can be seen as a politically astute posture. Her colleagues among the other women of client families at court (like Lady Nii and her daughters) cannot seriously fault her for clinging to the memory of Toba's father, and such an attachment could not offend the Murakami Genji, who were Horikawa's kinsmen. But the strain of this balancing act is everywhere apparent. An unusually oppressive awareness of the gaze of other court figures—their judgments and probable gossip about her—weaves in and out of the narrative of her memories of Emperor Horikawa. When we consider the level of political discontent at court during the years between Horikawa's death and the birth of Toba's first heir, as well as the ignominy in which her career ended, it appears that her anxieties were well grounded.

Toba's enthronement in 1107 aggravated tensions between Shirakawa and Prince Sukehito. As already mentioned, Shirakawa had passed over Sukehito twice for the position of crown prince—in 1072 at the birth of Horikawa and again in 1103 after the birth of Horikawa's son Toba. In refusing to recognize Sukehito's claims to the throne, Shirakawa was flouting the express wishes of their father, GoSanjō, and frustrating the ambitions of the Murakami Genji. Although the imperial house and the Murakami Genji had joined forces in the effort to undermine the hegemony of the Fujiwara regents in GoSanjō's day, Shirakawa was as wary of Sukehito's maternal relatives as his father had been of the Fujiwara regents. Fearing the resentment Toba's accession engendered in Prince Sukehito and the Murakami Genji, Shirakawa enlisted warriors from another branch of the Minamoto clan, the Seiwa Genji, to provide policing on the day of Toba's accession.[18] The Sanuki handmaid would have been aware of the anticipation of violence at Toba's accession ceremony, and though the memoir does not lay out these matters explicitly, it is equally likely that a contemporary court readership would have been able to read between her lines.

The eleven years between Horikawa's death and the birth of Toba's first heir were fraught with instability. The issue was still imperial succession. After Toba's accession, Shirakawa continued to leave the position of crown prince vacant, this time ignoring the obvious candidacy of

Sukehito's son Arihito, who had been born in 1103, the same year as Toba. Even if the memoir had been composed as late as 1118, the year before her dismissal from court (which was also the year Sukehito died and Toba's heir was born), the Sanuki handmaid would still have reason to consider her own position a delicate one, tied as her fortunes were to those of Toba, still a youth and still very much under the thumb of his grandfather Shirakawa, who had many enemies. Shirakawa's consistent refusal to recognize the claims of Sukehito won for him (and by default for Toba) the enmity of the Murakami Genji.

As already mentioned, the only detailed account of the Sanuki handmaid's possession is given in the *Chōshūki*, a *kanbun* diary by Minamoto Morotoki, under the entry for the twenty-third day of the eighth month of Gen'ei 2 (1119). The identity of the diarist as a member of the Murakami Genji family immediately raises a number of interrelated problems of interpretation. Morotoki was (like most of the courtiers whose private diaries have been preserved from the Heian period) no objective bystander commenting on events at court merely for the sake of keeping a record. Though it is not my purpose to explore all the possible political interests his diary may indicate, a general review of his position at court will show just how politicized his account of the affair is likely to have been.

To begin with, Morotoki was the son of Minamoto Toshifusa (1053–1121), the head of the Murakami Genji and a longtime supporter of Prince Sukehito and his heir, Arihito. Toshifusa and his sons were interested in seeing the throne occupied by their kinsman. Intent on keeping the imperial succession within his own branch of the family, Shirakawa was equally eager to curb the strength of Sukehito's Minamoto supporters. Like the imperial client families, though initially with greater success, Toshifusa's family had vied with the Fujiwara regents for key positions at court for a few generations. Although the Fujiwara still managed to monopolize the regency during those years, the leadership of the family had passed in 1101 to Fujiwara Tadazane (1078–1162) when he was still quite young and inexperienced. When Tadazane assumed the regency in 1105, he found himself outranked and overshadowed by Minamoto Toshifusa, who had been minister of the left for twenty-three years. At the time of Horikawa's death, Murakami Genji leaders occupied seven of the twelve key ministerial positions at court. Given their ties to the imperial clan through the late Horikawa and the still very much alive Sukehito, they posed a serious threat to Shirakawa's hegemony.

In 1114, five years before the date of the diary entry, the diarist Morotoki, his brothers Moroshige and Moroyori, two of his other brothers,
Ninkan and Shōkaku, and their father, Toshifusa, were all implicated in a
plot to kill Emperor Toba. Shirakawa's investigation of the plot exposed
as the mastermind Morotoki's brother Ninkan, a priest who, one commentator interestingly notes, had once served as imperial exorcist for
Prince Sukehito.[19] Shirakawa exiled Ninkan to Izu for seventeen years,
while Toshifusa and his three nonclerical sons (including Morotoki) were
stripped of office and forbidden to attend court for a year. The banish-
ment of Toshifusa and his sons was intended to weaken significantly the
Murakami Genji threat to Shirakawa's control of the imperial succession.
Thus, the reader may readily imagine with what interest Morotoki would
still have listened, four years later, to any gossip suggestive of serious rifts
between Shirakawa and Toba, particularly if that gossip even remotely
concerned the legitimacy of the child who was the firstborn of Toba's
heirs. Indeed, a closer look at the account in *Chōshūki* reveals its particular concern with the implications of the incident for relations between the
reigning emperor, then still a youth of sixteen, and his imperial grandfather, Shirakawa.

A further, very fundamental question raised by the entry concerns the
problem of audience for the genre of courtiers' diaries in Chinese. If we
can assume that courtiers' diaries were written with the intent to be
more than just private memoranda, to what end did the diarist record
gossip about his contemporaries and rivals at court? Whose eyes did
Morotoki imagine perusing his diary? Issues of readership and rhetorical
convention in the *kanbun* diary tradition are generally overlooked by
literary scholars who employ Heian courtiers' diaries as reliable historical sources against which to verify events recounted in Heian court
women's memoirs, a genre that is regarded as inherently more "literary"
(read: fictionalized and apolitical). I would argue that although fragmentary, the second- and thirdhand accounts of the incident as recorded
in Morotoki's diary have more to tell us about the gossipers, and gossip
as text, than about the events themselves. Morotoki's account of the affair is an elaborately wrought network of rumors and speeches within
speeches. It also includes reports on the contents of other equally enigmatic written documents—an order from Shirakawa's office of the retired emperor (*in no chō*) and a letter (but from whom?) to Lady Nii,
whose daughter had recently become Toba's new empress and the
mother of his first male child.

The entry immediately calls attention to its own obfuscated (and obfuscating) nature; one imagines how it might have served to intensify the scent of scandal already in circulation. Morotoki begins by qualifying the origin of his information as a story told him by "the governor of Iyo" (Fujiwara Nagazane), who, qualifying his own story as "something that has already become a big issue," identifies his source as a certain "high priest." The names of these other gossipers, of course, pose further questions. What was the nature of Fujiwara Nagazane's interest in the affair, and what were his ties to Morotoki? What or who is implied by Nagazane's mention of the high priest who told him the story? Are we to imagine the priest was an exorcist or the associate of an exorcist brought in at the time of one or more of the handmaid's episodes of possession? Was he connected by blood or political ties to the Murakami Genji clan or to any other of Shirakawa's enemies or client families? The potential for distortion becomes greatest at the heart of the story, where the diarist reports the gossipers' reports of fragments of the speeches made by the handmaid when she was under possession. What we read is a translation into Chinese of the Japanese speech of an imperial handmaid whose words are ostensibly not her own but those of the possessing spirit of a dead emperor as retold to Morotoki, who had it in turn from Nagazane, who had it from an unspecified priest who may or may not have been present to witness or to officiate as exorcist at the time of one or more of the handmaid's possessions.

Both grammatically and syntactically, the possessed handmaid's speech creates further ambiguities, which are themselves difficult to evaluate without reference to the generic conventions of spirit-possession narratives. These conventions may be modified or elaborated depending on the embedding context, that is, on whether the possession is described as an episode in an overtly fictional tale or whether, as in this instance, it purports to be the account of an actual event, on whether it appears in a memoir in Japanese or Chinese or is narrated from the perspective of victim, medium, witness, or interested gossiper. Roughly translated, the speech goes something like this:

I am the spirit of the former emperor. It is true that many times I have appeared to this woman and given her commands. To comply with my commands is what I ordered of this lady-in-waiting. Therefore, she should be rewarded according to her requests; otherwise, the resulting resentment in her heart could become a terrible thing. What is it that is desired? That my elder brother Michitsune be appointed governor of Ōmi province. Moreover, since my residence burned down, I have no place to live. Build a residence for me in the rear quarters of the imperial palace.[20]

The speech ends with a vow to "haunt to death the descendants of Lady Nii" if these requests are not granted.

First-person-singular pronouns pepper the Chinese text, and their referents shift in a fascinating way, the ultimate identity of the "I" in the first part of the speech being the spirit of Horikawa referring to his own medium using third-person locutions ("this woman," "this lady-in-waiting"). The spirit's statements about its identity and relationship to the medium are followed by the question "What is it that is desired?"—an utterance whose speaker, whose "I," is necessarily ambiguous, given the diary context in which the question is embedded. Is it the spirit or is it the diarist-narrator (or one of his informants) who asks the question? When a definite "I" appears again in the next sentence, its referent is clearly the Sanuki handmaid, who goes on to demand material compensation for her brother and for herself in the first person. The sentences are declarative and syntactically simple; in fact, compared to other parts of the diary entry, the spirit's speech comprises one of the most readily comprehensible sections in the entry as a whole.

The entry continues with insinuations about the conflict the incident engendered between Toba and Shirakawa. Shirakawa ordered the Sanuki handmaid's withdrawal from court. Emperor Toba, on the other hand, the diarist notes, "because he is always closeted talking with his handmaid," was inclined to listen to the handmaid's speeches sympathetically. Morotoki implies that Toba initially opposed the Sanuki handmaid's dismissal and even threatened to cease visiting Empress Taikenmon'in if the handmaid were removed from court.

It was, after all, Toba's father's ghost for whom the handmaid-as-medium claimed to speak. To judge from later mentions of the affair, however, there would have been more at issue for Toba than a simple belief in the ghostly authority of the handmaid's requests and threats. The motives of his grandfather Shirakawa were deeply entangled in the marriage politics of the day, and Toba's reported reactions to the event suggest that he was well aware of that. Toba's new empress had been raised as the foster daughter of one of Shirakawa's own consorts, Gion no nyōgo.[21] Not only was Taikenmon'in thus Shirakawa's protégée, but also it was rumored that her relations with her foster father had been sexual as well as familial. But for that story we have to turn to other sources. Morotoki does not explicitly pursue this line of interpretation, or any other for that matter, in this entry from *Chōshūki*. Nonetheless, it became common gossip, recorded in later years, that Empress Taikenmon'in's first child was not Toba's son at all, but rather his half-uncle, the result of her earlier sexual intimacy with Shirakawa.[22]

Perhaps Shirakawa wished to have Toba's handmaid dismissed in an effort to prevent her from further manipulating rumors about the new empress and the paternity of the infant prince. Or perhaps the whole story of the handmaid's possession was concocted by Shirakawa or others who had an interest not in stirring up paternity rumors but rather in discrediting those that had already spread. Whatever the case, the upshot of the affair was the dismissal of the Sanuki handmaid and further friction between Shirakawa and his reigning grandson. Shirakawa's wishes prevailed, and his continued overshadowing of Toba in affairs at court was perpetuated by Toba's abdication in favor of the child, who acceded to the throne four years later as Emperor Sutoku (1119–64; r. 1123–41). And the friction did not die away with the death of Shirakawa in 1129. The question of Emperor Sutoku's paternity eventually contributed to the political rivalries between him and Retired Emperor Toba that finally culminated in the Hōgen Rebellion of 1156, one year after Toba's death.[23]

Is it conceivable that the handmaid could have given such a speech? Are we to understand that she made her demands for a reward (not to mention the subsequent threat to kill Lady Nii's descendants, should the demands not be met) in her own voice (whether or not under the guise of spirit possession)? And if so, what are we to make of the gossipers' perception of her possession? This is different from asking whether she in fact did make such a speech or whether she actually experienced or staged an episode of possession (questions that are probably not even answerable). What is at issue here is the degree of verisimilitude such a *story* would possess. How plausible could such an account be in terms of the handmaid's social and personal identity? How was spirit possession understood in the memoirist's day? Any answer to this question has to involve some notion of the range of believable discursive performances and of sociopolitical norms for a woman in her position at the twelfth-century Heian court.

One of the biggest difficulties bedeviling discussions of spirit possession in Heian literature is the ambiguity of the phenomenon itself as it is represented in Heian texts. Particularly ambiguous is the figure of the *miko* (shamaness or medium, also called *yorimashi*), a role generally played by a woman or child who acts as a mouthpiece for the gods (*kami*) or spirits of dead ancestors in a number of related scenarios of spirit possession and exorcism. The word *miko* is sometimes used in Heian texts to describe the women who served as priestesses at Shinto shrines or at the Imperial Palace. The institution of shrine and imperial palace priestesses is related to the ancient pre-Heian figure of the shamaness, whose trances are understood as self-induced—not necessarily mediated or facilitated by the spells and chants of an exorcist.[24] The word *miko* is also used to designate the mediums who assisted Buddhist priests.

Anthropologists distinguish between the self-induced trances and discourse of shamanistic practice and the more or less passive reception of spirits while in a trancelike state by the Buddhist medium, also called *miko*, in Tendai and Shingon rites of exorcism, which begin to be mentioned frequently in writings starting in the tenth century. The women or girls who accompanied Tendai or Shingon priests, or alternatively, unaffiliated, itinerant Buddhist exorcists (these latter referred to as *genza, genja,* or *hijiri*), acted as mediums by receiving the possessing spirits originally afflicting some third person, often a pregnant woman or a woman in childbirth or a person of either sex suffering from illnesses of various kinds. Among Japanese anthropologists, the distinction between the two types of *miko* is sometimes characterized in terms of her discourse while under possession. The self-induced speech of Shinto priestesses is understood as "self-generated speech" (*hitorigatari*), while Buddhist *miko*, whose speeches under possession are solicited and guided by spells and questions uttered by a priest, produce "solicited speech" (*toigatari*). It was usually only after the possessing spirit had been transferred from the victim to the Buddhist *miko* that it could be induced to reveal its identity, speak its grievance, and in some instances, name terms for its own propitiation. Examples of this type of medium abound in mid-Heian texts, and the terminology used to describe them is diverse. One such medium, brought to court to little avail in attempts to exorcize possessing spirits during Emperor Horikawa's final days, is referred to in the *Sanuki no suke nikki* as simply "the person to be possessed" (*monotsuku mono*) (NKBZ 18: 374; Brewster, 59). Thus, in the Buddhist exorcism rites that became common beginning in the tenth century, the female medium provided a crucial means for the verbal communication of grievances and unsatisfied desires ostensibly thought to emanate, not from the gods, but from either spirits of people who had died bearing some sort of grudge (*goryō*) or the dissociated living spirits (*ikiryō, ikisudama*) of someone whose resentment is so intense that his or her spirit leaves the body and attacks the object of its resentment or someone dear to that person. The possibilities for cynical manipulation of these rites as a means of gaining a more or less public hearing for politically motivated or otherwise inadmissible demands should be obvious, and they did not escape the notice of Heian writers of fiction, as will be discussed below.

Heian narratives about spirit possession, whether overtly fictionalized or reported in diaries and memoirs, do not always involve representations that fall neatly into the category of either self-induced or mediated possession. There were other possibilities in Heian practice, judging from the accounts of spirit possession seen in Heian women's memoirs and tales. Particularly common are accounts of ladies-in-waiting on hand at sickbeds and scenes of possession who spontaneously fall into trances and speak for the spirits presumably possessing the mistress or master without the intervention of exorcists. There are also victims who suddenly blurt out grievances and/or the identity of the spirit possessing them with no priest or medium attending them at all. The Heian term for this type of speech is "unsolicited talk" (*towazugatari*). Though the term seems to have originally referred to the speech of the possessed, it was also used loosely, as we have already seen in the *Kagerō nikki*, to describe a woman's angry or jealous outbursts.

Gender arrangements on the scene of possession are equally diverse. Both men and women fall victim to possessing spirits, though it is usually women who serve—either by training or by virtue of their spontaneous response at the scene of a possession—as mediums for the possessing spirits. The possessing spirits themselves are usually also identifiable as either male or female, and they may be presented as the spirits of living or dead people. Many of the possessing spirits that figure in the long historical tales like the *Eiga monogatari*, the *Ōkagami*, and the *Masu kagami* are dead but still disgruntled male courtiers or ministers who never got the post they wanted or who are angry because their survivors have not been well treated politically.

As texts, reports and stories about spirit possession display a rich variety of narrating perspectives. Sometimes possessions are narrated from the point of view of an interested or personally implicated onlooker. When Genji's principal wife Aoi is lying prostrate in the clutches of an as yet unidentified malign spirit, her possession is portrayed from Genji's viewpoint, including snatches of interior monologue that suggest Genji's own speculations about the identity of the possessing spirit and the stirrings of a guilty conscience on his part (*NKBZ* 13: 33–34 and 36; S, 168–69). They might also be described as superficial spectacles

from the standpoint of unimplicated onlookers. Sei Shōnagon gives a
vivid description of an exorcism, complete with a fashion-conscious critique of what the priest and the medium were wearing and musings on
how awful it would have been for the medium if she had had any idea
of how disarrayed she looked while under possession (*SNKBT* 25: 341–
43).[25] Narratives that involve unsolicited outbursts (*towazugatari*) explore the possibility of conflating the roles of victim and medium: the
victim speaks in the voice of the possessing spirit, perhaps even taking
on the appearance of the other who possesses her. This is true of Genji's
wife Aoi in the possession scene mentioned above (*NKBZ* 13: 33; S,
168). Still other narratives explore the phenomenon from the perspective of the person accused of possessing another. Examples of this, again
from *The Tale of Genji*, are to be found in the passages describing Lady
Rokujō's interior monologues after she gets wind of the gossip about
her part in Aoi's illness and death by possession (*NKBZ* 13: 29–31 and
35–36; S, 167 and 169).

Finally, the phenomenon of spirit possession is evaluated in a variety
of ways, ranging from the pious, reverential treatment of it in ideologically conservative works like the *Eiga monogatari*—where it is presented simply as a supernatural event, or the will of the gods—to works
like *Yowa no Nezame*, a late-eleventh-century tale that hints at the idea
of a false medium (*namamiko*), hired by the heroine Nezame's enemies
and told to name her as the spirit possessing their mistress.[26] The novelist Enchi Fumiko wrote an important novel that revolves around this
theme of duplicitous spirit mediums. Its title, the *Namamiko monogatari* (which translates as "A Tale of False Mediums") plays on the in-
triguingly ambivalent nuances of the word *nama*, which can mean "raw
and immature . . . natural and unspoiled" as well as "appearing to have
certain qualities that one does not actually possess," hence "false."[27]
The very concept of the *namamiko*, like that of *towazugatari*, encompasses both innocence and falsehood, outraged ingenuousness and duplicitous manipulation of the innocent.

As already noted, the malign spirits (*mononoke*) described in Heian
spirit-possession narratives are usually gendered, but their gender identity may be either male or female. There are distinctions to be made,
however, depending on the text or even the gender identity of the au-
thor(s) and the primary audience. In an essay that has long been considered basic reading in English on the subject, William McCullough
makes interesting observations about the gender of possessing spirits in
Genji, as opposed to other Heian accounts. McCullough's essay is typi-

cal of the critical tendency to oversimplify Heian spirit-possession narratives in a particular way.[28] In his reading, Lady Rokujō's career as a vengefully jealous "living spirit" (*ikisudama*) attacking Genji's other wives and lovers becomes a norm for describing Heian spirit-possession narratives in general. In fact, I would argue that the *Genji* text is rather atypical, if read against other Heian accounts in which the possessing spirits tend to be identified as male and the issue is court appointments. Against the backdrop of the many possessions recounted in the *Eiga monogatari*, *The Tale of Genji* appears radical in its interest in female ambitions, the thwarting of feminine desire, and the social and psychological consequences of thwarted feminine desire for both men and women. The gender arrangements involved in the *Genji* spirit-possession narratives are striking. Often no Buddhist priest is involved at all to facilitate (or manipulate) the show; female characters occupy all three roles—possessed victim, possessing spirit, and medium. Under possession, Yūgao and Aoi interact directly with Genji, the latter uttering unsolicited speeches that suggest the identity of the possessing spirit and implicate Genji's provocative behavior as the ultimate source of its unrest. Murasaki's possession by Lady Rokujō involves a girl acting as medium, who expressly sends the priest and all others away so that the spirit/medium may speak with Genji alone (*NKBZ* 15: 225–28; S, 617–18). Only Ukifune is alone at the time of her supposed possession; her possessing spirit appears to be male, and her case is maverick to the *Genji* in other ways as well. As Matsumoto Yasushi points out, the Sanuki handmaid's speech under possession as represented in *Chōshūki* also appears to be an "unsolicited speech," because no medium other than the sick handmaid herself speaks for the possessing spirit.[29]

Our cultural and temporal distance from the Heian accounts exacerbates the problem of interpretation. Were the spirit-possessed figures dramatized in Heian *monogatari* or reported in male courtiers' diaries in Chinese seen simply as involuntary victims of aggressive, wandering spirits? Or was the victim's possession regarded as representing some position halfway between intentionality and victimization by another? Was spirit possession as a phenomenon understood on some level to represent, as Bargen has argued for its textual representations in *The Tale of Genji*, an "oblique aggressive strategy" for calling attention to the victim's otherwise unspeakable needs and demands? In the case of stories about possessions by living spirits especially, might it have been seen as a form of collusion, however unwitting, between possessor and possessed in order to express a shared grievance directed at a third party connected to both?[30] Given the Heian origins of the concept of the *na-mamiko* (the false/innocent medium), how can we unquestioningly read the medium as simply the passive vehicle for the voice of a possessing spirit? May she not also speak for her own interests (or the interests of others connected to her) under the guise of voicing the interests of the dead?

Bargen has argued that *The Tale of Genji* dramatizes these issues. Although I do not find all the details of her analysis convincing, I think the general thrust of her argument is worthy of serious consideration. My point is that the *Genji* is not the only Heian text to suggest links between the supposedly supernatural phenomenon of spirit possession and the more prosaic but no less compelling forces of repressed desire and political discontent. As we have seen, the *Chōshūki* account touching on the *Sanuki* memoirist's possession suggests sophisticated readings and manipulations of spirit possession by the memoirist's contemporaries and perhaps by the memoirist herself. My readings of the *Sanuki no su-ke nikki* further suggest that the pose of the *miko* is part of a repertoire of ways to obviate social taboos against feminine self-display and the articulation of feminine desire. A court woman who can claim spirit possession avoids breaking the taboo against making a spectacle of herself by presenting herself as not herself, in the grip of a malign spirit. The woman under possession is able to sustain the gaze of even the most critical spectator by masking herself as other, that is, possessed (and to some extent concealed) by an other. This phenomenon need not be explained as an either/or proposition, pathology on the one hand or the cynical, highly premeditated manipulation of others by the medium acting independently or in collusion with accomplices on the other. The *miko* as discursive pose enables the writer to negotiate the intertwined issues of commemoration and self-disclosure—both of which are, in the context of Heian women's writing, desirable literary goals that are nonetheless fraught with anxiety and the threat of censure and that require a tightrope walk between indecorous self-exposure and alluring self-display. In the particular case of the Sanuki handmaid, the *miko* and related poses served pragmatic as well as aesthetic ends. It is the aesthetic profile of these poses that we will turn to next.

The scholarly tradition of seeking connections between the mysterious demise of the Sanuki handmaid's career at court and stylistic aspects of the memoir she is thought to have written some ten years earlier begins with Tamai Kōsuke's brief remarks that the "mental illness" she suffered in later life should prove useful to the deeper appreciation of aspects of the memoir itself.[31] What I find especially interesting about this interpretation is its positioning of the figure of the *miko* as the (sick) source of the memoir-narrative rather than as a deliberately assumed literary pose (the writer/memoirist as medium) or as simply an apocryphal story told about the memoirist in later life. The danger that such interpretations will lead to an understanding of the memoirist as simply the victim of her own infirmities (and the memoir as a product of its writer's pathology) has been borne out by the direction that commentary on it has taken in the past thirty years.

Aside from the way such readings obscure the complex political contexts in which many memoirs may have been written and read, they engender particular distortions in the portrait of Heian court women—not only regarding their conscious participation in the political intrigues of the day but also the question of their consciousness itself as writers. The more obvious the links between the handmaid's text and her possible motivations as a patronage-seeking agent, the more creative the commentators become in neutralizing images of her as such. Predictably, among the scholars who read the story of the Sanuki handmaid's possession as evidence of something other than the archaic, superstitious beliefs and practices of an only superficially sophisticated age, the debate polarizes around the issue of the handmaid's agency and will. The image of her as a self-interested manipulator (however unwitting or unconscious) of the credulity of her contemporaries or of her own insider's guesses regarding Empress Taikenmon'in's sexual history was apparently at odds, for Ikeda Kikan, with the docile, self-effacing image of the memoirist that he saw inscribed in the *Sanuki no suke nikki*.[32] Following Tamai on the other hand, commentators after Ikeda argue for continuity between the image of the Sanuki handmaid as memoirist and her identity in later life as the victim of spirit possession. A decidedly twentieth-century perception of spirit possession as a form of mental illness or emotional imbalance underlies these arguments. Inaga Keiji considers that the incident signifies, like the memoir itself, the handmaid's frustrated and long unvented desire to have borne Horikawa a child.[33] As already noted, Matsumoto Yasushi finds evidence of the memoirist's susceptibility to obsessive behavior in the prose style of the text. Matsumoto's essay moves from a summary of the *Chōshūki* passage to argue that not only the content but also the rhetorical style (or lack of style) in the *Sanuki no suke nikki* suggests that the handmaid was possessed of "an unusual facility for assimilating herself to the personality of others." For Matsumoto, the memoirist's personality is more accurately

characterized as a lack or a fluidity of personality that he also associates, via reference to folklorist Hori Ichiro, with Japanese women in
general throughout history. He argues that this is most noticeable in
passages describing Emperor Horikawa. His readings identify instances
of what he terms "shamanistic style" (*miko teki buntai*) in the frequent
shifts among descriptions of Horikawa's external appearance, direct
quotations of the dialogue between the emperor and the handmaid, and
a kind of indirect free style used to convey the emperor's unspoken
thoughts.[34] An obvious critique of Matsumoto's point is that the fluidity
of narrating perspective or point of view that he finds characteristic of
the "shamanistic style" peculiar to this memoir sounds too much like
the shifting narrative perspectives characteristic of other major mid-
Heian narratives, as *Genji* scholars in the past fifteen years have so pro-
lifically demonstrated. Other stylistic features and flaws for which the
memoir has long been faulted, such as its dearth of included *waka*, its
inexpert and scant use of such standard rhetorical devices as *hikiuta* (the
embedding of poetic allusions within prose passages), and *honkadori*
(allusive variation within individual *waka*) and its overuse of lexical
repetitions, are all marshaled as symptomatic of the memoirist's shamanistic "personality."[35]

The operating assumption is that the traces of shamanistic propensi-
ties that surface as stylistic mannerisms bespeak fundamental, unconscious manifestations of the *Sanuki* memoirist's overly suggestible personality. All these interpretations assume the absence of the memoirist's
control as artist and as a politically motivated writer. Not surprisingly,
then, the most conventionally and overtly rhetorical passage in the
memoir—the prologue—is precisely the passage whose authenticity as
the work of the Sanuki handmaid remains under serious debate.[36] Similarly, the scholarly consensus on her inferiority as a *waka* poet has done
nothing to encourage readers to ask an obvious question: Might not the
image of the writer as an obsessive mourner compulsively absorbed in
contemplation of the past, with a propensity for losing herself in reverie
to which even her lexical and structural repetitions testify, be itself part
of a studied pose, the mark of the memoirist's artistry rather than of her
pathology? Why should we not read the play with mediumship—both in
the memoir and perhaps in the handmaid's actual involvement in spirit
possession—as a deliberately artificed literary pose? Yet another possibility is to read the posture of mediumship as both artistry *and* pathology. Might it not be that pathology, whether we understand it as a pre-

disposition toward assimilating herself to the personality of another or simply as a gender-related "lack of strength," designates what is conventionally sanctioned in a woman's writing, as it is in many other modes of female behavior? What could be more feminine than to succumb to the influence of what is, according to the conventions of the day, an angry spirit from the Other World, or—also in the language of the day—to the demon in her own heart (*kokoro no oni*)?

Heian court women seem to have seen themselves as other, or possessed by the will of another, particularly at moments when they felt most strongly the need to speak up for their own interests. To account for this show of strength using the language of possession is a supremely conventional move. Even so bold a character as the *Kagerō* memoirist imagines that her husband will read her explanation of her flight to Narutaki as a "weird, unasked-for tale" (*ayashiki towazugatari*), the unsolicited outburst of a woman possessed by the strength of her own desires (*NKBZ* 9: 259). The readings that follow will attempt to demonstrate that the *Sanuki* memoir presents us with a curiously canny sort of medium. There is a nervous mobility in its narrator-heroine's gaze; her words anticipate the responses of her future readers even as she conjures the things of the past. We can only speculate about what she intended her memoir to accomplish and how it might have been perceived by her contemporaries, but I will argue that it is informed by far more complex and carefully premeditated images of the handmaid as medium than those with which it has been traditionally credited.

Problems of Commerce

What images of the writer and of commemorative writing preside over the opening passages of the *Sanuki no suke nikki*? What political and aesthetic codes are at work here? In the prologue to the memoir, the topoi of vision (of looking, being spied upon, hiding from the critical eye of others, gazing longingly) figure prominently in the image the memoirist creates of herself, newly bereft of a patron and anxious to find a place for herself in the world she has been left behind in. The second volume discloses a similar figure: a woman who inhabits a threshold space between the past and the present, whose actions (both voluntary and involuntary) facilitate the intrusion of a lost or forgotten time into a present world that, in keeping with the discourse of both elegiac poetry and political anxiety, appears bent on forgetting.

The skies of the fifth month are gloomy with clouds, and the workers out planting the paddies will be hard pressed to dry their hems—all in keeping with the season it seems, a time of year that would dampen my spirits even if things were not as they are. But here in the stillness of my old house, more so than on other days, my mind keeps turning over things of the moment and thoughts of the past, and I feel the deep sorrow of it all.

When I look out across the veranda, there are banks of clouds and a dark-ening sky, and cloud formations that crowd together as if to return my gaze with knowing faces. Now I understand the woman who sang of "a dwelling place in clouded skies" and I feel myself plunged into a groping darkness. Even the drops trickling from the sweet-flags hung along the eaves are no different from these; and the mountain cuckoos raise their cries with mine. One after an-other, the fleeting summer nights turn to dawn and pass, while memories of times long gone, themselves faded with age like the abandoned capital Isono-kami, rise up in my mind as my tears fall unabated.

When I recall the days I waited on the late emperor—surveying the flowers in spring and the maple leaves in autumn, gazing at the moon in cloudless skies, attending him on mornings when the snow had fallen (each season of the eight years I spent in his service so full of the many splendid things we did together), in the mornings, his voice in prayers, in the evenings, the music of his flute—I find much that is hard to forget. And so I go on writing down the things that come back to me in the hope that it might bring some consolation. But I am shut in by a mist through which I can no longer even see where to set my brush. Tears drop and mingle with the water in the inkstone—they will wash away even the traces of this watery reed, I think—and with that thought weep all the harder. This is something I started in the hope that trying to write would take my mind off things, but like the one who gazes on the moon at Mount Oba-sute, I am beyond all comfort, and find it hard indeed to go on. (NKBZ 18: 371–72)

A flow of poetic allusions associated with the fifth month governs this evocation of memoir writing. In the Heian capital it is the season of long rains (nagame) and idle gazing (also nagame; the two terms are homophonous, though written with different characters). The figure who writes is a court lady away from court, a woman secluded at home in a room festooned with the sweet-flags customarily hung in honor of the sweet-flag festival (tango no sechi), held on the fifth day of the fifth lunar month.[37] The lexicon of elegiac poetry (aishō no uta) provides a conventional vocabulary for describing both a landscape and a state of mind, and it is used here with unusual skill to foreground a network of themes and allusions that center around that peculiar confusion of boundaries between this world and the next that characterizes mourning in Heian literature.[38]

The narration begins by depicting inner and outer weather in terms of each other: the cloudy skies of the rainy season match the handmaid's gloom, and the rustic image of the rice planters' wet hems (*tago no mosuso*) rhymes with the tear-soaked sleeves of the court lady in mourning.[39] As she gazes outward at the scene beyond her veranda, the correspondences she discovers between her melancholy thoughts and the brooding skies intensify. Clouds gather in the growing darkness, signaling the approach of night or more rain coming on, and she discerns among them some that seem to gather together like faces that recognize and reflect her own thoughts (*omoishirigao ni kumoi gachi naru*). Distinctions between inner and outer, emotion and atmosphere, past and present, and finally, looking, writing, and remembering grow more and more indistinct.

The allusive exchange the narrator's words carry on with other elegists and memoirists dissolves other kinds of boundaries. Haunted by the things that are "hard to forget" (memories of eight years as assistant handmaid to Emperor Horikawa, images of mourning in the external world), the narration attunes itself to the voices of an array of literary predecessors, the ghosts of other bereaved writers whose words reappear in the intricate web of poetic allusions interlacing the prose. The line "a dwelling place in clouded skies" (*kumoi no sora*) recalls the phrasing of other elegiac poems, perhaps in particular one by Izumi Shikibu. Like the *Sanuki* prologue, Izumi Shikibu's poem, written after the cremation of her lover, Prince Atsumichi, figures death and grief as a blurring of distinctions among the world, the mourner, and the deceased, who, turning to smoke upon cremation, dissolves all distinctions between self and world:

> Hakanakute   Because of one
> keburi to narishi   who turned to smoke
> hito ni yori   so fleetingly,
> kumoi no kumo no   how dear to me are
> mutsumashiki kana   the clouds in the cloudy sky.[40]

Following immediately upon this allusion, another poetic voice intrudes into the prose, this time unmarked and unannounced within the compass of an emphatically brief sentence: "Even the drops trickling from the sweet-flags hung along the eaves are no different" (*noki no ayame no shizuku mo kotonarazu*). The sentence represents only a slight variation on a line ending a poem by Tachibana Toshitsuna (1029–94),[41] the *hikiuta* melding the narrator's words with Toshitsuna's, her emotions with those of other poets and with the emotionalized weather engulfing the quiet house she describes. Next invoked is the cuckoo (*hototogisu*), a bird that conventionally figures in Heian *waka* as a creature who passes back and forth over the mountain of death (*shide no yama*) with news of dead loved ones.[42] But although many earlier poets apostrophized the *hototogisu* from afar, here the narration underscores the lack of distance between this mourner's cries and those of her messengers to the dead. They cry together (*morotomo ni*), and their weeping is a kind of conversation (*kataraite*). Like the raindrops that, as water and as remembered lines from an old poem, fall and mingle indistinguishably with her own words, tears, and ink, the narrator's sobs and the cries of the cuckoo join together in a kind of dialogue that bemoans an excessive commerce with the world of the dead. What begins as a notation of correspondences among the mourner, the rainy landscape, and the poetic topoi of the fifth month gives way to an assertion of metaphoric identities. The raindrops are "no different" (*kotonarazu*) from the mourner's tears; the memoirist as *hototogisu* brings us word of the world beyond the mountain of death.[43]

In the final lines of the prologue, anxiety about the future gradually overwhelms preoccupation with the past. The narrating voice turns to the equally urgent problem of commerce with the living. Who will read this memoir, who will be able to make sense of such overwhelming grief? "I go on writing down these things that come back to me in the hope that it might bring some consolation," she explains; what makes her doubly disconsolate, however, is the fear that the intensity of her own sorrow will render the memoir illegible, that the text itself will dissolve like mist or vanish with her tears: "[My tears] will wash away even the traces of this watery reed I think, and with that thought weep all the harder." The poetic toponym Obasuteyama calls up the inconsolable sorrow of the man who carries off the kindly aunt who raised him and abandons her so that she will die alone in the mountains. The allusion here recalls the details of the old story in a problematic way, however, raising the question always implicit in mourning the death of someone on whom one has depended materially. Who has abandoned whom? The Obasute topos touches lightly but deftly on the significance of the emperor's death for the memoirist. She has been left bereft of her patron.

This weepy writing scene engages a topos of the gaze common to classical Japanese courtly love poetry, elegy, and literary evocations of the rainy season of the lunar fifth month—*nagame*, which means both "long rains" and "staring" or "brooding" (literally, "long gaze"). As "staring," the verb *nagamu* connotes a kind of aimless gazing, suggesting a desire that is free-floating and without object. But a survey of the *nagame* motif in *Genji* and earlier texts confirms folklorist Origuchi Shinobu's observations that the image involves more than simply staring vaguely outside. It is also conventionally used to indicate a gaze underlain by the psychic state of the gaze-bearer's unfulfilled desire.[44] Of interest here is the way the prologue manipulates the *nagame* topos to tease out metaphors for commemorative writing. Aimless, objectless staring across a rainy landscape and the writing of a memoir become analogous activities: the stare of the mourner dissolves, through the imagery of falling rain and tears, into the image of a kind of blind writing, writing that takes place in the dark, its reading rendered impossible by the illegibility of the text thus produced.

The imagery of seeing and being seen also follows an unhappy trajectory through this passage, from the tentative possibility of reciprocity and mutual recognition ("[I see] banks of clouds . . . and cloud formations that crowd together as if to return my gaze with knowing faces") to blockage of vision ("I am shut in by a mist through which I can no longer even see where to set my brush"). The memoirist is not simply blinded by tears; her blindness threatens to render her unrecognizable to the reader. The danger here is not the penetrating or appropriating power of the gaze of others, but the impotence of that imagined gaze in the face of the writer's inarticulate grief and her text's illegibility. Worse than being looked at for this court lady is being away from court, at home ("in the stillness of my old house"), where one is not only invisible but also blind and unreadable, where all commerce with human society is blocked.

The idea of a blocked commerce with the world activates another facet of the *nagame* topos—its resonance with rainy season taboos (*nagame imi*) originating in the agricultural practices of rice production. As Origuchi has pointed out, the lunar fifth and ninth months were crucial to rice culture. Recurring in a number of *waka* as early as the *Man'yōshū*, the rustic figure of a man cloaked in a straw raincoat visiting a woman's house has its roots in the folk belief that the god of the rice fields manifests itself biennially to visit the rice paddies during the fifth and ninth months. According to agrarian customs, all women qualified as shamans (*miko*) during those months, and therefore were expected to abstain from sex in order to be ritually ready to entertain the god. Traces of the taboo against sexual encounters during the long rains persist in Heian court literature, as Hayashida Takakazu has so fully documented, and at the imperial palace the rainy season of the fifth month was still marked in the mid-Heian period by the nominal observance of taboos involving sexual abstinence.[45] Apparently, in life as in literature, the rainy season occasioned much listless gazing among lovelorn Heian aristocrats, both male and female.[46] In *The Tale of Genji*, the fifth month in particular is portrayed as the time for amusing oneself with substitute diversions—for men, telling tales about women (as in "The Judgments of a Rainy Night"), and for women, reading and copying tales other women have supplied them with (as in "The Defense of Fiction"). In 1102, at the court of Emperor Horikawa, the rainy fifth month was celebrated with a special poetry contest in which teams were divided up according to gender. On the second day of the month, the men's team presented the women's with poems proposing love (*keshō no uta*), to which the women composed replies. On the seventh day the women initiated the exchange with poems of resentment (*urami no uta*), to which the men replied.[47]

The prologue to the *Sanuki no suke nikki* elaborates on and darkens the traces of archaic rainy-season taboos. If commerce with the world of men is blocked in this scene of writing, commerce with the world of spirits is actively solicited. Remembering the dead, staring blindly across wet paddies for a glimpse of a figure who does not appear, the *Sanuki* memoirist conjures an image of herself as a spirit medium poised to receive visitation from the world of the spirits. The imagery of the prologue, like many of the tropes that structure the second volume of the memoir, positions the handmaid in a threshold space between two worlds, attending to memories of the dead emperor while she occupies herself watching over his son.

The Passageways of Memory

Tears, like commemorative texts, can be read and interpreted by the living. And the *Sanuki no suke nikki* is a text that claims to have emerged involuntarily, like tears, under the pressure of emotions that could not be pent up. But written words have a way of channeling the free flow of tears and memories, and no one who reads the second volume of the *Sanuki no suke nikki* in the context of earlier Heian women's memoirs will fail to notice that the temporal flow of this narrative pursues an unusually intricate course.

The act of narration is continually emphasized in this memoir, particularly in volume two. One is made to envision the *Sanuki* narrator sitting alone in the gloom of an empty chamber, recording scenes that still unfold before her eyes, scenes that were played out—often in the same room—months or years before. Terse, even clumsily childlike in style,[48] but enlivened by tiny, very human details, her renderings seem bereft of everything but those elements that haunt the rememberer. They have the sparse, loaded quality of dream imagery. And many of them are, like dreams, highly visual. An insistence on making the reader see the same things the narrator herself recalls animates these scenes.

In the prologue, the act of writing seems to occur simultaneously with the feelings and scenes the narrating voice describes; the image of the mourner's symbiosis with her surroundings is reinforced at the temporal level by the illusion of a synchronicity of language and experience.[49] The temporal distance between story and discourse has narrowed to the vanishing point; the temporal distance between reader and narrator also disappears in the illusion of immediacy produced by the tenselessness of the terminal verbs and adjectivals, an illusion that, moreover, extends throughout volume one as well, where terminal verbs are unmarked for tense.[50] As others have pointed out, a "non-past, 'tenseless' propensity" is typical of the prose style of most mid-Heian women's writings, especially memoirs (*nikki*), and "produces an enunciating perspective that gives the illusion that the events being recounted are happening at the very moment of telling."[51]

Volume one, presumed to have been written soon after Horikawa's death, from memory or from notes the memoirist may have scribbled in the moments she did not spend nursing the dying emperor, gives a detailed account of the stages of the emperor's illness from its inception in the sixth month of 1107 to his death at the end of the seventh, structuring time in a pattern familiar from earlier linearly structured *kana nikki*. As in the *Kagerō* and *Sarashina nikki*, events of the past recalled by the narrating voice conform to the order of their occurrence in a past that is not, however, overtly marked as past. Except for scattered asides to the reader, any disjunctions between the (past) events narrated and the narrating present are effaced by the tenselessness of the discourse and what it implies of an immediate presentation of events in the sequence in which they arose.

A very different, and rather elaborate, set of temporal structures organizes volume two. What these structures involve, and what purpose they might serve, will be the focus of the remainder of this chapter. Vol-

ume two opens as the Sanuki handmaid is recalled to court to participate in Emperor Toba's accession ceremony. It is the twelfth month of
1107; with the new year she will resume her former duties as assistant
handmaid, this time in service to Toba. This volume chronicles her life
at court during the twelve months of that year (1108) and closes with
several undatable passages probably referring to episodes that postdate
1108.[52] But the temporal structure of volume two is only partly determined by this linear chronicling of the year after Horikawa's death. The
account of the Sanuki handmaid's first year back in court service is also
interlaced with a discontinuous series of flashbacks, scenes of memory
recalled, not in the order of their occurrence in a distant past but in the
order of their recurrence as memories that intrude on the narrating present. As a result, their link to the temporal macrostructure of the memoir
is highly associative, with each remembered anecdote closely tied to the
narrator's description of events connected with the position she has re-
sumed under Emperor Toba. Thus, although the account of the annual
cycle of festivals and rituals performed at court (*nenjū gyōji*) provides a
broad, chronological framework for the volume as a whole, within this
linear order the forward momentum of the narrative is periodically
halted and reversed. Time becomes peculiarly chopped up and static in
volume two. Descriptions of individual months and festivals open up
like spaces in time, commemorative *loci* recalled for what they offer as
windows on the same months in other years. The narration is concerned
with obsessive memories of Emperor Horikawa and with the way these
memories continue to overshadow, and at times overwhelm, the narration of the handmaid's experience of her current duties at court.

   In this respect, volume two of the *Sanuki no suke nikki* recalls the
structure and themes of "The Wizard" (*Maboroshi*) chapter of *The Tale
of Genji*. As Genji passes a year mourning the death of Murasaki, each
festival and change of season recalls those of the past and provides the
occasion for the extensive use of *waka* and poetic allusions, which
heighten the lyricality of the narrative and deepen the pathos of Genji as
mourner.[53] Genji's young grandson, Niou (like the boy Emperor Toba
with the Sanuki handmaid), is "the sole companion" (*NKBZ* 15: 515–
16) during this year of intense reverie, his pranks and innocent remarks
providing a poignant counterpoint to the aging Genji's melancholy.
Though its slight, intricate sketches cannot compare with the *Genji*'s
majestic weave of *waka*, prose, and poetic allusion, the *Sanuki no suke
nikki* develops a number of interesting possibilities left unexplored by
the densely lyrical prose of *Genji*.

The structural complexity of volume two consists of more than the interpolation of simple flashbacks to scenes from the remembered past. The memoir further complicates the temporal linearity by introducing a third level of past time, which one Japanese commentator terms "the remote past" (*dai kako*).[54] In the language of narratology, these passages constitute what might be called double analepses: they are remembrances of occasions that themselves embed remembrances of yet earlier events. In other words, the narrator in volume two has a propensity for recalling moments that were already moments of recollection. Remembering her own earlier moments of remembrance, the memoirist places the reader at a third remove from the instant she wishes to evoke.

Examples of this trope occur here and there throughout volume two, but when the narrator recounts her impressions upon returning to the imperial palace at the end of the year-long mourning period for Emperor Horikawa, the mediations of memory become especially involved. The result is a passage about unreflective departures and unpremeditated returns, about actual gateways as liminal spaces in time, and it is one of the most complexly layered evocations of memory in a text that delights in wandering among different strata of the past. As with many of the other scenes of memory recounted in this volume, the past rises up here by virtue of its association with a particular place, a site that opens out dizzily onto the vision of earlier moments of reverie that occurred there in other years. The linear movement of time is both checked and reversed, as the narration slides from a description of Toba's procession through the central gate to the imperial palace in the seventh month of 1108 to the memory of the handmaid's own momentary halt at the same gate en route to visiting Horikawa's grave at Kōryūji the year before, which in turn embeds the recollection of her recalling on that occasion, Horikawa's last trip out through the gate. Grammatically, this multilayered evocation of the past is accomplished by a shift from a discourse of verbals without aspectuals (or involving -*nu* alone) to one involving -*ki* or -*keri* modal aspectuals. The perfective -*ki* suddenly obtrudes as the governing, terminal verbal auxiliary when the topic shifts from the tenseless account of Toba's procession to the description of the handmaid's past pilgrimage to Kōryūji. Tenseless narration resumes with the final clauses of the passage, after "And though I thought then":

When darkness had fallen completely, we departed. I rode with Emperor Toba, and before long we drew up at the palace. From the moment we enter the Cen-

tral Gate, I am plunged into gloom, just as I imagined I would be. On a pilgrimage to Kōryūji I had stopped there once to look in and had thought: "This
is the gate I went in and out of, at morning and evening. Just after the twentieth
of the twelfth month the year before last the late emperor moved to the Horikawa Palace. I went through this gate with him then, you see, never supposing
it was the end of our days together there." And though I thought then, "Now,
no matter what happens, I shall not pass through it anymore in this world,"
here I am, returning through the same gate again, and me, the same as I ever
was. How it saddens and depresses me. (*NKBZ* 18: 433–34)[55]

In erecting its elaborate nonlinear framework for reminiscence, the
second volume of the *Sanuki no suke nikki* clearly breaks with the
precedent of other *kana nikki* and with its own practice in volume one.
What might these breaks with convention mean? Ishino Keiko argues
that the maverick architectonics of the *Sanuki no suke nikki* point to the
memoirist's underlying ambivalence about leaving behind a work that
might be read simply as a record of her reminiscences of Emperor Horikawa.[56] She associates the structural eccentricity of volume two with
another feature for which the *Sanuki no suke nikki* has long been singled out: its extreme consciousness of its readers, a consciousness that,
as Imai Takuji and others have noted, manifests itself also in the narrator's repeated insistence on her own belated gratitude to Emperor Horikawa, her frequent asides to the reader, and her explicit description of
the ideal reader for the memoir at the end of volume two.[57]

Ishino argues that this heightened consciousness of the reader bespeaks the *Sanuki* memoirist's apprehensiveness about readerly censure
rather than the more general "literary consciousness" with which it has
been traditionally identified. She points out that the memoirist's impulse
to commemorate her relationship to the late emperor was complicated
(perhaps even rendered inauspicious) by her ongoing public role as assistant handmaid to Emperor Toba. Her duties at court demanded attention to the needs of the present, and this made a preoccupation with the
events of Horikawa's reign unseemly.[58] Her summary recall to court
service before the end of the mourning period (a call she could not, perhaps for pragmatic and political reasons, refuse to answer) threatens to
obliterate all public memory of her claim to the status of mourner, a
member of the inner circle of the bereaved, someone who (like Horikawa's wet nurses and his empress) could expect recognition of her
right to grieve. At the same time she seeks to forestall misinterpretation
on the opposite account. She fears that perhaps it will appear she had
been too eager to answer the summons to return to court service. As

Ishino notes, there is a degree of self-justification implicit in her insistence, especially in the early sections of volume two, not concerning her inner obsession with the past but her public acts of mourning and the grateful recognition of them by the more politically prominent mourners who had been allowed to stay behind at the Horikawa mansion.[59]

In short, if the structure of the second volume of the memoir is problematic, it may be so partly because the memoirist took up her brush hoping to leave behind not only a record of her reminiscences of Emperor Horikawa but also an image of herself as one who was renowned for remembering and whose acts of remembrance were sanctioned and appreciated by more powerful members of Horikawa's former entourage. The underlying desire here is clear. The one who is renowned for fondly remembering wishes herself to be remembered gratefully by the powerful.

The memoirist portrays her behavior as stubbornly commemorative, a persistent, willful kind of mourning that draws others' criticism as well as their praise. The narrator recalls the words of another lady-in-waiting, an attendant in service to Horikawa's empress Atsuko, who was moved to hint that the Sanuki handmaid's tenacious mourning was inappropriate to her station. The handmaid had accompanied her elder sister Tōsanmi (Kaneko) to the Horikawa mansion for the memorial readings of the sutras conducted there in the third month of 1108. Summoning Tōsanmi, the lady-in-waiting hints that perhaps the Sanuki handmaid should be excluded from the empress's presence. "'Lady Sanmi is requested to approach the empress. But the way things are now, I feel hesitant about calling in Lady Sanuki.'" The suggestion won the lady-in-waiting a rebuke from the empress herself, who, as the narrator is careful to recall, immediately sprang to her defense, though her voice was choked with sobs: "'But it is precisely she who has shown us her profound regard. It is she who always remembers to call at this dismal house that the others seem to have forgotten'" (*NKBZ* 18: 425).

Let us assume that the memoirist's fear of censure from several different factions made it necessary for her to defend what might appear to some to be an inappropriate preoccupation with the past (or a disingenuous one, given her present political affiliations). Then the narrative structure of volume two may also imply, as Ishino further argues, that she tried to accomplish this defense rhetorically. She thus created a record that carefully quarantines disruptive, fragmentary memories of her former life, subordinating them to the linear narrative of her new life at Toba's court. Yet if this is in fact the strategy employed in the *Sanuki no suke nikki,* it is a profoundly ambivalent one, if only because the narrative suggests so strongly the flimsiness of its own structures. Though volume two chronicles the annual round of events at court in 1108, it also quite clearly acts as a thin frame, providing the context for the return and the retelling of other tales of other years. I disagree with Ishino's understanding of the memoirist's success at subordinating anecdotes about Horikawa to the framework of annual observances at court. But I would not argue that she was simply unsuccessful at accomplishing the neat and organized compositional goals Ishino ascribes to her. I would argue instead that the presentation of the past in the *Sanuki no suke nikki* is so obtrusive as to be suggestive of mental disorder, and that this effect is the result of conscious artifice.

The elaborate structure of reminiscence in volume two gains the memoirist a certain advantage in one crucial respect. Because the volume inscribes annual court rituals and the cycle of the seasons as the catalysts of reverie, it also creates an image of the handmaid as an involuntary medium of the past. Having stressed the unavoidable circumstances of her return to court service, the narration then figures the handmaid's bouts of reverie as the unwitting response to specific sites and occasions, and so presents her not only as one who staunchly remembers when the occasion demands, but also at other times as *one who is forced to remember*: the past speaks to her in the material things that surround her at court. As with the self-effacing figure of the *miko* through whom the possessing spirit speaks, the process of reminiscence overwhelms her and speaks through her like the spirit of an other. The question of her agency is suspended; she suffers remembrance half-unwillingly, first because she has no control over the circumstances that brought her back to these sites of her former life and second because she fears the public censure that her obsession with Horikawa's reign may provoke.

The narration distinguishes carefully between instances of willed and involuntary memory, marking the differences between deliberate acts of commemoration (both public and private) and those instances in which the handmaid finds herself impelled, by circumstance and an irresistible presence of the past, to reminisce in spite of all public expectations to do otherwise. The relations between these two kinds of memory are not simply complementary, however, because all representations of involuntary memory point back to the hand that held the brush and ultimately suggest another level of covertly voluntary self-commemorative action.[60] The structure of time in volume two thus emphasizes the role of involuntary memory on one level, even as its neat and carefully deliberated organization undermines the impression of a spontaneous eruption of the past into the present.

The fascination with evocative sites and with the commemorative quality of court festivals is equally involved with the desire that the reader also be made to remember. Volume two is full of beautiful and vivid descriptions of particular scenes. But its art doesn't just lie in its inventorying of the images that memory brings to light. It also lies in the way the narrative retraces the movements and repetitions of the hand-maid's memory as she wanders the same rooms of her former life at court and witnesses the yearly round of festival preparations. Something of what Walter Benjamin called "the dark joy of the place of finding" permeates this volume.[61] Remembrance is more than a means of turning up a clutch of vivid anecdotes. It also becomes, in an astonishing way, both the subject and the goal of the memoir. The memoir cleverly stages the experience of memory itself—its repetitions and returns, the vertigo of involuntary recollection—at the level of narrative sequence and repetition:

It is evening on New Year's Day when I arrive at the palace, and as my carriage enters the gate, thoughts of the past rise up in me, and I am plunged into gloom. Upon reaching my quarters I have the impression that the emperor has gone somewhere else. The night passed without incident.

When I get up and look about the next morning, a deep snow has fallen, and it is still coming down heavily. Looking in on the emperor's chambers it seems to me that very little has changed, and just as I am musing about how strange it is that he should be here, I hear a tiny voice piping "flurry, flurry, powder snow." Who's that! Whose child—? I start, and then remember—of course. But to think that this is the one I am supposed to rely on and serve as master? Wretched indeed, for I can see in this child no one to lean on. (*NKBZ* 18: 418)

The strangeness of this passage hinges partly on its portrayal of the handmaid as a figure wavering on the threshold of two different worlds and partly on the way it manages to impose, if only momentarily, the sensation of her disorientation upon the reader. Confronting the emperor's apparently empty room, the handmaid feels "that very little has changed," or more literally, that there is "nothing much different there" (*bechi ni tagaitaru koto naki kokochishite*). But different since when? we want to ask. Since the evening before, when Emperor Toba vacated it temporarily? Or is this a description of how the handmaid recalls some other snowy morning when Emperor Horikawa would have occupied this same room? Our hesitation is over in an instant—the handmaid's thoughts may well have been on the ghostly possibility of Horikawa's presence, for the voice of the child startles her into fretting about the insecurity of her present position, but we have been caught up for a moment in a kind of doubt that reenacts the handmaid's hesitations.

No reader of the *Sanuki no suke nikki* can fail to notice the artful recurrence of specific images that intrude again and again as the narrative doubles back to them to find new discoveries concealed beneath old ones. Of these, perhaps the most richly evocative are memories of snowfalls, and snowy mornings in particular (*yuki no ashita*). Emperor Toba's incantatory "flurry, flurry, powder snow" (*fure, fure koyuki*) would seem to have lodged in the memory of at least one prominent reader of the *Sanuki no suke nikki* some two hundred years later.[62] That particular scene resonates with two other snowy mornings recounted sequentially in later sections of volume two, and all three scenes are neatly foreshadowed by a phrase in the prologue: "attending the emperor on snowy mornings" (*yuki no ashita ni ontomo saburaite*).

The imagery of snow in Heian *waka* and in Heian women's writings in general often occurs in conjunction with scenes of memory and forgetting.[63] Both the beginning and the closing passage of "The Wizard" chapter in *The Tale of Genji* feature striking snow scenes.[64] Of special note is the first, in the opening pages of the chapter, which describes a moment in early spring, the plum trees already in blossom, when Genji falls into a fitful sleep, sadly recalling a snowy morning when he had returned from the Third Princess's bed to Murasaki's quarters before dawn. He had hurried back, alarmed after seeing Murasaki's face in a dream, and he remembers especially the chill of the dawn air as he waited outside her doors. Suddenly the voice of a lady-in-waiting surprised by the heavy snow as she returns to her own rooms awakens him—from his sleep and from his remembrance of the past—to the sight of another snowy dawn: "He heard a voice call out, 'Just look at how deeply the snow has piled up!' and he feels in that moment just as he had that other dawn, but she was gone from his side now and his loneliness was a sorrow beyond words" (*NKBZ* 15: 510).

The reader who follows the trajectory of Genji's musings back into the memory of his past life with Murasaki (the past of *The Tale of Genji*) will also falter, like Genji, at the voice of the lady-in-waiting astonished at the depth of the snow, because the syntax of the passage enacts the involuntary slippages between past and present to which Genji in his mourning is prey. In this way, the reader is made to participate in the same disorientations that plague the mourner.

There are signs of experimentation with a related trope in the later pages of volume two of the *Sanuki no suke nikki*, where we come across a sequence of two passages ordered by something that might be called a syntax of involuntary remembrance. The topic in both passages is, at least superficially, the Gosechi festival that took place annually at court. The context that catalyzes the narrator's remembrance is the Gosechi festival of 1108. But the handmaid recalls two earlier festivals as well, each linked to the other by the reference to snow:

The year before—perhaps because it was the last time?—Emperor Horikawa was unusually taken by it all, and from the evening the dancers arrived at court he was up, bustling here and there. Then there was the rehearsal until late that same night, so he slept longer than usual the next morning. But when he heard that it had snowed, up he got. The empress was also with him that time—they were going to send letters to the Gosechi dancers—and since I was in attendance, we made the decorative hair garlands together, and they tied and fastened them; we are in the empress's chamber, with thoughts of the past welling up in me till I am blind and deaf to all else. (*NKBZ* 18: 441–42)

Because of the structure of this passage (which reads as one long sentence in the original), we cannot place the narrating voice, and thus cannot know what site triggers her reminiscence until we read through to the end. The scene of narration is the empress's chamber, where the handmaid is sitting when the reconvergence of a particular site and time of year dissolves for a moment the distance between past and present, setting the stage for reminiscence.[65]

In the passage immediately following, we are led through an even more radical slide from reportage into recollection. Momentarily drawn back to the events of 1108 by young Emperor Toba's fascination with the carpenters who have come to build the bridge for the Gosechi dancers, the narrator plunges again, this time in midsentence, deep into a sustained evocation of yet another snowy morning during the Gosechi festival of yet another year. Unlike the passage quoted above, which signals recollection with the temporal marker "the year before" (*hitotose*; more literally, "a certain previous year"), in this passage the transition to the scene of memory is completely unmarked. Without signaling the change in temporal perspective, the narrating voice shifts abruptly from talk of Emperor Toba's delight in this year's Gosechi preparations to how Emperor Horikawa had overslept one snowy morning during the same festival in an unspecified year. (In the translation that follows, I have identified the two emperors by name in brackets; no such distinction is made in the original.) The empress and all other attendants are excluded from this deeper layer of the past. This second return to the topos of snow and memory, which transpires as the handmaid attends Toba, nets her an idyll of nearly perfect intimacy between herself and Horikawa:

The carpenters came to construct the long veranda the dancers use to mount into the palace; it was the usual sort, linking the steps at the southwest corner of the Sogyōden to the edge of the northeast corner of the Seiryōden, just as in times past. The emperor [Toba] finds it all very novel, and since he is watching them I stay with him until it gets dark—there was that snowy morning he [Horikawa] had still been asleep when we heard the news of a very deep snowfall— that was the morning we got up to see the snow together, because I had spent the night before at his side. And though I always find snowfalls beautiful, this one was especially so; why, even the commoners' poor hovels were a sight to behold in all that whiteness, but how much more so was the imperial palace, gleaming like a polished jewel or mirror, and we two gazing together at the scene—if I had been a painter, I would have painted it just as it was without changing a jot, and shown it to the others—when he had the shutters opened, we found where we supposed tree-tops to be that the snow had piled up so much it was hard to say which one of them was a plum. The stand of bamboo in front of the Jijūden was bent over till it looked like it had snapped. Even the fire-huts by the palace were buried, and I marveled at how even now the snow was still falling down out of the gloom. How lovely it was, lodged in the interstices of the wattle fence in front of the guards' quarters.

He was radiant—was it because of the moment? or because my own heart made me see him that way? I became embarrassed at the thought of how disarrayed I must appear. "This is a morning to make a person wish she might look more beautiful than usual," I exclaimed.

He seemed amused by this, and replied, "But you always do look so." I feel I could be there before him even now, facing that bright, smiling countenance he had as he spoke to me. I was wearing the kind of things one wore for the Gosechi season, a pale mauve Chinese jacket, I believe it was, over a brilliant layering of maple-leaf robes that ranged from yellow to scarlet, colors made all the more splendid by their contrast to the glowing white of the snow. The emperor gazed on at me, unable to go back inside.

Then we heard women's voices, servants from the guard house it seemed, who had come close to the wattle fence by the guards' quarters. They seemed to be looking at the snow, and we heard one call out, "Just look at how high this awful stuff has piled up! What are we going to do? We can't get through it in these skirts." The emperor heard them and laughed. "Listen to that," he said; "it's just that it created such a bother for them that they are raising a fuss. I feel I've been jolted awake from a splendid dream of snow." And I was remembering these things, completely caught up in their contemplation, when the boy tugs at me with an uncomprehending stare: "Ask that workman for that thing he's got. Hurry up and go on out there! Go on before he goes away and ask him for it. Ask him, hurry!" I felt I had been roused from all my dreams of beauty. Answering his questions distracted me for a while, but when I said, "I'd like to retire," the others muttered among themselves, "Isn't she awful! Why leave now, without even seeing anything of the performance?" (*NKBZ* 18: 442–44)

The narration glances here at last on an episode of unequivocal intimacy, which is, however, repeatedly brought to precipitous closure by the intrusion of others, initially and long ago by the serving women approaching from the guards' quarters, commenting loudly on the snow, which they found to be "just awful" (*ana, yuyushi*), and finally by the intrusion of the present, in the person of the boy emperor tugging on the handmaid's sleeve with "an uncomprehending stare." As if to replay in little the old paradigms of the handmaid's intermittent intimacy with Horikawa, the narration embeds reminiscence in a narrative frame that is a latticework of interruptions and broken illusions. The reverie intrudes abruptly into the account of Emperor Toba's delight in the carpenters; it is brought to a sudden end, just as Emperor Horikawa's delight in the snow was, by the intrusive cries of people around the handmaid (Emperor Toba asking her to fetch one of the workman's tools; the remarks of the other ladies-in-waiting, who find her retiring behavior to be, as the snow was to the other women long ago, "just awful," *ana, yuyushi*).

The slippage between the narrative frame and the scene of memory draws the reader into the world of reminiscence, and it is a highly visual one, deftly executed, with swatches of bright color framing the hero and heroine, as in an illustrated tale, against the dazzling backdrop of the snow.[66] Whatever the origins of the language of painting here, the entire scene is shot through with dramatic concerns that are equally characteristic of the *monogatari* tradition as verbal narrative: the peculiar pleasure of stolen glimpses, the joy of seeing and self-display, and anxieties about being caught unaware by the gaze of others. The long, lingering look the emperor bestows on the handmaid climaxes the passage, elaborately realizing the compulsion to portray her as the object of another's approbation. But the problematic nature of this compulsion in the context of a memoir is evident in the way the idyll collapses, threatened by an imbalance of the very tensions that generated it in the first place. The pleasure of being admired by the emperor gives way to the impropriety of allowing oneself to be seen as the object of his admiring gaze and the indecorum of portraying oneself as obsessed with the memory of that regard.

In the Shadow of His Knees

One of the most distinctive rhetorical features of the second volume of the *Sanuki no suke nikki* is to be found in the way the narrating voice repeatedly recalls images of the handmaid in the disempowered pose of a woman unwittingly caught by the unsolicited gaze of another in the spontaneous gestures or revealing attitudes of an unguarded moment. At first glance, there seems to be nothing remarkable about this. Certainly the memoir's obsessive portrayal of the handmaid as someone "to be looked at" merely reinforces the socially given constructions of her gender and class identity. But at the same time, by focusing the reader's attention on the interiority of the handmaid who is looked at (and who as narrator also portrays herself as fully aware of her potential status as the object of critical censure), this text complicates conventional motifs of literary voyeurism. It is as though one of the shadowy *Genji* narrators should have stayed the narrative of Genji's pursuit of other heroines long enough to recount (for the space of a short memoir, perhaps) how he turned to her from time to time, to stare at her, speak to her, even shelter her from the gaze of other men and the gossip of other women. Although it is an erotically or politically empowered other who is usually portrayed looking at her, it is the handmaid's subjectivity, her thoughts and reactions, that provide the focus of narrative interest. Here desire and interiority are located, not simply in the one who sees, but in the double-voiced figure of the narrator-handmaid, the one who is seen and who sometimes speaks about being seen. In this way, what it feels like to be looked at as a lady-in-waiting in court service emerges as one of the most haunting and problematic motifs of the memoir.

What the handmaid sees when she herself looks is no less important to the organization of the memoir. What she "sees" are events of the past no longer visible to the others around her. And what she sees she recounts, with the express desire of making the reader see the same scenes: "Had I been a painter," as she assures us breathlessly in the midst of the passage just quoted, "I would have painted the scene, just as we saw it together, without changing a jot of it and shown it to someone" (*NKBZ* 18: 442–43). Predictably, it is precisely this double-edged gesture of seeing and showing on her part that becomes the focus of others' censure of her and the focus of the narrative.

The memoir is punctuated by the narrator's expressions of belated gratitude for the recognition Emperor Horikawa showed her during his lifetime. Indeed, the payment of this debt figures largely among her expressed motives for writing. But although much seems to depend on the debt of affection, the anxieties it generates center less on the impossibility of recompensing the dead than on the double problem of convincing readers that there did indeed exist such a bond and forestalling questions about her claim to imperial patronage by anticipating them. The narrator recalls being disturbed, in the initial shock of the emperor's death, that she alone could find no tears, and her recollection of the moment toward the end of volume one attempts to restore a voice to the silent image of herself as Horikawa's handmaid, sitting mute and motionless among the rest of the self-forgetful crowd of his weeping nurses and attendants: "I stayed by his side, pressing my own face with the paper I had been using to wipe away his sweat. My feelings for the emperor were no less than what theirs must have been, or so I had thought over the years, but now I wondered if perhaps my affection was weaker after all, since I could not cry out the way his other ladies did" (*NKBZ* 18: 400).

The image is deeply involved, as is the memoir as a whole, with the desire that others perceive the singularity of the handmaid's relationship to Horikawa and with the delicate problem of guiding their vision without appearing to do so. There is something irreducibly equivocal about the figure of the exhausted court lady pressing a sweat-sodden scrap of paper to her face. To recount such a gesture—and accounts of other, similar gestures are repeated in different forms throughout the text—betrays a struggle with contrary impulses, the desire both to disclose and to mask the nature of the handmaid's relationship to the emperor. The trope of simultaneous concealment and revelation is merely repeated, not resolved, by her ambivalent commentary on the memory: "But now I wondered if perhaps my affection was weaker [than theirs] after all." The narration revolves around the question of how she compared with the other women on the scene and how she will appear in the eyes of future readers.

As already noted, an unusually oppressive awareness of the not so benign gaze of other court figures permeates this memoir. Indeed, what the narrator seems to find hardest to forget is not so much—or at least not solely—memories of the dead emperor, but rather the problematic image of herself as the object of others' gazes, both in the anecdotes and images she recalls from Horikawa's lifetime and in the accounts of the events at Toba's court that provide the immediate context for narration. The image of the handmaid as the object of others' high regard, and the anxiety that so often surrounds that image in the narration, suggests both the desire for self-display and the opposite of that desire: the fear of revealing too much, of obliterating commemoration of the emperor with self-disclosure (or self-promotion). On the one hand, the narrative consistently underlines others' recognition of the handmaid's ties to Horikawa; on the other, there is an expressed anxiety that such images of her will draw criticism. The image recurs because it answers to both fear and desire. To see how it accomplishes this, we need to attend closely to the way the narration constructs its scenes of looking and display.

Many of these scenes take the shape of little cautionaries, exempla that suggest how we might read the singularity of the handmaid's behavior. Remonstrating with herself for her past ingratitude, the narrator recalls how she once threw down a fan in front of Horikawa in a fit of pique, breaking up a game she had herself suggested postponing till morning so that she should not "miss seeing people's expressions because of the dark" (NKBZ 18: 429). Anticipating the pleasure of catching others out in a moment of envy or disappointment, she is herself caught out when she draws the least lovely fan of the bunch. The would-be seer becomes the seen, a reversal that reduplicates the shift in the handmaid's own position from the one who looks after Emperor Horikawa in volume one to disempowered court lady imperiled by the censuring gaze of others in volume two. The memory is the source of both shame and pride, since she is exonerated first by Horikawa and then by another court lady who plays the role of sympathetic spectator. Amused by her petulance, the emperor laughs at her indulgently, and the narrator's closing comment on the anecdote is conventionally contrite. But what sticks still in her memory, and what is apt to stick with the reader as well since it is related in the vivid language of quoted speech, is the comment the incident provoked from the sympathetic court lady who was happily witness to the handmaid's momentary loss of face: "Everyone was quite amused when the woman called Lady Tajima said, 'Isn't that just like a girl who's been raised in the palace [ie no ko]? A different woman would not have been allowed to do that.' At the time I didn't even think about it, but today I wonder how I ever did that—it seems so impudent" (*NKBZ* 18: 429).

We are being asked to note, as readers, that others once recognized and favorably interpreted the special quality of intimacy that existed between the handmaid and Horikawa, an intimacy so much a part of everyday life that it could be the object of casual remarks. She is proud to have been known as an *ie no ko* (literally, a "child of the family," someone raised in the palace as a close retainer of the imperial house) and privileged by that familiarity to have been the object of the emperor's indulgence. Her ostensible shame cloaks but thinly her yearning, not just for their lost intimacy, but also for others' *recognition* of their social bonds. Her exoneration by sympathetic spectators—which provides a happy ending to the fan-game anecdote—suggests the kind of response she desires from the reader of the memoir. And Lady Tajima will not be the only empathetic witness memory enlists to give an instructive "reading" of that relationship and to model an appropriate response for the audience of the memoir. The desire to manipulate the gaze of the reader is tightly woven into the pattern of reminiscence itself, emerging again and again like the dominant figure in the design of an intricate carpet.

Let us consider what seems to be the most obsessive of all images in the memoir, the handmaid lying next to Horikawa, half-hidden behind his raised knees. The days when she could depend on him to warn her of the Fujiwara regent's frequent entrances and shelter her from his gaze she discovers have long passed when one morning, in the middle of serving Emperor Toba his breakfast, she finds herself confronted with the regent's imminent approach. Her desire to maintain propriety and flee the room is held in check by the fear that leaving the child to feed himself might also raise eyebrows. She decides to stay in the end, we are given to understand, out of contrition for all the years she had spent never really appreciating Emperor Horikawa's consideration for her. Thus, the narration masks a thoroughly premeditated breach of propriety as an act of penance (not so surprising, really, for a handmaid whose penitential preoccupation with the past often borders on the indecorous). The act of self-exposure becomes an explicitly commemorative gesture then, the decision to stay and submit to the regent's gaze a reenactment of another day during Horikawa's last illness when the regent surprised the handmaid in the imperial presence. The account of the earlier incident occurs in volume one:

Since the emperor's condition was [grave], the regent was constantly coming to inquire after him both night and day. I felt I was making such an uncouth spectacle of myself [lying by his side], but Lady Sanmi told me, "It's only natural, given the circumstances. When things have gone this far, why should you fret over appearances?" Since there was nothing I could do about it, I stayed as I was. When the regent approached, the emperor raised up his knees and hid me behind them. Drawing my unlined gown over my head I lay down, and listened to the regent. (*NKBZ* 18: 380–81)

As on the previous occasion, the handmaid remains as she is, and the regent enters the room. With thoughts of flight and concealment still apparently much on her mind, she finds herself slipping into a characteristically irreverent reminiscence even while listening to the regent's words. A parodic variant of the proper court lady's impulse to flee flashes across her mind. The fleeing figure she recalls, however, is neither she nor any other lady-in-waiting, but the former emperor. As the regent approaches, the handmaid is silently remembering how "Once some years back, the emperor had asked, 'Who is going to serve the meal?' and when he heard [it was the regent], he had stuck out his tongue, hiked up his trousers and fled" (*NKBZ* 18: 421). Now, however, her silent presence in full view of the regent as she attends the boy emperor ultimately achieves its desired effect. The regent's gaze is not critical. He speaks to her and ends by proving himself to be another of her sympathetic spectators, for he too remembers what she wishes him to remember—the image of her as the cherished beneficiary of the emperor's esteem:

What an unforeseen turn of events! I certainly never thought I would come near you like this to talk about things. There were those days when the emperor was not himself, and I visited him as you lay by his side, but the emperor raised his knees and hid you in their shadow. I certainly had no idea then that things would come to this. Indeed, now he too is hidden in shadows. Such is the way of things in this world. (*NKBZ* 18: 421)

The image of the late emperor physically concealing the handmaid from the regent's eyes with his own body haunts the narrative, and thus the reader as well. It appears three times, as if to remind us that the death of the emperor, figured as the absence of his body as screen, has left the handmaid exposed to the gaze of others. Faced with this loss, her defense is to recall the memory of his gone body. And we are not left much in doubt as to what response might be desired from the reader of that image. Insofar as we read this memoir in its pragmatic context, we can see in these passages the bid for patronage, the gestures of a supplicant who hopes to work a kind of sympathetic magic on future benefactors by presenting them with idealized images of her relationship to the dead patron. The narrator would have her reader recognize and repeat the esteem in which she was held by Emperor Horikawa.

Soliciting the Gaze: The Memoirist and the Patron

Kouru ma ni	And if the old year closes
toshi no kurenaba	with you still yearning for
naki hito no	the one who is no more
wakare ya itodo	how much farther that last parting
tōku narinamu[67]	will sink into the past.

—Tsurayuki, to Kanesuke, on the death of the latter's wife.

Toward the end of the *Sanuki no suke nikki*, we read of the handmaid's feelings as the twelfth month of 1108 draws to a close. It is the end of the first full year following Horikawa's death, a year she has spent, reluctantly it would seem, treading the rooms of her former life. Away from court for a brief rest at home, she has just received a message from the retired emperor Shirakawa summoning her back to serve the young emperor his meals on New Year's Day. It is the same sort of message that had recalled her to court service before the end of the mourning period the year before, and she receives it with something of the same mix of emotions she describes having felt then. The women around her busy themselves with preparations for her return to the imperial palace, while she alone among them, always with her mind on the past, stands outside the excitement turning over in her mind a fragment from an old poem: *wakare ya itodo*, "how much [farther] will our last parting?" (*NKBZ* 18: 453).

The line alludes to the *waka* by Ki no Tsurayuki quoted above, a poem that Tsurayuki composed on the last day of the year and addressed to his patron Kanesuke, who was still in mourning for the death of his wife. The memoirist may have come across it in the final volume of the *Gosenshū*, where the lines appear as the last poem in the anthology, in reply to the *waka* by Kanesuke that immediately precedes it:

Naki hito no	If this were a year
tomo ni shi kaeru	when I could go home
toshi naraba	with my beloved,
kureyuku kyō wa	the gathering twilight today
ureshikaramashi[68]	would make me happy.

Kanesuke's poem begins with an allusion to his dead wife (*naki hito*) but veers uneasily by means of the hypothetical *naraba* at the end of the third line away from direct reference to the loss encompassed in the first line. The shift registers the motions of a mourner's sensibility: a turning away from bereavement toward the self-consoling hypothesis of a (new) year in which he would return home (*tomo ni shi kaeru toshi*) with the wife who is, in fact, no longer alive. Shunting aside grief with a fiction of intimacy and return, the final three lines proceed on the trope of a contrary-to-fact situation. Kanesuke evokes the reality of his loneliness as well as his own inability to find words for his grief by naming the opposite of that reality—the pleasant dream of returning home with his wife in the evening of the last day of the year.

Tsurayuki's reply seizes directly on the unnamed emotions skirted in Kanesuke's poem. It reprises and translates the dream of a homecoming (*naki hito no tomo ni shi kaeru toshi*) back into the reality Kanesuke's poem wishfully aspires to deny: *naki hito no wakare* ("your parting with the one who is gone"). Figuring the beloved's death as an event constantly regressing away from Kanesuke in time (*itodo tōku narinamu*), Tsurayuki's poem inscribes grief as a problem of complex temporal disorientations in the consciousness of the mourner.

Both poems draw on a thematic convention of elegiac *waka* according to which the mourner laments outward signs of the passage of time because they clash so strongly with the steadfastness of his own grief. The turning of the old year was one such sign, as was the end of the mourning period when the day came to put off mourning robes and return to regular court dress. As a poetic topos, *fuku nugu* (changing out of mourning robes) is associated with the figure of a mourner, whose grief exceeds the short space of the mourning period. Still immured in his memories, he feels displaced in time and can only watch bitterly as those around him put off the past and their grief along with their mourning clothes.[69] He laments the pain of isolation and loss. Grief is measured by the psychological distance separating the mourner from those who have already begun to forget the dead. Unable to find any who share his inner anguish, he is doubly bereaved. Kanesuke's *waka* laments the coming of the new year, because this outward sign of the passage of time underscores the distance that stretches between the present and the death of his wife and the emotional distance between him and those who greet the new year as an occasion for happiness. His own desires place him in opposition to the onrush of the new year (which he sees as the gathering darkness of today's twilight: *kureyuku kyō*), while the longing to move backward in time lodges in the fabrication of an impossible return (*naki hito no/tomo ni shi kaeru*).

Tsurayuki's *waka* presses even further in this vein, intensifying the imagery of unbridgeable distance between the mourner and the dead. In his hands, the image of a retrogressive movement against the current of time suggests more than the turning of a mourner's consciousness away from the living world around him. Here the past itself also seems to move in an infinite regression away from the mourner, while he in his turn is propelled forward in time, despite the retrospective bent of his desire. But is it not the context of Tsurayuki's poem as a reply to Kanesuke that makes it so strangely memorable to the handmaid? Tsurayuki's poem seems to imply that Kanesuke's yearning will only serve to increase his isolation, as though the mourner's yearning itself might be partly to blame for the distance he sees widening inexorably between him and the scenes of memory to which he would cling. Yet the gesture Tsurayuki's *waka* makes is a profoundly empathetic one, for his words, in their vivid projection of the very dislocations Kanesuke's poem refrains from naming, recognize what is at stake when one grieves for an irrecoverable past. He offers his poem as proof of the empathy whose absence Kanesuke's poem anticipates.

It would seem that public expectations regarding the mourner change at some point in the mourning process. Even Tsurayuki's poem to his patron suggests there is a point beyond which excessive mourning becomes indecorous, even inauspicious or somehow damaging to the mourner and the memory of the dead. Although it does not seem likely that Tsurayuki intended his poem as a censuring of his patron's grief, it may be with something of a self-censuring intent that the Sanuki handmaid recalls lines from Tsurayuki's *waka*, perhaps in an effort to preempt the criticism of her readers, "the people who may chance to see these pages" whom she imagines in such anxious terms in the penultimate passages of the memoir.

The fragment of this poem as it appears in the *Sanuki no suke nikki* is enigmatic at best; it becomes more so when we try to imagine the influence its original context may have exerted on the memoirist's memory.[70] And what are we to imagine the handmaid is thinking, muttering the verse to herself in the bustle of preparations for the New Year celebration? Like so many of the fragments and scenes of memory recounted in this text, the line presents itself as an involuntary association, something called up by the occasion. It is the end of the old year, the moment of the handmaid's return yet again to a palace that had become for her, in

many ways, a problematic place. The narrator recounts setting out on
New Year's Eve and how the sight of the Horikawa mansion, standing
empty and masterless on the road to the imperial palace, calls up the
memory of yet another old poem.[71] But it is the first poem, the one she
could not initially completely remember, that continues to haunt her.
And like a number of other half-remembered images and associations
recalled and re-recalled in this text, this is one to which the narration is
destined to return. The line surfaces again, at the end of the next passage, in a *waka* that differs from Tsurayuki's in only one detail:

People who chance to see these pages may speak ill of me among themselves:
"It irks me the way she goes on—and she a mere lady-in-waiting—acting like
she knows so much." But I have merely written things as they were, just as they
have come back to me, and even the bits about the way of the Law were things
I was always hearing from his lips in the course of idle talk in the mornings and
evenings. You must not criticize me for that. But how will it look to those who
do not cherish him? In my gratitude and longing for this one man's kindness of
heart, I simply continued jotting matters down (surely such a thing is of the
very nature of ladies-in-waiting) just as they remain in my memory, never forgotten for a moment.

Nagekitsutsu	If this year spent
toshi no kurenaba	lamenting him draws to a close
naki hito no	how much further will
wakare ya itodo	that last parting with the one who is no more
tōku narinamu	sink into the past.

(NKBZ 18: 453–54)

The reader who has followed the interweavings of memory this far
through the pages of the *Sanuki no suke nikki* will find much that is familiar in the prose passage that precedes this poem. Present desires and
fears rise to the surface of a text that claims to be simply a transcript of
memory: "I have merely written things as they were, just as they have
come back to me" (*koto no arisama, omoiideraruru mama ni kakita-
runari*). The narrator worries that the memoir will fall into the wrong
hands, that it will be mistaken and misread. The close, competitive
world of the other women in court service, many of them from competing client families, is almost palpable in the hypersensitive projection
of the likely responses of those "people who may chance to see [these
pages]" (*uchi min hito*). The narration renders them in the language of
direct speech, as though the overheard voices of the other ladies-in-
waiting were already ringing in the handmaid's ears: "It irks me the way

she goes on—and she a mere lady-in-waiting—acting like she knows so much" (*nyōbō no mi nite, amari monoshirigao ni, nikushi*). Then there are the censuring eyes of "those who do not cherish him," arguably another group of readers entirely, disinclined to favor a lady-in-waiting who insists so much on her past ties to Horikawa. The passage ends by excusing her on the very grounds her imagined detractors use against her. Surely such fond scribblings of memory are simply (and innocuously) "of the very nature of ladies-in-waiting" and nothing for which she should be singled out for criticism.

Coming as it does at the end of such a passage, the memoirist's poetic performance, if indeed she intended the poem not as a citation of Tsurayuki but as a *honkadori*, her own variation on the original, suggests more than her skill (or lack of skill) as a poet. Appropriating the words of another ostensibly to address herself, but also in anticipation of her readers, preempting their reading of her by a strategy of self-deprecation, her *waka* addresses problems of repetition and return and the paradoxical power of memory both to recover the past and to distance the rememberer from the things recalled. Her lines (which are also Tsurayuki's lines to his patron) underscore the dangers of excessive memory and hint that mourning alone may only serve to widen the gap between past and present. The mourner reaches back, in her grief, to the face she remembers, but the dead are never simply gone from sight. They are receding from us constantly, and each passing year drags them yet farther away (*itodo tōku*). The bright treasures of memory wear and fade. Grief itself loses its edge, one parting takes on the contours of other partings in our memory, and we express ourselves in the coinage of others' lines till even our own sorrow is all but indistinguishable from the sorrows of others.

We have already noted in passing the critical consensus on the *Sanuki* memoirist's lack of skill as a composer of *waka*. Commentators regularly remark that the memoir is unique among other examples of the genre for the aesthetic meagerness of its included poetry. The first volume is completely devoid of all *waka*, a fact attributable to its subject. The matter of Horikawa's illness and death is assumed to have been too emotionally immediate and taxing a subject to accommodate the insertion of *waka*. Volume two, on the other hand, contains a total of twenty-three *waka*, a sum that, as Miyazaki has pointed out, creates a prose-to-poetry ratio comparable to that in four other major Heian female-authored *nikki*.[72] What really sets the *Sanuki no suke nikki* apart is the extent to which it relies on *waka* by others and *waka* that represent only minimal variations on poems by someone else. Only eleven of the twenty-three *waka* included in the memoir are considered to be the work of the memoirist's own hand (five *dokuei* and six *waka* composed as part of poetic exchanges between the handmaid and someone else). Of the five *dokuei*, four present only minor variations on a more illustrious original (as in the *waka* quoted above). In the *Sanuki* memoirist's hands, the conventionality of poetic language itself sets up a kind of screen, an opacity into which the images of the individual mourner and the dead man she mourns join a category of conventionalized mourners and mourned. The *waka* included in the *Sanuki no suke nikki* conceal the handmaid's feelings; quoting old poems, she hides the face of her own grief in the shadow of others' lines.

The gesture of self-effacement her *waka* embody should not distract us from the import of the text's final image. In the closing lines of the memoir, the narrator reverts to her favorite idyll. The old, familiar pleasure of displaying herself before Horikawa and those who understood her intimacy with him surfaces again, but this time as the explicit desire to be read. What the *Sanuki* memoirist wished to see writ large cannot be disengaged from the image of the late emperor, and the image of other readers, or perhaps just one ideal reader who remembers him and her relationship to him:

My thoughts revolved around this problem: if I were to look over these pages with someone who cherished the emperor just as I do, who would that person be, assuming there is such a one? If I showed it to someone who did not care for me, it could cause trouble should word get out, and that would never do; yet even were I to show it to someone who held me in esteem, if she had no friends or patrons I would feel my lines had not gotten the attention they deserve. Pondering these things I realized that Lady Hitachi alone was the person to meet my three conditions. (*NKBZ* 18: 456)

The memoir strives to invoke the liminal trance of memory, to serve, in the right hands, as a medium of that lost world, a kind of transmissible reverie in which one could move and breathe, where one might even linger, for the space of a day, reading out loud with a friend who would also remember: "I sent for her and, just as I envisioned she would, over she came, with a gentle graciousness that was quite touching. We spent the whole day together, reminiscing until it grew dark" (*NKBZ* 18: 456).

The final passage resolves the fraught issue of the gaze of the other by offering an alternative scenario of looking. The reader's gaze is directed elsewhere, away from the image of the handmaid herself. What the final lines delineate is a scene in which the handmaid's gaze, and the gaze of the reader (with Lady Hitachi as our proxy and model), join together to look at the same thing. The memoir wishfully resolves the problem of others by envisioning a scene of reading, a communal act much involved with the seeking and winning of patronage by women at the Heian court and in its surrounding aristocratic salons.[73]

We see the Sanuki handmaid and her relation to Horikawa through the eyes of those who censured her grief and circumscribed their intimacy—or at least, her memoir invites us to do so, again and again. Do we see her as she wished to be seen? Like other commentators before me, I am struck by the naïveté of many of these passages, not only in terms of their syntax and diction, but also as a rhetorical means of soliciting the approbation of the reader. I cannot help but suspect they would have appeared even more heavy-handed to those who knew her or who competed with her for favor during Toba's reign or those to whom, in the person of Lady Hitachi, the memoir was ideally addressed. Could she really have been so naive, so unsophisticated, as the memoir and the commentators make her out to be? Or was not the appearance of naïveté itself, in her unsettled day, something only to be achieved with the greatest of cunning?

6 ☙ The Poetics of Voyeurism
in *The Pillow Book*

Although individual aristocratic Heian women may not have actually hated being looked at directly in the face, the prose writers among them participated eloquently in the construction of the literary convention that they did. They also created some of the most memorable images of the aristocratic Heian male as voyeur. I will be arguing in this chapter that these writers' portraits of women also show them to be more than just the passive objects of male visual pleasure. Careful consideration of Heian court women's writings suggests abundantly that Heian women did not refrain from representing themselves in acts of desirous looking. How they looked, who they looked at, what the literary motifs of feminine looking might be, and what connection these motifs bear to different modes of writing and desire—such questions have been only partially addressed by current discussions of voyeurism in Heian court literature.

To date most discussions have focused on the thematics of "peeping through the fence" (*kaimami*), particularly as that topos is played out in the love stories of *The Tale of Genji*. The topos conventionally involves scenes in which a man looks at a woman who remains more or less unaware of his gaze. Understood at the level of the characters within the story, the *kaimami* topos appears simply to showcase a conventional heterosexual configuration of visual pleasure and narrative desire. A fictional man peeps longingly at a fictional woman; the reader's gaze conflates momentarily with that of the voyeuristic male figure and the reader wants to read on to see what happens next. Is a strictly feminine gaze absent from such scenes? Does it emerge only when we pull back from events in the narrative to consider how the narrative frame constructs a kind of looking game that engenders the reader, drawing her (or his) gaze and heightening—for possibly different reasons—his or her interest in reading on? This essay will try to complicate our understanding of voyeurism in the Heian women's tradition by looking first at conventional *kaimami* scenes and the critical commentary they have generated and then beyond these normative paradigms to explore *kaimami* scenes that invent new games out of old conventions. I have singled out *The Pillow Book* as textual anchor for this exploration because I believe important questions about relations among looking, desire, and gender are both posed, and find answers, in this text.[1]

According to the self-assured, not to say pretentious, narrating persona that readers since Murasaki Shikibu have come to identify as "Sei Shōnagon," when it comes to participation in the risky pleasures and advantages of looking and being seen, everyone at court, both male and female, emperor to female underling, gets involved:[2]

These ladies who sit at home, lacking any venue for future growth, while taking seriously joys that are really only counterfeit—imagining them I am overcome with scorn! How indeed I would love to have their daughters mingle among us and make them see the way things are in this world, even if it meant they should be made to serve as assistant handmaids for a while.

And I really hate these young men who think and say that the women who serve at court are shallow and disreputable. Then again it is surely only natural. From their majesties on down through the senior nobles and the courtiers, to say nothing of the fifth- and fourth-rankers, there are very few people indeed *who do not see her/whom she does not see*. Then there are the messengers of the ladies-in-waiting who come from their homes, female domestic servants, the women who clean the latrines, all the way down to underlings who are no more fussed over than pebbles and tiles: when do they hide their faces in shame? But these young lords, don't they too have to deal with such things?[3]

The passage is a famous one, sometimes referred to among twentieth-century Japanese scholars as Sei's "defense of the career girl," or, to use a less anachronistic idiom, her "discussion of service at court" (*miyazukae ron*). On the surface, Sei seems intent on defending the moral reputations of "women who serve at court." The structure of the passage implies that an odious comparison has already been made between women who live at home, complacent because they are unaware of what they are missing, and women in court service. The cure Sei wishes for these benighted, housebound females involves their seeing and her showing: "How I would love to have their daughters mingle among us and make them see the way things are in this world, even if it meant they should serve as assistant handmaids [*naishi no suke*] for a while" (*SNKBT* 25: 27).

What is Sei doing in wishing on these women service at court in the position of assistant handmaid? The fantasy reveals her dispensing wisdom to women potentially above herself in court rank and office and in family affiliations. Though lower-ranking than principal handmaids, assistant handmaids were counted among the upper echelons of an emperor's ladies-in-waiting, and they generally were made up of daughters of middle-ranking senior nobles (*kugyō* or *kandachime*) and courtiers (*tenjōbito*). In other words, their fathers were mostly men of the fourth rank or above.[4] Sei herself served as a lady-in-waiting (*nyōbō*) to Empress Teishi. And although Sei's father, Kiyowara Motosuke (908–90), enjoyed a good reputation as a poet and literary scholar in his time, his rank and family name (a Kiyowara in a world where Fujiwara and Minamoto men stood the best chances of prospering) place Sei squarely in the tradition of daughters of the middle ranks.[5] Aside from her desire to pull rank on women nominally above her in the social scale at court, Sei's fantasy positions her as one in possession of a certain kind of authority: the one who *shows* "the way things are in this world." In fact, this is precisely what she accomplishes in writing a text in which she figures prominently as the one who looks and tells. The minor ladies-in-waiting who people the margins of Heian tales are always sighing about how they long to "show" their exquisite mistresses to discerning aristocratic male eyes. In Heian court women's memoirs, the writer's claim that she wishes to reveal the talents and beauty of her mistress (a claim that lodges the desire to show off her own discursive talents) is a common motif, and *The Pillow Book* is no exception. But against this conventional theme of voyeuristic pandering the wishes Sei expresses here appear slightly off-center, didactic, and perhaps even protofeminist, given the implied interest in female spectatorship. What Sei claims she wants to show is "the world," and the eyes she imagines showing it to belong to women of the upper ranks of the aristocracy. What she actually displays is her own connoisseurship.

The explicit insult against which Sei defends herself and other women who serve at court is that of "superficiality" of feeling or sensibility. The word is *awa awashi*, an adjectival whose root connotes literal lightness or thinness (of color or flavor) and points to the anxiety about oppositions between superficiality and depth developed here and elsewhere in *The Pillow Book*. The woman in court service is vulnerable to the charge of frivolity (with its connotations of indiscretion or immodesty) for two possible reasons: first, because she is seen by so many and second, because she looks at so many. The phrase that ends *minu hito wa sukunaku koso arame* ("there are very few people indeed who do not look [at her]/[whom she] does not see") cunningly exploits the ambiguity produced by the lack of a clearly marked subject for the sentence and the negative attributive form of the verb *miru* ("to see"). Who looks at whom here? Most commentators opt for one interpretation over the other. The *SNKBT* editors, assuming that the taboo against a woman allowing herself to be seen is uppermost, understand the line to mean "From their Majesties on down . . . there are very few people indeed who do not look at [the woman in court service]." But it is equally possible to read the sentence as meaning "From their Majesties on down . . . there are very few indeed whom [the woman in court service] does not look at."[6] Morris's translation follows the latter line of thinking and even elaborates on it by calling attention to the "brazen" behavior of the ladies-in-waiting who "walk about, looking openly at people they chance to meet."[7] I prefer to preserve the ambiguity of the phrase.

Regardless of how one reads its intent, the passage highlights the fraught relation between women and acts of looking, and by extension, the relationship of women to knowledge and desire. The conventionally ideal woman, the one who lives at home, her gaze chastely confined and her body safely hidden from view, neither looks nor is seen beyond her own house and carriages. Part of Sei's project was to demonstrate that the apparent shallowness of the highly visible and visually active woman in court service in fact belies a superior depth of experience and knowledge—a knowledge associated specifically with the faculty of seeing (and at times seeing through) surfaces, spectacles, people, and things in all their amusing, splendid, or odious variety. The passage epitomizes the disadvantages suffered by women who live secluded in private residences in terms of their ignorance, especially their nonfamiliarity with court spectacle (the Gosechi festival is the example given). But it is not simply a matter of all the things the secluded woman never sees and therefore has to ask others about when requested to present her own daughter at court. More insidious and significant, the woman who contents herself with remaining hidden lives blind to the limits of her own perspective. She "sees" only "mock joys" or "counterfeit happiness" (*esezaiwai nado mite*). Overturning woman's traditional status as merely an object of another's gaze, Sei hints at the possibilities that might be realized once the woman exercises the gaze herself. While the woman who lives at home must rely on "what she gathers from others about the things she doesn't know" (*iishiranu koto nado hito ni toikiki nado*), the woman who serves at court gains real vision because she is able to look for herself at the "way things are in this world." Looking inscribes knowledge, and self-display connotes not shame but power in *The Pillow Book*. Vision potentially invests a woman with the power to understand, if not the power to possess. As to the potential shame of her being seen (which is different from self-display), that is what happens to everybody at court, as the final lines quoted plainly assert.

The only truly formidable target of criticism here, and perhaps a key segment of the text's implied audience, is the antagonistic, aristocratic male. Interwoven in her defense of the court woman's acts of looking and exposing herself to the gaze of others is a challenge to the idea of the gaze as a male prerogative. Far more radical than the scopophilic remedy Sei recommends for the housebound woman is her depiction of the imperial palace as a kind of house of mirrors where neither gender nor any particular class monopolizes the pleasures and risks of seeing and being seen. Life at court is a spectacle in which the spectators themselves are also expected to participate. *The Pillow Book* describes in many of its passages a dissemination of the gaze across class and gender boundaries. With its hierarchically arranged list of ranks and categories of high-ranking male courtiers down to the brief but suggestive enumeration of female menials and hangers-on, the passage subtly emphasizes the engagement of all eyes and all bodies on the stage of life at court, though it singles out for special mockery the hypocritical gaze of the detestable men who presume to judge women in court service. The gaze circulates, the exclusive property of neither gender and available to all, regardless of class distinctions.

Feminine Spectacle and Female Spectatorship: Murasaki Shikibu and Sei Shōnagon

It is interesting to compare Sei with her contemporary Murasaki Shikibu in this respect. Murasaki also finds fault with the young nobles (*kindachi*) whose perceptions take an objectionable form in their comments on the elaborate spectacle of the Gosechi dancers. The passage comes in the middle of her lengthy, painstakingly detailed description of the Gosechi festival of 1008, a section memorable for its almost obsessive and anxious empathy with the feelings of the four female dancers and their female attendants, each the focus of intense scrutiny by the emperor, the senior nobles, and the courtiers, to say nothing of the sharp-eyed and highly competitive ladies-in-waiting, Murasaki among them.[8]

The memoirist describes each of the four principal dancers in detail and singles out for extended comment certain of the female attendants (*warawa*) as well. In such a context, the reported remarks of the young men appear crude indeed:

And now all these young lords talk about are the charms of the Gosechi dancers' quarters. "Even the edges and fittings of their blinds show differences in style, and the way their hair falls when they are sitting down, and the way they carry themselves, they are each so distinctive, you see." So they go on, in a manner most unpleasant to hear. (*NKBZ* 18: 214)

What the memoirist (like the narrator of the "Judgments of a Rainy Night" in *The Tale of Genji*) finds "unpleasant to hear" (*kikinikushi*) in these remarks is what they betray of the young men's presuppositions. That they should be so amazed at the individual differences distinguishing the Gosechi dancers from one another suggests the unflattering reverse side of the coin—that the young men assumed the women would be otherwise, that is, that they would be more or less interchangeable with one another. Surely the author of *The Tale of Genji* is censuring the commodification of women in court ritual and Heian marriage politics, a critique that works not by openly challenging the men themselves but by obliquely indicating what is distasteful about their perspective and then by offering (as an alternative to the young nobles' fascination with mere surface detail) an embedding context that probes the anxieties of the women who draw the male gaze.

The differences on this point between the rhetorical strategies of *The Pillow Book* and the *Murasaki Shikibu nikki* are telling. Offended by a (male) presumption of sameness among young female newcomers to court, Murasaki as memoirist sets about to show the limits of their perceptions by highlighting the intricate distinctions the aristocratic male gaze fails to discern. But Murasaki's gestures also underscore the limits inherent in the looking game itself. Her memoir is full of brief but subtle characterizations of other women in the service of her mistress, Empress Shōshi, and even some women (like Sei herself) from competing female salons, known to her probably only by their writings and reputations. As memoirist, her musings revert again and again to the inner sufferings and aspirations of other women, and not merely those most likely to inspire male passion. Descriptions repeatedly wander toward figures sitting on the sidelines of great events. Capping the portrayal of the Special Festival at the Kamo Shrine in 1008 is the image of one Kura no myōbu, former wet nurse to Michinaga's second son, Norimichi, who served that year as the imperial messenger to the Shrine Priestess. Norimichi's mother, Rinshi, makes a point of coming to the palace to watch him depart for the Shrine—but instead of zeroing in on Rinshi or her impressive son, Norimichi, or even simply on the spectacle of mother looking at son, the narration moves tangentially. The person who stands out most memorably for the narrator, and thus for the reader of the memoir, is Kura no Myōbu: "Seeing him there looking very grown-up and imposing with artificial wisteria flowers in his hair, his old wet nurse, Kura no Myōbu, had no eyes for the dancers; she just gazed at him, tears running down her cheeks" (*NKBZ* 18: 220).[9]

The narration, too, "has no eyes for the dancers," in this case, male dancers. Yet while the *Murasaki Shikibu nikki* appears preoccupied with female figures from its author's own class of middle-ranking ladies-in-waiting, at bottom, what still seems central is the relation between the feminine and the look that predominates in *The Tale of Genji*. The one who looks may be first and foremost an identifiably feminine and middle-ranking narrating voice, and the way she exercises her gaze raises the art of looking at women to new levels of sophistication and sensitivity, but women in Murasaki's memoir are still represented primarily as something to be looked at. And when a woman (and particularly the narrator) exercises the gaze, it is she herself (or another more or less marginalized woman like her) at whom she is most likely to look.

In this respect Murasaki's memoir presents a far different content from *The Pillow Book*, where even the most cursory glance reveals that while an interesting assortment of men traverse its pages, the only other woman besides Sei who receives sustained narratorial attention is Empress Teishi. In sharp contrast to Murasaki, Sei turns the tables on her frequently male opponents, meeting and often beating them at their own game. Instead of offering an exemplary pattern for the deeper scrutiny of other ladies-in-waiting or women at court in general, Sei looks back at the male courtiers, and in doing so, reverses the rules of the game in which men look and women are scrutinized.

But we should consider what this kind of transgressive looking has cost her (or won her, depending on your aesthetic allegiances): a reputation as a writer obsessed with surfaces. Mark Morris's remarks provide a neat summary of the contrast between Murasaki and Sei on this point:

Sei's "world," in contrast [to the world of *Genji*], is noticeably one of exteriors. This can be applied to her attachment to occasional forms of verse or to the values she demands in the occasional, decorous lover. To *Genji* devotees this dwelling on the surface of things has tended to deprive *Makura no sōshi* of high seriousness in the crucial dimension of human emotion. But to a reader who comes to Sei's book straight from *Genji*, from a series of highly charged scenes rich in the hemmings and hawings of frustration or guilt, where two or more complicated interior psychological worlds have once again failed to make contact, the style of *Makura no sōshi* can strike you like a gust of fresh air.[10]

Is there any doubt that Sei precisely anticipated this sort of judgment about her writing? Aside from her own attempts to preeempt such commentary by making it herself, the (at times reductive) characterization of Sei as a writer of surfaces is nowhere stated more memorably than by Murasaki Shikibu, whose criticism of Sei Shōnagon's writing focuses exactly on issues of appearances, ways of looking, and the kinds of discernment these things imply. At issue for Murasaki is Sei's unfeminine breaching of literary gender norms. Murasaki's censuring of Sei moves hand in hand with the anxiety I have already noted in her description of the young men at the Gosechi festival. Alive to the deceptiveness of surface appearances, Murasaki disdains the insincerity and superficial manner (*ada ni naru sama*) of people who, like Sei (or like the young men commenting on the Gosechi dancers' quarters), go out of their way to display their own connoisseurship. Who indeed would be more personally affronted by the way Sei exaggerates the image of herself as exquisitely sensitive to nuance and detail than so enormously nuanced a writer as Murasaki Shikibu?

Sei Shōnagon! Now there was someone with an insufferably knowing look about her. She appeared to conduct herself with such wit, and laced her script with Chinese letters, but when you take a good look, you find much of it not quite up to the mark. A person like that, who imagines herself so different from all the rest, is bound to appear inferior and she will wind up getting worse and worse; a person accustomed to such showiness, who pursues the pathos and won't overlook the charm of even random occasions, she will herself become inappropriate and superficial. The end of such a trifling one as she, how could it turn out well? (*NKBZ* 18: 238)

Setting aside for the moment the question of how these contrasts in style and content have contributed to a critical privileging of Murasaki's talents over Sei's, the comparison of the two writers returns us to the issue of looking and its relation to gender and desire in Heian women's writing. Does Sei's interest in surface detail indicate what is merely a mocking, feminine parody of patriarchal models of the look, or does her play with literary conventions of looking suggest aspirations toward an alternative poetics of voyeurism, a different fiction to challenge the he-

gemony of the fiction that fine women neither look nor allow themselves to be seen? One way to begin answering these questions is to look
at Sei looking, to examine who and what it is she examines and how she
portrays herself in relation to that object.

This strategy has led me to a consideration of Sei's depiction of her
male contemporaries, and more generally, to questions about the relation of eroticism to narrative structure in *The Pillow Book*. How is difference, and the suspense created by deferment—both so necessary to
the dynamic of erotic as well as to narrative tensions and their fulfillment—constituted in a prose text whose narratives are seldom sustained
beyond the confines of the discrete anecdote? How is tension built and
pleasure heightened in a world where everyone looks and is seen? Clearly gender, as well as the fine gradations of court rank and office, remains
a potent source of erotic difference, as the carefully respected hierarchies
in the passage from *The Pillow Book* quoted above suggest. But in addition to these matters, one must look and talk about looking in a special
way. Inventing the opinionated voice of Sei Shōnagon, the writer found
her most potent strategy for showing and telling: an antiheroine who is
the bearer of an almost prankishly discerning gaze—an eye for telling
details. In the figure of "Sei Shōnagon" as narrating persona, as well as
in those select others mentioned in her text whom she occasionally holds
up for the reader's admiration, *The Pillow Book* assigns value and
power (erotic and otherwise) to the eye that sees surfaces clearly and
recognizes in appearances what those with lesser powers are unable to
detect. Before we can turn to our examination of the creativity in *The
Pillow Book*'s challenges to the fiction of woman as passive object of
voyeuristic desire, we will need to make an excursus into the very heart
of that fiction. *The Tale of Genji*, and recent writing on voyeurism in
Genji, will provide us with vantage points.

The Critic as Voyeur: Vicissitudes of the Feminine Gaze in Contemporary Readings of *The Tale of Genji*

The voyeuristic appeal of *kaimami* scenes for the implied reader of tale
literature should be apparent. For the actual reader, the narrative of a
desirous man looking at a desirable woman serves as a representation of
reading as voyeuristic looking, creating a dizzying sensation of (self-)
recognition the moment the reader identifies his or her own position as
voyeur mirrored in the scene.[11] To a great extent, critical recognition of

the possibility of feminine-oriented modes of voyeurism in Heian literature has been hampered by the privileging of the *kaimami* topos and especially by the appropriative, masculine mode of desire that topos is
understood to signify in its working out in different episodes from *The
Tale of Genji*. The association of the look with acts of physical, political, and sexual possession (*ryōyū*) has roots in early Japanese culture
and myth, notably the mythic motif of *kunimi* (surveying the land) and
the *kumimi uta* (poems on the *kunimi* topos) found in the *Kojiki* and
elsewhere.[12] While I do not wish to scant the importance of the motif
and its significance for Heian literary representations of looking and desire (especially the *kaimami* topos), I would call attention to an over-
preoccupation with it among scholars in Japan and elsewhere. The concern with gazes that signify a transgressive desire to possess has led to a
disregard of other scenes of voyeuristic looking and other modes of desire in a tradition that is unusually rich in its play with figures of seeing
and display. Notions of female spectatorship and feminine voyeurism
have received relatively little critical attention, despite the fact that
much of what is now considered the most interesting texts of the Heian
tradition was written by and for women. Where do we locate figures of
feminine voyeuristic pleasure in Heian court literature? Can we really
say that the feminine gaze in these texts is generally figured as passive or
merely flattering to its object? And if not, what kinds of agency and desire does it suggest? Before turning to these questions, we need to review
the main points at which current discussions of the gaze in Heian court
literature have engaged the possibility of feminine voyeurism.

Generally speaking, the upshot of these discussions has been an understanding of the construction of the feminine gaze in *Genji* as taking
one of two patterns. It is characterized as the largely passive, flattering-
to-its-object perspective of the lady-in-waiting who gazes with admiration on someone (often male) far above her in social standing.[13] A second model addresses the feminine tendency to perceive the self as an
object meant to be looked at. Norma Field's analysis of "seeing and
being seen" in the Uji chapters of *The Tale of Genji* provides a sustained
example of this model.[14] According to her reading, the Uji princesses
employ the gaze as though they had internalized—to borrow the terms
of John Berger's critique of voyeurism in Western visual arts—the con-
ception of themselves as sights to be seen rather than as subjects in possession of their own power to look and to desire.[15] Particularly in its
analysis of the *Genji* heroine Ōigimi and her relation to the gaze, Field's
study presents a far more nuanced reading of the gender dynamics of

looking than do Berger's polemical essays. But it is not so clear that her readings (or *Genji* itself) offer something fundamentally different from the image of the female as surveyed object and surveyor of herself, though certainly the vocabulary of images and the patterns of production and consumption of Heian narrative differ in important ways from their counterparts in Western visual arts. When they gaze at all, most of the *Genji* heroines appear to gaze most intensely at themselves. And what the *Genji* heroine is most apt to see is what she thinks (or fears) others see when they look at her. However, I do not think that a focus on the *Genji* heroines can even begin to suggest the entire range of Heian response to the cultural fiction that women are to be looked at. As I hope these chapters have already demonstrated, Heian court women's writings reveal a variety of creative negotiations with the limits of the aristocratic woman's conventional position as a desired object rather than as a desiring subject.

What follows is a brief examination of some important critical essays and statements on the topoi of looking in Heian tales (*monogatari*), made with an eye to filling in some of the gaps in the current discussion of scenes of looking in Heian court women's narrative. My argument assumes the importance of working from a more elaborate description of the narrative forms of literary voyeurism, one that encompasses not only the gazes exchanged or denied among characters within the story but also the discourse of the narrator as a perspective that operates in ways sometimes analogous to the gazes exchanged among the characters.

On the basis of his survey of the motif of the "surreptitious glimpse" (*nozokimi*) in *The Tale of Genji* and earlier works, Shinohara Yoshihiko formulated a typology of three basic scenarios of furtive looking in classical Japanese literature.[16] These categories are underlain by a thematics of transgressive appropriation, a notion of the gaze and of desire as forces that work furtively to possess or to expose their object. Shinohara's interest in the theme of transgressive looking has a profound impact on what he is able to recognize and admit as part of his typology of the look. From the outset, his formulation of the relation between desire and the look rules out gazes that are not furtive and underplays desires that are not primarily appropriative.

In Shinohara's first category, whose locus classicus is the *Kojiki* tale of Toyotamabime, both characters in the scene are superhuman, and the stolen, transgressive gaze of one on the other reveals the unrecuperable Otherness of the object of the gaze. Toyotamabime, the daughter of the god of the sea, forbids her lover to look at her while she is giving birth to their child. At the crucial, transgressive moment of vision, Toyo-tamabime, the tabooed object of her lover's gaze, appears in the monstrous, inhuman form of a crocodile. His desirous act of looking at once exposes her in her "true form" and violates her own desire to remain hidden. According to the logic of this scenario, the act of looking precipitates a breaking of relations between the seer and the one who is seen.[17]

Shinohara finds examples for his second category of looking in the scenes surrounding Kaguyahime, the "Shining Princess" of the *Taketori monogatari* ("The Tale of the Bamboo Cutter," completed by the first decade of the tenth century). Here, the object of vision is a heavenly creature transformed into a beautiful human being. The act of looking at her (and I use the feminine pronoun pointedly, though Shinohara himself does not make explicit the role gender plays in his own typology) may result in either union or separation of seer and seen. He devotes the bulk of his article to this scenario, since his survey reveals it to be the type most frequently exploited by *The Tale of Genji*. As he sees it, the focus of narrative interest here is less the princess than the voyeur himself and the emotional turmoil into which he is plunged by his discovery of a beautiful woman. This privileging of the psychic state underlying the actions of the voyeur in the *kaimami* scene provides Shinohara with a framework for exploring the topos in terms of conventional, masculine, heterosexual triangulations of desire. Consequently, Shinohara moves on to discuss Yūgiri's spying on Genji's principal wife, Murasaki, as part of the larger tale of Yūgiri's rivalry with his father. In this respect his argument bears comparison to René Girard's rereading of the Oedipal complex.[18] In Girard's theory of "mimetic desire," it is not so much the intrinsic value of the (feminine) object as it is the presence of a (masculine) rival that confers value on the object and thus arouses desire in the bearer of the gaze. Girard argues that a homoerotic structure of sublimated desire for the rival as model is the basis of all heterosexual triangles: "The subject desires the object because the rival desires it. . . . The rival, then, serves as a model for the subject . . . in regard to desires. . . . Desire itself is essentially mimetic, directed toward an object desired by the model."[19]

Shinohara's model can be critiqued from a feminist standpoint on the same grounds that Girard's has been. As Toril Moi has demonstrated, Girard's revisions of the Oedipal triangle are based on an exclusion of the mother (and thus of the possibility of feminine desire) from Freud's classic model of the origin of desire and sexual difference.[20] Shinohara's argument slides toward a Girardian understanding of the gaze insofar as he implies that Yūgiri's real interest in spying on Genji's ladies has less to do with the intrinsic interest of the women themselves than with Yū-giri's desire to transgress his father's authority and indirectly view what it is about his father that has remained hidden from view (the women he treasures, his sexuality).

Both Shinohara and Girard describe a configuration that Joan DeJean has characterized as a "triangulation of desire [that] act[s] to objectify Woman, [and thus] to deny her an active role in the economy of desire."[21] There are a number of crucial differences, however, in the kinds of texts that Shinohara and Girard choose to examine. Girard concentrates on male voyeurs in novels written by men and triangles in which the gender arrangements are typically male-male-female.[22] Shinohara is primarily concerned with triangles in *The Tale of Genji*, a work by a woman written for a primarily female audience. His relatively lengthy discussions of the male-male-female triangulation of Genji-Yūgiri-Murasaki (and later, in the same essay, of Genji–Kashiwagi–the Third Princess) stand out all the more given the text he is examining. Further reflection on the examples cited in his survey actually reveals a preponderance of male-female-female triangles in *Genji*. Certainly the motif of the *yukari* (literally, "link," refer-ring to the daughter or other female relative who is sought as an erotic substitute for her own mother, aunt, and so on, in a man's affections) sug-gests that the normative voyeuristic configuration in the *Genji* involves an amorous man remembering as he gazes, not a hidden male rival, but an-other woman whom the woman before his eyes appears to resemble. In some important ways the story that remains only partially elaborated in *Genji* (especially the early chapters, up to *Nowaki* ["The Typhoon"]) is the tale of male jealousy and masculine rivalry, the more or less amicable competition between Genji and Tō no Chūjō notwithstanding. The figures depicted as chronically suffering from the presence of rivals (and at times reacting in response to them) are markedly the female figures. I would suggest that the emphasis on a prior female rival in the typical *Genji* trian-gle indicates one of the ways in which a preoccupation with feminine per-spectives and interiority inflects scenes apparently about male voyeurism in *Genji*.

And yet, regardless of the gender of the third party in the erotic tri-angles of *The Tale of Genji*, Shinohara's analyses, like Girard's, do sug-gest a primarily passive relation of women to the gaze in *Genji* and ear-lier texts. His typology appears to reveal a binary, gendered opposition:

men look and women are to be looked at. Shinohara's first two categories imply that feminine desire, if it can be said to be represented at all, appears only as the negative wish to avoid being seen. The woman, as passive, perceived object of the male voyeur's desire, is usually viewed externally in the *kaimami* scenes in *Genji*. And because the rationale for Shinohara's typology and his selection of individual instances of literary voyeurism spring from a special interest in the subjectivity of looking as appropriation or (erotic) possession, scenes of men transgressively gazing at women become the norm against which other scenes of looking are understood and evaluated.

It is therefore as a deviation from the norm that we can best grasp the position Shinohara implicitly assigns his third category of stolen glimpses, the *nyōbō sanbi* type. In scenes belonging to this category, the seer is of a lower status, typically a lady-in-waiting (*nyōbō*), who gazes with admiration (*sanbi*), usually at a man who is superior to her in rank. Ukifune's mother gazing surreptitiously at her daughter's first suitor and subsequently at Prince Niou are paradigmatic examples of the type. Despite her act of looking, however, the gaze of the lady-in-waiting is powerless to reverse the usual patterns of erotic dominance. Her admiring stare serves only to confirm the beauty of her object, because the narrative does not then proceed to describe her (sexual) passion (which for Shinohara would mark it, like conventional *kaimami* scenes, as a topos initiating a tale about desire).

Not surprisingly, Shinohara leaves relatively unexplored this third category of furtive glimpses, though he does make a brief, interesting reference to the possibility that the female voyeur of the typical *nyōbō sanbi* scene serves as a surrogate for the reader in the text.[23] Although he does not explain why this type of seer but not the others should strike him as a proxy for the reader, we might speculate that it concerns the marginal position of these seers within the tale. The ladies-in-waiting are all minor characters, peripheral to the main story. In this respect their gazes might be said to mimic the gaze of the implied reader of the tale, who may "witness" the actions of textual figures but whose own participation is always only vicarious. The fact that their gazes represent the only category of exclusively female gazes in the typology is also significant. Shinohara does not touch explicitly on the possible erotic content of these scenes, but again, his identification of the voyeuristic lady-in-waiting as a surrogate for the reader is suggestive. I suspect that her appreciative scoping of various heroes is a textualization of heterosexual desire on the part of the court women who made up the *Genji*'s original primary readership.

One can question Shinohara's description of the *nyōbō sanbi* category further by comparing it to his two other categories in terms of an
economy of power. ("Power" is to be understood here as an attribute of
the subject in voyeuristic fantasies in which looking constitutes a transgressive exposure or results in erotic possession of what is seen.) Both of
Shinohara's first two categories involve the transgression of a taboo by
a (usually male) seer, which may then result in the disempowerment of
the one who is seen (usually female) either through the disclosure of her
monstrous Otherness (as in the tale of Toyotamabime) or through her
erotic possession by the desirous voyeur who moves from looking to
taking (as Genji did with the young Murasaki). It is striking that all
three of Shinohara's categories are named for the female figure involved,
regardless of whether she plays the role of seer or seen. Is this perhaps
because the critic, like the usually male bearer of the gaze in Shinohara's
first two categories, objectifies the woman in the scene without regard
for the role she actually plays? However, although the lady-in-waiting
in the *nyōbō sanbi* scenes plays the role of voyeur, what transgression
does she commit when she steals a peek at a handsome courtier? We are
left to assume that the female voyeur transgresses social codes simply by
usurping a male, upper-class prerogative.

We need to first ask, however, whether the gaze is typically figured as
an upper-class male prerogative in the Heian prose tradition. Can the gaze
of the lady-in-waiting, which must have been a ubiquitous fact of daily life
for both men and women of the upper class in Heian court society, even
be categorized as a type of "furtive glimpse" (*nozokimi*)? How transgressive could such a gaze be, regardless of whether the (male) object of it was
aware of being watched?

Second, it is significant that whatever its relation to gender norms,
the gaze of the voyeuristic lady-in-waiting, at least in Shinohara's reading, lacks the power to transform or appropriate its object. The (male)
object of her gaze is never violated or erotically possessed as a result—
indeed for him, being seen from the low-angle perspective of the female
attendant usually results only in an affirmation of his power, figured in
the narrative by typically favorable descriptions of the man's physical
appearance. And the gaze of the lady-in-waiting is never translated into
action, at least so long as the "action," the playing out of visual pleasure, is conceived of only in conventional fantasies of possession or violation.[24] Although Shinohara does not spell this out, his categories themselves imply that the *nyōbō sanbi* scenario is an asymmetrical inversion
of the *kaimami* topos. Though the gender of the gaze-bearer shifts, re-

versing the usual pattern of male subject versus female object, the one who possesses power in the scene is still decidedly the male—despite the fact that he now plays object to a female subject.

These asymmetries bear further consideration. In discussing the *nyō-bō sanbi* scenario, Shinohara is quick to highlight the difference in status between the subject of the gaze and the object, noting that the female subject is usually of a lower rank than the object of her gaze (as in Ukifune's mother staring with admiration at Niou). But what about the status differences between seer and seen in his other two categories? He mentions that the female figures who are objects of the gaze are usually taken to be of superhuman or unearthly origin, or at least as retaining vestiges of that origin by virtue of their exquisite beauty or association with some other woman of great beauty, but he doesn't elaborate on the actual class differences between the *Genji* heroes and heroines whose voyeuristic encounters fall into his second category. He also does not note that the otherworldly seer and seen in his first category are equally divine or superhuman. Perhaps one of the reasons why the issue of status does not enter into his descriptions of the first two categories is because it is linked to gender in a way that renders it invisible. Women are already socially subordinate to men by virtue of gender, so their double subordination—when it occurs because of class differences—goes more or less unnoticed.

The intersection of femininity and lower social status is a constant in all three of Shinohara's categories, regardless of who exercises the gaze. Although his survey reveals examples of lower-class men spying on higher-ranking women (Kashiwagi spying on Genji's young wife, the Third Princess, most notoriously), examples of the opposite case—high-ranking women spying on and desirous of men of equal or lower social rank—are conspicuously absent. It would seem from this survey that the privileges of class did not count for the female characters of *Genji* and its intertexts in early Japanese literature. In fact, it appears that, as a female, the woman is typically prey even to men below herself in the social hierarchy. As the cautionary tales of Genji and Fujitsubo and Kashiwagi and the Third Princess suggest, she exhibits herself to them at her own peril and at the risk of imperiling the very fabric of society and family. The feminine gaze, on the other hand, is class-specific, typically represented by a middle-ranking woman who serves as lady-in-waiting (often one who may aspire to, but not achieve, something higher, as in the case of Tamakazura watching the Reizei Emperor from afar during the imperial procession in "The Royal Outing" [*Miyuki*]).[25] Such a gaze inscribes only a passive appreciation of its object; it will never translate into passionate action, and thus it resembles the gaze of the emperor's subjects on the emperor himself. The only outcome is a reaffirmation of the power of the one who is beheld.

In many ways, Norma Field's discussions of "seeing and being seen" in *The Tale of Genji* open the door to a more detailed consideration of the relation between voyeurism and gender in *Genji*. She argues that although Genji is portrayed as the Peeping Tom par excellence, his interiority, unlike that of other male voyeurs (notably Yūgiri, Kashiwagi, and Kaoru), remains curiously sealed off from the narrator, the narrative, and the reader, projected instead onto the women whom Genji desires.[26] Drawing on yet other examples from *Genji*, Field properly rephrases the sexual bipolarity in other discussions of voyeurism in terms of gender rather than physiology, a tension between "masculine" and "feminine" positions with respect to the gaze, thus challenging the unexamined conflation of sexual and gender identity implicit in the arguments of both Bowring and Shinohara. Her discussion demonstrates how the *Genji* narrative complicates the gender and class arrangements of classic scenes of voyeuristic looking, arguing that late in *The Tale of Genji*, Genji himself (like Kashiwagi before him, though under different circumstances) plays a feminized role in "The Wizard" (*Maboroshi*) when, deep in mourning for the dead Murasaki, he assiduously avoids the gaze of others.[27]

Following through on her own contention that interiority in *Genji* is projected from Genji onto the heroines (except when Genji himself plays a feminized role), Field discusses at length the issue of feminine self-consciousness within traditional *kaimami* scenes. In her readings of the Uji chapters, feminine looking and subjectivity, at least in the form of the woman's awareness of her status as object in the eyes of a male voyeur, become key issues.[28] Her argument provides an important counterweight against both Shinohara's special interest in masculine voyeuristic interiority and Bowring's assertion that for most of the feminine figures in the *kaimami* scene, "a knowledge of their capacity to generate emotion [in the male voyeur] is cruelly hidden from them."[29] Field's analysis allows us to restate the situation thus: the *Genji* typically idealizes, in its amorous heroes, a lover whose interiority remains opaque to his women (though often quite transparent to the narrator and reader).[30] The question of the woman's awareness of her capacity to "generate emotion" in the man is seldom raised as such. But when it is, as in the case of Ōigimi and the Uji chapters in general, masculine desire (in the

figures of Kaoru and Niou) comes in for relentless questioning and resistance. At Uji, the romance plots that Kaoru devises run amok, while the
figures of Ōigimi and Ukifune bring the question of feminine resistance
and desire out of the shadowy interstices and into the forefront of the
narrative.

Field's reading radically parts company with Shinohara's and, at least
on this issue, does not warrant Morris's hints that she fails to address
the problem of "what such furtive voyeurism is doing in a tale ostensibly written by and for women."[31] Yet the broader implications of Morris's critique of Field deserve serious attention. While Morris suggests
that the voyeurism of the *Genji* text signals one of the more ideologically conservative, even reactionary, aspects of the narrative, Field
seems bent on rescuing *Genji* from just such aspersions. Her argument
tries to find in the *kaimami* topos something that, though certainly not
feminist or even protofeminist, does not simply suggest further instances
of women turning themselves into sights to be beheld by the male
viewer.

What is difficult to follow is her contention that this longing in the consciousness of the (usually male) seer, which creates beauty in the (usually
female) object of the gaze, also constitutes the seen as subject. The most
extended example she gives is that of Ōigimi, who becomes painfully
aware of her own appearance after Kaoru has intruded on her and continued, despite her resistance, to pursue her. It seems that Field here equates
self-consciousness with subject status and agency, pointing out that
Kaoru's amorous gaze compels Ōigimi to look at the women around her
and at herself in a mirror and to draw disturbing comparisons.[32] One
could argue, echoing John Berger's polemics, that what Ōigimi sees is only
the reflection of what Kaoru sees. The figure of Ōigimi seems rather to
signify a woman's painful and not wholly successful internalization of her
own status as surveyed object (and surveyor of her own femininity) because she does not, on the other hand, look for herself desirously or ap-
praisingly at Kaoru.[33] Her response thus delineates a classic, but far from
revolutionary, moment in *Genji*. In this scene Ōigimi is "engendered" as a
heroine along the lines of so many other female figures who are forced to
recognize their own similarity (in the hero's eyes) to other women whom
the hero has already desired.[34] What makes her special, what marks her as
an object worthy of male regard, is also paradoxically her resemblance to
other special women before her, an interchangeability with them (at least
from the masculine perspective) that is itself perilously contingent on her
own youth and the whims and peculiar history of the man who gazes at

her. In short, what Ōigimi "sees" is herself as she is constituted in the eye
of the other. Her act of looking at herself in the mirror and in the faces of
the older women does not suggest a subjectivity through which she can
express her own desire. She still only plays object to subject Kaoru's objectifying gaze.

Yet Ōigimi's story, as Field so compellingly argues, will be to move
from this recognition of her deceptively special place in Kaoru's erotic
vision to create herself through self-annihilation, thus effectively removing herself from the objectifying gaze of her would-be lover. Ōigimi
stages her own disappearance through self-starvation and death. Field
understands Ōigimi's manipulation of her body, the mirrorlike surface
image onto which Kaoru projects his desire, as heralding the emergence
of an exaggeratedly feminine psychological depth, one that can only be
created at the cost of self-destruction. Needless to say, the feminine
subjectivity that the suicidal figure of Ōigimi exaggerates almost to the
point of parody embodies a fiction complicitous with traditional gender
ideologies. Yet it tugs at their seams. Ōigimi represents a heroine who
does finally translate what she sees (and hears) into action (if only the
self-destructive action of suicide).[35] But her story highlights a self-dis-
empowering quality in feminine agency, its despairing tendency toward
introversion. The ideological message of her tale is clear. Dire consequences await the woman who recognizes her conventional place (as ex-
changeable and interchangeable object) in the patriarchal economy of
Heian marriage arrangements. Field's reading demonstrates that Ōigimi's tale resists the conventional polarity between an active masculine
gaze and a passive feminine spectacle. But it also makes clear that Ōigimi's story offers little in the way of an alternative inscription of the play
of gender and desire. The final passages of Ōigimi's tale encompass a
description of her final face-to-face interview with Kaoru, in which she,
playing the resisting lady with her last ounce of strength, covers her face
and eyes with her sleeve, preventing both herself and Kaoru from fully
seeing. Removing the heroine from view (without, on the other hand,
establishing any alternative venue for the story of her own desire), her
tale aspires toward the blockage of all desire. In the process of resisting
masculine desire, feminine desire is left with no place to go.

So, is *The Tale of Genji* to be found in fact bereft of all traces of an
alternative to the fiction of the feminine as simply passive, erotic spectacle? I find a more promising demonstration of Field's assertion that the
Genji constitutes both seer and seen as subjects in her reading of the
scene in which Kaoru spies on Nakanokimi, Ōigimi, and their atten-

dants when the two sisters are in mourning, a *kaimami* scene that ironically exposes Kaoru's act of looking and in so doing lays bare the mechanisms of masculine voyeurism sentimentalized in the earlier chapters of the *Genji*. Field argues that it does this by deploying the gaze of the female characters. The first is a metaphorical one, represented by the verbally expressed viewpoint of one of the sisters' ladies-in-waiting who believes the two princesses are in no danger of being spied on by so pious a visitor as Kaoru. The female who actually engages in pleasurable looking is Nakanokimi, depicted as gazing out beyond the veranda at Kaoru's male attendants and finally turning back into the room, unwittingly giving Kaoru a full frontal view of her smiling face.[36] As Field puts it, Kaoru as viewer is "transfixed by the gaze of the viewed."

My understanding of the role of feminine agency in this scene differs somewhat from that of Field, who locates the gaze only at the level of the characters in the story, not the narration. In my view, the feminine gaze(s) within the scene (both Nakanokimi's actual peeping through the blinds and the metaphorical view of things represented by the lady-in-waiting who comments, "Oh, he wouldn't rush over for a peek") are blind. In fact, none of the characters who is party to the scene fully sees. Neither the women (who remain unaware they are being watched) nor even Kaoru fully "sees," because Kaoru remains blind to his own mixed motives and is himself, in Field's words, "peculiarly incorporated into the scene."[37] Ultimately both Kaoru and the women are mediated and enclosed by the ironic perspective of the narrating voice who reveals all of them to her by now self-consciously voyeuristic readers: Nakanokimi's undisguised pleasure in viewing Kaoru's attendants, the women in their mistaken vision of what Kaoru is capable of, Kaoru in his obliviousness to their disdain of him as amorous hero.

The two apparent voyeurs within the story (Nakanokimi looking at the men, Kaoru looking at the sisters) are each exposed in turn: Nakanokimi by the admiring Kaoru, and Kaoru, rather disadvantageously, by the elusive, feminine narrating perspective whose counterpart on the scene—the cavalier lady-in-waiting who comments on his boring propriety—has already debunked Kaoru as a hypocrite, given the voyeuristic role he actually plays. It is not that both seer and seen are constituted as subjects. Rather, both are constituted as objects in the "eye" of a narrating figure whose perspective governs the presentation of the scene to the voyeuristic implied reader. In its radical shifting between different points of view, the narration in the Uji chapters exposes the voyeuristic mechanisms idealized (and masked) by the steadier conflation of narrating perspective with the perspective of the male voyeur in less complex *kaimami* scenes. Given this constant shifting of perspective in the Uji chapters, the reader is denied the simple pleasure of identifying with the voyeur and is instead forced to watch him (and watch him critically, ironically) in the act of looking.

The voyeurism of reading itself—always implicit in earlier chapters— now becomes peculiarly marked by the cautionary example of Kaoru as viewed voyeur. Only the one who remains hidden retains power; to be exposed unwittingly is to lose power. If Kaoru and Niou emerge as lesser men than Genji, they do so in part because the narrating perspective has become less empathetic to their interests as would-be lovers. What emerges instead is criticism of the masculine gaze and the desire it signifies, both within the story (the ladies-in-waiting whose mistaken assumptions give the lie to Kaoru's otherwise scrupulous behavior) and within the narrative frame by means of the narrator's critical mediation of Kaoru's peeping. We do not merely see him seeing; we also watch while being relentlessly reminded of the voyeuristic nature of our own reading.

Not only is the passage not focalized simply through his perspective, but also the whole dynamic makes a subtle mockery of the privileges of gender and status with respect to the gaze. A middle-ranking feminine narrating perspective (properly deferential in terms of the honorific language she uses to describe the high-ranking characters' actions) nonetheless relates an image of the amorous hero as fool. At the very moment when a figure like Genji would be accorded a kind of narratorial romanticization of his lust, despite the suffering it might cause the women who are its objects, Kaoru and the hypocrisy of his behavior are held up, the unwitting object of a critical, middle-ranking feminine gaze. *Nyōbō sanbi* indeed!

We can speculate further on the "gaze" of the narrating figure and its relation to desire. Though the tales it presents are often enough stories about looking, getting, and keeping, the narratorial gaze in *Genji* exposes its object not in order to appropriate it but rather to interrogate it, while at the same time suggesting the complexity of looking and desire. The thrust of the narrative works constantly to guide the reader's attention elsewhere, both away from the feminine narrating voice and away from an exclusive focus on either the hero or the heroine. Attention shifts instead from one to another and back to the narration itself, so that the reader's gaze must encompass both seer and seen within the discursive context of storytelling. The philosophical seriousness of this project is masked by the terms and the apparent frivolity of the context (*monoga-tari*) in which it is embedded. The persona of the *Genji* narrator(s) is that of the gossip, and a gossip who increasingly shows less and less loyalty to the figures she reveals.[38]

I have been concerned that the preoccupation with *kaimami* in *Genji* has blinded us both to the role of other motifs of looking and to the way the *kaimami* motif itself is complicated by different generic contexts and by the fact that Heian women's narrations are marked by class and gender. Just because women were discouraged from exercising the gaze does not mean they did not use it, and not all feminine voyeurs in Heian women's writing can be categorized as simply passive, peripheral, admiring figures. Feminine figures who more actively appropriate the gaze are not foreign to—and may not even be unusual in—this tradition, and they do not do so only from the coyly evasive, half-hidden perspective of the feminine *monogatari* narrator-as-gossip.

Clearly, the issue of the gaze in *The Tale of Genji*, to say nothing of the larger tradition of Heian court women's writing, could easily occupy a book of its own. *The Pillow Book*, Sei Shōnagon's memoirs of life in attendance on Empress Teishi, provides a very different but equally rich sourcebook for exploring the topoi of looking and visual pleasure in this tradition. We turn to it now because it appears to be a text intensely interested in the articulation of a feminine gaze and of the desires and diversions created when a woman looks at others. It is not within the scope of this essay to give an overview of the many passages in *The Pillow Book* that raise questions about feminine looking and desire. The readings that follow are meant rather to suggest an alternative vantage point for further explorations of the poetics of voyeurism in Heian women's writings.

The Gaze Returned: Men and Narrative in *The Pillow Book*

As topoi in which acts of looking signify the play of desire, *nagame* (the brooding gaze) and *kaimami* (peeping through the fence) share an obvious one-sidedness. Granted, desire is free-floating and unfocused in the vacant staring of *nagame*, whereas it finds direction and a definite object in the *kaimami* scene. Yet both topoi connote anxieties about fulfillment and reciprocation. In both scenarios, desire remains unmet and unfulfilled. This feature renders them both highly appropriate as figures to preside over the inception of narratives. As Hayashida has pointed out, the *kaimami* topos frequently initiates love stories.[39] I would suggest that the *nagame* topos also operates as a figural means of beginning memoirs and memoirlike tales, especially those with an elegiac cast (*Sanuki no suke nikki, Kenreimon'in Ukyō no Daibu shū*, or "The Wizard" [*Maboroshi*] chapter of *Genji*). All these texts circulate around the problem of absent objects: dead or otherwise lost lovers or patrons, the blindness of grief or regret, and blocked desire.

In contrast, consider the trajectories of the gaze and its implications for plots of desire in the topos that folklorists identify as *maguhai*. Hayashida notes that the term *maguhai*, signifying marriage, is etymologically related to the homophonous term *maguhai/meguhai,* which denotes the locking or mutual exchange of gazes by a man and a woman.[40] If *nagame* and *kaimami* often initiate narratives that begin in dysphoria of one sort or another (desire aroused but unfulfilled), *maguhai* suggests itself as a ludic motif, a matching of gazes and agency, scenarios in which a character's object status in the eye of the other is coincident with his or her own accession to subject status. Looking at each other, both characters employ the gaze that signifies to each his or her own desire simultaneously. Each assumes the position of subject, and each plays object to the other at once. Gazes meet; figures both see and freely allow themselves to be seen in a condition of reciprocity that establishes an end to the game of hide-and-seek in which one subject's voyeuristic desire is expressed at the cost of the effacement or violation of the other's desire. The topos appears highly appropriate to narrative closure, especially euphoric closure. However, happy endings, like returned gazes and happy marriages, are rare in Heian women's narratives. In fact, closure itself, at least in forms recognizable to contemporary sensibilities, appears foreign to Heian narrative.

The Pillow Book offers no exception to the rule of paratactic sequences that resist closure, so common to Heian narrative. In fact, it outdoes other Heian tales and memoirs in the radicality of its parataxis. Yet it does so without engaging in the usual *monogatari* and *nikki* strategies for infinitely linking section to section. Long tales like *Utsuho* or *Genji* typically involve a tiny handful of heroes who move in and out of relations with dozens of heroines. Court women's memoirs, on the other hand, often use the device of a single female protagonist as a means of linking sometimes quite disparate kinds of passages and episodes. Seldom, however, do they portray the heroine as moving blithely (or otherwise) through a series of enticing men.[41]

When it comes to narratives about men, women, and desire, the memoir passages of *The Pillow Book* remain at odds with the strategies of both *nikki* and *monogatari*. Though these passages are full of men, perhaps none of them is especially Sei's man, though we might just as easily say that all of them are hers. And while the critic may talk about Sei's men and their relation to her as objects of her romantic interest or not, Sei does not often present herself as the object of their *erotic* interest, nor as particularly wanting to be. One of the consequences of this at the thematic level in *The Pillow Book* is the absence of conventional figures of femininity, especially the image of the heroine as passive recipient of transient, unstable masculine desire. This has long frustrated Sei's readers, who remain nonetheless indefatigable and undaunted. If she won't provide us with conventional plots of romantic intrigue, we will fill in the gaps in her nonnarratives so that they read like conventional tales anyway. Among the questions perennially asked by commentators on *The Pillow Book* is, Just who was Sei's greatest love? And which—if any—of the various men whom *The Pillow Book* describes was ever actually Sei's husband, and which were her lovers (and of these latter, which were the most important, as lovers or as patrons)?

These questions represent a time-honored scholarly pursuit, but one overemphasized in the study of female writers and perhaps underemphasized in the case of male writers. In some ways, such questions completely miss the point with a writer like Sei. Must we see her as having had a great love? We might revise the question and consider how the reader's desire to read Sei as a woman who secretly longed for one man in particular reflects the power of the convention that the heroine be defined by her relation to one especially compelling man. The resistance, in *The Pillow Book*, to outlining a conventionally plotted erotic itinerary moves hand in hand with the resistance to extended narrative. It may also concern the necessity of her self-censure on matters that were implicitly political. Here I am assuming, of course, that the question of who slept with whom was a political one at the Heian court.

One of the strategies most often adopted in trying to make sense of Sei as a writer has been to attach heightened significance to the silences in *The Pillow Book*. Typically it is assumed that Sei deliberately elided references to tragic events that formed the central, half-hidden mainsprings of her life, career, and text (for example, the inaccessibility of a particularly important lover or the erosion of her mistress Teishi's position as imperial favorite). Though not scholarly, author Ogino Ayako's popular study of the men in *The Pillow Book* spells out and pursues, with refreshingly unabashed directness, some of the implications of the more scholarly biographical speculations on Sei Shōnagon's (unhappy) love life. Thus Ogino concludes that the man Sei mentions least is probably also her "greatest love."[42] By her count, *The Pillow Book* contains eight passages concerning Fujiwara Tadanobu, five on Fujiwara Yukinari, with only three on Tachibana Norimitsu (b. 965), the man who is thought by some scholarly commentators to have been her erstwhile husband. The man least mentioned is the poet and courtier Fujiwara Sanekata (d. 998). There are only three passages on him, of which two are only one or two lines long. Sanekata's suitably tragic official career further qualifies him as Sei's secret favorite. According to one of the many legends recounted about him in other Heian texts, he was divested of his post as middle captain and sent off to become governor of Mutsu in 995 after publicly quarreling in the Courtiers' Hall at the imperial palace with none other than Sei's witty friend Fujiwara Yukinari (972–1028).[43] As noted above, there is the similar problem of her conspicuous silence about the tragedy of Empress Teishi's career, a feature that is singled out for special note by readers at least as early as the *Mumyōzōshi* (early thirteenth century).[44] I will return to the significance of Sei's "silences" on personal and political matters.

Despite readers' insistence on finding a one-man woman (or a servant whose adoration of Teishi approached the "pathological")[45] under Sei's mask of sophisticated connoisseurship, there is nonetheless an unspoken consensus on seeing her as very much the agent of her own passions, however much *The Pillow Book* masks those passions, at least where they concern specific men. Playing cultural arbiter, Sei certainly makes no bones about telling her reader precisely what sort of snow she prefers, or rain, or Buddhist priest. Why should she have treated the topic of lovers differently? No one imagines Sei desiring to be desired, like Michitsuna's mother or Takasue's daughter. The question that underlies all the other questions does do her some justice: Who was it she desired? That question is a fair one. Many of the few narratives included in this radically nonnarrative text are about men, or men in relation to women. One way to explore the innovations *The Pillow Book* makes in the old story of desire between court men and women is to examine its handling of the topoi of looking and gender in these passages.

Anecdotes and fantasies concerning encounters with men in *The Pillow Book* often work as anti-*monogatari* on various levels. Consider, for example, the figure of the *matsu onna*, literally, the "woman who waits" (for her errant lover), so ubiquitous in Heian tales and memoirs that it influences, as these essays have repeatedly suggested, the way readers perceive not only Heian fictional heroines but also Heian women writers. Again, the differences between *Genji* and *The Pillow Book* in their treatment of this figure are telling. One of the themes that gets underplayed in *The Tale of Genji* is that of male jealousy and female infidelity. How can any amorous Heian hero know who else may be visiting in his absence the woman who keeps her own room, her own secrets, her own existence separate from his in her own or her parents' mansion (even if—or perhaps especially because—that mansion is buried in weeds in an obscure corner of the city)? Sei picks up this thread, this twist in the skein of upper-class Heian sexual arrangements in her vignette about the lover peeking in on a woman whose lover has just left her and reflecting that another man may be spying at that very moment on the woman whose room he has himself just left.[46] Though the figure of the woman in the scene Sei paints toes the line of feminine propriety (she responds to the man but does not initiate anything), the dimly visible figure of the woman who wrote the passage itself is another matter. Her text powerfully suggests, if not the reversibility of erotic opportunities for men and women in Heian marriage, then the hand of a writer who can play with the seams of the polygynous system, exposing the looseness of it, the fictionality of the image—oppressively dominant in *Kagerō nikki*, idealized in *Genji*—of the upper-class woman as isolated and passive, cut off from any alternative to simply waiting for one man and that man only.

Contrary to what one might expect, Sei is also given to using herself as raw material for subversive deflations of cultural fictions about women. The reader who approaches *The Pillow Book* for the first time with Murasaki Shikibu's unflattering appraisal of Sei's conceitedness ringing in his or her ears may be surprised to find there are at least a few major areas in which Sei presents a markedly modest—even self-deprecating— version of herself. Significantly, one of the most conspicuous of these is the matter of her own physical appearance. Commentators have tended to take these passages at face value. Sei's references to her appearance are traditionally understood in the context of her greater age relative to Empress Teishi and the other ladies in attendance on her. Though Sei's birth and death dates remain unclear, it is speculated that she entered court service sometime in the early to mid-990s, after having been married and when she was already around age thirty, a late age to make a first appearance in court service. She would have been roughly ten years Teishi's senior.

Yet it seems possible that there is more afoot in these passages than
mere autobiographical exactitude. Sei's emphasis on her age and lack of
physical appeal suggests also a longing, in this writer of surfaces and exteriors, to transcend questions of appearance, especially narrow, corpo-
real standards for evaluating feminine appeal. *The Pillow Book* seems to
wish to establish other measures for judging women, or perhaps more to
the point, other measures for evaluating Sei Shōnagon. *Dan* (section)
79, regarding a meeting between Sei and Fujiwara Tadanobu (967–
1035), involves a rhetorical move that is characteristic of certain of Sei's
narratives about her relations with her male friends. The visual appeal
of Tadanobu's costume and bearing are detailed with an obvious delight
in the man as erotic spectacle, while Sei's self-description, by contrast,
deliberately short-circuits the convention of the heroine as desirable object. Calling attention to the potency of her appeal as a writer, Sei's
marked self-irony suggests a reverse snobbery about her own physical
appearance.

Though I was all a-flutter, I opened the top of the lattice door on the east fa-
cade of the Umetsubo and said, "Over here." How splendid he looked as he
approached. His figured, cherry-colored outer robe was brilliant, the lustrous
purity of its lining beyond description; his deep, dusty-lavender trousers were
wildly woven with a striking pattern of wisteria tendrils—its scarlet gloss just
glittered; layered severally beneath all of this, underrobes of white and pale lav-
ender. The veranda was narrow, so he sat with one foot touching the ground,
leaning close in against the lower end of the hanging blinds. It looked just like
one of the splendid episodes from the tales that they depict in paintings.
    The plum blossoms outside the palace—white ones on the west, red ones on
the east—were a bit past their peak but all the more charming for that, tran-
quilly glowing in the bright daylight. I longed to show it to someone. Inside the
blinds, it would have been even more picturesque had there been a young lady-
in-waiting with lustrous, flowing hair making her replies to him. Instead there
was this faded woman well past her prime whose hair, frayed and loose here
and there, looked as though it might not even be her own. (*SNKBT* 25: 94–95)

What Sei as an antiheroine does is even more compelling than how
she appears. Not only does she not look like a conventional heroine, but
she also doesn't act like one and delights in showing herself as quite capable of thwarting at will, and by her own design, the would-be amorous hero. Her description of encounters with Taira Narimasa (b. 950?)
during Empress Teishi's lying-in at his residence in Sanjō in 999 deploys
the feminine gaze with a directness that the author of *The Tale of Genji*

would not have dreamed of allowing her heroines (or herself as heroine of her own memoir).

The passage opens with a description of the arrival of Teishi and her women in carriages at Narimasa's residence. Four-pillared gates on private residences were normally only allowed to men of the second rank and above, and Narimasa, though a senior steward in the empress's household, was at this point only the governor of Tajima. He had been granted special allowance to build a four-pillared gate on the east side so that it would be large enough to accommodate the empress's carriage. But the north gate, through which the carriages of the ladies-in-waiting had to pass, was modest, in keeping with Narimasa's status. Sei is irritated; what sets the tone and terms for her verbal exchanges with Narimasa is the fact that the north gate to Narimasa's house is in fact so narrow that the carriages of the ladies-in-waiting cannot be drawn up adjacent to the house. Instead the women have to get out and walk across mats spread for them in the garden while being watched by a group of men: not only *tenjōbito* but also *jige*, gentlemen of lower rank—usually sixth rank or below. Sei is angry at being caught off guard and made to show herself when she is not prepared. The issue is decidedly that of appearances and what those appearances signify. Some of the women, Sei explains, "who hadn't done up their hair," chafed all the more at being caught in disarray because they had assumed they wouldn't be seen at all. The affront to the pride of the ladies-in-waiting is indicative of a more serious one that is *not* directly mentioned: Teishi should not have been lodged at Narimasa's residence at all, given her rank as empress and standing as Emperor Ichijō's (former) favorite. But her father has been dead since 995 and matters at the imperial palace increasingly under the sway of her uncle Michinaga, whose own daughter Shōshi is on her way to being Ichijō's unrivaled favorite. Sei will see to it that somebody be made to repay in kind—in this case, it will be Narimasa (even if readers clued into the political context may already suspect he is a paper tiger). If he has been insensitive to the empress's ladies-in-waiting, causing them to be seen at a disadvantage, Sei as "mistress of the chamber" (*tsubone aruji*), as Narimasa himself styles her later, will engineer his exposure twice over. Her strategies are both verbal and visual, and her tools the same ones theoretically available to her male opponent: ready wit, informed by intimidating references to Chinese literature, and the power of the gaze.

Having apprised the empress of her complaints against Narimasa and his gate, Sei determines to make him into a laughing-stock: *mieba wara-wamu* ("I'll have a laugh [at his expense] when he shows up"). And so she does, scolding him about the narrowness of his gate in a way that manages both to dazzle and entice him. She portrays Narimasa as taken aback by her erudition. At her allusion to an overweening official of the former Han dynasty he exclaims, "How frightening!" (*Ana osoroshi*), while the empress, noticing the speed of his retreat asks, "What's going on? Narimasa was so agitated" (*Nani goto ni zo, Narimasa ga imijiu ojitsuru*).

And yet somehow, in what seems to be testimony both to his foolishness and to Sei's charm, the exchange also inspires Narimasa to try pursuing the conversation with Sei in private later that night. The women have all gone to sleep, unaware that the sliding door on the north side of the western anteroom is missing its doorlatch. But Narimasa, as Sei wryly notes—"since he was master of the house, was well aware of this and opened it." As with the gate whose narrowness necessitated the women's exposed stroll from carriage to house, a certain inadequacy of architectural detail emerges again as metonymic evidence of Narimasa's shabby contrivances to have a peek at the empress's women. And again, architectural flaws point back to Narimasa's less than impressive rank and position.

"How would it be if I were to come in?" he repeated over and over in an oddly throaty, rasping voice. I started awake and looked, and there he was, plainly visible in the light of the lamp set up outside the curtain of state. He was speaking through the sliding door, which he had open about five inches. . . . I jostled awake the women next to me and said, "Look at him! Now this is something you don't see every day." Sitting up, they peered out at him and laughed heartily. "Who is that, standing there so boldly?" I asked.

"Oh—it's not what you think. As master of the house I have something to settle with the mistress of the chamber."

"I was speaking to you about your gate, but did I say anything about your opening the sliding door?"

"As a matter of fact, it is exactly the business of the gate that I would like to discuss. How would it be if I were to come over there?"

Laughing as she spoke, one of the women piped up, "How unseemly! No, he certainly cannot come in!"

"Ah—there are young women there with you." After he closed the door and left, how we laughed! Having opened the door, why didn't he just come in? But to beg permission?! Is there any woman who would say, "Oh, sure, come on in"? It was really so amusing! (*SNKBT* 25: 11–12)

The tropes of feminine looking in this passage work to expose, humiliate, and resist the amorous male. Sei deploys her own gaze, and enlists those of the women around her to undercut unwanted male attention and to make of the would-be hero fodder for amusing anecdotes. In this latter respect especially, her look suggests not simply resistance but mastery, and this not merely at the level of the individual scene or anecdote. The organization of the passage as a whole locates Empress Teishi as the third member of a triangle comprised of Sei as both provocateur and gossip, Teishi as wise but gentle listener (sometimes scolding Sei for giving Narimasa such a hard time), and Narimasa as the laughable "text" the women manipulate and judge. All of Sei's several anecdotes about Narimasa in this passage are framed or capped by the empress's response to Sei's narrations. Sei appears particularly focused on (and successful at) entertaining Teishi, and she does not hesitate to use Narimasa for this purpose, exposing his shortcomings as matter for the empress's amusement. For the reader who is pursuing the subtext of Teishi's tragic destiny, the anecdote also deftly underscores Teishi's grace under pressure. She deserved better than a lying-in at Narimasa's residence. Yet confronted with shabbiness and buffoonery at each turn, she remains a model of graciousness and *miyabi* (courtly elegance).

Was Sei also writing with the further edification of her male readers in mind? The almost didactic closing remarks on the incident quoted above ("But to beg permission?! Is there any woman who would say, 'Oh sure, come on in'?") mockingly highlight Narimasa's miserable failure to follow the code of courtly love, to take advantage of the prerogative of entrance and erotic possession the heroes of the *kaimami* scenes in *monogatari* conventionally win for themselves once they successfully steal a glimpse of the unsuspecting female. Not that *The Pillow Book* elsewhere details encounters between Sei and men that quite fit that code. Yet the closural reference to an opened door, and a sheepish man who beats a hasty retreat to the accompaniment of loud female laughter, recalls a very different but no less maverick playing out of the *kaimami* topos in a series of anecdotes concerning Sei and Fujiwara Yukinari, to which we now turn.

Dan 46 is one among several concerning Sei's encounters with the courtier and famous calligrapher Fujiwara Yukinari (972–1028).[47] It is especially rich in its varied use of the topoi of looking. Where Narimasa retreated under the humiliating gaze of Sei and the other ladies-in-waiting, Yukinari, having engaged Sei in protracted banter, inserts himself without waiting for an invitation. At least one commentator sees this as a perfect working out of the folk belief on which the *kaimami*

topos as inception of the love story is founded: the woman must accept
the amorous attentions of the man who succeeds in seeing her.[48] But a
closer look suggests that the scene is far more complex than that. Certainly the climax to this long passage about looking, deliberately not
looking, hiding, and deferred display seems to be a face-to-face meeting
with minimal barriers between Sei and Yukinari. But there the story
ends, at precisely the point where the love story initiated by *kaimami*
conventionally begins. But it does not end simply with Yukinari looking
at Sei. Sei also looks at Yukinari. In short, the passage closes on a mutually gratifying moment of reciprocal looking and self-revelation: the
ideal of *maguhai*, the returned gaze. What makes it both erotic and
amusing is everything that comes before this last look. The entire passage is laced with subsidiary scenes of spying and sallies of talk about
premeditated self-display. The passage as a whole traces an extended
foreplay of withheld gazes, while creating suspense about Yukinari's desire to look—a suspense that depends for its urgency on a gradual development of the image of both Yukinari and Sei as people who can see
the true value and nature of others despite appearances.

The story opens with Sei looking at Yukinari (presumably from a
vantage point that renders her invisible to him) as he "stands chatting
for a long time with a lady by the garden fence of the Empress's Office."
She then "advances" (*sashi idete*), though still remaining screened from
full view (possibly she merely advances to the edge of her chamber, remaining on her own side of the blinds or screens or both), and from this
remove demands to know the identity of the other woman. So begins
the rhythm of looking and talking that will structure the entire passage,
the narration enlivened by direct quotations of the dialogue—witty and
erudite—between Sei and Yukinari, a banter full of references to Chinese classics, that notorious feature of Sei's writing that Murasaki so
loathed. The impression that Sei has met her match (and Yukinari his) is
evident in the verbs used to describe their quotations from the classics.
Neither one outdoes the other: "he speaks with me" (or "his opinions
dovetail with mine," *iiawasetamaitsutsu*), and a kind of harmony develops between the two that excludes the disgruntled younger ladies-in-
waiting in Teishi's salon.

In content, the banter between Yukinari and Sei, as well as the remarks of Yukinari and the other ladies-in-waiting about one another,
revolve around the fraught relationship between external appearance
and interiority. Sei, of course (with her superior vision), holds the key to
these deeper realities. Her perceptions are set off by the contrasting

viewpoints and remarks (framed as self-serving and unflatteringly self-revealing) of the other ladies-in-waiting, while her own opinions are, as in so many other passages evaluating men in *The Pillow Book*, authorized and confirmed by those of Teishi, who always agrees with Sei regarding Yukinari:

Never making a show of his own appeal, Yukinari lets others take him as being simply what he appears to be, so that everyone knows only that about him. But since I have seen deeply into his heart, I would even say to the empress, "he is no ordinary man." And the empress recognized that herself. He and I were always saying to each other: "A woman makes up her face for the one who takes pleasure in her; a gentleman dies for the one who really understands him. . . . Yet the young women at court openly declare Yukinari particularly ugly. "What an ugly gentleman he is!" they say. "Why can't he recite poems and sutras like other people? He really is a bore." (*SNKBT* 25: 65)

The woman who would alter her appearance, and the scholar-gentleman who would sacrifice his life, each for the sake of the one who truly appreciates her or him—these figures represent a quotation from the *Shih chi* that reverses the order the lines follow in the original. Ivan Morris remarks that the reversal reflects the greater importance attached to relations between men and women over relations between a lord and his vassal in Heian society.[49] And so it may, or at least it suggests their greater importance in the world of Heian society according to Sei Shōnagon. But the misquotation also keeps in the forefront the linkage between facial exposure (and more precisely, a calculated, artful display of the female face) and pleasurable erotic encounter. The parallel line about the gentleman who will die for the sake of "the one who understands him" (*shiru mono/chih jen*) sets up implicit equivalences between knowing someone and taking pleasure in a woman, being willing to die for the true friend and knowing how to present one's face in answer to a lover's desire.

The preoccupation with appearances, deeper understanding, and desire gets elaborated to the point of parody in the lines that follow. As if in response to the younger ladies' sour judgment of his own ugliness, Yukinari remarks:

"You see, I could long for a woman even if she had eyes that turned up, eyebrows growing up all over her brow, and a nose that spread sideways, just so long as she has a charming mouth, an alluring chin and noble neck, and a voice that isn't unpleasant. Of course, it is depressing when a woman has an unattractive face." After that, the women—especially those with narrow chins and less than charming mouths—became remorselessly hostile to him and even spoke ill of him to the empress. (*SNKBT* 25: 65–66)

Yukinari singles out only a few features that are requisite for arousing his desire, all of them precisely those that a woman would ordinarily be able to keep hidden by a deft deployment of the fan or sleeve. As Hayashida points out, it is the brow that usually determined a woman's beauty.[50] Discounting those regarded as the benchmarks of feminine beauty (eyes, eyebrows, nose), Yukinari deliberately targets the features normally hidden—a ploy perhaps designed to provoke into self-disclosure any woman with illusions about her own below-brow loveliness. The ploy comically backfires; Yukinari's words make bitter enemies of the ladies-in-waiting—especially those who (at least according to the unkind Sei) are unattractive below the brow. And how, the reader has to wonder, did Sei herself measure up in all of this? We are left to imagine that she, "who has seen deeply into his true nature," sees through Yukinari's mock pontifications about a woman's appearance and understands it to be a ploy. Or else we are to guess that she is above concern because she, fulfilling Yukinari's below-brow requisites, has a good mouth, chin, neck, and a pleasant voice. Whatever the case (perhaps she wanted her reader to assume both), Sei would be the last person from whom we can expect the real story on her own appearance.

The subsequent lines demonstrate the mutual admiration society that develops between Sei and Yukinari as a function of Yukinari's reliance on Sei as a favorite messenger for his communications with the empress: a triangular arrangement typical of the memoir passages of *The Pillow Book* that highlights Sei's special position with regard to both Teishi and whatever man is in question. Yukinari returns to the issue of Sei's appearance. What next develops is a collusive game of reciprocal self-concealment by the two eccentrics, whose physical attractiveness, however, is now seriously in question. The younger ladies-in-waiting (though perhaps themselves long of chin and unlovely of mouth) have not refrained from expressing even to the empress their opinion that Yukinari is extremely ugly. Sei, for her part, is anxious to convince Yukinari that her hesitancy to show herself to him has everything to do with her fear that her face would place her in the category of those women whom he would be "incapable of loving" (*eomowaji*):

"Even with people saying that we are on intimate terms, if we talk together like this, what is there to be ashamed of? Come now, show yourself to me."

And in reply: "I would hate to do that, after what you said about 'not being able to love that kind of woman'—because of that, I just cannot."

And his rejoinder: "Is it really that bad? If that's the case, then please don't let me see you."

After that, even when he could have seen me, he covered his own face, and just when I thought he really wouldn't look, and had spoken with sincerity [*magokoro*] and not in jest [*soragoto*] . . . (*SNKBT* 25: 66–67)

Sei's reply is wonderfully two-pronged, allowing her to play the woman's part and coquettishly deny Yukinari a peek even as she informs him that she wants to be among the women he longs for. But her confession, so carefully calculated to whet male interest in her appearance, apparently backfires just as brilliantly as Yukinari's ploy to draw out the young women. His reply is in turn cleverer still and just as backhandedly flattering. He now avoids all opportunity to look but makes it clear he does so because he too would not wish Sei's unattractiveness to disqualify her from the category of women he could love. His strategy allows her to pretend he has put her off her guard while simultaneously preventing her from losing face on the issue of his desire to desire her. But of course his reply leaves provocatively unallayed the anxiety about appearances: their power to determine a woman's value and their power to mask the man's intentions and desires. Is Yukinari really serious in his fear that a less than lovely chin and mouth could destroy his delight in the likes of a figure like Sei, or is *magokoro* here really *soragoto*?

At this point, the reader is primed for the final anecdote with its dizzying array of complications concerning hiding, surreptitious spying, and self-display. The emperor and the empress surprise Sei and a fellow lady-in-waiting called Shikibu around daybreak but before the two women have properly had a chance to get up from sleep. The royal couple wants to hide in the ladies' chamber for the express purpose of spying on the courtiers who approach the women's blinds to banter with them. Once their majesties have exited, the women chat away, despite their promise to follow once they've "made up their faces." As they continue to sit and talk, both become aware of the silhouette of a man peering in on them through a screen near a sliding door in a corner of the room. Assuming it's only Noritaka, they are unfazed, an insouciance that suggests either the finely tuned rank- and class-bound limits of Heian conventions about the need for female modesty before men of lesser rank, or else a flouting of them on Sei's part. Apparently, the prurient gaze of some courtiers may be blithely ignored; but is this because of the man's rank or relation to the woman, or because the woman in question is the unabashedly indomitable Sei?[51]

But wait—a second glance at the peephole reveals not Noritaka's gaze, but the far more discomfiting gaze of Yukinari. When Yukinari then thrusts forward his own face, visibly beaming (*ito yoku emitarugao no sashiidetaru mo*) and revealing his identity as voyeur, he also reveals that he has witnessed not only the spectacle of the ladies themselves (with just the very sort of unmade-up morning faces he had come in hopes of glimpsing) but also the spectacle staged by the imperial couple with the ladies as decoys. The multilayered embedding of viewers and viewed becomes comically vertiginous at this point, food for laughter rather than for the darker passions of longing. It may be that one of the greatest contributions *The Pillow Book* makes to the Heian women's tradition is its linking of eroticism with humor and, most strikingly, feminine laughter and pleasure. How seldom women laugh in *Genji*! And when men are romantically involved with them, female laughter dies away completely.

We have come to the suspended closural moment in a delightfully extended game in which both Sei and Yukinari defer looking and showing in order to draw out the pleasure of verbal and visual teasing. The passage plays itself out as a contest of averted faces, talk of women with frightful brows but alluring mouths, men who die for the one who understands them, and above all, the center-staging of a singularly perceptive woman who agrees that "women make up their faces for those who take pleasure in them"—even as she artfully presents herself as having been caught in the final scene without makeup.

The erotic (which involves here a mutual recognition of the worthiness of the other as opponent) is emphatically a part of the image on which the passage closes. In the end, Yukinari raises the *sudare* over his shoulders and inserts the upper part of his body into the room—a classic gesture that in *monogatari* often heralds a sexual encounter. There is, of course, no doubt which of the two women is singled out by Yukinari's advances into the room. Shikibu, as Sei has already carefully noted for our information, "had been facing the other direction." Questions about the desirability of Sei's appeal, if not her appearance, seem happily resolved, since Yukinari now sticks his body in for a closer look. But what is at issue here is less his positive appraisal of her appearance than hers of his behavior. He is not treated with the disdain a man like Taira Narimasa wins under similar circumstances, and he is not resisted.[52] Yukinari follows a script Sei approves (and may well have simply invented). It is her approbation of him that we are finally shown. At the end of the passage, the two are poised for the moment of *maguhai*, a meeting and returning of gazes between the man and the woman, though the woman may further defer things by moving to hide her face:[53]

After the emperor and empress left, Shikibu and I were still sitting and talking over how magnificent they looked when we noticed there was something dark filling a slight gap in the hanging blinds just where they brushed up against the protruding handle of our curtain of state near the sliding door on the south side of the room. It seemed to be Noritaka, so we didn't look any closer and kept on talking about various things. Even when he thrust his face forward, absolutely beaming at us, I still thought it was Noritaka and glanced over only to find it wasn't his face at all. Astonished, we laughed and bustled about readjusting the curtain of state to hide ourselves—it was in fact Yukinari! How irksome after all the fuss about resolving not to let him see me. The lady with me had been facing the other way so her face couldn't be seen.

Standing up and moving further in he said, "What a perfect view I got!"

"I just ignored you because I thought you were Noritaka," I explained. "But why in the world, after all you said about determining not to look at me, did you stare so intently?"

"I've heard that the face of a woman who's just gotten up from sleep is especially beautiful. So I came, thinking I might be able to get such a glimpse if I went to peep at the chamber of a certain lady-in-waiting. You didn't realize it, but I was watching even while the emperor and empress were here."

Then it seems he put the blinds right over his shoulders. (SNKBT 25: 67–68)

Erotic desire between men and women becomes a game for skilled players on both sides in *The Pillow Book*, with the woman playing as active a role as her male counterpart. The irreversible, one-way desire of *kaimami* is only part of the story. Though the notion of voyeuristic peeping is everywhere in this passage, even coming to the surface in Yukinari's own explanation of his behavior to Shikibu and Sei ("I came, thinking I might be able to get such a glimpse if I went to peep at the chamber of a certain lady-in-waiting"), none of the multiple *kaimami* scenes is focalized through the gaze of the voyeur. Yukinari may have good reason to consider himself the voyeur par excellence (who watches not only Sei and Shikibu but also the courtiers being watched by them, who are in turn being watched by the emperor and empress, whom he also sees). But the real adept is Sei, who, though momentarily caught unaware of the identity of Yukinari as viewer, gets the last laugh and the last word by relating the scene for others to peruse in *The Pillow Book*. Voyeurs literally surround Sei, but the controlling gaze throughout remains firmly sited in the narrating voice, even as she speaks from the standpoint of a woman who plays the highly conscious object of others' gazing. The subjectivities of the apparent voyeurs (the imperial couple, the courtiers, Yukinari) remain subject to the (self-)disseminating gaze and discourse of Sei, who, as narrator, antiheroine, and memoirist "sees" (and shows to her reader) the entire scene.

Epilogue: Telling Details and Significant Silences

> A reader may be forgiven for thinking hers the only dry eye, or at least hers the only dry sleeve, in Heian Japan. . . . If Sei Shōnagon did not exist, there would be no one to invent her.
> —*The Princeton Companion to Classical Japanese Literature*

> So we have Sei Shōnagon, who left this world, bequeathing only her carefree laughter and ready wit on that splendid paper she received from Empress Teishi. *The Pillow Book* is truly, and through and through, the legacy in prose of "a skilled performance." How many tears of blood did she shed over its pages?—no one can sneak a peek inside the bamboo blinds of a thousand years ago.
> —Ogino Ayako, *Makura no sōshi: Sei Shōnagon o torimaku otokotachi*

Oppositional pairings, like that of *The Tale of Genji* and *The Pillow Book*, have much to tell about what is both feared and covertly desired by a readership. Not that we must choose one over the other or imagine that we cannot look beyond the limits and possibilities of the particular pairing of Murasaki and Sei when we think about Heian women writers. But what might the oscillation between the two signify? It is possible that Sei's reputation as a writer and as a woman obsessed with surfaces has won *The Pillow Book* its equivocally privileged place in the tradition of Heian women's writings, as that tradition is currently understood. At the head of the canon is *The Tale of Genji*. Memoirs like the *Kagerō nikki*, with its proto-*Genji* interest in the feminine as interiority, also stand out as masterpieces of women's literature (*joryū bungaku*). Sei's work, on the other hand, occupies an ambivalent spot in terms of both gender and genre, an ambiguity that testifies to its positive strengths as much as to its refusals and its silences. Sei has been regarded, particularly since the reappropriation of Heian court women's writings by scholars and Japanese women writers since the Meiji period, as having a narrower range than Murasaki as a writer. I suspect that this negative view of her range has much to do with her refusal to present herself (and other women) as surveyed, penetrable objects, and to offer instead (presumptuous) versions of herself as voyeur and cultural arbiter. Such tactics are bound to be called into question when they appear as the product of feminine agency.

Critical commonplaces about Sei's singularity as a woman and as a writer mirror the difficulties her text has always posed for those who would like to categorize it generically. We seem to believe we should be able to account for the extreme eccentricity of *The Pillow Book* on the grounds of Sei's extreme eccentricity as a woman, and vice versa. Let me be clearer about these terms. Sei's particular brand of singularity is not to be confused with marginality. There is little common ground, in this respect, between Sei Shōnagon as memoirist and the self-consciously marginal persona of Takasue's daughter in her memoir, the *Sarashina nikki*. Similarities in the biographical backgrounds of the two women serve only to underscore radical differences in their individual destinies as writers. Both women were born and brought up in the households of hereditary scholar-bureaucrats, one the daughter of a Kiyowara and the other the daughter of a Sugawara. Both made unremarkable matches in marriage, and in the long run, their marriages were of far less significance to their identities than their writings have been. Both came to serve as ladies-in-waiting at court relatively late in life, when they were already in their thirties. But there the similarities end. Two more different outlooks on (and memoirs about) court society, fictional tales, men, religion, and life could hardly be imagined, at least within the narrow compass of the Heian court context. Sei Shōnagon and *The Pillow Book* inscribe an eccentric, not simply a distanced, orbit from that which is central and normative in Heian cultural fictions about women and their writings. They go their own way around the center.

The Pillow Book achieves this in part by negative means, presenting an image of its author-narrator as antiheroine, a woman defined in terms of her defiance of convention. The other, more compelling face her text displays is that of the virtuoso, a woman who knows the codes so well she can run circles around everyone else, while she herself remains outside the game (and the text) as its mistress of ceremonies: hers is the only dry sleeve in Heian Japan. What we are shown of Sei in *The Pillow Book* is someone who makes an art of exposing as artifice what others would present as natural. If Sei had not existed, there would be no one to invent her, because no one could invent her so well as she invented herself. To play out the wonderful logic of the epigraph from the *Princeton Companion*, we should pause a moment to remember the Latin origins of the word *invent*: it comes from *invenire*, to come upon, to discover, to find. Because Sei positioned herself as self-textualizing subject, there have been many since who have tried to discover her in reading her book. Readers have repeatedly rediscovered and reinvented her because she once invented herself so ingeniously.

Speculating on the possible influences of the *Kagerō nikki* on the memoir passages of *The Pillow Book*, one scholar muses that Sei's memoirs, like Michitsuna's mother's, revolve around the relationship of a couple (the central "couple" being Sei and Empress Teishi).[54] Certainly the relation of Sei to Teishi, memoirist to mistress, evokes a far different tale than the woeful one of Michitsuna's mother with her husband, Kaneie. Creative as the comparison is, the remark bears serious consideration. Like the *Kagerō* author, Sei is in some sense writing against *monogatari*, but in a more powerful, less equivocal way than Michitsuna's mother did. It is not fictionality that she abhors so much as plottedness, or at least the unhappy plot type so favored by the *monogatari* tradition: a man pursues a woman, the woman surrenders, a brief period of happiness ensues until the man's affections attenuate, "wavering in an unforeseen direction," the man neglects the woman as his affections stray to another, the woman waits as his visits become less frequent, and the plot and the man move on. Nothing is closed or resolved; the story simply continues with a change of (female) personnel. What Sei refuses in refusing *monogatari* is a certain range of classic Heian feminine poses. The unplottedness of her text highlights the oppressiveness (as well as the artificiality) of the image of the high-born Heian woman as isolated and immobilized. What we are given instead is a wealth of bright details about things, a plurality of interested and interesting men, and glimpses of a stable, female couple—Sei and Teishi— around which all the details and the stories may once have coalesced. Announcing its heroine's own assertive possession of the gaze, *The Pillow Book* underlines what is perhaps obvious, but never so openly flaunted in other Heian court women's memoirs: the one who looks and talks about what she sees is a woman who is trying to imagine and to write alternative ways of seeing things.

The peroration of Ogino Ayako's essays on *The Pillow Book*, from which my second epigraph is drawn, sounds like an elegy for someone who is not simply gone from this world. Even Sei's physical death and distance from us in history are envisioned in terms of agency on Sei's part. Sei Shōnagon "left the world" (*yo o satta,* the language of a resolute religious ritual of turning away), and what she left behind in departing she left as a legacy—something she meant to pass on—the rec-

ord of her "skilled performances." How strongly sensed, in this characterization, is Sei's will. Her text is seen as the trace of her masterful improvisations; its author prepared for her own absence in advance by
writing herself. Begotten of Sei Shōnagon's social and material relation
to Teishi (that splendid paper that was Teishi's gift to Sei), *The Pillow
Book* remains as the scriptive testimony to a certain very calculated repertoire of poses, one that highlights the performer's wit and laughter.
What Sei leaves out of the account is what remains somehow inside it,
hidden by time and the cunning discursive devices of her day, bamboo
blinds from the last millennium. Was the laughter carefree and real? Or
was it a cover-up for the ubiquitous tears of blood, laughter's opposite,
which we seem so easily able to find everywhere else in Heian women's
writings?

In the daylight, bamboo blinds work to the advantage of those on the
inside who want to see out. In the dark, they are capable of betraying
the occupants of even the most dimly lit interiors to the probing gaze of
outsiders. Unfortunately, being in the dark and outside the bamboo
blinds of the Heian imperial court does would-be voyeurs little good in
this day and age. Contemporary readers of Heian women's writings will
always feel their own vantage point to be on the blind side. But being in
the dark has its own advantages at times. Readers can more easily see
what they wish to see in the opacity of a text. I am tempted to recall
Erich Auerbach's terminology for the pregnant silences in biblical narrative and to say that *The Pillow Book* is "fraught" with the evoked presence of everything it doesn't say.[55] But here again we run up against the
problem of eccentricity. What is central and normative to Sei's world, or
the world of the Heian court, has little to do with Greek antiquity or
ancient Israelite culture, whose own centers are elsewhere. What *The
Pillow Book* does make present is a plethora of surface details, the
world of objects that Auerbach associated with Homeric epic, the antithesis of biblical narrative.

Perhaps we should say that *The Pillow Book* externalizes and thereby
exoticizes interiority. What is seen and talked about—externalized as
discourse—always implies the inner springs moving the one who sees.
What is evoked, of course, is never proffered to full view. Nonetheless,
its presence—her presence as an enigma—is almost palpable. Sei's suffering, the extent to which she was a creature of her female body (how
many tears of blood?), an unwitting victim of the dominant fictions of
femininity ("moving, but without strength"), is what readers have felt
invited to imagine in all the welter of material detail.

Unquestionably, Sei Shōnagon's destiny was shaped by the political misfortunes of her mistress's family—misfortunes she is often understood to have expressed by means of "eloquent silence." What she doesn't say suggests loudly and clearly how deeply involved her world must have been in the dramatic social and political disasters suffered by Empress Teishi and her backers: the death of Teishi's father Michitaka in 995, the exile of her elder brothers, Korechika and Takaie, in 996, and most strikingly of all, the death of Teishi herself in childbirth a few years later—after witnessing her own eclipse as Emperor Ichijō's favorite by her younger cousin Shōshi. Like many other readers, Mark Morris notes the conspicuous absence of reference to the matter of Teishi's death in *The Pillow Book*, and he finds in it a possible motivation for Sei's "enterprise" as memoirist and list maker, a "recourse to language to preserve and communicate things and feelings now ruined for her in reality. Sei's [enterprise] . . . needs to be balanced against a persistent and eloquent silence, because even in the diary-like passages she only vaguely alludes to the passing of Michitaka, never to that of the woman around and through whom she had shaped not just a book but her very existence."[56]

Depth is conferred by the hint of things that are left hidden and unsaid. Such readings of *The Pillow Book* bespeak a tradition of interpretation at least as old as *Mumyōzōshi* (ca. 1196–1202):

It is in *The Pillow Book* that [Sei Shōnagon's] character comes out, and it is delightful. Leaving out nothing that was charming, full of pathos, impressive, or splendid, she wrote in minute detail about everything having to do with the magnificent flowering that was Empress Teishi's reign, yet it seems she was prudent to the point that she said nothing at all about the ruin brought on by the death of Michitaka and the exile of Korechika. Perhaps because she had lost her most reliable patrons, she went off to stay in the countryside with her wetnurse's daughter. Someone glimpsed her going out in the fields to dry some sort of greens and muttering to herself: "It's the figures wearing those court robes I cannot forget." She was wearing a plain robe and a headcloth of rags. So sad! Truly, how she must have longed for the past.[57]

Of course, one can justifiably argue Sei's silences away as a function of the manner in which her book may have been composed: on a day-to-day basis as things happened—not more or less retrospectively like the *Kagerō nikki*, the *Sarashina nikki*, or the *Sanuki no suke nikki*. One might also ask, given her apparent choice to eschew both *waka* and the narrative mode: Was she really so interested in preserving the past, or did her book not aim rather to preserve its author in the present and secure her future? In other words, to what extent was the writer, in her significant silences as well as in her flattery of men like Yukinari and Tadanobu, governed by the need to let go of the past and to solicit the patronage of the presently powerful?

Perhaps it isn't really so much the silence as the raucousness in *The Pillow Book* that has impelled its readers to acts of interpretation. Such lightness seems to require chastening—her readers won't let her get away with being simply happy. She was a woman, after all, and Tsura-yuki's vision of the poetry of women as "moving, and without strength" provides an important set of terms for the relation of Heian women as writers to canonical, dominant ideologies of the feminine. It also carries implications for their relation to the world of court politics, which the love poetry of the *Kokinshū* and the erotic plots of *monogatari* aestheti-cized, masking relations of power in the dysphoric rhetoric of courtly love. Given the ideological context (then and now, in different ways), it is no wonder that Murasaki Shikibu has recently been reinvented as a subtle spokeswoman whose narrative lays bare, with a critical and ironic eye, the inner workings of Fujiwara marriage politics and its psy-chological effects on the women who suffered as its more or less com-plicit victims. Heian culture valued sorrow because it was aesthetically pleasing, especially in women. We value it as a sign of intelligence. But if Murasaki and *The Tale of Genji* have long represented the favored half of the pair, the pair itself has always only inscribed a hierarchy within the already subordinate class of female writers. Sei Shōnagon and *The Pillow Book* represent the Other of the Other, the difference within the difference.

What has possessed us, her contemporary readers, that we should try to efface her distinctiveness (along with the subtler distinctions among other Heian women writers) by reading *The Pillow Book* as secretly the same old story of feminine suffering masked by an unusually bravado show of gallant silence? What if Sei was actually satisfied (or indifferent) in love? What if she took Teishi's eclipse in stride and didn't suffer in her old age, hopelessly lamenting the loss of the past? What if, instead, she spent her later years amusing herself (and gaining or cementing a comfortable pa-tronage relationship) by putting her delightful *Pillow Book* into (dis)-order? Can we handle so irreverent a departure from the fiction of Heian women's literature as an "aestheticization of suffering," so simple an im-age of the female writer as powerful, yet not particularly appropriative, in other words, someone who was more or less free and able as a writer to challenge the gender and genre codes of her day?

The question of what Sei Shōnagon and the other Heian women who left memoirs behind represents for us now is no less important than asking what they may have signified for readers throughout history. In some ways, the former question is the more pertinent. But the questions and their answers are not easily separated, and I am not suggesting that it would be fruitful to try. Critical commonplaces about Sei Shōnagon's appeal as a writer bring us up short, if we take them seriously at all. If she still speaks to us, it is at least in part because the limits and the possibilities that shaped her world still shape ours. Her place in literary history, her struggles and her contradictions, her details and her opacities, resemble ours because they have helped to form the basis on which we understand ourselves and our own world. This can only become more rather than less true as the boundaries of our different worlds—past and present, Japanese and non-Japanese, East and West, female and male, continue to be called into question.

Reference Matter

☞ Notes

Introduction

1. For a succinct discussion in English of the history and usage of *nikki* and related terms and forms, plus synopses of numerous individual Heian *nikki* by male and female practitioners of the genre, see Cranston, *Izumi Shikibu Diary*, pp. 90–125. The number of Japanese scholarly works devoted in whole or in substantial part to mapping the vague boundaries of the genre and its near neighbors in Heian *monogatari* (fictional or historical narrative prose in Japanese), *uta monogatari* (Japanese prose narratives centering on included poems or *uta*), and *shikashū* or *ie no shū* (poets' personal *waka* collections) is legion. A recent handbook on Heian court women's *nikki* edited by Akiyama Ken contains a useful annotated bibliography of these. See his *Ōchō joryū nikki hikkei*, pp. 176–93. Other important discussions in English concerning *nikki* and the problem of genre may be found in Miner, *Japanese Poetic Diaries*, pp. 3–20; Harries, trans., *Poetic Memoirs*, pp. 28–62; Bowring, *Murasaki Shikibu*, pp. 19–41; and Konishi, *Early Middle Ages*, pp. 251–394.

2. Michele Marra provides a concise, provocative discussion of the parallel (though differently motivated) construction of dichotomies between the discourse of the "literary/aesthetic" and the "political/historical" in both modern Western (post-Kantian) and early modern Japanese writers beginning with Motoori Norinaga (1730–1801). See his *Aesthetics of Discontent*, pp. 1–13.

3. This is most noticeable in the *Kagerō nikki* and the *Sarashina nikki*, where the relation between *monogatari* and *nikki* become explicit themes, but it is also apparent in texts like *Mumyōzōshi*, where fictional tales are analyzed in part on the basis of evaluations of individual figures—especially the male and female figures—around whom romantic plots evolve.

4. The phrase "image-repertoire of poses" is borrowed from Doane, who uses it in reference to a genre of Hollywood films consciously aimed at a primarily female audience. See *Desire to Desire*, p. 4.

5. For a thoroughgoing feminist reading of the relation between women's salon literature and the history of the French novel, see DeJean, *Tender Geographies*.

6. "The Tale of Genji." Murasaki's shadow graces the pages of *A Room of*

One's Own three years later as well, where the eleventh-century Japanese "nov-elist" becomes part of "the short and partial" history that is of only partial help to the aspiring female writer in 1929: "When [those early-nineteenth-century novelists] came to set their thoughts on paper . . . they had no tradition behind them, or one so short and partial that it was of little help. For we truly think back through our mothers if we are women." See Woolf, *A Room of One's Own*, p. 79.

7. The author of the *Kagerō nikki* was the daughter of the provincial gover-nor Fujiwara Tomoyasu (d. 977) but is remembered and usually identified as Michitsuna no haha, "the Mother of [Fujiwara] Michitsuna" (955–1020). Her own given name, like those of most Heian women writers, has not survived. Her dates are also uncertain but are guessed to be ca. 936–95. Her *nikki*, a work in three volumes, covers a period of some twenty years, from 954 to 974, and was probably completed within a few years after 974.

The *Sarashina nikki* was written by the daughter of the provincial governor Sugawara Takasue (ca. 973–?), and is known conventionally as Takasue no musume, "Takasue's Daughter." She is also identified as the niece of the *Ka-gerō* author. She was born around 1008, and her single-volume *nikki*, which covers a period of about forty years (ca. 1020–60), is thought to have been be-gun and completed not long after the last datable events recorded in the *nikki*: her husband's death in 1058. The date of her own death is not known.

8. The author of the *Sanuki no suke nikki*, Fujiwara Nagako (ca. 1079–after 1119), was the daughter of Fujiwara Akitsuna, the head of a client family (*kinshin*) of the imperial household. She served as assistant handmaid (*naishi no suke*) to two emperors, Horikawa (1079–1107) and his son Toba (1103–56). Her *nikki*, which survives in two volumes chronicling approximately two years in her life (her final months of attendance on Horikawa and her first year of service to Toba), is thought to have been completed sometime not long after 1108.

9. Sei Shōnagon's birth and death dates are unknown though guessed to be ca. 966–after 1017. She was the daughter of the poet and minor court official Kiyohara Motosuke (908–90) but made a name for herself during the last dec-ade of the tenth century as lady-in-waiting to Empress Teishi (976–1000) and later as the author of *The Pillow Book*. Her one-volume text, which concerns her experiences at court during the 990s, is not usually classified as a *nikki*. Though it contains many passages considered "*nikki*-like," many others, nota-bly the passages of lists that occupy a third of most recensions of the text, are unique to it. Sei Shōnagon was a near contemporary of Murasaki Shikibu (ca. 970–?), the author of *The Tale of Genji*, and lady-in-waiting to Teishi's young-er cousin and political rival, Empress Shōshi (988–1074). As early as the *Mu-myōzōshi* (ca. 1196–1202), these two talented ladies-in-waiting and their texts were being paired as contrasting exemplars of the heights that Japanese women had achieved as writers. The question as to which of the two can be considered the superior writer has been the subject of sporadic but persistent debate since at least the Meiji period. The two continue to be the best-known and most widely translated writers of Heian court literature.

10. The translation is Donald Keene's (*Essays in Idleness*, p. 20). See also *Tsurezuregusa*, pp. 108–9.

Chapter 1: The Staging of Feminine Self-Disclosure

1. Miyake, "*The Tosa Diary*," p. 42.

2. *Tosa nikki*, ed. Matsumura, *NKBZ* 9: 29. Two complete translations of the memoir in English are available: "The Tosa Diary," in Miner, *Japanese Poetic Diaries*, pp. 57–91; and "A Tosa Journal," in McCullough, ed., *Classical Japanese Prose*, pp. 73–102. An earlier version of McCullough's translation appears in her *Kokin Wakashū*, pp. 263–91.

3. For the specialist, less rigid versions of the story of Tsurayuki's "sources" for the female narrating persona of the *Tosa nikki*, including the possibility that Tsurayuki was aping the originally feminine genre of *nyōbō nikki* (memoirs by ladies-in-waiting), have also been debated. At issue is the ambiguous positionality of the *Tosa* narrating voice, which seems to speak from the viewpoint of a lady-in-waiting or former nurse in the Tosa governor's entourage. See Horiuchi, "Nikki kara nikki bungaku e," p. 10. It has been speculated on the basis of fragments of an early-tenth-century *kana nikki* quoted in the *Kakaishō* (a fourteenth-century commentary on *The Tale of Genji*) that one of the duties of ladies-in-waiting was the task of keeping records in Japanese prose on the doings of their mistresses. The fragment is from a record entitled *Taikō onki*, which seems to have contained daily entries centering on Fujiwara Onshi (872–907), empress to Emperor Daigo (897–930), and is thought to have been authored by one or several of her ladies-in-waiting. The term *nyōbō nikki* (memoirs by ladies-in-waiting) was coined by Miyazaki Sōhei to describe *Taikō onki*, and, more broadly, developments in later *kana* records written by women who served as ladies-in-waiting and wrote from the viewpoint of their positions as ladies-in-waiting. Those records are thought originally to have focused, not on the thoughts and doings of the writer herself, but rather on those of her mistress. Thus, according to Miyazaki's scheme, *The Pillow Book* (*Makura no sōshi*), and the *Murasaki Shikibu nikki* (the *Memoir of Murasaki Shikibu*) may be described as "descended from" the tradition of the *nyōbō nikki*. See Miyazaki, *Heian joryū nikki bungaku no kenkyū, zoku hen*, pp. 66–111.

4. For examples of interpretations of the feminine persona as a device allowing Tsurayuki paradoxically greater freedom for the expression of "self," see Hagitani, *Tosa nikki zenchūshaku*, p. 491, and Kimura, "Nikki bungaku no honshitsu," pp. 99–126. Implicit in these readings is the assumption that interiority and/or emotional expression is to be identified with the feminine and with writing in the mother tongue. Corollary to this is the idea that Tsurayuki's adoption of a feminine narrating persona for this memoir reinforces oppositions between writing in Japanese, the feminine, interiority, and the private self, on the one hand, and writing in Chinese, masculinity, and an external, public self or set of concerns, on the other.

5. See Miyake, "*The Tosa Diary*," pp. 41–73; and Butler, *Gender Trouble*.

6. *Kokinwakashū*, ed. Ozawa, *NKBZ* 7: 59 (my emphasis).

7. Although, as John Timothy Wixted has pointed out, disparagement of female poets was something of a convention already in the classical Chinese treatises on which both the *mana* (Chinese) and the *kana* (Japanese) prefaces to the *Kokinshū* drew in the interest of proving their own legitimacy as treatises on poetry. See "The *Kokinshū* Prefaces," p. 233. The trouble with literary conventions is that they often have roots in and effects on conditions in the extratextual world irrespective of the designs of the writers who manipulate them. Female poets were generally underrepresented in the imperially commissioned *waka* anthologies of the Heian period, and no woman was chosen to compile any of the imperial anthologies. Two centuries after the compilation of the *Kokinshū*, the fictional ladies of the *Mumyōzōshi* (ca. 1196–1202) are bitterly complaining about this and citing by contrast *The Tale of Genji*, *The Pillow Book*, and the genre of *monogatari* in general as a corpus of texts in which women had been able to come into their own despite their gender and gender-related lack of social status. See *SNKS* 7: 104–5. See also Marra, "*Mumyōzōshi*, Part 3," pp. 421–22.

8. For the first position, see Bowring, *The Tale of Genji*, pp. 11–12. For the second position, see R. Okada, *Figures of Resistance*, p. 14.

9. *NKBZ* 18: 238 and 244–45; see also Bowring, trans., *Her Diary and Poetic Memoirs*, pp. 131–33, 139.

10. *NKBZ* 14: 412. The translation is S, 519.

11. Hayashida, *Genji monogatari no hassō*, p. 240.

12. The *Utsuho monogatari* is a long, late-tenth-century narrative of uncertain (and probably composite) authorship, sometimes attributed to Minamoto Shitagō (d. 983). All citations refer to *Utsuho monogatari*, ed. Kōno, *NKBT* 10–12 (Iwanami shoten, 1959–60).

13. See *Ōkagami*, ed. Matsumura, *NKBT* 21: 174–75.

14. *NKBZ* 18: 238, 237; Bowring, *Her Diary and Poetic Memoirs*, pp. 131–33.

15. Notable among other post-Heian writers who participated in a philologically oriented nostalgia for the literature of the imperial court in its heyday is Yoshida Kenkō (ca. 1280–1352), whose miscellany, *Tsurezuregusa*, makes reference not only to *The Pillow Book*, but also to what are now considered far more obscure memoirs like the *Sanuki no suke nikki*. See *Tsurezuregusa*, ed. Nagazumi, *NKBZ* 27: 236; also Keene, *Essays in Idleness*, p. 156.

16. See *SNKS* 7: 109–11; and Marra, "*Mumyōzōshi*, Part 3," p. 424. *Mumyōshō* (after 1212), on the other hand, a collection of notes on poetry by Kamo no Chōmei (1153–1216), cites *Ōkagami* as an exemplary model of the *nikki* genre. *Ōkagami* (which modern scholars classify as a *rekishi monogatari* or "historical tale") is a prose narrative concerning the doings of important figures at the Heian court, written in *kana* but traditionally thought to be the work of a man. See *Mumyōshō*, ed. Hisamatsu, *NKBT* 65: 93; also Katō, "The *Mumyōshō* of Kamo no Chōmei," p. 420.

17. *NKBZ* 13: 368–69 and 377–81; S, 310–11 and 314–16. Morita Kane-

yoshi speculates that the inspiration for the triumph of Genji's illustrated *nikki* in "The Picture Contest" may be traced to the triumph of Toshikage's *nikki* in the scene from *Utsuho* described above. See his *"Utsuho monogatari ni ega-kareta nikki bungakuteki sakuhin,"* p. 45.

18. See "At Writing Practice" (*Tenarai*) and "The Floating Bridge of Dreams" (*Yume no ukihashi*) in *The Tale of Genji* and the discussion of Uki-fune's writerly accomplishments by Field, *The Splendor of Longing*, pp. 286–93.

19. *The Tale of Sagoromo*, ca. 1069–72, attributed to Saiin Baishi Naishin-nō no Senji (?1022–92), a lady-in-waiting to Princess Baishi (1039–96). See *Sa-goromo monogatari*, ed. Mitani and Sekine, *NKBT* 79: 456–62.

20. *NKBZ* 18: 195; Bowring, *Her Diary and Poetic Memoirs*, p. 83.

21. Of course, a number of these memoirists appear to have been commis-sioned by others to compile their accounts. The *Murasaki Shikibu nikki* is thought to have been at least begun in response to Fujiwara Michinaga's re-quest that an account be written of his daughter Empress Shōshi's lying-in and the birth of her first son.

22. It is on this point that my understanding of distinctions between mid-Heian women's *nikki* and *monogatari* echoes, albeit distantly, those proposed for *kana nikki* and *monogatari* by Konishi in *The Early Middle Ages,* chap. 8. At issue here is Konishi's stress on differences in content between *monogatari* and *nikki*. For Konishi, the *kana nikki* can be characterized by its tendency to concentrate on a single protagonist, regardless of whether that protagonist is considered to be an image of the author or of someone else. *Monogatari*, on the other hand, typically involve a more complex personnel: "The subject of a *nikki*, then, is a kind of 'real event,' the life and experiences of a historical indi-vidual; in this respect *nikki* narrative differs from *waka* narrative (*uta monoga-tari*). The difference between the *monogatari* and the *nikki* is not so much one of fiction versus nonfiction; rather, the criterion is whether the narration is con-cerned with a single protagonist." See Konishi, *Early Middle Ages*, p. 252.

23. Mayne, *Woman at the Keyhole*, p. 9.

24. Bowring, *Tale of Genji*, p. 16.

25. Bowring, *Tale of Genji*, p. 13. As Miyake suggests, it is precisely this motif of the *matsu onna* (the woman who waits)—a conventional pose in court women's *waka*, and a common figure in *monogatari*—on which Bowring's gen-eralizations run amok: "Bowring appropriates woman's literary self-representa-tion as a *matsu onna*, conflates it with her role in society and history, and des-ignates it as the entire representation of woman." See her "Review of *Murasaki Shikibu*," p. 351.

26. Following the work of Tania Modleski, Janice Radway, and others on soap opera and contemporary Gothic and Harlequin romances, Mark Morris makes this same point to great effect, though he places particular emphasis on the voyeurism of the implied (female) audience of *Genji monogatari* when he asks "what such furtive voyeurism is doing in a text written by a woman osten-sibly for other women. . . . The crucial act of voyeurism involved in *Genji* is that of the reader, an ambiguous type of identification facilitated by shifting

subjective points of view and response." See his "Desire and the Prince," p. 302.

27. Bowring, *Tale of Genji*, p. 12 (emphasis mine).

28. *NKBZ* 12: 142; S, 25 and *NKBZ* 14: 207; S, 438–39.

29. In the latter case, see, for example, the memoirist's complaints that Michinaga, stole her copy of *Genji* and passed it on to his second daughter, Kenshi (*NKBZ* 18: 205; Bowring, *Her Diary and Poetic Memoirs*, p. 95); also Emperor Ichijō's approbative remarks on Murasaki's erudition after hearing the *Genji* read aloud to him (*NKBZ* 18: 244; Bowring, *Her Diary and Poetic Memoirs*, p. 137).

30. Mayne, *Woman at the Keyhole*, p. 9. Recent volumes compiled by members of the Monogatari Kenkyūkai, especially the collection on "lines of sight in *monogatari*," contain essays that approach the problem from precisely this direction. See especially the essay by Mitani Kuniaki, "Monogatari bungaku no 'shisen,'" pp. 89–108. Takahashi Tōru's study of narrating perspective in *Genji* as analogous to that of a possessing spirit (*mononoke*) captures the shifting, elusive, alternately transcendent and immanent positionality of the narrating voice/gaze in that work, but as a critical model for the *Genji* narration, it emphasizes issues of focalization, free indirect discourse, and the postmodern deconstruction of the subject rather than strictly feminist readings of aspects of gender. See his *Monogatari to e no enkinhō*, especially chap. 3.

Chapter 2: The Engendering of the Heroine

1. No *shahon* (handwritten copies) survive from the Heian or Kamakura periods. The earliest more or less complete version of the text that survives dates from the reign of Emperor Reigen (1663–87). For rigorous scholarly discussions of the textual history of the *Kagerō nikki*, I have found helpful Ishihara Shōhei, "Kagerō nikki: shuyō kenkyū bunken annai" and Kakimoto Tsutomu, "Kagerō nikki no denbon to shomei." Uemura Etsuko's foreword to her nine-volume compendium of commentaries on the *Kagerō nikki* is briefer but more evocative of the quixotic nature of the quest to reconstruct (in some places create) a scholarly edition of this Heian classic. See Uemura, *Kagerō nikki kaishaku taisei*, 1: 1–6.

2. *NKBZ* 12: 134. My translation of this remark follows the definition of the adjectival *kikinikushi* given in a standard classical Japanese dictionary: "*Kiita kanji ga yoku nai*." See Ono Susumu et al., eds., *Kogo jiten*, p. 355. Tamagami Takuya translates it similarly as *kikigurushii koto* (things that are unpleasant or vexing to hear). See his *Genji monogatari hyōshaku*, 1: 174. The *NKBZ* editors are a bit more specific about just exactly what variety of unpleasantness was involved, identifying these "things" as *mittomonai hanashi* (indecent, disgraceful, disreputable, even scandalous stories). See *NKBZ* 12: 134, n. 16. Seidensticker's translation is perhaps the most interpretive of all, contributing to a rather vivid characterization of the narrator: "The discussion progressed, and included *a number of rather unconvincing points*" (S, 23).

3. The term in Japanese is *uchi no onmonoimi*, which involved, among other things, a temporary abstinence from sexual relations. No wonder the gentlemen were so busy *talking* about women. The fifth month, the rainy season under the Heian lunar calendar, sets the stage for at least two other important classical discussions of romantic relations between men and women and the tales that specialized in that topic: the dialogue on *monogatari* (*monogatari ron*) in the "Fireflies" (*Hotaru*) chapter of *Genji* and *Mumyōzōshi*, the early-thirteenth-century fictional dialogue on *monogatari* and women, attributed to the daughter of Fujiwara Shunzei (ca. 1171–after 1252). For further discussion of the literary significance of the fifth month and folk beliefs associated with it, see the discussion in Chapter 5.

4. *Kagerō nikki*, ed. Kimura, NKBZ 9. All translations are mine unless otherwise noted. For complete English translations of the text, see Seidensticker, trans., *The Gossamer Years*, and Sonya Arntzen, trans., *The Kagerō Diary*. See also H. McCullough, trans., "The Gossamer Journal," in H. McCullough, ed., *Classical Japanese Literature*, pp. 102–55, for her translation of the first volume of the *Kagerō nikki*.

5. The suggestion that the *Genji* author was alluding to the *Kagerō nikki* in the guards' officer's speech has been made by the editors of the NKBZ edition of *Genji*, among others. See NKBZ 12: 143, n. 21.

6. For a detailed account in English of the conventions (and lack thereof) surrounding Heian marriage and housing arrangements, see W. McCullough, "Japanese Marriage Institutions in the Heian Period," pp. 103–67, and Nickerson, "Meaning of Matrilocality," pp. 429–67.

7. There are three other wives of Kaneie mentioned in the memoir. The first is the woman who lived near Machi no kōji (*Machi no kōji no onna*), an unrecognized daughter of an unrecognized imperial prince, whose only child by Kaneie dies young (a fact that is cause for rejoicing in the heroine's household). See NKBZ 9: 150. Also mentioned is the daughter of another provincial governor, Fujiwara Kuniaki, identified in the memoir as "the Ōmi woman." And, finally, there is the daughter of Fujiwara Kanetada, mother of the girl the *Kagerō* memoirist records adopting.

8. See NKBZ 9: 311.

9. Early in this century the so-called *Narutaki komori* ("Seclusion at Narutaki") became the focus of scholarly debates on the "formation" (*keiseiron*) of the memoir. Following in the footsteps of the Meiji critic Fujioka Sakutarō, Kita Yoshio speculated that the memoirist's retreat to and return from Narutaki was the event that precipitated her writing of the memoir. Arguing that she began and completed volumes one and two soon after her return from Narutaki, Kita's theory was for many years influential, although it was challenged by equally influential scholars like Ikeda Kikan and Oka Kazuo, who believed the entire *nikki* to have been written in retrospect sometime after 975, when the last datable events recorded in the third and final volume took place. See Ishihara, "*Kagerō nikki*: shuyō kenkyū bunken annai," pp. 175–79. Uemura Etsuko, in her authoritative *Kagerō nikki no kenkyū*, summed up scholarship on the dat-

ing of the three volumes as generally divided between two groups: those who believed the entire text was written retrospectively (Ikeda, Oka, Imai Gen'e), and those who posited that only the first volume was compiled and written retrospectively, with the second and third written from a standpoint more or less close in time to the events themselves. The current consensus seems to be that each of the three volumes was composed at a separate time, with the second (containing the account of the seclusion at Narutaki) thought to have been written soon after the memoirist's return from Narutaki, during the fall of 971, or between the end of that year and the early months of 972. See Moriya, "*Kagerō nikki*," pp. 36–37.

10. Oka, *Michitsuna no haha*, p. 5. Oka pointed out that the first volume, with its preponderance of poetic exchanges, is stylistically similar to *kashū*, or personal poetry collections, and the third volume, with its concentration on the romantic fortunes of the memoirist's son and adopted daughter, resembles *monogatari*. These observations continue to exert influence on the directions of *Kagerō nikki* scholarship.

11. *NKBZ* 9: 257–84.

12. For example, *Man'yōshū* 1809, a poem on the Unai maiden theme, attributed to Takahashi Mushimaro, relates one of these. See *Man'yōshū*, ed. Kojima, *NKBZ* 3: 440–42. Episode 147 of *Yamato monogatari* provides a similar suicide tale that was probably known to the *Kagerō* author. See *Yamato monogatari*, ed. Takahashi, *NKBZ* 8: 382–88. It would be left to Murasaki Shikibu, in the Uji chapters of *Genji* (especially the tale of Ukifune), to explore the theme of female suicide with the subtle instrument of the long *monogatari*.

13. Connections between Kintō and the memoirist's own family no doubt played some part in that poet's enduring appreciation of Michitsuna's mother. Her younger brother, Nagayoshi (946?–1017?; also pronounced Nagatō), a noted poet in his own right, was associated as a poet with both Kintō and Nōin. Some commentators speculate that it was Nagayoshi who compiled the memoirist's *kashū*, a private collection of about fifty *waka* appended to some redactions of the memoir.

14. To mention only the most prominent of these, there were five of her *waka* included in *Jidai fudō utaawase* (compiled by GoToba'in [r. 1183/4–98]), and three in *Nyōbō sanjūrokunin utaawase* (compiled between 1272 and 1278). Both Fujiwara Shunzei (1114–1204) and his son Teika (1162–1241), arbiters of poetic style in the late Heian and early Kamakura period, acknowledge her famous "Nagekitsutsu" poem by including it in their collections of exemplary poems, *Korai fūteishō* (compiled by Shunzei, 1197), *Hyakunin isshu* (compiled by Teika, ca. 1235), and *Hyakunin shūka* (also by Teika, ca. 1229–36).

15. Uemura, "Michitsuna no haha," pp. 216–19.

16. *Ōkagami*, ed. Matsumura, *NKBT* 21: 174–75. The translation is by H. McCullough, *Ōkagami*, p. 166.

17. See for example Murai, *Kagerō nikki zenhyōshaku*, p. 81.

18. Moriya's remarks are representative: "Her poetic style, reflecting per-

haps someone who possessed an extreme degree of fastidiousness, reveals an austere moralistic sincerity." See his entry "Michitsuna no haha," p. 945.

19. Sansom, *A History of Japan to 1334*, chap. 9, "The Rule of Taste."

20. She goes on, interestingly enough, to touch on the works two contemporary male authors succeeded in making out of their readings of the *Kagerō nikki*: Hori Tatsuo's *Kagerō no nikki* and *Hototogisu*, and Murō Saisei's *Kagerō nikki ibun*. Though Enchi does not develop the argument herself, it seems worth noting that her metaphors imply that female novelists (like herself), whose relation to their novels "has often been characterized by the image of the umbilical cord" (*heso no himo*) connecting mother to unborn child, do not make novels out of other (women's) novels, but only out of themselves. See Enchi, "Ōchō josei bungaku to gendai bungaku," pp. 209–10.

21. Setouchi, *Watashi no suki na koten no onnatachi*, pp. 69, 71.

22. The most virulent I have run across are those of Tamagami Takuya, quoted in part by Nomura Seiichi in a relatively recent collection of general essays on Heian women's *nikki*. Tamagami's diatribes, developed over the course of several essays and articles, feature dismissals of the *Kagerō nikki* as "something the author probably undertook with little or no idea of what she was doing," and "the chatter of a woman who just won't stop chattering once she gets started." See Nomura, "*Kagerō nikki*: hyōgen no ronri," pp. 37–45, especially pp. 40–42.

23. Prefaces written in the third person are common in the personal poetry collections (*shikashū*) of the day and are related to the *kotobagaki* or prose headnotes of poetic anthologies in general, including the imperially commissioned anthologies (*chokusenshū*). It should also be noted that the preface is not the only place where the *Kagerō* narrator uses the third person to refer to the protagonist. See Konishi, *Early Middle Ages*, pp. 288–94, for an account in English of the equivocation between first- and third-person "point of view" in the *Kagerō nikki* and other late-tenth-century texts. For a close reading of the preface and the opening poetic exchanges that follow it, with emphasis on their relations to those of contemporary *shikashū*, see Ishihara, "*Kagerō nikki no hassō*," pp. 277–96.

24. Compare the *Ise monogatari*: "there was a man" (*otoko arikeri*) and the *Taketori monogatari*: "there was a person called the 'Old Bamboo Cutter'" (*Taketori no okina to iu mono arikeri*). See *Taketori monogatari, Ise monogatari, Yamato monogatari, Heichū monogatari*, ed. Katagiri et al., NKBZ 8: 134, 51.

25. Kimura notes that the opening passage of the *Kagerō nikki* differentiates itself from the opening tropes of contemporary *monogatari* by focusing on the interiority of the central figure in the narrative rather than on genealogy or other "external" biographical details. See his "*Izumi Shikibu nikki* keisei ron," p. 242.

26. Matsuhara Kazuyoshi speculates that the first volume of the *Kagerō nikki* was composed around 974 with the memoirist's adopted daughter in mind as a reader, and the *nikki* as a whole completed about 990 with her granddaughter Hōshi as intended reader. See "*Kagerō nikki* no tenkai to keisei," pp. 109–20.

27. Or it was written at least after the completion of the first volume of the *nikki*. On the question of dating the *Kagerō* preface, see Ishihara, "*Kagerō nikki* no hassō," pp. 282–86.

28. All the major extant *monogatari* predating or roughly contemporary to the *Kagerō nikki* (the *Taketori monogatari*, the *Ochikubo monogatari*, the *Utsuho monogatari*) are considered to have been written by men. In the case of the *Ise monogatari* and the *Yamato monogatari*, which are understood as works by several hands, the gender of their creators remains a subject of debate. The rise of *monogatari* and *nikki* by women is considered largely a late-tenth- and early-eleventh-century phenomenon.

29. *Heianchō nikki no kenkyū*, p. 105.

30. The Cinderella plot of the *Ochikubo monogatari* has often been cited in this regard, but Masuda singles out the example of Emperor Daigo's (r. 897–930) mother, whose "success story" is recounted in *Konjaku monogatarishū*. See *NKBZ* 23: 192–202. He also notes that the career of Tokihime, Kaneie's principal wife and the *Kagerō* author's longest-standing and most successful rival, is another case in point. As already mentioned, Tokihime, though slightly better off on her mother's side than the *Kagerō* author was, began as a daughter of the provincial-governor class but saw her own daughters married to emperors. Her eldest, Chōshi, bore to former Emperor Reizei a son who became Emperor Sanjō; a second daughter, Senshi, bore to Emperor En'yū a son who became Emperor Ichijō. As mother to an emperor, Senshi herself went on to become a figure of considerable political influence. See Masuda, *Kagerō nikki sakusha*, pp. 16, 73–84.

31. *That* story will be left to her niece, the daughter of Sugawara Takasue, to explore in the *Sarashina nikki*. See Chapters 3 and 4.

32. The poem reads in its entirety:

Nagekitsutsu	Weeping and weeping
hitori nuru yo no	through the nights I lie alone
akuru ma wa	waiting till dawn breaks;
ika ni hisashiki	have you any idea
mono to ka wa shiru	how long a time that is?
	(*NKBZ* 9: 136)

33. Enchi, "Ōchō josei bungaku to gendai bungaku," p. 209.

34. Fujii Sadakazu speculates that since *sukigoto* carries a nuance of mendacity, the narrator mentions them in the opening line of the *nikki* in order to hint that she never expected that Kaneie's early correspondence would materialize into anything more than a dalliance, something that eventually would have been either dropped or properly pursued through a female go-between. See his "*Kagerō nikki* to Heianchō no kon'in seido," pp. 173–74.

35. One hundred and twenty-three *waka* are quoted in volume one. In addition, the volume includes two *chōka* (long songs) and one *renga* (linked poem). Only four of the *waka* are quoted as *dokuei* (poems composed in solitude). The second volume, by contrast, includes only fifty-five poems (including one *chōka*

and one *renga*), with sixteen of them *dokuei*. The third and last volume of the memoir contains eighty poems, all of them *waka*, and most of them exchanged between Michitsuna and two women with whom he was corresponding. See Uemura, "Michitsuna no haha," p. 212.

36. *Ōkagami*, ed. Matsumura, *NKBT* 21: 96. The translation is by H. McCullough, *Ōkagami*, p. 115.

37. Frye, *Anatomy of Criticism*, p. 271.

38. For a meticulous examination and analysis of Chinese sources for both Tsurayuki's *Kanajo* and Yoshimochi's *Manajo* (preface to the *Kokinshū* written in Chinese), see Wixted, "Chinese Influences," pp. 387–400. For a discussion of the tradition of classical Chinese poetics that is sensitive to tensions between the assumptions modern English-speaking readers bring to the reading and translation of Chinese poetry and the assumptions hinted at in classical Chinese essays and statements on poetics, see Owen, *Traditional Chinese Poetry and Poetics*, pp. 54–77.

39. *Kokinwakashū*, ed. Ozawa, *NKBZ* 7: 49.

40. Wixted, "Chinese Influences," p. 400.

41. M. Morris, "Waka and Form, Waka and History," p. 555.

42. Recent books by Marra and R. Okada pursue the pragmatic and political contexts of *waka* aesthetics and praxis. See Marra, *The Aesthetics of Discontent*, and Okada, *Figures of Resistance*.

43. The line appears in the famous letter to Izambard (the "lettre du voyant"): "C'est faux de dire: Je pense: on devrait dire on me pense.—Pardon du jeu de mots." (It's false to say: I think: one should say I am thought.—Pardon the play on words.) Rimbaud, *Poésies, Une saison en enfer, Illuminations*, p. 200.

44. The *Eiga monogatari* (completed ca. 1092) is a long narrative treating historical figures and events from the reign of Emperor Uda (887–97) to Emperor Horikawa (1086–1107). The bulk of the tale is attributed by some to Akazome Emon (fl. ca. 976–1041), a contemporary of Murasaki Shikibu, who also served as a lady-in-waiting to Murasaki's mistress Empress Shōshi.

45. *Kokinwakashū*, ed. Ozawa, *NKBZ* 7: 49.

46. Uemura, ed., *Kagerō nikki kaishaku taisei*, 2: 587. Following up on related work by Yamaguchi Hiroshi and Moriya Shōgo, Joshua Mostow takes this line of thinking a step further. He argues that the *Kagerō nikki* may be fruitfully read as the product, at least in part, of its author's having been commissioned to produce a work commemorating Kaneie as a *sukibito* or ladies' man, since the ideal of the skilled lover was, given the importance of a politically ambitious courtier's marital connections, a crucial element in Heian notions of the politically successful nobleman. See his "The Amorous Statesman and the Poetess," pp. 305–15. Moriya Shōgo surveys earlier personal poetry collections to find evidence of the image of the *sukibito* as organizing principle in works antedating the *Kagerō nikki*. See his "*Kagerō nikki* zenshi," pp. 43–61.

47. Mitani Kuniaki notes of this episode that it reads like "a kind of parable on the power of *waka*." See his "*Kagerō nikki* no jikan ishiki," p. 222.

48. There is a theory that during this period (964), Kaneie was visiting the daughter of Fujiwara Tadamoto, who became the mother of his fourth son, Michiyoshi. See Kimura, *NKBZ* 9: 164, n. 3.

49. Kaneie responds in kind with an answering *chōka*, but as Nishihara Kazuo notes, it is quite possible that both poems were written by the memoirist and inserted into the *nikki* retrospectively at the time she composed the first volume as a whole. See Uemura, *Kagerō nikki kaishaku taisei*, 1: 389.

50. Commentators writing in English have criticized the *Kagerō* memoirist (as they did Jane Austen for her unconscionable failure to discuss the French Revolution) for a deplorable indifference to Kaneie's political career. See especially Seidensticker, *Gossamer Years*, pp. 14–16. I would argue, on the contrary, that her memoir suggests she was well aware of the ups and downs of his life at court, at least insofar as those changes influenced the frequency of his visits to her. For example, the passage referred to here begins with this line: "His years as Shōnagon passed, and since he was promoted to Fourth Rank . . ." (*NKBZ* 9: 156). As to her apparent inattention to events at court, why should she (how could she?) have written interestingly about them? It was a world from which she was effectively barred by her gender and her private lifestyle. More pertinently, we need to question the questioner and ask why a Fujiwara woman's preoccupation with the frequency of her husband's visits should be viewed as having nothing to do with politics. Presumably the frequency of Kaneie's visits with Tokihime contributed in large measure to the latter's success as a bearer of politically useful sons and daughters.

51. Chōshi (d. 982) was the eldest daughter of Kaneie and Tokihime.

52. Perhaps this is because the differences in status were becoming so marked as to place Tokihime out of reach. See Masuda, *Udaishō Michitsuna no haha*, p. 84.

53. On the vested interests of ladies-in-waiting in the success of their mistress's marital ties, and the exploitation of this theme in *Genji*, see Akiyama, "Nyōbōtachi," pp. 450–63. *The Tale of Genji* elaborates further on the technique of contrasting the mistress's viewpoint and aspirations with those of her household women. As Haruo Shirane notes in a discussion of the "fallen princess" episodes in *Genji*, "The *nyōbō* are more materially oriented than their mistresses and tend to view the suitor as an indispensable source of social and financial support. The struggle that emerges between the woman and her *nyōbō* . . . becomes a manifestation of the larger conflict between the woman's personal concerns and the pressures of the external world." See his *Bridge of Dreams*, p. 145. One should also note that *nyōbō* often had their own personal interests at stake as well; subplots involving erotic liaisons between a woman's female attendants and men in her husband's or lover's entourage are common. Consider Koremitsu (Genji's wet nurse's son) with Ukon (Yūgao's wet nurse's daughter) in the "Evening Faces" (*Yūgao*) chapter of *The Tale of Genji*.

54. *Kagerō nikki*, ed. Kawaguchi, *NKBT* 20: 155, n. 22.

55. Kawaguchi notes the possibility here of an allusion to *KKS* 583, a *waka* by Tsurayuki, which activates the metaphor latent in *chigusa*: "various weeds or grasses." See *Kagerō nikki*, *NKBT* 20: 155, n. 20.

56. Spacks, *Female Imagination*, p. 62.

57. Compare *The Tale of Genji (NKBZ* 17: 177; S, 1006), in which the narrator comments on Ukifune's suicidal fantasies as though they are indicative of her uncouth provincial origins—certainly not something that would occur to a proper lady of the capital. But again we have to wonder, would the *Kagerō* heroine have appeared as excessive in her own day, as comparisons with the literature of the succeeding generation make her appear?

58. Gyōgi Bosatsu (668–749) was a popularizer of lay Buddhism legendary for the practical and public works he initiated in his efforts to spread Buddhist compassion and teachings to lay believers (e.g., founding hospitals and orphanages, etc.). Tales concerning his good works appear in collections like *Nihon ryōiki* and *Sanbōe*. See Nakamura et al., eds., *Bukkyō jiten*, p. 172.

59. Kimura notes its conspicuous frequency. See *NKBZ* 9: 261, n. 15.

60. The same expression appears in her husband's *chōka* to her in the first volume. In both instances, there is a play on a famous line by Po Chü-i: "Human beings are not like trees and stones, all have feelings." See *NKBZ* 9: 154–55, n. 15.

61. As Arntzen notes, "This is the first time in a long time that Kaneie has answered with a poem. She has succeeded in getting his attention." See *The Kagerō Diary*, p. 232. The translation is by Rodd with Henkenius, *Kokinshū*, p. 350.

63. Kimura, *NKBZ* 9: 261, n. 14.

64. According to the memoir, Michitsuna had received Junior Fifth Rank, Lower Grade, at the Daijō'e festival of 970. See *NKBZ* 9: 245, n. 17.

65. Kimura, *NKBZ* 9: 264, n. 7.

66. As Arntzen notes, the letter she sends to her husband the morning following his first attempt to take her back to the capital is "remarkably conciliatory. . . . Withholding is her only weapon in this struggle of wills. So although this note seems to indicate that she is not opposed to going back home, it will be very difficult for her to actually do so." See her *The Kagerō Diary*, p. 236.

67. Kimura reads these lines as the heroine's words, not her aunt's. See *NKBZ* 9: 266, n. 3.

68. The translation is taken, with only minor changes, from Seidensticker, *Gossamer Years*, p. 103.

69. Kimura suggests she is thinking Kaneie instructed the messenger to adopt this tone for the ulterior purpose of persuading her not to return, but to stay. See *NKBZ* 9: 271, n. 17. Kawaguchi speculates she suspects the machinations of a female rival, perhaps Tokihime. See *Kagerō nikki, NKBT* 20: 228, n. 10.

70. Rodd with Henkenius, *Kokinshū*, p. 195.

71. "Heian bungaku ichimen oboegaki," in Akiyama, *Ōchō joryū bungaku no sekai*, pp. 1–10, especially pp. 9–10. Akiyama goes on to argue that the technique of foregrounding narrative events with lyric utterances and allusions forms one of the striking differences to be noted between earlier, presumably male-authored *monogatari* and the "feminine prose spirit" (*joryū sanbun seishin*), which begins to emerge in writings by women in the mid-tenth century.

Akiyama's call here and in earlier essays for an exploration of the history of this development, which he believes forefigures the achievements of *Genji*, stimulated a surge of inquiries into stylistic connections between the *Kagerō nikki* and other contemporary and near-contemporary autobiographical *kashū* and *nikki* by women writers who had been hitherto overlooked or scanted: i.e., Kamo Yasunori no musume, Hon'in Jijū, Nakatsukasa, Ise. See, for example, Moriya, "Ise ni okeru nikki bungaku keisei."

72. The phrase "the pinks are in the pink" is Seidensticker's translation for *nadeshiko wa nade oshitari ya*. See his *Gossamer Years*, p. 112.

73. Kimura, *NKBZ* 9: 285, headnote.

74. The girl is thought to have been Kaneie's daughter by the daughter of Kanetada, but little is known about her subsequent career. Some commentators believe she was later given a position as attendant to Senshi, Kaneie's younger daughter by Tokihime, thus making her the figure identified as "the *senji* of Grand Empress Senshi's time" in the *Ōkagami* account of Kaneie's offspring. See *Ōkagami*, ed. Matsumura, *NKBT* 21: 170; also H. McCullough, *Ōkagami*, p. 164. The *Eiga monogatari* also mentions a *senji* in service to Senshi who claimed to be Kaneie's daughter. See *Eiga monogatari*, trans. Matsumura and Yamanaka, *NKBT* 75: 103, and McCullough and McCullough, eds., *Flowering Fortunes*, p. 136. In any case, whatever her real parentage, the career of the *Kagerō* memoirist's adoptive daughter in no way measured up to that of the colorful Ōmi lady's colorful daughter Suishi. The Ōmi lady apparently bore a daughter to Kaneie's son Michitaka as well. Her daughter by Kaneie, Suishi, carries on in her mother's footsteps in this respect. The account of Suishi's career in *Ōkagami* repeats the motif of doting father and licentious daughter that characterizes the description of the Ōmi lady in the *Eiga monogatari*: "[The Ōmi lady] was of undistinguished birth, but it seems that her doting father, the Senior Assistant Governor-General, had spoiled her badly, allowing her to develop into a passionate, flirtatious woman." See the *Eiga monogatari*, ed. Matsumura and Yamanaka, *NKBT* 75: 104; the translation is by McCullough and McCullough, *Flowering Fortunes*, p. 137. Like mother, like daughter; Ōmi's story is repeated with variations in the *Ōkagami* account of her daughter Suishi's career: Suishi, having been made a consort to Crown Prince Okisada (later Emperor Sanjō) by her doting father, Kaneie, subsequently became pregnant by Consultant Minamoto Yorisada. She then fell from royal favor, and Yorisada's privileges at court were curtailed during Sanjō's reign as a result. See *Ōkagami*, ed. Matsumura, *NKBT* 21: 171–72; and H. McCullough, *Ōkagami*, pp. 164–65.

75. As if to signal the preoccupation with the absence of another child and the inexorable passing of her childbearing years, reference is made a couple of times to the heroine's menstrual periods in the accounts of the years 971 and 972.

Chapter 3: Fictions of Desire

1. The *Sarashina nikki* is thought to have been written sometime between 1058 and 1065 by Sugawara Takasue's daughter (ca. 1008–after 1059). Cita-

tions from the text refer to *Sarashina nikki*, ed. Inukai Kiyoshi, *NKBZ* 18. All translations are mine. For a complete English translation see I. Morris, trans., *As I Crossed a Bridge of Dreams*. Translations in French and German are also available: Sieffert, trans., *Les Journaux poétiques de l'époque de Heian: Le journal de Sarashina*, and Kemper, trans., *Sarashina-nikki: Tagebuch einer japanischen Hofdame aus dem Jahre 1060*.

2. *Genji monogatari o yomu tame ni*, pp. 8–9.

3. The blurring of distinctions between author and heroine has been standard in critical commentary on the memoir, whether the critic is Western or Japanese. Ivan Morris's remarks, reflecting views that dominated Japanese scholarship on the *Sarashina nikki* in the first two decades after World War II, provide a succinct example of this tendency in English. Though noting elsewhere that the memoir is believed to be a work of the author's late middle age, Morris remarks, "The *young girl who wrote the Sarashina diary* . . . gives some breathless descriptions of Mt. Fuji and of the other natural wonders she had seen on her journey to the Capital." See his *World of the Shining Prince*, p. 34 (my emphasis).

4. Compared to the other memoirs treated in this book, the textual history of the *Sarashina nikki* is relatively straightforward. After the memoirist's death, the text seems to have been kept in the closely guarded possession of the Sugawara family, not circulating until the early part of the Kamakura period (1185–1333). The survival of the *Sarashina nikki* owes much to the influence of Fujiwara Teika (1162–1241), who first mentions the memoir in 1230, in a notation in his *kanbun* diary, *Meigetsuki* (1180–1235). All the extant manuscript and woodblock print versions of the text derive from the same textual line as Teika's holograph; no text originating from a different textual family has been discovered. The development of scholarly commentaries on the memoir from the Edo period on was bedeviled by the obvious disorder of the text in seven different places. The text was not unscrambled until this century, when Tamai Kōsuke made a careful examination of Teika's holograph and published his findings in *Sarashina nikki sakkan kō*. For a concise account of Tamai's process, see Mitsuno Yōichi, "*Sarashina nikki* no sakkan wa dono yō ni shite tadasareta ka," p. 93.

5. See R. Okada, *Figures of Resistance*, esp. pp. 177–78, for a useful summary and critique of the debates in Japanese scholarship concerning the nature of "reading" *monogatari* in mid Heian.

6. Again, Ivan Morris's comments provide a convenient summary of the earlier wisdom on the *Sarashina* memoirist's motives: "Thwarted and saddened by the real world, with all its deaths and partings and frustrations, Lady Sarashina protected herself by a barrier of fantasy. Her girlish craving for romantic tales, which for a time became almost obsessive . . . was an attempt to escape from harsh reality into a rosier, more congenial realm." See *As I Crossed a Bridge of Dreams*, p. 11.

7. *Sarashina nikki*, ed. Akiyama, *SNKS* 39: 141–43.

8. Actually, a careful examination of the social backgrounds of the mem-

oirist and her favorite heroines reveals more differences than similarities. The memoirist's father, Sugawara Takasue, was a rather unsuccessful provincial governor. Ukifune's father was the Eighth Prince. Despite his refusal to recognize her, Ukifune comes from royal stock. Yūgao's father was a Middle Captain (see NKBZ 12: 259 and 261). Her social rank thus would have been higher than that of a provincial governor's daughter, despite the straitened economic circumstances she finds herself in as a result of her father's absence.

9. Inukai, "Takasue no musume ni kansuru shiron," p. 164. A similar reading is given by Imai Takuji, "Genji monogatari to Sarashina nikki," pp. 91–96. This view is more or less echoed and elaborated on by Tada Kazuomi, who extends the lines of these arguments to suggest that during girlhood in the eastern provinces, the appeal of monogatari stemmed from their power to open a window on the capital, to serve as a source of knowledge about the interactions of men and women in capital society. See Tada, "Sugawara Takasue no musume," pp. 350–51.

10. Field, Splendor of Longing, pp. 128–36.

11. Ibid, p. 131.

12. R. Okada, Figures of Resistance, p. 230.

13. See Becoming a Heroine. Brownstein's argument concerns female readers of the novel (both actual readers, and the female readers figured as heroines in novels themselves) primarily in the nineteenth- and twentieth-century Anglo-American context. Field's study of The Tale of Genji proceeds on some of the same assumptions as Brownstein's book, which Field also cites. See Field, Splendor of Longing, p. 130, n. 80.

14. NKBZ 9: 125.

15. Imai, Heianchō nikki no kenkyū, p. 105.

16. Masuda, Kagerō nikki sakusha, p. 16.

17. Harper, trans., quoted in "Motoori Norinaga's Criticism," p. 27. See also Sanbōe Chūkōsen, SNKBT 31: 6. Sanbōe was compiled and presented to Imperial Princess Sonshi (966?–985) as an illustrated collection of Buddhist didactic tales demonstrating the virtues of the "Three Jewels" (the Buddha, his clergy, and his teachings/the Dharma). For a complete translation and discussion in English, see Kamens, Minamoto Tamenori's Sanbōe.

18. Mitsuno, "Uta manabi to uta monogatari," pp. 28–34.

19. Tada, "Sugawara Takasue no musume," p. 350.

20. Ono et al., Kogo jiten, p. 1325.

21. R. Okada, Figures of Resistance, p. 19. See also Konishi, Early Middle Ages, pp. 282–304, and Stinchecum, "Who Tells the Tale?"

22. Akiyama Ken's seminal essay, "Nikki bungaku ron: sakka to sakuhin ni tsuite," in Ōchō joryū bungaku no sekai, pp. 166–92, marks the beginning of a response among scholars of nikki bungaku to the (old) New Critical critiques of Genji that were starting to emerge in Genji scholarship in the late sixties and early seventies in response to the writings and debates of scholars like Tamagami Takuya and Konishi Jin'ichi on monogatari dissemination and reception. Akiyama's essay marshaled, among other things, the nineteenth-century French

poet Verlaine's distinction between the poet and the man in order to argue that what is needed in future critiques of *nikki bungaku* is a theory that will unify what one can know of the writer as artist, which is revealed only in his or her works (*sakuhin*), and what is known of the writer (*sakka*) himself or herself, as embodied in the "facts" of his or her "life." The conceptual problems here should be immediately apparent. For most of the Heian female memoirists, what we know about the facts of their "lives" depends largely on reading their "works," the *nikki* themselves. In general, scholarship on *nikki bungaku* continues to lag behind *monogatari* scholarship in its assimilation of Western and contemporary theoretical models and analytical tools. Mitani Kuniaki's study of "temporal consciousness" in the *Kagerō nikki* provides an early exception to this trend ("*Kagerō nikki* no jikan ishiki"). Despite recent work by Mitani and other scholars associated with the Monogatari Kenkyūkai, biographical and autobiographical readings that do not explicitly address the assumptions and issues of narratology, feminism, and poststructuralism continue to dominate mainstream scholarship on Heian *nikki*.

23. Ukifune, the *Genji* figure to which the *Sarashina nikki* explicitly refers four times, was an unassuming girl from the eastern provinces whose bizarre destiny occupies center stage in the final six chapters of the *Genji monogatari*. She seems to have been born, not in Azuma, but in the house of the Eighth Prince, and like the *Sarashina* heroine, she returns to her birthplace near the capital after a childhood in the east, specifically Hitachi, the "province at the end of the Eastern Road."

24. *SNKS* 39: 136.

25. In fact, the account of their return to the capital embeds at least one explicit reference to the trip down to Kazusa four years earlier, at Hamanagawa; see *NKBZ* 18: 295.

26. *SKT* 2: 239.

27. Tsumoto Nobuhiro notes that this initial emphasis on the girl's exceedingly remote origins finds an echo in the opening passage of one of the surviving volumes of *Hamamatsu Chūnagon monogatari*, a work that at least since Teika's time has been attributed to Takasue's daughter, though the attribution is under debate (as is indeed the whole concept of *monogatari* as works that may be understood as attributable to single "authors"). See *Sarashina nikki no kenkyū*, p. 301. Volume 3 of *Hamamatsu* begins with the same trope that opens the *Sarashina nikki*: the naming of a place even more remote than the place that has become an exemplar (*tameshi*) of remoteness: "The mountains of Yoshino are well known for their seclusion, but the monk's retreat took Chūnagon into the even more distant recesses of Miyoshino." See *Hamamatsu Chūnagon monogatari*, *NKBT* 77: 264. The translation is from Rohlich, trans., *Tale of Eleventh-Century Japan*, p. 133. The heroine whose provincial origins are thus disclosed is the Yoshino princess, a character whose intertextual relationship to Ukifune exceeds even that of the *Sarashina* heroine in its complexity.

28. The opening lines of the *Sarashina nikki* provide a good example of the fusion of *waka* and prose and what Komachiya Teruhiko terms the "long-

winded" thought and style typical of *The Tale of Genji*. See his "Joryū bungaku no dentō to *Genji monogatari*," p. 72. As my own translation implies, I think it would not be faithful to what I imagine to have been the norms of Heian women's prose to attempt to render this passage in two excessively long English sentences. But I do think that Morris's translation deflates the energy of the passage unnecessarily by truncating the final phrases of the second sentence and shifting them down, where they head (his) second paragraph. This conveys the impression of an orderliness that is, I would argue, absent for important reasons in the Japanese. The passage is, to use an idiom the *Sarashina* memoirist would not have recognized, "built for speed" and suggests to my mind a deliberate mimicry of childlike narrative rhythms, on the order of ". . . and then, . . . and then, . . . and then."

29. It should be pointed out in passing that few readers take her at her word here. Since it is difficult to imagine a Heian girl carving out of wood a Buddha the size of herself, commentators have tended to take *tsukurite* as causative in connotation (a usage that can be found in *Genji*) and to interpret the line to mean that she had someone else make it for her. Given the girl's age and material circumstances (she was an assistant governor's daughter, somewhere between nine and twelve years old, living in the remote eastern provinces), it seems unlikely, though not impossible, that she would have commissioned such an icon. Provincial governors and their families were notorious for making up in material wealth what they lacked in social prestige. It is also possible, as Tsumoto argues, to understand the figure as signifying a painted image of Yakushi rather than a statue, and in that case possibly one the girl made herself. Indeed, the latter scenario resonates interestingly with a dream recounted later in the memoir in which she is informed of a prior life as a *busshi*, a maker of Buddhist icons. See Tsumoto, *Sarashina nikki no kenkyū*, pp. 339–41. Setting aside the perennial questions about the material makeup and genesis of the icon, Kubo Tomotaka has pointed out a possible allusion here to Sugawara family history. Both Sugawara Kiyokimi (770–842), the grandfather of the memoirist's illustrious ancestor Sugawara Michizane (845–903), and the latter's father, Koreyoshi (812–80), were noted for their devotion to Buddhism in later life. The monk Saichō (767–822), founder of the Tendai sect, was an associate of Kiyokimi and sailed with him to China in 803–4 on the penultimate mission the Heian court sent to Ch'ang-an. The supposed allusion to Sugawara family history here is the memoirist's offhand reference to having a Buddha made to match her own height. There is an image of the Yakushi Buddha that measures five *shaku* and five *sun* enshrined at Enryakuji, which is thought to have been built to correspond to Saichō's height. See Kubo, "*Sarashina nikki* no Yakushi Botoke," pp. 198–202. Robert Borgen's excellent study of Sugawara Michizane also contains brief studies of the lives of Kiyokimi and Koreyoshi. See *Sugawara Michizane and the Early Heian Court*, pp. 30–67. For details on the mission to China and the connections between Kiyokimi and the Tendai founder Saichō, see Borgen, "Japanese Mission to China." Oblique allusions to Sugawara family history can be found elsewhere in the memoir too, and we cannot overlook

the fact that whatever other purposes Heian women's memoirs served (as re-positories of *tameshi* for future female readers, literary diversion, personal ex-pression, etc.), many also explicitly claim to have been motivated in part by the desire to commemorate the literary, cultural, and sociopolitical reputations of the memoirist's own family, a motive that Japanese scholars refer to in terms of the memoirist's "clan" or "house consciousness" (*ie no ishiki*). In the case of Sugawara Takasue's daughter, the Sugawara clan's close association with the Tendai sect of Buddhism is frequently mentioned.

30. Akiyama, *SNKS* 39: 136–37.

31. In his disquisition on *monogatari* in *The Tale of Genji*. See *NKBZ* 14: 204.

32. Akiyama also draws attention to the implicit link between these two passages in a headnote commenting on the latter. See *SNKS* 39: 44.

33. Katagiri Yōichi notes that although the term *utamakura* seems frequent-ly to have referred to poetic diction in general (*kago*) and to handbooks con-taining lists of poetic words, there exist some sources, such as the late-Heian *Kojidan*, which demonstrate its usage in the narrower sense of poetic toponyms (*meisho utamakura*). A famous contemporary of Takasue's daughter, priest Nō-in (908–1050), left behind a handbook known as *Nōin utamakura*, which, to judge from the surviving seventeenth-century versions, was arranged according to provinces rather than *dai* (topics). See Katagiri, "Utamakura no seiritsu," pp. 22–23. The tendency to conflate the place itself with its poetic place-name is il-lustrated by the *Kojidan* account of Narihira's journey to the east (*Azuma ku-dari*), in which he is described as "going to see the *utamakura*" (*utamakura o mi ni yuku*). See Morimoto Shigeru, "Utamakura to meisho," pp. 14–21.

34. R. Okada, "Unbound Texts," p. 20.

35. *Figures of Resistance*, p. 150.

36. Or, better yet, consider Arabella in *The Female Quixote* (1752) by Charlotte Lennox. Though it refers to a radically different set of literary-historical contexts, I have found Patricia Meyer Spacks's reading of Lennox's novel ("Subtle Sophistries of Desire: *The Female Quixote*") particularly illumi-nating to my own explorations of the relation of fiction and desire in the *Sara-shina nikki*. See chap. 1 of Spacks, *Desire and Truth*.

37. See, for example, Akiyama, *SNKS* 39: 138–39, and Tada, "Sugawara Takasue no musume," pp. 351–52.

38. *Heian kōki nikki bungaku ron*, pp. 7–22. Moriya does not make the dis-tinctions I have been making between the presumed historical author of the *Sara-shina nikki* (Takasue's daughter), the narrator (or narrating voice) that recounts the story, and the figure of the traveler-heroine around which this part of the memoir is woven. As is the case for much mainstream *kokubungaku* scholarship, Moriya's use of terms implies a more or less unproblematic identity among the historical author, the narrating voice in the *nikki*, and the main character.

39. Tsumoto, *Sarashina nikki no kenkyū*, pp. 192–211.

40. See *Yamato monogatari*, ed. Katagiri et al., *NKBZ* 8: 403–4, and *Kon-jaku monogatarishū*, ed. Mabuchi et al., *NKBZ* 24: 506–11.

41. See Tsumoto, *Sarashina nikki no kenkyū*, p. 198, and Moriya, *Heian kōki nikki bungaku ron*, p. 10.

42. Mitani Eiichi outlines variations of this and other archetypical plots of classical Japanese fiction in his *Monogatarishi no kenkyū*, pp. 77–96. Discussions in English of these plots and their importance to the development of classical Japanese literature may be found in Field, *Splendor of Longing*, pp. 33–39, and Shirane, *Bridge of Dreams*, pp. 3–4.

43. Moriya, *Heian kōki nikki bungaku ron*, p. 10.

44. The image of the burning house as a metaphor for blind attachment to the passions of this world originates in the well-known parable from the *Lotus Sutra* in which a father tries to persuade his children to leave off their indoor amusements, flee the house (which is burning, unbeknownst to them), and get into the carriage (a metaphor for the Dharma, the "vehicle" of Buddhist teachings or law). See Takakusu Junjirō et al., eds., *Taishō Shinshū daizōkyō*, 9: 14b, and Hurvitz, trans., *Scripture of the Lotus Blossom*, pp. 68–70.

45. Though the memoir does not specify this statue as an image of Miroku, it can be identified on the basis of the *Sekidera engi*, which describes a Miroku Bosatsu, five *chō* (about fifteen feet) in height, commissioned by priest Genshin (942–1017), author of *Ojōyōshū*, and promoter of Amida devotion. See Akiyama, *SNKS* 39: 30, n. 7. Begun in 1018, the statue was finished and dedicated in 1022. The memoirist would have seen it first in the twelfth month of 1021, the year before its dedication.

46. The consistent linkage made between Kannon and Amateru onkami (Amaterasu) in the *Sarashina nikki* appears to be an early instance of what had become a commonplace of popular religious belief by late Heian. See Matsumoto, "Haha isaku no kagami o itasasete." According to the syncretic doctrine of *honji suijaku* ("original ground, manifest trace") that was then evolving in Japanese Buddhism, the native sun goddess, Amaterasu, patron deity of the imperial family, was also regarded as a local manifestation of Kannon, the bodhisattva of mercy, who is sometimes figured as feminine. In an essay that adds some interesting footnotes to Matsumoto's important article on the *honji suijaku* conflation of Kannon and Ise Amaterasu in the *Sarashina nikki*, Ouchi Kazuaki identifies Inari (who is mentioned in a dream the heroine has on a pilgrimage to worship the Kannon at Hasedera, *NKBZ* 18: 348) as yet another Shinto manifestation of Kannon. See "'Amateru onkami o nemushimase' no yume." The *Sarashina nikki* consistently refers to Amateru, rather than Amaterasu, but commentators believe that the two names were interchangeable at this point in Heian history.

47. Kondō Hajime, "*Sarashina nikki* no saigimmi: sono shūkyō ishiki ni tsuite," pp. 172–79.

48. Matsumoto, "Haha isaku no kagami," p. 11.

49. Moriya, *Heian kōki nikki bungaku ron*, p. 92.

50. Harper, "Motoori Norinaga's Criticism," p. 49.

51. That the concern about the dangers of literary fictions extended to both consumers and producers of *monogatari* is evident in *Genji ippon kyō* (ca.

1166 by the monk Chōken, 1126–1203), a text "written in Chinese in the form of a sutra . . . [and] meant as a prayer for the repose of the souls of Murasaki Shikibu and the readers of *The Tale of Genji*. They were presumed to be suffering in hell for having spent their idle hours with frivolous works of fiction." See Rohlich, trans., *Tale of Eleventh-Century Japan*, p. 4.

52. *NKBZ* 14: 205; S, 438.

53. Examples of these tales, drawn from *Ima kagami* (ca. 1170), *Hō butsushū* (ca. 1179), and *Ima monogatari* (after 1239), are translated and quoted in Harper, "Motoori Norinaga's Criticism," pp. 50–55, 58.

54. *SNKS* 7: 22–23 and 13. See also Marra, "*Mumyōzōshi*: Introduction and Translation," pp. 137, 132.

55. See Hosono Tetsuo, "*Sarashina nikki* shoko." The memoirist's father, Sugawara Takasue, represents a break in this family tradition of scholarly bureaucrats. He began and ended his career in less distinguished provincial governor posts, first in Kazusa and finally in Hitachi, and never, unlike his father and his son, held the post of *daigaku no kami*.

56. Hosono, "*Sarashina nikki* shoko," pp. 33–34.

57. The following description of the *Kangaku'e* ceremonies is based on that of McCullough and McCullough, *Flowering Fortunes*, pp. 506–7, n. 46, which is itself based on a description that appears in the late-tenth-century tale collection, *Sanbōe*. On the fourteenth and fifteenth nights of the third and ninth months, scholars chanting lines from Po Chü-i's poem "The Seed of the Way to Nirvana," gathered at a temple where they were joined by monks from Mount Hiei singing a hymn of praise to the *Lotus Sutra*. On the night of the fifteenth (the full moon), expositions of the *Lotus Sutra* were followed by group composition of poems in Chinese on the *Lotus* and the recitation of lines from Po Chü-i's important recantatory poem "In This Life":

> In this life profane literature has been my occupation.
> I have followed the mistaken path
> of indiscriminate words and ornate language.
> My desire is to transform my faulty writing
> And make it in this world and the next
> An instrument for praise of the Buddha's teachings,
> A vehicle for exposition of the dharma.

Po Chü-i's poem would have been known to mid-Heian readers—including those (especially women) who might not read Chinese—via Fujiwara Kintō's influential anthology of Japanese and Chinese poems for chanting, *Wakan rōeishū* (ca. 1013). The translation here is by McCullough and McCullough, *Tale of Flowering Fortunes*, pp. 506–7.

58. The first subcategory explicitly named *shakkyōka* in the *chokusenshū* (imperially commissioned *waka* anthologies) appeared in the fourth anthology, the *Goshūiwakashū* (1086) as part of the twentieth and final book of *zōka* (miscellaneous) poems. However, poems that could later be categorized as *shakkyōka* appear even earlier, in the third anthology, the *Shūishū* (1006).

With the seventh anthology, the *Senzaishū* (1188), *shakkyōka* comprise their own formal category and continue to be included as such in all subsequent anthologies until the last one was compiled in 1439. See S. Miller, "Religious Boundaries in Aesthetic Domains," pp. 105–10. See also Morrell, "Buddhist Poetry in the *Goshūishū*."

59. Edward Kamens's translation and study of the collection provides a richly detailed rhetorical and historical analysis of this poetic work and its implications for the status of women in Buddhism in mid Heian. See *Buddhist Poetry of the Great Kamo Priestess*.

60. Ultimately, Buddhist commentary on *Genji* moves toward accommodation rather than rejection of the potential religious meaning inherent in *monogatari*. As Thomas Harper puts it (in reference to the later and somewhat more specialized context of traditional *Genji* commentaries), far from discrediting such masterpieces of fiction as *Genji monogatari*, "the main object of most Buddhist criticism . . . is to justify rather than to condemn the author's having written the novel and the reader's having enjoyed it." The earliest surviving examples of Buddhist commentaries on the tale date from a somewhat later period than the *Sarashina nikki* (beginning with *Genji monogatari shaku*, ca. 1160). See Harper, "Motoori Norinaga's Criticism," pp. 55–56.

61. Kondō, "*Sarashina nikki no saigimmi*," p. 178.

62. For an extended discussion of this structural balance, addressing it primarily in terms of its connection to the memoirist's aesthetic rather than religious preoccupations, see Takahashi Bunji, "*Sarashina nikki shoken.*"

63. Kubo, "*Sarashina nikki no Yakushi Botoke*," pp. 183–207.

64. Kubo's argument is weakened by the fact that he bases it largely on the reconstructed layouts of only two eleventh-century temples (Jōruri and Hōjōji), neither of which figures in the *Sarashina nikki*.

65. Elaborating on a suggestion offered by Takahashi, who notes in passing that the Yakushi Buddha's eighth vow concerns the promise that all women will achieve Buddhahood, Kubo also points out possible numerological links between the numbering of Amida's vows and the *Sarashina* heroine's age at different junctures in her "pilgrimage." She begins her journey to the west in the most remote of the eastern provinces, where she is seen off, at the age of *thirteen*, by an image of the Yakushi Buddha, which faces her, and thus faces west, as she looks back longingly toward him and her old house, separated from him by "a dreadfully bleak mist" (*NKBZ* 18: 284). After the circuitous tale of her comings and goings in the capital—from house to house as her father's fortunes rise and fall, commuting back and forth to serve as lady-in-waiting to an imperial princess and finally off on this and that pilgrimage to various temples beyond the capital in her own later life—her journey ends, as does the memoir, years and pages later with the pilgrim widowed and alone, an aging, abandoned aunt in a weed-grown garden far to the west of her childhood home. The strikingly precise dating of her dream encounter with Amida (the only passage in the memoir so explicitly dated)—the *thirteenth* night of the tenth month of the third year of the Tengi era—reveals that she has this vision at the age of

forty-eight. In the dream, she recognizes Amida, who stands on a lotus-blossom pedestal in the garden, glowing with a golden light. Mist clouds her vision here as it did at her parting with the Yakushi image years ago in far off Azuma, but this time she is separated from the Buddha only "as though by a single layer of mist" (*kiri hitoe hedatareru yō ni*), through which she can, by straining her eyes, dimly make out his figure. His hands are fixed in an *inzō*, or *mudra*, one of the conventional signs by which Buddhist icons represent specific vows made by the various Buddhas and bodhisattvas. One hand is lowered, and the other makes a sign with joined fingers, recalling thus the *thirteenth* of Amida's *forty-eight* vows: to come for those who call upon his name and lead them into the Western Paradise (*NKBZ* 18: 360). Takahashi's suggestion is made in his "*Sarashina nikki* shoken," p. 105. For Kubo's elaboration of this vein of interpretation, see his "*Sarashina nikki* no Yakushi Botoke," pp. 204–5.

66. It was widely believed that the year 1052 would usher in the "Latter Days of the Law" (*Mappō*), the era in which people have degenerated so much that Buddhist teaching and practice is no longer comprehensible to them.

67. Tsumoto, *Sarashina nikki no kenkyū*, p. 27. The memoirist's step-mother was the daughter of Takashina Nariyuki. The stepmother's paternal uncle, Takashina Nariaki, was married to Murasaki Shikibu's daughter. By 1021 the memoirist's stepmother, having separated from Takasue after their return to the capital in 1020, was again moving in court circles as a lady-in-waiting to Emperor Goichijō's Empress Ishi (999–1036; r. 1016–36).

68. The five obstacles indicate the five forms of "rebirth" that women cannot experience, including rebirth as a Buddha. See Hurvitz, trans., *Scripture of the Lotus Blossom*, pp. 199–201, and Takakusu et al., eds., *Taishō Shinshū daizōkyō*, 9: 35bc.

69. Nichiren, the charismatic founder of his own mass sect of Buddhism in the Kamakura period, cited this passage as the basis of his assertion, itself a re-iteration of an assertion made by Chih-i, the Chinese founder of T'ien-t'ai (Tendai) Buddhism, that "other sutras are written for men only. This [the Lotus] sutra is for everyone." Quoted in Rodd, "Nichiren's Teachings to Women," p. 9.

Chapter 4: The Desire for Fiction

1. Haraoka Fumiko notes allusions to passages bearing on the Akashi lady in the *Sarashina nikki*, but since that heroine is never explicitly named in the memoir, I have chosen not to pursue the issue. See Haraoka, "*Genji monogatari* no eikyō: in'yōsareru bungaku," pp. 190–91.

2. *SNKS* 7: 31–32. The delightfully arch remark about Tamakazura from *Mumyōzōshi* may be a deliberate rewriting of the line from *The Tale of Genji* in which Ukon mentions to Genji that the lovely girl she found by chance at Hasedera may be "the link [*yukari*] to the dew on the evening faces [Yūgao] which vanished so fleetingly." See *NKBZ* 14: 114; S, 401.

3. The topos here is *monomi*, "spectacle viewing," which involves spectatorship rather than voyeurism on the part of the onlookers. The nobles and

courtiers whose presence creates a spectacle for viewing at court festivals and imperial processions engage in deliberate self-display; the gaze of their onlookers is solicited.

4. Or are we to understand that she finally does fulfill it after a fashion when, at a much later date, she manages to make a successful match between her own daughter and Reizei? See *NKBZ* 16: 95–97; S, 770–71.

5. For a discussion of the half-hidden wifely side of Takasue's daughter's life, see Inukai, "Takasue no musume ni kansuru shiron," pp. 164–65.

6. Bargen's study of the Yūgao possession first appeared in her "Yūgao: A Case of Spirit Possession," pp. 15–24. She elaborates her readings of the four other major *Genji* spirit-possession episodes in *A Woman's Weapon*.

7. Field, *Splendor of Longing*, p. 118.

8. The bibliography on the *Sarashina* memoirist's admiration for Ukifune is extensive. I have found particularly useful and informative the essay in Tsumoto, *Sarashina nikki no kenkyū*, pp. 298–312. For annotated lists of other materials on this topic, see Ishihara, "*Sarashina nikki* kenkyū shoshi," pp. 319–23 (especially pp. 322–23), and Itō, "Ōchō joryū bungaku kenkyū no kiseki to tenbō."

9. Even a cursory reading of late-Heian tales like the *Hamamatsu Chūnagon monogatari* and the *Torikaebaya monogatari* reveals the persistent fascination with Ukifune-like figures and Uji-like locales. We have already touched on the intertextual resonances between Ukifune and the Yoshino princess in the *Hamamatsu Chūnagon monogatari*. See Chapter 3, n. 27. Ukifune's lover Kaoru also gets rewritten and replayed as a hero in late-Heian fiction with far more imagination than Genji or Niou. The articulate, opinionated ladies-in-waiting whose critiques of *monogatari* make up the bulk of *Mumyōzōshi* find the Hamamatsu Middle Counselor to be "ideal in appearance and character ... a wonderful man, the same type as Captain Kaoru." See *SNKS* 7: 74; and Marra, "*Mumyōzōshi*, Part 2," p. 302. The central figure of the first two volumes of the *Torikaebaya monogatari* too (the biological "sister" who irresolutely masquerades as her own brother until pregnancy and motherhood leave her stranded in seclusion at Uji) presents a further, parodic rewriting of Uji intertexts that manages to combine in one figure both the Kaoru and the Ukifune prototypes. See *Torikaebaya monogatari*, ed. Suzuki, and Willig, trans., *Changelings*.

10. DeJean, "Female Voyeurism: Sappho and Lafayette," p. 202.

11. See *NKBZ* 18: 336–41.

12. I. Morris, trans., *As I Crossed a Bridge of Dreams*, p. 11.

13. The *Torkikaebaya monogatari* exaggerates the theme of sexual and gender ambivalence almost beyond recognition. The complications generated by the sexual reserve that its gender-ambiguous central figure (a sister masquerading as her own brother, who then eventually returns to her original identity as sister) maintains before "his" own wife dominates the narrative of volume two of that tale.

14. Field, *Splendor of Longing*, p. 287.

15. The translation is by Field, *Splendor of Longing*, p. 286. See also *NKBZ* 16: 329; S, 1069–70.

16. *NKBZ* 13: 250–51; S, 264. Genji and Murasaki exchange *e nikki* ("illustrated *nikki*") during Genji's exile at Suma. Murasaki's *nikki* is thus associated with Genji's affair with the Akashi lady and his subsequent confession of it to her. Genji's Suma *e nikki* triumphantly resurfaces in "The Picture Contest" (*Eawase*), where its excellence helps win the day for Akikonomu's faction (*NKBZ* 13: 368 and 377–78; S, 310 and 314). In "A Branch of Plum" (*Ume ga e*), Genji considers passing on his Suma *nikki* to his daughter, the Akashi princess, but decides she is still too young for it—this while he is preparing a library for her quarters at court (*NKBZ* 14: 414–15; S, 520). Murasaki's anguished jottings (*tenarai*) appear in "New Herbs, part one" (*Wakana jō*), in the context of Murasaki's attempts to both vent and hide her anxiety about Genji's wandering affections (*NKBZ* 15: 81–82; S, 564).

17. Brownstein, *Becoming a Heroine*, p. xv.

18. For an extended meditation on the poetic and religious associations of Ukifune's name, see Miner," Heroine," pp. 64–67.

19. For a discussion of the *sasurai* motif (and other motifs of "wandering") and their thematic importance in the *Genji* and other Heian narratives, see Fujii, *Genji monogatari no shigen to genzai*, pp. 180–219.

20. It is passages like the above that have led some scholars to postulate the direct influence of Murasaki's diary on the *Sarashina nikki*, though Koyano Jun'ichi makes a strong case against it in *Heian kōki joryū nikki no kenkyū*, pp. 174–94. For Sei Shōnagon's account of her first attendances on Empress Teishi, see *SNKBT* 25: 222–28. For Sei, the anxiety about being seen is balanced—even in this passage about her experiences as a newcomer at court—by her evident pleasure in looking.

21. The memoir itself indicates the heroine's young patroness at court by means of a very laconic metonym, *yukari aru tokoro*, literally, "the place where the *yukari* is" (with *yukari* presumably used here to indicate a blood relative—in this, as in many cases, a daughter). See *NKBZ* 18: 327. Teika glosses the passage with a name for the *yukari*, Imperial Princess Yūshi, also mentioning her mother, the late Empress Genshi, and the Fujiwara Chancellor Yorimichi, who was patron and foster father to both mother and daughter. The new Iwanami edition of the text, edited by Yoshioka Hiroshi, handily provides Teika's glosses in an appendix keyed to page and line numbers in the memoir. See *Sarashina nikki*, ed. Yoshioka, *SNKBT* 24: 469–70.

22. By this reckoning, the memoirist would have been thirty-three years old at the time of her marriage. See *Sarashina nikki*, ed. Akiyama, *SNKS* 39: 128. I. Morris's dating of Takasue's daughter's marriage to 1043, when she was, in his words, "about [age] thirty-six," reflects the judgments of commentators earlier in this century. Morris himself specifically names Miyata Kazuichirō, *Sarashina nikki hyōshaku* (Kyoto, 1931), and *Sarashina nikki*, ed. Nishishita Kyōichi, *NKBT* (Iwanami, 1964). See *As I Crossed a Bridge of Dreams*, pp. 7, 89, 138, n. 158.

23. *Sarashina nikki no kenkyū*, pp. 93–95.

24. Saigō, *Genji monogatari o yomu tame ni*, pp. 70–71.

25. Tsuzuki, "Yorimichi seiji to joryū bungei saron: sono ichi."

26. *Rokujō Saiin monogatari utaawase, SKT* 5: 91.

27. Tsumoto, *Sarashina nikki no kenkyū*, p. 103.

28. Teika identifies Shūshi's residence as that of her mother's Biwa mansion. See *Sarashina nikki*, ed. Yoshioka, *SNKBT* 24: 469.

29. The reader should bear in mind that the sun goddess, Amaterasu, was the patron deity of the imperial family. Prayers directed to her suggest prayers for a position in the imperial household. There was historically a distinction between Amaterasu ōmikami, the sun goddess enshrined at Ise at the end of the seventh century as patroness of the imperial family, and Amateru onkami, a nature deity associated with Ki province and the Ki clan, but the two seem to have been regarded as one by mid Heian. See *SNKS* 39: 37, n. 16, and 65, nn. 19, 20. See also Inoue, "*Sagoromo monogatari* no 'Amateru onkami' hyōgen o yomu," pp. 107–13. In fact, the belief that the Ki province deity (Amateru onkami), Ise Amaterasu, and the Amaterasu enshrined in the Sacred Mirror Room in the Naishidokoro of the imperial palace are all manifestations of the same goddess is made explicit in the *Sarashina nikki* by the explanation the heroine is given when she asks who Amateru is, whether god or Buddha, and where she might be enshrined. See *NKBZ* 18: 324–25.

30. Tsumoto, *Sarashina nikki no kenkyū*, p. 104.

31. *NKBZ* 9: 256.

32. Kubo, "Sarashina nikki no Yakushi Botoke," p. 196.

Chapter 5: The Problem of Others

1. *Sanuki no suke nikki*, ed. Ishii, *NKBZ* 18: 371–456. All citations from the memoir refer to this edition. All translations mine. For a complete English translation, see Brewster, trans., *The Emperor Horikawa Diary*.

2. See his *Kyūtei joryū nikki bungaku*, p. 302.

3. Thus Tamai Kōsuke: "This entry concerns an attack of mental illness [*seishinbyōteki hossa*] on [the handmaid's] part, and indicates she had a predisposition toward clairvoyance [*senrimanteki soshitsu*]." See his *Sanuki no suke nikki zenchūkai*, p. 227. The study was originally published in 1936, under the title *Sanuki no suke no nikki tsūshaku*.

4. The term is Yuzawa Shōji's in his "*Sanuki no suke nikki* no buntai to ishiki," p. 213.

5. Fujiwara Nagako, the author of the *Sanuki no suke nikki*, is unique among the memoirists treated in this book by virtue of the fact that her first name has been preserved. In general, unless they were imperial consorts or the wives of high-ranking ministers, Heian women's names were not recorded and passed on to posterity; neither, it appears, were their names generally known to nonintimates in their own day.

6. The confusion arose in part because Nagako is not listed among her fa-

ther's offspring in *Sonpi bummyaku*, an important medieval genealogical work, and in part because a contemporary courtier's diary in Chinese (*Chūyūki*, by Fujiwara Munetada) incorrectly identified Kaneko as the handmaid chosen to raise the curtains at the accession ceremony for Emperor Toba (see below). See *Chūyūki*, *Shiryō taisei*, 10: 292, and Ikeda, *Kyūtei joryū nikki bungaku*, pp. 276–79. An article by Tamai Kōsuke ended the confusion in 1929 ("*Sanuki no suke nikki* sakusha ni tsuite," *Shigaku zasshi* 50 [September 1929]). For a summary of the authorship debate in English see Brewster, *Emperor Horikawa Diary*, p. 49, n. 81.

The confusion was further exacerbated by a passage from the memoir. After Horikawa's death, when the handmaid is recalled to court service and appears for the first time before the new emperor, Toba, the boy is told that the woman before him is his father's "breast sibling" (*onmenotogo*, literally, the "[imperial] wet nurse's child"). Wet nurses often suckled and reared their own children together with their charges. The intimate relationship thus established between the two children could then be formalized in adulthood by other sorts of ties. In later life, breast siblings frequently served as close attendants to their higher-ranking foster siblings. Some infer from this passage that Nagako had been adopted by her sister, Kaneko, and had been known at court as the latter's foster daughter; her position at court as assistant handmaid (*naishi no suke*) to Horikawa is seen in this light as the logical extension of her earlier relation to him as breast sibling. See *NKBZ* 18: 419, n. 19; also Brewster, *Emperor Horikawa Diary*, pp. 30, 89.

7. I am following McCullough and McCullough, *Flowering Fortunes*, in rendering both *sesshō* and *kanpaku* as *regent*. In fact, *sesshō* is the title taken by the regent during the emperor's childhood. After the emperor comes of age, the title is formally *kanpaku* ("civil dictator").

8. For fuller discussions in English on the ramifications of matrilineal inheritance patterns among aristocratic families in the mid-Heian period, see McCullough, "Japanese Marriage Institutions," Nickerson, "The Meaning of Matrilocality," and Wakita, "Marriage and Property in Premodern Japan."

9. Emperor Horikawa was assigned four different wet nurses, all of them from imperial client families and/or the Murakami branch of the Minamoto clan: the memoirist's sister, Fujiwara Kaneko; Daini no sanmi Ieko, also known as Hitachi no suke; Oidono no sanmi, wife of Minamoto Masazane, who was brother to Horikawa's mother, Minamoto Kenshi; and Lady Nii (referred to in the memoir as Ben no sanmi), the wife of Fujiwara Kinzane, who was the head of one of Retired Emperor Shirakawa's client families.

10. Imai Gen'e, "*Sanuki no suke nikki*," p. 74. As Inaga Keiji also points out, there were living examples of assistant handmaids who bore children to the emperors they served close at hand. Among the Sanuki handmaid's contemporaries at court, her own cousin, the daughter of Fujiwara Tokitsuna, bore Emperor Horikawa a son, later known as priest Saiun (1104–62). See Inaga, "*Sanuki no suke nikki* no shi to sei," p. 81.

11. *Chōshūki*, *Shiryō taisei*, 6: 158–59.

12. *Sonpi bummyaku* records Akitsuna's date of death as 1103, but Hagitani Boku has disputed this on the basis of research in contemporary courtiers' diaries and records of poetry contests in the first decade of the twelfth century. The year 1107 is now the accepted date for his death. See Brewster, *Emperor Horikawa Diary*, pp. 49–50, n. 83.

13. The Sanuki handmaid had three elder brothers: Iemichi, Arisuke, and Michitsune. The memoir does not specify which of the three may be indicated here. It is Michitsune's career she seems anxious to further—as governor of Ōmi—during one of her episodes of possession.

14. *"Sanuki no suke nikki,"* p. 105.

15. Prince Sukehito was the son of Emperor Gosanjō and his Murakami Genji consort, Minamoto Motoko. Horikawa's mother, though formally the adopted daughter of the Fujiwara regent Morozane, was Minamoto Kenshi, daughter of Minamoto Akifusa, minister of the right.

16. Toba's mother, Shishi, was the daughter of Fujiwara Sanesue, Shirakawa's maternal uncle.

17. Tsunoda, *Taikenmon'in Tamako no shōgai*, pp. 17–18.

18. Brewster, *Emperor Horikawa Diary*, p. 25.

19. Hurst, *Insei*, pp. 138–39.

20. *Chōshūki, Shiryō taisei* 16: 159.

21. Tsunoda, *Taikenmon'in Tamako no shōgai*, pp. 7–21.

22. The rumor is recorded in the *Kojidan*, compiled ca. 1212–15, a collection attributed to the (Murakami Genji) poet and courtier Minamoto Akikane (1160–1215). See *Kojidan*, ed. Kuroita, *Kokushi taisei* 18: 40.

23. Hurst speculates on the triangular relations that obtained among Shirakawa, Empress Taikenmon'in, and Toba and the way sexual rivalries between grandfather and grandson contributed to later conflicts between Toba and his supposed son Sutoku. However, his account does not touch on the Sanuki handmaid's possession. See his *Insei*, pp. 154–77.

24. For discussion of the status of *miko* serving at Shinto shrines in the Heian period, see Okada Seiji, "Kyūtei miko no jittai." Carmen Blacker gives a more general account of spirit possession and related practices in Japanese history and culture in her *Catalpa Bow*.

25. The medium in this passage is referred to as *utsubekihito*: "the person to whom the spirit could be transferred."

26. More specifically, the implied culprit is an Empress Dowager, mother-in-law to the man who is Nezame's would-be lover. The man suspects his mother-in-law has instructed the medium to falsely accuse Nezame in a desperate attempt to rekindle his interest in her daughter while undermining his passion for Nezame. See *Yowa no Negame*, ed. Suzuki, *NKBZ* 19: 407–9; also Hochstedler, trans., *The Tale of Nezame*, pp. 122–24.

27. See Gessel, "The 'Medium' of Fiction," for a summary and analysis of Enchi Fumiko's development of this Heian motif in her novel *Namamiko monogatari*.

28. W. McCullough, "Spirit Possession in the Heian Period." McCullough's

article, published more than twenty years ago, makes a number of observations whose implications have yet to be pursued in scholarly circles. McCullough notes that accounts of spirit possession become common beginning in the early tenth century. Texts predating that (*Kojiki, Nihongi, Man'yōshū*) contain accounts of apparently spontaneous shamanistic possessions by priestesses but no references to anything like the sort of illness- and death-producing possessions so numerous in Heian literature (though he notes one reference in *Shoku Nihongi*: in 746, Priest Genbō is reported to have died because of possession by the spirit of Fujiwara Hirotsugu). McCullough cites as reason for this tenth-century shift the appearance of a Chinese medical encyclopedia (*Ishinhō*, in Japanese) that was partially translated into Japanese in the tenth century. *Ishinhō*, made up largely of quotations from various Chinese sources, was put together by Tanba Yasuyori ca. 982–84 for reference at the imperial palace. What might the shift imply regarding new strategies on the part of the Buddhist clergy for their involvement in political intrigues at court? What connection might there be here with the tenth-century rise of the Fujiwara-authored system of imperial marriage politics, with its feminine power base?

As McCullough notes, the most commonly reported motivation for spirit possession was the disappointment at court of a recently deceased ancestor. Long-held political grudges were expressed and assuaged by both the symbolic and the practical rituals of exorcism and propitiatory prayers and material recompense to descendants. Those who suffered as a result of possessing spirits, those who participated most centrally in the "staging" of spirit possession, either through their illness or through their mediumship, were primarily women. Typically, then, women play the role of mouthpiece for the ambitions of disgruntled male ancestors or relatives at the mid-Heian court. This suggests another area in which women could play potentially pivotal roles in court politics.

29. See Matsumoto, "Sanuki no suke no seikaku," pp. 289–90.

30. Doris Bargen explores these issues at length in the context of *The Tale of Genji* in her book *A Woman's Weapon*.

31. *Sanuki no suke nikki zenchūkai*, ed. Tamai, p. 227.

32. Ikeda, *Kyūtei joryū nikki bungaku*, p. 302.

33. Inaga, "*Sanuki no suke nikki* no shi to sei," pp. 79–85.

34. Matsumoto, "Sanuki no suke no seikaku," pp. 281–84.

35. Yuzawa Shōji raises important questions about the way similar rhetorical devices and stylistic tics in other court women's memoirs historically have received different interpretations. See "*Sanuki no suke nikki* no buntai to ishiki," pp. 215–16.

36. Among textual scholars, the debate over the authorship of the prologue is a long-standing one that centers on the greater allusive density and rhetorical sophistication of the prologue as compared with the rest of the memoir. Citing stylistic similarities between it and certain later sections of volume two, some scholars argue that not only the prologue but other parts of the text as well, particularly in the second volume, are the work of a later hand. This theory, formulated by Ikeda in his *Kyūtei joryū nikki bungaku*, pp. 269–70, has been

taken up again more recently by Kusakabe, *Sanuki no suke nikki,* pp. 10–15. Moriya scrutinizes the passages singled out by Ikeda and Kusakabe as suspect and concludes the opposite, i.e., that they are in fact quite characteristic of the style of the rest of the *nikki* and not likely to be by another hand. See his *Heian kōki nikki bungaku ron,* pp. 300–319. For my purposes, I think it unnecessary to take sides on the issue. I assume that the prologue is either the Sanuki hand-maid's composition or the composition of a sensitive later reader who con-structed the passage as one which might be read as hers, that is, mimicking, re-iterating, and elaborating the voice and themes inscribed in the body of the *nikki,* so that the prologue, whether actually indited by the handmaid or not, might pass in the world (as indeed it did for centuries) as a plausible product of her hand.

Of course, the prologue may well be the work of a later hand—perhaps someone inspired by the legend of the memoirist's possession by Horikawa's ghost to compose a suitably literary foreshadowing of that incident ex post facto. Some scholars have suggested Teika as a plausible candidate for this bit of literary forgery, in part because he was the great-grandson of her sister Kaneko (Kaneko's daughter married Fujiwara Toshitada and bore him four sons, one of whom was Fujiwara Shunzei, Teika's father.)

37. *Tango no sechi* was observed annually at court and was celebrated in private residences. Among the practices involved was that of decorating the eaves of the house with sweet-flags and their roots. The plant was valued as a medicinal herb. The point of the festival was to ward off illnesses associated with the onset of rainy season. The long, tuberous roots of the sweet-flag were also associated with longevity.

38. *Aishō no uta* (songs of lament) comprise one of the conventional cate-gories of *waka* in the imperially commissioned anthologies (book sixteen of the *Kokinshū* is devoted to them). See Shirane, *Bridge of Dreams,* chap. 9, for a discussion of the relation of this genre of poetry to narrative topoi in *Genji mo-nogatari.*

39. Tamai Kōsuke suggests that the image of the rice planters' hems may specifically echo the *Kagerō* memoirist's use of it, a gesture that serves the fu-rather purpose of inserting the *Sanuki no suke nikki* into the lineage of earlier memoirs. See *Sanuki no suke nikki,* ed. Tamai, p. 113, n. 1. The passage in the *Kagerō nikki* appears in the context of that memoirist's ironic description of her propensity for sleeping soundly during the fifth month in the third year of Ten-roku (972): "Nowadays, the banks of clouds are restless and I find my thoughts going out to the farmers in the paddies with their wet hems. But I haven't heard the voice of the cuckoo. They say that people who brood can't even doze off for a nap; how strangely [at peace] my sleepy appearance must make me seem" (*NKBZ* 9. 333). Other possible sources for the allusion appear in the personal poetry collections (*shikashū*) of Ise no Ōsuke (fl. ca. 1000–25), a lady-in-wait-ing who was a contemporary of Murasaki Shikibu, and Ōe Masafusa (1041–1111), a well-known poet in the Sanuki handmaid's own day, who served as tu-tor to Emperor Horikawa and others. See *SKT* 3: 340 and 403, respectively.

40. Izumi's line is *kumoi no kumo*, however: "the clouds in the cloud-dwelling [sky]." See *Izumi Shikibu shū, Izumi Shikibu zokushū*, ed. Shimizu, p. 54.

41. *Goshūiwakashū* 208:

Tsurezure to	Idle and endless
oto taesenu wa	is the sound of raindrops
samidare no	trickling from the irises
noki no ayame no	hung among the eaves
shizuku narikeri	in the fifth month.

42. Thus Ise no Ōsuke (*Shūiwakashū* 1307):

Shide no yama	Come back from over
koetekitsuramu	the mountain of death
hototogisu	hototogisu
koishiki hito no	give me some word of
ue kataranamu	the one I love.

43. A complicated combination of poetic devices and allusions defying concise explication climaxes this passage on the memoirist's symbiosis with the atmosphere of the fifth month and the world of the dead:

One after another the fleeting summer nights turn to dawn and pass, while memories of things long gone, themselves grown old like the abandoned capital at Isonokami, rise up in my mind, and my tears fall unabated. (*hakanaku akakuru natsu no yo na yo na sugimote isonokami furinishi mukashi no koto o omoiiderarete, namida todomarazu*)

Isonokami is a poetic toponym (*utamakura*) designating the site of an ancient, long-since abandoned capital in the Furu district of Tamba province. Predating Nara as the site of the capital, Isonokami served as seat of the Yamato state in the fifth century. Isonokami also functions as a "pillow word" or poetic epithet (*makurakotoba*) conventionally associated with poetry on the topos of abandoned capitals and thus gives rise to the next word in the sentence, the verb (not the place-name) *furu* ("to grow old"). *Furu* (used here with the perfective aspectual auxiliary *-nu* and the modal aspectual auxiliary *-ki*: thus, "to have grown old," *furunishi*) in turn modifies the "things of the past" (*mukashi no koto; koto*, "things," may mean words or events). Finally, the concurrence of references to the voice of the *hototogisu* and the old capital at Isonokami recalls a famous *Kokinshū* poem by priest Sosei (fl. late ninth century), who lived at Isonokami temple, an allusion that further underlines the image of the narrator as solitary mourner of the past (*KKS* 144):

Isonokami	O hototogisu
furuki miyako no	in the old capital
hototogisu	Isonokami
koe bakari koso	your voice alone
mukashi narikere	recalls the past.

44. See Origuchi, "Daijō matsuri no hongi," and "Kodai ni okeru gengo denchō no suii," in *Origuchi Shinobu zenshū*, vol. 3, pp. 174–240 and pp. 438–50. Cited in Hayashida, *Genji monogatari no hassō*, p. 62, n. 2.

45. The "Judgments of a Rainy Night" in "The Broom Tree" (*Hahakigi*) chapter of *Genji* take place during the rainy season of the fifth month, on a night while the court is "in retreat," observing this particular taboo. See Chapter 2.

46. I note in passing that the critical tendency to analyze topoi of literary voyeurism primarily in terms of their relation to masculine looking and desire plays itself out in Hayashida's survey of the *nagame* topos, despite his recognition of the folk belief underlying the topos according to which the woman's role in the rainy season is that of a *miko* (medium or shamaness), a figure defined by her posture of waiting and watching over the flooded rice paddies for signs of a divine visitor's approach. Hayashida concentrates his survey of *The Tale of Genji* and its predecessors on passages in which it is a male figure who stares off longingly. See Hayashida, *Genji monogatari no hassō*, pp. 66–73 (or, more inclusively, pp. 61–86).

47. The result was the text known as *Horikawa'in ensho awase*, regarded as one of the finest testimonials to the talents of an emperor who, though sickly and short-lived, is remembered by literary historians for his poetic skill and for the salons that centered around him, his empress Atsuko, and their relatives among the Minamoto and imperial client families. See *Utaawase shū*, ed. Hagitani and Taniyama, *NKBT* 74: 263–70.

48. Imai Gen'e, quoted by Ishino Keiko in "*Sanuki no suke nikki*," p. 106.

49. Kimura Masanori notes that the technique with which the prologue to the *Sanuki no suke nikki* opens is one it shares with the opening passages of the *Izumi Shikibu nikki*, the *Murasaki Shikibu nikki*, individual tales in the mid- to late-eleventh-century collection the *Tsutsumi Chūnagon monogatari*, and in certain late chapters of *The Tale of Genji*. Kimura draws on Tsukahara Tetsuo's eight-part typology of temporal structures and conventions of opening passages in *monogatari*, expanding and modifying it to encompass opening strategies apparent in *nikki*. Kimura stresses that the memoir's strategy for beginning, with its omission of references that would place the origin of the discourse in some moment or event of the past (e.g., formulaic references to the tale's source in a nonspecific or remotely distant past [*ima wa mukashi, izure no ontoki ni ka*], or specific details on the biography of the main character, etc.), has the effect of placing the reader immediately into the world of the narrative. See "*Izumi Shikibu nikki* keisei ron," pp. 231–61.

50. Instead, sentences end with verbal auxiliary suffixes (*jodōshi*) like *-tari* (which denotes an incomplete action and its resultant state) or *-nu* (not a past-tense marker but a perfective, denoting a completed action). The appearance in sentence-terminal position of *-keri* and *-ki* (verbal auxiliary suffixes that have been termed "narrative modal aspectuals") is rare in the *Sanuki no suke nikki*. One survey discovers only seven instances of *-ki* as a terminal auxiliary in the memoir, all of them occurring in volume two. In this respect, the *Sanuki no*

suke nikki resembles many other mid-Heian *kana nikki*, in which tenseless narration is the norm. According to this same survey, the *Tosa nikki* shows only two instances of sentence-terminal use of *-ki*, volume one of the *Kagerō nikki* shows but one, the *Sarashina nikki* two, and the *Izumi Shikibu nikki* none. The exception to this rule is the *Murasaki Shikibu nikki*, where *-ki* and *-keri* in sentence-terminal position emerge as a distinctive feature of that narrative (*-ki* occurs thirty-seven times, while *-keri* appears at the end of sentences thirty-five times in that memoir). See Horikawa Kō, "Jikan no mondai," p. 166.

51. See R. Okada, *Figures of Resistance*, p. 18.

52. Stylistic differences and a chronological gap in the sequence of events narrated in the two surviving volumes have led many scholars to argue the original existence of a third volume, now lost. The fact that the *Honchō shojaku mokuroku* (a late Kamakura–early Muromachi catalogue of books) describes the *Sanuki no suke nikki* as a text in three volumes lends external evidence to this argument.

Those who posit a third volume are divided in their opinions as to where the lost one would have fit into the sequence of the extant two. Tamai (*Nikki bungaku no kenkyū*, pp. 335–37) and Miyazaki (*Heian joryū nikki bungaku no kenkyū*, pp. 373–76) argue the lost volume was a final one. Others, among them Ozaki Satoakira (*Sanuki no suke nikki*) and Morita ("*Sanuki no suke nikki* no seiritsu"), speculate that the missing volume covered events immediately following Horikawa's death in the seventh month of 1107 up to the eleventh month of the same year, thus filling the chronological gap between volumes one and two.

But radical ellipses and chronological leaps in narrative are not an uncommon feature of *monogatari* and *nikki* of the Heian and Kamakura periods. The absence of a chapter recounting Genji's death in the *Genji monogatari* is a famous example, as is the chronological gap between books three and four of *Towazugatari*. My point is that the ellipsis may not imply a lost volume at all.

53. See Shirane, *Bridge of Dreams*, chap. 9, for a discussion of "The Wizard" (*Maboroshi*), its links to the *aishō no uta* cycle of the *Kokinshū*, and to the tradition of women's *nikki*.

54. Ishino, "*Sanuki no suke nikki* ni okeru jikan no kōzō," p. 252.

55. Compare Lady Rokujō's musings on her dead husband and now-vanished chances for further social ascendancy as she reenters the gate of the imperial palace en route to Ise with her daughter in the "Sacred Tree" (*Sakaki*) chapter of *Genji monogatari*, NKBZ 13: 85; S, 189–90.

56. Ishino, "*Sanuki no suke nikki* ni okeru jikan no kōzō," p. 254.

57. Imai Takuji argues that the *Sanuki no suke nikki* contains a larger number of direct addresses to the reader than any of the other four major Heian *nikki* by women writers (the *Kagerō nikki*, the *Murasaki Shikibu nikki*, the *Izumi Shikibu nikki*, the *Sarashina nikki*). See his *Heian jidai nikki bungaku no kenkyū*, p. 202.

58. Ishino does not speculate explicitly on any possible political reasons for the memoirist's anxiety about the issues of unseemliness or divided loyalties.

59. Ishino, "*Sanuki no suke nikki*," p. 105.

60. Hence Marian Ury's comment that the *nikki* reads like an "examination essay. . . . If there is something not quite right about this diary it is that it is too well schooled [in the art of narrative]. One becomes too easily aware of the management of time, of the balancing (as in *Tosa nikki*) of long against short episodes, fleeting remembrance against extended revery." See Ury, "Review of *The Emperor Horikawa Diary*," p. 223.

61. Benjamin was drawing a distinction between the art of reminiscence and the narrative techniques of more conventionally structured linear autobiographies when he wrote in "A Berlin Chronicle": "He who seeks to approach his own buried past must conduct himself like a man digging. This confers the tone and bearing of genuine reminiscences. He must not be afraid to return again and again to the same matter; to scatter it as one scatters earth, to turn it over as one turns over soil. . . . True, for successful excavations a plan is needed. Yet no less indispensable is the cautious probing of the spade in the dark loam, and it is to cheat oneself of the richest prize to preserve as a record merely the inventory of one's discoveries, and not this dark joy of the place of the finding itself. Fruitless searching is as much a part of this as succeeding, and consequently remembrance must not proceed in the manner of a narrative or still less that of a report, but must, in the strictest epic and rhapsodic manner, assay its spade in ever-new places, and in the old ones delve to ever-deeper layers." See Benjamin, *Reflections*, p. 26.

62. See Yoshida Kenkō's *Tsurezuregusa*, ed Nagazumi, NKBZ 27: 236.

63. Kenreimon'in's former handmaid is watching the snow cover the traces of the autumn world with a blank whiteness when the sight of a snow-covered orange tree obliterates momentarily the distance between past and present and launches her into the memory of a morning when Sukemori offered her a snow-covered orange-tree bough. This is a doubly suggestive image, as orange trees (especially the scent of orange blossoms) were also associated with memory. See *Kenreimon'in Ukyō no Daibu shū*, ed. Hisamatsu, NKBT 80: 483. See also Harries, trans., *Poetic Memoirs of Lady Daibu*, p. 225.

64. The penultimate passages of the chapter describe the Festival of Names in the twelfth month and Genji's first public appearance since Murasaki's death. A heavy snow has fallen and the plum trees are just beginning to bloom as the narrative of Genji's year of seclusion comes back around full circle to the moment of its own beginning in the early spring of the previous year. Genji exchanges poems on snow and plum blossoms with the priest in charge of the services, an old friend from the days at Rokujō mansion, whose hair, he notices, after all these years, has also begun to go white. See *Genji monogatari*, NKBZ 15: 535.

65. Brewster's translation obscures this effect by rationalizing it. Her rendering of the passage *begins* with lines that appear only at the end of the passage in the original: "I was in the chamber used by the Empress on her visits to the Emperor, so absorbed in memories of the past as to be heedless of the current festivities." See Brewster, *Emperor Horikawa Diary*, p. 104.

66. The painterly description of the scene recalls the iconography of illus-trated *monogatari* and *nikki*. Perhaps what we are reading here is in fact the textual frame for a now lost or never accomplished illustration for the memoir. Joshua Mostow's study of this phenomenon in the *Kagerō nikki* sheds new light on some of the more visually descriptive passages in that memoir, connecting them to the now largely lost tradition of illustrated *nikki* and *monogatari*. His study carries implications for similar passages in other Heian memoirs and tales. See his "Self and Landscape in *Kagerō Nikki*."

67. Ki no Tsurayuki, *Gosenwakashū* 1426; also *Shūiwakashū* 1309.

68. *Gosenwakashū* 1425.

69. Note, for example, the *waka* by Bishop Henjō (composed at the end of the mourning period for Emperor Nimmyō), which the handmaid recalls at the end of the mourning period for Emperor Horikawa. See *NKBZ* 18: 432, and Brewster, *Emperor Horikawa Diary*, p. 98.

70. And how indeed is one to identify an "original context" in the intertex-tual maze of Heian *waka*? In singling out Tsurayuki's exchange with Kanesuke, I have followed the example of most Japanese commentators, for reasons that will become clear below. Other precedents that resonate interestingly with the use of this poem in the *Sanuki no suke nikki* appear in the *Genji monogatari* (the Suma chapter; *NKBZ* 13: 161) and the *Eiga monogatari* (Matsumura and Yamanaka, eds., *NKBT* 76: 391).

71. By priest Nōin, *Goshūiwakashū* 553. See *NKBZ* 18: 453, and Brewster, *Emperor Horikawa Diary*, p. 112.

72. In fact, according to Miyazaki's calculations, there is a higher propor-tion of *waka* to prose in the second volume of the *Sanuki no suke nikki* than there is in the second volume of the *Kagerō nikki*, while the *Murasaki Shikibu nikki* has a much lower percentage overall than does volume two of the *Sanuki no suke nikki*. See his *Heian joryū nikki bungaku no kenkyū*, pp. 351–52.

73. The logical question to ask here is, Who was Lady Hitachi? Does the name refer in fact—or provide clues to—the patron or patrons this memoir originally sought? Unfortunately, her identity remains a puzzle, though many commentators speculate that she was Fujiwara Ieko, who is referred to fre-quently in the first volume of the memoir by her court sobriquet, Daini no sanmi. She was one of Emperor Horikawa's four wet nurses, and one of the three ladies-in-waiting, including the memoirist, who attended him daily during his final illness. Note, for example, the long, impassioned speech she gives at his deathbed (*NKBZ* 18: 398–99). Moriya Shōgo reviews the debate on her iden-tity in his *Heian kōki nikki bungaku ron*, pp. 284–99.

Chapter 6: The Poetics of Voyeurism

1. Mitamura Masako's work on "seeing, being seen, and showing" in *The Pillow Book* did not come to my attention until after I had developed my own arguments on voyeurism in this text, so I have not attempted to incorporate them here. The reader is advised to read her *Makura no sōshi: hyōgen no ronri*,

especially the chapter entitled "Miru/mirareru/miseru: *Makura no sōshi* no shisen kōzō," for a wide-ranging analysis of the dynamics of looking in Sei Shōnagon's work.

2. I will be referring to both the author and the narrator-heroine of *The Pillow Book* hereafter as either Sei Shōnagon or simply Sei in keeping with current conventions in English-language scholarship by which Murasaki Shikibu is sometimes referred to simply as "Murasaki" rather than "Shikibu." "Sei" is the sinitic reading for the first character of the memoirist's family name, Kiyowara. "Shōnagon" means "minor counselor," a position in the court bureaucracy that was probably held by one of Sei's male relatives around the time she first entered Empress Teishi's service. Murasaki refers to Sei in her *nikki* as "Sei Shōnagon." Within *The Pillow Book* itself, Sei is often addressed by her mistress Empress Teishi as simply "Shōnagon."

3. *Makura no sōshi*, ed. Watanabe, *SNKBT* 25: 27–28. All translations are mine unless otherwise indicated. All citations from the text will be keyed to the *SNKBT* edition, with page numbers provided in parentheses. For a complete English translation, see I. Morris, trans., *The Pillow Book of Sei Shōnagon*, 2 vols. Cross-references to Morris's translation will be keyed to the often reprinted and widely available Penguin paperback abridgment of the same translation: I. Morris, trans., *The Pillow Book of Sei Shōnagon*.

4. *Naishi no suke* refers to the second of the three categories of female officials in the Naishi no Tsukasa (Palace Attendants Bureau). The other two are *naishi* (handmaid) and *naishi no kami* (principal handmaid). As noted in Chapter 5, *naishi no suke* and *naishi no kami* were posts usually filled by women who were also imperial concubines and thus generally of very high rank—in Sei's time, Junior Third Rank for *naishi no Kaman*, Junior Fourth for *naishi no suke*, and sometimes even higher in both cases. At the end of the tenth century, handmaids (*naishi*) were usually Junior Fifth Upper Rank.

5. Sei's father, Motosuke, was numbered among the compilers of the second imperial anthology, *Gosenshū*, and, together with Minamoto Shitagō and three others, took part as one of the "Pear Palace Five" (*Nashitsubo no gonin*), a group of poet-scholars that produced glosses for the *Man'yōshū*. In terms of rankings in the court bureaucracy, however, Motosuke never rose above Junior Fifth Upper Rank and achieved that only very late in a career that involved a number of provincial governorships.

6. This is pointed out in the *NKBZ* edition of *The Pillow Book*. See *Makura no sōshi*, ed. Matsuo and Nagai, *NKBZ* 11: 92, n. 3.

7. I. Morris, *Pillow Book*, p. 39.

8. A look at relations among the ladies-in-waiting themselves, at least as the *Murasaki Shikibu nikki* depicts them, should be enough to dispel any temptation to paint that world or its most famous commemorator as a community imbued with putatively "feminine" virtues of mutual nurturance and empathy. Murasaki's memoir is full of anecdotes illustrating the unkind pranks ladies-in-waiting played on one another—particularly targeting aged colleagues whose behavior, appearance, or even mere presence call attention to the fact that they

are well past their prime and ought not to allow themselves to be seen at all. See especially the passages regarding Chikuzen no myōbu and Sakyō no muma in *Murasaki Shikibu nikki*, NKBZ 18: 195 and 216–18, and in Bowring, *Her Diary and Poetic Memoirs*, pp. 83 and 109–11.

9. The translation is from Bowring, *Her Diary and Poetic Memoirs*, p. 113.

10. M. Morris, "Sei Shōnagon's Poetic Catalogues," 40–41.

11. The gender of the reader may affect the degree and/or quality of his or her identification. Following the rereadings of Freud and Laura Mulvey by the film theorist Teresa de Lauretis, we might hypothesize that for the female reader, the identification is double: she experiences herself as both the seer and the surveyed simultaneously or else oscillates between identification with each. De Lauretis's work also exposes the complexity of identification for male readers/viewers instead of assuming that for them, identification is simply and straightforwardly with the (male) voyeur. Why should men be any less complicated than women in their self-identifications with respect to desire and the desire to be desired, passivity and activity, the subject versus the object position? See De Lauretis, *Alice Doesn't: Feminism, Semiotics, Cinema*, chap. 5.

12. See Nakanishi Susumu's widely cited essay on the significance of motifs of looking in early Japanese writings: "Miru: kodai teki chikaku."

13. Shinohara Yoshihiko discusses at length this motif, which he terms *nyōbō sanbi* (the admiring gaze of the lady-in-waiting) in his "*Genji monogatari* ni itaru nozokimi no keifu," p. 63. We will take it up further below.

14. Field discusses themes of voyeurism in *Genji* at various points throughout her study of the *Genji* heroines. She addresses the issue of feminine voyeurism and the gaze of female characters directly in chap. 4 of *The Splendor of Longing*, esp. pp. 251–57 and 269–76.

15. Berger contends that, particularly since the Renaissance invention of the individual as consumer of art, the "ideal" spectator in Western visual arts has been male. Images of women in the visual arts are crafted to appeal to his gaze and to his desire to possess. Material possession of the work of art (particularly the representation of the female nude) becomes a metaphor for erotic possession of Woman. Woman herself (as spectator, and, more recently, as potential consumer of art, cinema, and advertisement) is understood "to consider the surveyor and the surveyed within her as the two constituent yet always distinct elements of her identity as a woman." See his *Ways of Seeing*, p. 46.

16. Shinohara, "*Genji monogatari* ni itaru nozokimi no keifu."

17. Hayashida Takakazu gives a similar interpretation of the same scene (though without acknowledging Shinohara's previous work) in his essay on the "arts of *kaimami*" in *Genji monogatari no hassō*, pp. 242–44. We will take up Hayashida's remarks on other topoi of the gaze below.

18. Girard develops his theories on desire in literature over the course of several books beginning with the publication of *Mensonge romantique et verité romanesque*.

19. Girard, *Violence and the Sacred*, pp. 145–46, quoted in Moi, "Missing Mother," p. 22.

20. Moi, "Missing Mother," pp. 27–29.

21. Joan DeJean, "Female Voyeurism," p. 201.

22. Both Moi and Ciriaco Moron-Arroyo have pointed out that despite his claim that the desiring subject is always masculine and thus theoretically may be a female whose gaze mimics the masculine model (a proviso necessary to keep his argument in line with his own claim that his theory of desire is "absolutely symmetrical in both sexes"), in practice Girard avoids dealing with women as subjects of the gaze and agents of desire. See Moi, "Missing Mother," pp. 24–25.

23. Shinohara, "Nozokimi no keifu," p. 63.

24. But note how Nakanishi Susumu's remarks on the dynamics of admiration (sanbi) suggest the very opposite configuration of looking and power for the nyōbō sanbi scene, i.e., that the one who looks is disempowered by the act of looking: "When it comes to admiration, the beholder ends up possessed by the beheld" (sanbi ni naru to iu no wa, jiko ga ta ni ryōyū sarete shimau). See "Miru: kodaiteki chikaku," p. 483. Takahashi Tōru has made a similar case by underlining the importance of reversed relations of possessor to possessed in the kaimami scene: "It has already been argued that the concept that 'seeing [miru koto] is possession' is fundamental to kaimami. What surfaces now is the importance of the complementary concept that 'to see is to be possessed.'" See his Monogatari to e no enkinhō, pp. 262–65.

25. See NKBZ 14: 281–86; S, 467–70. The topos in this case is monomi (looking at spectacles), not nyōbō sanbi. Imperial processions and many other festivals at court provided occasions for men (and women too) to engage in a controlled form of self-display: being seen was the goal; the admiring gaze of spectators was deliberately sought.

26. Field, Splendor of Longing, pp. 216, 253.

27. Ibid., p. 201. As Field implies elsewhere, The Tale of Genji seems peculiarly attuned to feminine interiority and in some respects conflates interiority and femininity. Hence Genji's interiority—when it does become the focus of narrative interest—coincides with passages in which his behavior (such as his desire to shun the eyes of others when in mourning for Murasaki) also mimics the feminine.

28. Field, Splendor of Longing, pp. 251–57, 269–76.

29. Bowring, Tale of Genji, p. 14.

30. In this respect the love stories in the Genji seem to arouse and allay some of the same anxieties that Tania Modleski argues are characteristic of contemporary Harlequin romances: "a good man is hard to detect," as Mark Morris has pointed out. See his "Desire and the Prince," p. 303. Until recently, commentators on Heian literature have tended to underplay the likelihood that anxieties about romance were fueled by anxieties of a more practical nature. Heian aristocratic women—both the real ones and the images of them that people the pages of The Tale of Genji—were probably less worried than we usually imagine in their interactions with men (whether real husbands or lovers or representations of them in fiction) about the man's "interiority" than about

his reliability—a quality that, though it might encompass questions about his romantic feelings for her (or for the heroines in the tales she was given to read), is not limited to them. What was worrisome was not so much questions about the perdurability of the hero's passion as the issue of his willingness to offer steady, practical support (social recognition of self and offspring, material help, prospects for the offspring's careers at court, etc.). Consider the shivery fate of Suetsumuhana and her aging ladies-in-waiting while she waited faithfully for Genji to remember her and come to call and make up for his appalling neglect by renovating her house and garden and providing warm clothes and coal for the winter.

31. M. Morris, "Desire and the Prince," p. 302.

32. Field, *Splendor of Longing*, p. 255.

33. Thus Berger, on the gender arrangements in Western culture: "Men look at women. Women watch themselves being looked at. This determines not only most relations between men and women but also the relation of women to themselves. The surveyor of woman in herself is male: the surveyed female. Thus she turns herself into an object—and most particularly an object of vision: a sight. . . . [Women] do to themselves what men do to them. They survey, like men, their own femininity." See *Ways of Seeing*, pp. 47, 63.

34. Shinohara argues that the technique so elaborately worked out in the *Genji* narrative of linking different heroines on the basis of visual associations between them in the memory of the hero is a technique it borrows from the *Utsuho monogatari*. See his "Nozokimi no keifu," pp. 63–64. I would add that the intensely emotional dramas of feminine discontent that the awareness of this "logic of [erotic] substitution" precipitates for *Genji* heroines like the Murasaki lady and Ōigimi resonate with pivotal passages in the *Kagerō nikki*. My discussion in Chapter 2 suggests the extent to which the crises occupying volume two of that memoir circulate around the development of the theme of the woman's traumatic recognition of what she may have in common with other women, in particular her perception of her own sameness (in the eyes of her husband) with her rivals, his other secondary wives.

35. Field notes the importance of the motif of hearing and overhearing by suffering, isolated *Genji* heroines in *Splendor of Longing*, p. 276. See also Mitamura Masako in her essay " 'Koe' o kiku hitobito." These two discussions bring to mind current debates in feminist literary theory that suggest the need to look more closely at other faculties of sense as metaphors for the narrative inscription of desire (especially feminine desire). Some feminists have challenged what they see as an overemphasis on specularity in contemporary discussions of desire, an emphasis that they single out as unquestioningly complicitous with phallocentric conceptions of desire and hence inadequate as a means of tracing the inscription of feminine desire. In the words of Luce Irigaray: "Within [the logic that has dominated the West since the time of the Greeks], the gaze is particularly foreign to female eroticism. . . . [Woman's] entry into a dominant scopic economy signifies . . . her consignment to passivity: she is to be the beautiful object of contemplation. . . . Woman's desire [does not] speak the same lan-

guage as man's. ... Woman takes pleasure more from touching than from looking." See her *This Sex Which Is Not One*, pp. 25–26. Though I object to the ahistoricizing and Eurocentric aspects of Irigaray's *cri de coeur* (not to mention her essentializing of "Woman's desire"), I would still join Irigaray in pointing out that the contemporary preoccupation with the dynamics of visual pleasure is questionable. Visual stimulation and scopic pleasure bear if not a greater, at least a different, kind of urgency for our own culture than they did for that of aristocratic Heian society and its cultural productions. The privileging of sight over other senses has been connected, of course, in psychoanalytic discourse since Freud with the origins of sexual difference—most dramatically with the little boy's discovery that what he has is more visible than what females have, which leads to his concomitant fear of castration and (in Freud's view) his assumption of masculinity. As Jane Gallop notes, Freud himself, in two lengthy footnotes to *Civilization and Its Discontents*, makes a tentative stab at connecting olfactory stimuli with female sexuality. For a playful yet serious consideration of the links between feminine desire/sexuality and the sense of smell, see Gallop's reading of Michele Montrelay with Jacques Lacan in chap. 2 of *The Daughter's Seduction*, esp. pp. 26–32. Given these hints, we might do well to pause to consider the way incense wafts so insistently through the air of the women's quarters in *Genji* and elsewhere.

36. See *Genji monogatari*, NKBZ 16: 208–10; and S, 819–20. Nakanokimi's gazing at Kaoru's men is not mentioned in Shinohara's survey.

37. Field, *Splendor of Longing*, p. 234.

38. One is reminded here of Tamagami Takuya's understanding of the *Genji* texts as the end product of a series of prior written texts, oral recitations and improvisations based on them by ladies-in-waiting, and subsequent transcriptions of those recitations. My understanding of the narrating voice as the voice of a gossip borrows a metaphor for narration from the opening passage of the *Kagerō nikki*: the text as *tameshi*, which can mean "precedent," "model," or "topic of gossip" (and thus, by implication, the narrator as purveyor of gossip). Okada's remarks are also to the point: "The ambiguity in the term *tamesi* will inform much of the *Genji* text: a narrative constituted by 'gossip' destined nevertheless to establish 'precedents.' " See his *Figures of Resistance*, p. 185. Tamagami's fruitful arguments concerning the *Genji* narrator(s) (the famous *ondokuron*, or "reading aloud" theory) were developed in a series of articles beginning in 1950. See the reprint of the first of these, "Monogatari ondokuron josetsu: *Genji monogatari* no honsei (sono ichi)," in Tamagami's *Genji monogatari kenkyū*, supplement 1, pp. 143–155. The essay stimulated a torrent of scholarship on the narrational complexities in *Genji* and other Heian *monogatari*. For extended discussion and analysis of this in English, see Konishi, *Early Middle Ages*, pp. 336–41, and Okada, *Figures of Resistance*, pp. 174–81. For a discussion that bears specifically on the narration in the Uji chapters, see Stinchecum, "Who Tells the Tale?" pp. 375–403. For a lucid and challenging critique of Okada's interpretation of Tamagami's theories, see Ramirez-Christensen, "Resisting Figures of Resisitance," especially pp. 182–91.

39. Hayashida, *Genji monogatari no hassō*, p. 242.

40. See ibid., pp. 247–48. See also Nakanishi, "Miru: kodaiteki chikaku," p. 482.

41. The Kamakura-period memoir *Towazugatari* (after 1313?), attributed to GoFukakusa'in Nijō, a concubine of retired emperor GoFukakusa, provides a striking exception to this rule. The mode of the heroine's movement through a series of men is represented, however, as anything but blithe.

42. Ogino, *Makura no sōshi*, p. 166.

43. For a summary of the various legends surrounding Sanekata's life and their sources, see Takehana Isao, "Sanekata," p. 398.

44. See *SNKS* 7: 110, and Marra, "Mumyōzōshi," pt. 3, p. 424. Naomi Fukumori argues that Sei did not simply eliminate "details about the political demise of her patron . . . details are laid out for the discerning reader to piece together, but without prior knowledge of the historical background, Sei's rhetoric . . . may seem simple or even superficial." See her "Sei Shōnagon the Essay/Eseist," pp. 72–73. Fukumori's reading draws also on the findings of Haraoka Fumiko, who demonstrates that Sei's strategy for masking the bleak political context of her text was not silence but laughter. Haraoka charts the occurrences of the adjective *okashi* (charming, amusing) and the verb *waru* (to laugh) in *The Pillow Book* and tries to correlate their occurrence with the approximate dates of the individual anecdotes in which they occur. Her study reveals that these words occur with much *greater* frequency in passages describing events that occurred after Michitaka's death and during the ensuing years of Teishi's decline, as though the author were deliberately trying to lighten the tone of anecdotes/events whose actual contexts may have been the very opposite of amusing. See Haraoka, *Genji monogatari: ryōgi no ito*, p. 311.

45. The adjective is I. Morris's, in *The Pillow Book*, p. 10.

46. See *SNKBT* 25: 48–50; and M, 61–62.

47. Kobayashi Shigemi dates the initial events described in the passage to somewhere between the sixth month of Chōtoku 3 (997) and the tenth month of Chōtoku 4 (998), and the final anecdote to the third month of Chōhō 2 (1000). If these speculations are correct, Yukinari was about twenty-six or twenty-seven and Sei about thirty-seven or thirty-eight. See *MSK* 2: 213.

48. Kobayashi, *MSK* 2: 215–16.

49. I. Morris, *Pillow Book*, p. 299, n. 153. Actually, Morris's point is more specific. He insinuates that Yukinari is trying to make a point about the greater importance of "a woman's obligations to her lover."

50. Hayashida, *Genji monogatari no hassō*, p. 240.

51. Some have speculated that what renders Noritaka's gaze impotent to Sei and Shikibu is the matter of his rank (and perhaps also, I would add, the women's inurement, as veteran *nyōbō*, to being viewed by male figures below them in the pecking order at court). Various guesses have been made as to the identity of the figure named Noritaka, who seems to have so little power to arouse female anxiety here. The *SNKBT* editors identify him as Tachibana Noritaka, who would have been a sixth-rank Chamberlain and thus one of the few

men of the relatively lowly Sixth Rank allowed admission to the Courtiers' Hall (*tenjō no ma*). See *SNKBT* 25: 67, n. 43. According to another theory, the man is Fujiwara Noritaka, elder brother of Murasaki Shikibu's husband, Fujiwara Nobutaka. See *Makura no sōshi*, ed. Matsuo and Nagai, *NKBZ* 11: 146, n. 20. Commentators who concur with this latter theory point to Sei's apparent disdain for Noritaka here as further motivation for the animus Murasaki Shikibu expresses in her comments about Sei quoted above.

52. *SNKBT* 25: 9–13.

53. The use of the verbal auxiliary -*meri* (conveying speculation or an indirect impression rather than direct sensory perception) in the final lines of the passage suggests vestiges of this last-ditch resort to a coquettish averting of the gaze on Sei's part.

54. Morimoto Motoko, "*Makura no sōshi* no gensen: nikki bungaku," in *MSK* 4: 193.

55. The distinctions between biblical narrative and the epic narrative mode of Greek antiquity are developed in chap. 1, "Odysseus' Scar," of Erich Auerbach's famous study *Mimesis*, pp. 3–23.

56. M. Morris, "Sei's Poetic Catalogues," p. 34.

57. See *Mumyōzōshi*, ed. Kuwabara, *SNKS* 7: 110–11.

⌒ Works Cited

The place of publication for all works in Japanese is Tokyo, unless otherwise noted. Abbreviations are as listed in the front matter. Primary texts are listed under their titles.

Akiyama Ken. "Nyōbōtachi." In Tamagami Takuya, ed., *Genji monogatari. Kanshō Nihon koten bungaku* 9: 450–63. Kadokawa Shoten, 1975.
———. *Ōchō joryū bungaku no sekai.* Tokyo Daigaku Shuppankai, 1972.
———, ed. *Issatsu no kōza: Kagerō nikki.* Yūseidō, 1981.
———, ed. *Kōza Nihon bungaku Genji monogatari.* 2 vols. Shibundō, 1978.
———, ed. *Ōchō bungakushi.* Tokyo Daigaku Shuppankai, 1984.
———, ed. *Ōchō joryū nikki hikkei.* Gakutōsha, 1986.
Arntzen, Sonya, trans. *The Kagerō Diary: A Woman's Autobiographical Text from Tenth-Century Japan.* Michigan Monographs in Japanese Studies, no. 19. Ann Arbor: University of Michigan, 1997.
Auerbach, Erich. *Mimesis: Representations of Reality in Western Literature.* Trans. Willard R. Trask. Princeton: Princeton University Press, 1974.
Backus, Robert L., trans. *The Riverside Counselor's Stories: Vernacular Fiction of Late Heian Japan.* Stanford: Stanford University Press, 1985.
Bargen, Doris. "Spirit Possession in the Context of Dramatic Expressions of Gender Conflict: The Aoi Episode of the *Genji monogatari.*" *HJAS* 48 (June 1988): 95–103.
———. *A Woman's Weapon: Spirit Possession in the Tale of Genji.* Honolulu: University of Hawai'i Press, 1997.
———. "Yūgao: A Case of Spirit Possession in *The Tale of Genji.*" *Mosaic* 19, no. 3 (1986): 15–24.
Benjamin, Walter. *Reflections.* Trans. Edmond Jephcott. New York: Schocken Books, 1986.
Berger, John. *Ways of Seeing.* London: BBC and Penguin Books, 1977.
Blacker, Carmen. *The Catalpa Bow: A Study of Shamanistic Practices in Japan.* London: George Allen and Unwin, 1975.

Borgen, Robert. "The Japanese Mission to China of 801–806." *MN* 37, no. 1 (Spring 1982): 1–28.

———. *Sugawara no Michizane and the Early Heian Court.* Cambridge, Mass.: Council on East Asian Studies, Harvard University, 1986.

Bowring, Richard. *Murasaki Shikibu: The Tale of Genji.* Cambridge, Eng.: Cambridge University Press, 1988.

———, trans. *Murasaki Shikibu: Her Diary and Poetic Memoirs.* Princeton: Princeton University Press, 1982.

Brewster, Jennifer, trans. *The Emperor Horikawa Diary by Fujiwara no Nagako.* Honolulu: University Press of Hawaii, 1977.

Brownstein, Rachel M. *Becoming a Heroine: Reading About Women in Novels.* New York: Viking Press, 1982.

Butler, Judith. *Gender Trouble: Feminism and the Subversion of Identity.* New York: Routledge, 1990.

———. "Performative Acts and Gender Constitution: An Essay in Phenomenology and Feminist Theory." *Theatre Journal* 40 (Dec. 1988): 519–31.

———, ed. *Nikki bungaku sakuhinron no kokoromi.* Kasama Shoin, 1979.

Chōshūki. In Zōho shiryō taisei kankōkai, ed., *Shiryō taisei,* vols. 16–17. Kyoto: Rinsen Shoten, 1965.

Chūko bungaku kenkyūkai, ed. *Genji monogatari to Heian bungaku.* Vol. 1. Waseda Daigaku Shuppanbu, 1988.

Chūyūki. In Zōho shiryō taisei kankōkai, ed., *Shiryō taisei,* vols. 9–15. Kyoto: Rinsen Shoten, 1965.

Cranston, Edwin A., trans. *The Izumi Shikibu Diary: A Romance of the Heian Court.* Cambridge, Mass.: Harvard University Press, 1969.

DeJean, Joan. "Female Voyeurism: Sappho and Lafayette." *Rivista di letterature moderne e comparate,* n.s., 40 (Aug.–Sept. 1987): 201–15.

———. *Tender Geographies: Women and the Origins of the Novel in France.* New York: Columbia University Press, 1991.

De Lauretis, Teresa. *Alice Doesn't: Feminism, Semiotics, Cinema.* Bloomington: Indiana University Press, 1984.

Doane, Mary Ann. *The Desire to Desire: The Woman's Film of the 1940s.* Bloomington: Indiana University Press, 1987.

———. "Film and Masquerade: Theorising the Female Spectator." *Screen* 23 (Sept.–Oct. 1982): 74–87.

Eiga monogatari, ed. Matsumura Hiroji and Yamanaka Yutaka. 2 vols. *NKBT,* 75–76. Iwanami Shoten, 1964.

Enchi Fumiko. *Namamiko monogatari.* Shinchōsha, 1993.

———. "Ōchō josei bungaku to gendai bungaku." *Kokubungaku* 10 (Dec. 1965): 208–13.

Field, Norma. *The Splendor of Longing in the Tale of Genji.* Princeton: Princeton University Press, 1987.

Frye, Northrop. *The Anatomy of Criticism: Four Essays.* Princeton: Princeton University Press, 1957.

Fujii Sadakazu. *Genji monogatari shigen to genzai.* Tōjusha, 1980.

————. "*Kagerō nikki* to Heianchō no kon'in seido." In Akiyama Ken, ed., *Issatsu no kōza: Kagerō nikki*, pp. 173–79. Yūseidō, 1981.

Fukumori, Naomi. "Sei Shōnagon the Essay/Ese-ist: Delineating Differences in *Makura no sōshi*." In Eiji Sekine, ed., *Proceedings of the Midwestern Association for Japanese Literary Studies*, vol. 3 (Summer 1997), pp. 66–88.

Gallop, Jane. *The Daughter's Seduction: Feminism and Psychoanalysis.* Ithaca, N.Y.: Cornell University Press, 1982.

Genji monogatari, ed. Abe Akio, Akiyama Ken, Imai Gen'e. 6 vols. NKBZ 12–17. Shōgakkan, 1970–76.

Gessel, Van C. "The 'Medium' of Fiction: Enchi Fumiko as Narrator." *World Literature Today* 62 (Summer 1988): 380–85.

Girard, René. *Mensonge romantique et verité romanesque.* Paris: Grasset, 1961.

————. *Violence and the Sacred.* Trans. Patrick Gregory. Baltimore: Johns Hopkins University Press, 1977.

Hagitani Boku. *Makura no sōshi kaishaku no shomondai.* Shintensha, 1991.

————. *Sei Shōnagon zenkashū: kaishaku to hyōron.* Kasama shoin, 1986.

————. *Tosa nikki zenchūshaku.* Kadokawa Shoten, 1967.

Hamamatsu *Chūnagon* monogatari, ed. Matsuo Satoshi. In Endō Yoshimoto and Mattsuo Satoshi, eds., *Takamura monogotari, Heichū monogotari, Hamamatsu Chūnagon monogotari.* NKBT 77. Iwanami Shoten, 1964.

Hansen, Miriam. "Pleasure, Ambivalence, Identification: Valentino and Female Spectatorship." *Cinema Journal* 25, no. 4 (Summer 1986): 6–32.

Haraoka Fumiko. "Genji monogatari no eikyō: in'yōsareru bungaku." In Suzuki Hideo and Fujii Sadakazu, eds., *Nihon bungeishi*, vol. 1, *Kodai*, pp. 189–92. Kawade shobō shinsha, 1986.

————. *Genji monogatari: ryōgi no ito.* Yūseidō, 1991.

Harper, Thomas James. "Motoori Norinaga's Criticism of the *Genji monogatari*: A Study of the Background and Critical Content of His *Genji Monogatari Tama no Ogushi*." Ph.D. diss., University of Michigan, 1971.

Harries, Philip Tudor, trans. *The Poetic Memoirs of Lady Daibu.* Stanford: Stanford University Press, 1980.

Hayashida Takakazu. *Genji monogatari no hassō.* Ōfūsha, 1980.

Heianchō bungaku kenkyūkai, ed. *Heianchō bungaku no shomondai.* Kasama Shoin, 1977.

Hochstedler, Carol, trans. *The Tale of Nezame: Part Three of Yowa no Nezame Monogatari.* Cornell University East Asia Papers 22. Ithaca, N.Y.: China-Japan Program, Cornell University, 1979.

Horikawa Ko. "Jikan no mondai: *Murasaki Shikibu nikki*." In Suzuki Kazuo, ed., *Tatta hitori no yo no naka: joryū nikki ron e no kokoromi*, pp. 165–85. Shibundō, 1973.

Horikawa'in ensho awase, ed. Hagitani Boku. In Hagatani Boku and Taniyama Shigeru, eds., *Utaawase shū.* NKBT 74: 263–70. Iwanami Shoten, 1965.

Horiuchi Hideaki. "Nikki kara nikki bungaku e: koten." *Kokubungaku kaishaku to kanshō* 649 (July 1985): 6–12.

Hosono Tetsuo. "*Sarashina nikki* shoko: sono bungeikan no haikei ni tsuite." *Kokugo to kokubungaku* 30 (Feb. 1953): 29–36.

Hurst, G. Cameron, III. *Insei: Abdicated Sovereigns in the Politics of Late Heian Japan, 1086–1185.* New York: Columbia University Press, 1976.

Hurvitz, Leon, trans. *Scripture of the Lotus Blossom of the Fine Dharma.* New York: Columbia University Press, 1976.

Ikeda Kikan. *Kyūtei joryū nikki bungaku.* Shibundō, 1926.

Ima kagami, ed. Takehana Isao. 3 vols. Kodansha, 1984.

Imai Gen'e. "*Sanuki no suke nikki:* Heian joryū nikki kenkyū no mondai ten to sono seiri." *Kokubungaku kaishaku to kanshō* 26 (Feb. 1961): 72–83.

Imai Takuji. "*Genji monogatari to Sarashina nikki.*" *Kokubungaku* 2 (Oct. 1957): 91–96.

———. *Heian jidai nikki bungaku no kenkyū.* Meiji Shoin, 1957.

———. *Heianchō nikki no kenkyū.* Keibunsha, 1935.

———, ed. *Sanuki no suke nikki: yakuchū to hyōron.* Waseda Daigaku Shuppanbu, 1986.

Imakōji Kakuzui and Mitani Sachiko. *Kōchū Sanuki no suke nikki.* Kasama Shoin, 1976.

Inaga Keiji. "*Sanuki no suke nikki* no shi to sei: Sanuki hara no onkotachi." *Kokubungaku* (Nov. 1965): 79–85.

Inoue Mayumi. "*Sagoromo monogatari* no 'Amateru onkami' hyōgen o yomu." In Monogatari Kenkyūkai, ed., *Monogatari kenkyū tokushū: katari soshite in'yō,* pp. 107–29. Shinjidaisha, 1986.

Inukai Kiyoshi. "Takasue no musume ni kansuru shiron: shu toshite sono chūnenki o megutte." In Nihon bungaku kenkyū shiryō kankō, ed., *Heianchō nikki* 2, pp. 163–71. Yūseidō, 1975. [First published in *Kokugo to kokubungaku* (Jan. 1955).]

Inukai Kiyoshi, Inoue Muneo, Ōkubo Tadashi, Ono Hiroshi, Tanaka Yutaka, Hashimoto Fumio, Fujihira Haruo, eds. *Waka daijiten.* Meiji Shoin, 1986.

Irigaray, Luce. *This Sex Which Is Not One.* Trans. Catherine Porter. Ithaca, N.Y.: Cornell University Press, 1985 [1977].

Ise monogatari, ed. Fukui Teisuke. In Katagiri Yōichi, Fukui Teisuke, Takahashi Shōji, and Shimizu Yoshiko, eds. *Taketori monogatari, Ise monogatari, Yamato monogatari, Heichū monogatari.* NKBZ 8: 131–244. Shōgakkan, 1972.

Ishihara Shōhei. "*Kagerō nikki* no hassō: bōtō bubun no zōtōka ni tsuite." In Heianchō bungaku kenkyūkai, ed., *Heianchō bungaku no shomondai,* pp. 277–96. Kasama Shoin, 1977.

———. "*Kagerō nikki:* shuyō kenkyū bunken annai." *Kokubungaku kaishaku to kanshō* 558 (Sept. 1978): 169–81.

———. "Nikki bungaku ni okeru kaisō: *Sanuki no suke nikki* ni miru shippitsu no imi." *Nihon bungaku* 32 (June 1983): 51–58.

———. "Nikki bungaku shippitsu no hito keiki: shi to kaisō." In Nihon bungaku kenkyū shiryō kankō, ed., *Heianchō nikki* 2: 304–13. Yūseidō, 1975.

———. "*Sanuki no suke nikki* kenkyū shoshi." In Nihon bungaku kenkyū shiryō kankō, ed., *Heianchō nikki* 2: 323–27. Yūseidō, 1975.

————. "*Sarashina nikki* kenkyū shoshi." In Nihon bungaku kenkykū shiryō kankō, ed., *Heianchō nikki* 2: 319–23. Yūseidō, 1975.

————. "Taiko onki no genkei: hatashite kambuntai ka." *Kokubungaku kenkyu* 31 (Mar. 1965): 14–27.

Ishihara Shōhei, Tsumoto Nobuhiro, and Nishizawa Tadashi, eds. *Kagerō nikki. Joryū nikki bungaku kōza* 2. Benseisha, 1990.

Ishino Keiko. "*Sanuki no suke nikki.*" In Nihon bungaku kenkykū shiryō kankō, ed., *Heianchō nikki* 2: 264–68. Yūseidō, 1975.

————. "*Sanuki no suke nikki.*" In Ōsone Shosuke, Kubota Jun, Hinokidani Akihiko, Horiuchi Hideaki, Miki Norihito, and Yamaguchi Akiho, eds., *Nikki, kikō bungaku Kenkyū shiryō Nihon koten bungaku* 9: 102–9. Meiji Shoin, 1984.

————. "*Sanuki no suke nikki* ni okeru jikan no kōzō." In Chūko bungaku kenkyūkai, ed., *Nikki bungaku sakuhinron no kokoromi*, pp. 241–61. Kasama Shoin, 1979.

Itō Moriyuki. "Ōchō joryū bungaku kenkyū no kiseki to tembō: *Ise shū, Sarashina nikki* o chūshin ni." *Kokubungaku kaishaku to kanshō* 51 (Nov. 1986): 144–53.

Izumi Shikibu nikki, ed. Fujioka Tadaharu. In Fujioka Tadaharu et al., eds., *Izumi Shikibu nikki, Murasaki Shikibu nikki, Sarashina nikki, Sanuki no suke nikki.* NKBZ 18: 81–157. Shōgakkan, 1971.

Izumi Shikibu shū, Izumi Shikibu zokushū, ed. Shimizu Fumio. Iwanami Shoten, 1983.

Izumoji Yoshikazu. *Kyoto koshaji shosetsu: Heian zenki hen.* Yūhō Shoten, 1974.

Jacobs, Lea. "The Woman's Film and the Female Spectator." *Camera Obscura: Journal of Feminism and Film Theory* 18 (1989): 53–66.

Joseishi Sōgō Kenkyūkai, ed. *Nihon joseishi.* Vol. 1. Tokyo Daigaku Shuppankai, 1982.

Kagerō nikki, ed. Kawaguchi Hisao. In Suzuki Tomotarō, Kawaguchi Hisao, Endō Yoshimoto, and Nishishita Kyōichi, eds., *Tosa nikki, Kagerō nikki, Izumi Shikubu nikki, Sarashina nikki.* NKBT 20. Iwanami Shoten, 1957.

Kagerō nikki, ed. Kimura Masanori. In Matsumura Seiichi and Kimura Masanori, eds., *Tosa nikki, Kagerō nikki.* NKBZ 9: 123–407.

Kakimoto Tsutomu. "*Kagerō nikki* no denbon to shomei." In Akiyama Ken, ed., *Issatsu no kōza: Kagerō nikki*, pp. 273–80. Yūseidō, 1981.

Kamens, Edward. *The Buddhist Poetry of the Great Kamo Priestess: Daisaiin Senshi and Hosshin Wakashū.* Michigan Monograph Series in Japanese Studies, no. 5. Ann Arbor: Center for Japanese Studies, University of Michigan, 1990.

————. *A Study and Translation of Minamoto Tamenori's Sanbōe.* Michigan Monograph Series in Japanese Studies, no. 2. Ann Arbor: Center for Japanese Studies, University of Michigan, 1988.

Katagiri Yōichi. "Utamakura no seiritsu: *Kokinshū* hyōgen kenkyū no ichibu toshite." *Kokugo to kokubungaku* (Apr. 1970): 22–33.

Katō, Hilda. "The *Mumyōshō* of Kamo no Chōmei and Its Significance in Japanese Literature." *MN* 23 (Autumn–Winter 1968): 321–430.

Keene, Donald. *Landscapes and Portraits: Appreciations of Japanese Culture.* Tokyo: Kodansha International, 1971.

——. *Travelers of a Hundred Ages.* New York: Henry Holt, 1989.

——, trans. *Essays in Idleness.* New York: Columbia University Press, 1967.

Kemper, Ulrich, trans. *Sarashina-nikki: Tagebuch einer japanischen Hofdame aus dem Jahre 1060.* Stuttgart: Phillipp Reclam, 1966.

Kenreimon'in Ukyō no Daibu shū, ed. Hisamatsu Sen'ichi. In Hisamatsu Sen'ichi, Matsuda Takeo, Sekine Yoshiko, and Aoki Takako, eds., *Heian Kamakura shikashū.* NKBT 80: 413–511. Iwanami Shoten, 1964.

Kimura Masanori. "*Izumi Shikibu nikki* keisei ron: sono bōtō o megutte." In Murasaki Shikibu Gakkai, ed., *Genji monogatari to joryū nikki kenkyū to shiryō*, pp. 229–61. Musashino Shoin, 1976.

——. "Nikki bungaku no honshitsu to sōsaku shinri." In Hisamatsu Sen'ichi, Aso Isoji, Ichiko Teiji, and Gomi Tomohide, eds., *Kōza Nihon bungaku no sōten* 2: 99–126. Meiji Shoin, 1969.

Kojidan. In Kuroita Katsumi, ed., *Ujishūi, Kojidan, Jikkunsho. Kokushi taikei* 18: 1–132. Yoshikawa Kōbunkan, 1965.

Kokinwakarokujō. SKT 2: 193–255.

Kokinwakashū, ed. Ozawa Masao. NKBZ 7. Shōgakkan, 1971.

Komachiya Teruhiko. "Joryū bungaku no dentō to *Genji monogatari*." In Akiyama Ken, ed., *Kōza Nihon bungaku Genji monogatari* 1: 56–75. Shibundō, 1978.

Kondō Hajime. "*Sarashina nikki* no saigimmi: sono shūkyō ishiki ni tsuite." 1949. In Nihon bungaku kenkyū shiryō kankō, ed., *Heianchō nikki* 2: 172–79. Yūseidō, 1975.

Konishi Jin'ichi. *The Early Middle Ages.* Trans. Aileen Gatten. *A History of Japanese Literature* 2. Princeton: Princeton University Press, 1986.

Konjaku monogatarishū, ed. Mabuchi Kazuo, Kunisaki Fumimaro, Kon'no Tōru. 4 vols. *NKBZ* 21–24. Shōgakkan, 1971–1976.

Koyano Jun'ichi. *Heian kōki joryū nikki no kenkyū.* Kyōiku Shuppan Sentaa, 1983.

——. "Sanuki no suke nikki." *Kokubungaku kaishaku to kanshō* 51 (Nov. 1986): 125–28.

Kubo Tomotaka. "*Sarashina nikki* no Yakushi Botoke: kōsō o tsukaeru saihō kensō no kinō." In Chūko bungaku kenkyūkai, ed., *Genji monogatari to Heian bungaku* 1: 183–207. Waseda Daigaku Shuppanbu, 1988.

Kusakabe Ryōen. *Sanuki no suke nikki: kenkyū to kaishaku.* Kasama Shoin, 1977.

Makura no sōshi, ed. Matsuo Satoshi and Nagai Kazuko. *NKBZ* 11. Shōgakkan, 1974.

Makura no sōshi, ed. Watanabe Minoru. *SNKBT* 25. Iwanami Shoten, 1991.

Man'yōshū, ed. Kojima Noriyuki, Kinoshita Masatoshi, and Satake Akihiro. 4 vols. *NKBZ* 2–5. Shōgakkan, 1971–76.

Marra, Michele. *The Aesthetics of Discontent: Politics and Reclusion in Medieval Japanese Literature.* Honolulu: University of Hawaii Press, 1991.

―――. "*Mumyōzōshi*: Introduction and Translation." *MN* 39, no. 2 (Summer 1984): 115–45.

―――. "*Mumyōzōshi*, Part 2." *MN* 39, no. 3 (Autumn 1984): 281–305.

―――. "*Mumyōzōshi*, Part 3." *MN* 39, no. 4 (Winter 1984): 409–34.

Masuda Shigeo. "Joryū nikki bungaku wa naze hassei shita no ka." *Kokubungaku* 29 (Nov. 1984): 67–73.

―――. *Kagerō nikki sakusha: Udaishō Michitsuna no haha.* Shintensha, 1983.

Matsuhara Kazuyoshi. "*Kagerō nikki* no tenkai to keisei: dokusha (yōjo, Hōshi) no sōtei." *Heian bungaku kenkyū* 59 (June 1978): 109–20.

Matsumoto Yasushi. "Haha isaku no kagami o itasasete: *Sarashina nikki* to Hasedera shinkō." *Kokugakuin zasshi* 80 (Apr. 1979): 1–12.

―――. "Sanuki no suke no seikaku: *Sanuki no suke nikki* to *Chōshūki*." In Nihon bungaku kenkyū shiryō kankō, ed., *Heianchō nikki* 2: 279–90. Yūseidō, 1975.

Mayne, Judith. *The Woman at the Keyhole: Feminism and Women's Cinema.* Bloomington: Indiana University Press, 1990.

McCullough, Helen Craig, ed. *Classical Japanese Prose: An Anthology.* Stanford: Stanford University Press, 1990.

―――, trans. *Kokin Wakashū: The First Imperial Anthology of Japanese Poetry; with 'Tosa Nikki' and 'Shinsen Waka.'* Stanford: Stanford University Press, 1985.

―――, trans. *Ōkagami: The Great Mirror: Fujiwara Michinaga (966–1027) and His Times.* Princeton: Princeton University Press, 1980.

McCullough, Helen Craig, and William H. McCullough, trans. *A Tale of Flowering Fortunes: Annals of Japanese Aristocratic Life in the Heian Period.* 2 vols. Stanford: Stanford University Press, 1980.

McCullough, William H. "Japanese Marriage Institutions in the Heian Period." *HJAS* 27 (1967): 103–67.

―――. "Spirit Possession in the Heian Period." In Ōta Saburō and Fukuda Rikutarō, eds., *Studies in Japanese Culture* 1: 91–98. Tokyo: The Japan P.E.N. Club, 1973.

Miller, Nancy K. *The Heroine's Text: Readings in the French and English Novel, 1722–1782.* New York: Columbia University Press, 1980.

―――. *Subject to Change: Reading Feminist Writing.* New York: Columbia University Press, 1988.

Miller, Stephen D. "Religious Boundaries in Aesthetic Domains: The Formation of a Buddhist Category (*Shakkyō-ka*) in the Imperial Poetry Anthologies." In Eiji Sekine, ed., *Proceedings of the Midwest Association for Japanese Literary Studies* 3 (Summer 1997): 100–120.

Miner, Earl. "The Heroine: Identity, Recurrence, Destiny." In Andrew Pekarik, ed., *Ukifune: Love in the Tale of Genji,* pp. 63–81. New York: Columbia University Press, 1982.

―――, trans. *Japanese Poetic Diaries.* Berkeley: University of California Press, 1969.

Miner, Earl, Hiroko Odagiri, and Robert Morrell. *The Princeton Companion to Classical Japanese Literature*. Princeton: Princeton University Press, 1985.

Mitamura Masako. "'Koe' o kiku hitobito: Uji jūjo no hōhō." In Monogatari Kenkyūkai, ed., *Monogatari kenkyū tokushū: katari soshite in'yō*, pp. 306–59. Shinjidaisha, 1986.

———. *Makura no sōshi: hyōgen no ronri*. Yūseidō, 1995.

Mitani Eiichi. *Monogatarishi no kenkyū*. Yūseidō, 1967.

Mitani Kuniaki. "*Kagerō nikki* no jikan ishiki: shijin no nikki arui wa wakateki jikan no bungaku." In Akiyama Ken, ed., *Issatsu no kōza: Kagerō nikki*, pp. 221–30. Yūseidō, 1981.

———. "*Makura no sōshi* no batsubun o megutte." *MSK* 2: 74–105. Yūseidō, 1975.

———. "Monogatari bungaku no 'shisen': miru koto no imi arui wa 'katari' no kyōen." In Monogatari Kenkyūkai, ed., *Monogatari kenkyū tokushū: shisen*, pp. 89–108. Shinjidaisha, 1988.

Mitsuno Yōichi. "*Sarashina nikki* no sakkan wa dono yō ni shite tadasareta ka." *Kokubungaku* 38 (June 1993): 93.

———. "Uta manabi to uta monogatari." *Kokugo to kokubun* 712 (May 1983): 28–39.

Miyake, Lynne. Review of *Murasaki Shikibu: The Tale of Genji* by Richard Bowring. *MN* 44, no. 3 (Autumn 1989): 349–51.

———. "*The Tosa Diary*: In the Interstices of Gender and Criticism." In Paul Gordon Schalow and Janet A. Walker, eds., *The Woman's Hand: Gender and Theory in Japanese Woman's Writing*, pp. 41–73. Stanford: Stanford University Press, 1996.

Miyazaki Sōhei. *Heian joryū nikki bungaku no kenkyū*. Kasama Shoin, 1972.

———. *Heian joryū nikki bungaku no kenkyū (zoku hen)*. Kasama Shoin, 1980.

———. *Sei Shōnagon to Murasaki Shikibu: sono taihiron josetsu*. Chōbunsha, 1993.

Modleski, Tania. *Loving with a Vengeance: Mass-Produced Fantasies for Women*. London: Methuen, 1984.

Moers, Ellen. *Literary Women*. New York: Oxford University Press, 1985 [1976].

Moi, Toril. "The Missing Mother: The Oedipal Rivalries of René Girard." *Diacritics* 12 (Summer 1982): 21–31.

———. *Sexual/Textual Politics: Feminist Literary Theory*. London: Methuen, 1985.

Monogatari Kenkyūkai, ed. *Monogatari kenkyū tokushū: katari soshite in'yō*. Shinjidaisha, 1986.

———, ed. *Monogatari kenkyū tokushū: shisen*. Shinjidaisha, 1988.

Morimoto Motoko. "*Makura no sōshi* no gensen: nikki bungaku." *MSK* 4: 185–95. Yūseidō, 1976.

Morimoto Shigeru. "Utamakura to meisho." *Heian bungaku kenkyū* 53 (June 1975): 14–21.

Morita Kaneyoshi. "*Sanuki no suke nikki* no seiritsu." *Kokugo kokubun* (Jan. 1963): 32–41.

———. "*Utsuho monogatari* ni egakareta nikki bungakuteki sakuhin: nikki bungakushi e no apurōchi no hitotsu toshite." *Heian bungaku kenkyū* 52 (July 1974): 34–45.

Moriya Shōgo. *Heian kōki nikki bungaku ron: Sarashina nikki, Sanuki no suke nikki*. Shintensha, 1983.

———. "Ise ni okeru nikki bungaku keisei no kanōsei ni tsuite." *Kokubungaku kenkyū* 5 (November 1969): 1–12.

———. "Kagerō nikki." In Ōsone Shosuke, Kubota Jun, Hinokidani Akihiko, Horiuchi Hideaki, Miki Norihito, and Yamaguchi Akiho, eds., *Nikki, kikō bungaku*, pp. 36–46. Meiji Shoin, 1984.

———. "*Kagerō nikki* kenkyū no dōkō to kadai." *Kokubungaku* 26 (Jan. 1981): 137–43.

———. "*Kagerō nikki* zenshi: kashū kara nikki keisei e no sobyō." In Ishihara Shōhei, Tsumoto Nobuhiro, and Nishizawa Tadashi, eds., *Kagerō nikki*, pp. 43–61. *Joryū nikki bungaku kōza* 2. Benseisha, 1990.

———. "Michitsuna no haha." In Inukai Kiyoshi, Inoue Muneo, Ōkubo Tadashi, Ono Hiroshi, Tanaka Yutaka, Hashimoto Fumio, Fujihira Haruo, eds., *Waka daijiten*, p. 945. Meiji Shoin, 1986.

———. "*Sanuki no suke nikki*: iki to shi no kiroku." *Kokubungaku kaishaku to kanshō* 50 (July 1985): 76–78.

———. "*Sanuki no suke nikki* saihyōka no hito shiten." In Chūko bungaku kenkyūkai, ed., *Nikki bungaku sakuhinron no kokoromi*, pp. 263–86. Kasama Shoin, 1979.

———. "*Sanuki no suke nikki* to waka." *Heian bungaku kenkyū* 5 (June 1977): 161–75.

Morrell, Robert E. "The Buddhist Poetry in the *Goshūishū*." *MN* 28, no. 1 (Spring 1973): 87–100.

———. *Early Kamakura Buddhism: A Minority Report*. Berkeley: Asian Humanities Press, 1987.

Morris, Ivan. *The World of the Shining Prince*. Harmondsworth, Eng.: Penguin Books, 1979 [1964].

———, trans. *As I Crossed a Bridge of Dreams: Recollections of a Woman in Eleventh-Century Japan*. New York: Harper Colophon Books, 1973 [1971].

———, trans. *The Pillow Book of Sei Shōnagon*. 2 vols. Oxford: Oxford University Press, 1967.

———, trans. *The Pillow Book of Sei Shōnagon*. Middlesex, Eng.: Penguin, 1971.

Morris, Mark. "Desire and the Prince—New Work on *Genji monogatari*: A Review Article." *Journal of Asian Studies* 49, no. 2 (May 1990): 291–304.

———. "Sei Shōnagon's Poetic Catalogues." *HJAS* 40, no. 1 (June 1980): 5–54.

———. "Waka and Form, Waka and History." *HJAS* 46, no. 2 (Dec. 1986): 551–610.

Mostow, Joshua S. "The Amorous Statesman and the Poetess: The Politics of Autobiography and the *Kagerō Nikki*." *Japan Forum* 4, no. 2 (Oct. 1992): 305–15.

————. "Self and Landscape in *Kagerō Nikki*." *Review of Japanese Culture* (Dec. 1993): 8–19.

Mumyōshō, ed. Hisamatsu Sen'chi. In Hisamatsu Sen'chi and Nishio Minoru, eds., *Karonshū, nohakuronshū*. NKBT 65: 35–98. Iwanami Shoten, 1961.

Mumyōzōshi, ed. Kuwabara Hiroshi. SNKS 7. Shinchōsha, 1976.

Murai Jun. *Kagerō nikki zenhyōshaku*. Yūseidō, 1978.

Murasaki Shikibu Gakkai, ed. *Genji monogatari to joryū nikki kenkyū to shiryō*. Musashino Shoin, 1976.

Murasaki Shikibu nikki, ed. Nakano Kōichi. In Fujioka Tadaharu, ed., *Izumi Shikibu nikki, Murasaki Shikibu nikki, Sarashina nikki, Sanuki no suke nikki*. NKBZ 18: 161–274. Shōgakkan, 1971.

Nagai Yoshinori. "*Kagerō nikki* 'otosede wataru mori' ko: Hase, Ise dōtai shinkō no genryū." *Hikkyōgaku kenkyū* 2 (March 1970).

Nakamura Hajime, Fukunaga Mitsuji, Tamura Yoshirō, and Kon'no Tōru, eds. *Bukkyō jiten*. Iwanami Shoten, 1989.

Nakanishi Susumu. "Miru: kodai teki chikaku." *Bungaku* 43, no. 4 (Apr. 1975): 479–89.

Nickerson, Peter. "The Meaning of Matrilocality: Kinship, Property, and Politics in the Mid-Heian Period." *MN* 48, no. 4 (Winter 1993): 429–67.

Nihon bungaku kenkyū shiryō kankō, ed. *Heianchō nikki*. 2 vols. Yūseidō, 1975.

Nomura Seiichi. "*Kagerō nikki*: hyōgen no ronri." In Akiyama Ken, ed., *Ōchō joryū nikki hikkei*, pp. 37–45. Gakutōsha, 1986.

Ogino Ayako. *Makura no sōshi: Sei Shōnagon o torimaku otokotachi*. Gakken, 1991.

Oka Kazuo. *Michitsuna no haha: Kagerō nikki no geijutsu kō*. Yūseidō, 1972 [1942].

Okada, Richard H. "Domesticating *The Tale of Genji*." *Journal of the American Oriental Society* 110, no. 1 (Jan.–Mar. 1990): 60–70.

————. *Figures of Resistance: Language, Poetry, and Narrating in The Tale of Genji and Other Mid-Heian Texts*. Durham, N.C.: Duke University Press, 1991.

————. "Unbound Texts: Narrative Discourse in Heian Japan." Ph.D. diss., University of California, Berkeley, 1985.

Okada Seiji. "Kyūtei miko no jittai." In Joseishi sōgō kenkyūkai, ed., *Nihon joseishi* 1: 43–74. Tokyo Daigaku Shuppankai, 1985.

Ōkagami, ed. Matsumura Hiroji. NKBT 21. Iwanami Shoten, 1960.

Ono Susumu, Satake Akihiro, and Maeda Kingorō, eds. *Kogo jiten*. Iwanami Shoten, 1974.

Origuchi Shinobu kinenkai, ed. *Origuchi Shinobu zenshū*. 32 vols. Chūokōronsha, 1954–59.

Ōsone Shosuke, Kubota Jun, Hinokidani Akihiko, Horiuchi Hideaki, Miki Norihito, Yamaguchi Akiho, eds. *Nikki, kikō bungaku*. Kenkyū shiryō Nihon koten bungaku 9. Meiji Shoin, 1984.

Ouchi Kazuaki. "'Amateru onkami o nemushimase' no yume: *Sarashina nikki* kaishaku shiken." *Gunma kenritsu joshi daigaku kokubungaku kenkyū* 2 (Mar. 1982): 12–27.

Owen, Stephen. *Traditional Chinese Poetry and Poetics: Omen of the World.* Madison: University of Wisconsin Press, 1985.

Pekarik, Andrew, ed. *Ukifune: Love in the Tale of Genji.* New York: Columbia University Press, 1982.

Radway, Janice A. *Reading the Romance: Women, Patriarchy, and Popular Literature.* Chapel Hill: University of North Carolina Press, 1984.

Ramirez-Christensen, Esperanza. "Resisting Figures of Resistance." *HJAS* 55 (June 1995): 179–218.

———. "The Desire for *Monogatari* in *Sarashina nikki.*" In Eiji Seleine, ed., *The Desire for Monogatari,* pp. 31–41. *Proceedings of the Second Midwest Research/Pedagogy Seminar on Japanese Literature.* Purdue University, 1994.

Rimbaud, Arthur. *Poésies, Une saison en enfer, Illuminations.* Paris: Gallimard, 1965.

Rodd, Laurel Rasplica. "Nichiren's Teachings to Women." *Western Conference of the Association for Asian Studies, Selected Papers in Asian Studies,* n.s., no. 5 (n.d.): 1–20.

———, with Mary Henkenius, trans. *Kokinshū: A Collection of Poems Ancient and Modern, Including a Study of Chinese Influences on the Kokinshū Prefaces by John Timothy Wixted and an Annotated Translation of the Chinese Prefaces by Leonard Grzanka.* Princeton: Princeton University Press, 1984.

Rohlich, Thomas H., trans. *A Tale of Eleventh-Century Japan: Hamamatsu Chūnagon Monogatari.* Princeton: Princeton University Press, 1983.

Rokujō Saiin monogatari utaawase. SKT 5: 91.

Rubin, Gayle. "The Traffic in Women: Notes on the 'Political Economy' of Sex." In Rayna R. Reiter, ed., *Toward an Anthropology of Women.* New York: Monthly Review Press, 1975.

Saeki Junko. *Yojo no bunkashi: hare no onnatachi.* Chūōkōronsha, 1982.

Sagoromo monogatari, ed. Mitani Eiichi and Sekine Yoshiko. *NKBT* 79. Iwanami Shoten, 1965.

Saigō Nobutsuna. *Genji monogatari o yomu tame ni.* Heibonsha, 1983.

———. *Kodaijin to yume.* Heibonsha, 1972.

Sanbōe. In Mabuchi Kazuo, Koizumi Hiroshi, and Kon'no Tōru, eds., *Sanbōe, Chūkōsen. SNKBT* 31: 3–226. Iwanami Shoten, 1997.

Sansom, George. *A History of Japan to 1334.* Stanford: Stanford University Press, 1978 [1958].

Sanuki no suke nikki, ed. Ishii Fumio. In Fujioka Tadaharu et al., eds., *Izumi Shikibu nikki, Murasaki Shikibu nikki, Sarashina nikki, Sanuki no suke nikki. NKBZ* 18: 365–459.

Sanuki no suke nikki, ed. Okazaki Satoakira. Ōfūsha, 1960.

Sanuki no suke nikki, ed. Tamai Kōsuke. Asahi Shimbunsha, 1953.

Sarashina nikki, ed. Akiyama Ken. *SNKS* 39. Shinchōsha, 1980.

Sarashina nikki, ed. Inagaki Taiichi. *Koten shinshaku shiriizu* 26. Chūdōkan, 1982.

Sarashina nikki, ed. Inukai Kiyoshi. In Fujioka Tadaharu et al., eds., *Izumi Shi-*

kibu nikki, Murasaki Shikibu nikki, Sarashina nikki, Sanuki no suke nikki.
   NKBZ 18: 283–362. Shōgakkan, 1971.
Sarashina nikki, ed. Nishishita Kyōichi. In Suzuki Tomotarō, Kawaguchi Hisao,
   Endō Yoshimoto, and Nishishita Kyōichi, eds., *Tosa nikki, Kagerō nikki,
   Izumi Shikubu nikki, Sarashina nikki. NKBT* 20: 463–542.
Sarashina nikki, ed. Yoshioka Hiroshi. In Hasegawa Masaharu, Imanishi Yūi-
   chirō, Itō Hiroshi, and Yoshioka Hiroshi, eds., *Tosa nikki, Kagerō nikki,
   Murasaki Shikibu nikki, Sarashina nikki. SNKBT* 24: 370–437. Iwanami
   Shoten, 1989.
Seidensticker, Edward, trans. *The Gossamer Years (Kagerō Nikki): The Diary
   of a Noblewoman of Heian Japan.* Rutland, Vt.: Tuttle, 1964.
————, trans. *The Tale of Genji.* 2 vols. New York: Alfred A. Knopf, 1976.
Setouchi Harumi. *Watashi no suki na koten no onnatachi.* Shinchō Bunko,
   1985.
Shinohara Yoshihiko. "*Genji monogatari* ni itaru nozokimi no keifu." *Bun-
   gaku gogaku* 68 (Aug. 1973): 56–67.
Shinozuka Sumiko. "*Sanuki no suke nikki* to jinsei: onhiza no kage." *Koku-
   bungaku kaishaku to kanshō* 46 (Jan. 1981): 55–59.
Shirane Haruo. *The Bridge of Dreams: A Poetics of the Tale of Genji.* Stanford:
   Stanford University Press, 1987.
Sieffert, René, trans. *Les Journaux poétiques de l'époque de Heian: Le journal
   de Sarashina.* Paris: Publications Orientalistes de France, 1978.
Spacks, Patricia Meyer. *Desire and Truth: Functions of Plot in Eighteenth-
   Century English Novels.* Chicago: University of Chicago Press, 1990.
————. *The Female Imagination.* New York: Alfred A. Knopf, 1975.
Stinchecum, Amanda Mayer. "Who Tells the Tale?—'Ukifune': A Study in Nar-
   rative Voice." *MN* 35, no. 4 (Winter 1980): 375–403.
Suzuki Hideo and Fujii Sadakazu, eds. *Nihon bungeishi.* Vol. 1, *Kodai.* Kawade
   shobō shinsha, 1986.
Suzuki Kazuo. *Tatta hitori no yo no naka: joryū nikki ron e no kokoromi.*
   Shibundō, 1973.
Tada Kazuomi. "Sugawara Takasue no musume." In Akiyama Ken, ed., *Ōchō
   bungakushi,* pp. 349–60. Tokyo Daigaku Shuppankai, 1984.
Takahashi Bunji. "*Sarashina nikki* shoko: Yakushi Botoke to shinbiteki
   imaaju." *Kokugo to kokubungaku* (Nov. 1987): 102–13.
Takahashi Tōru. *Monogatari to e no enkinhō.* Perikansha, 1991.
————. "Ōchō bungaku to hyōrei no keifu: kotoba no shamanizumu." *Koku-
   bungaku* 29 (Aug. 1984): 79–83.
Takakusu Junjirō and Watanabe Kaigyoku, eds. *Taishō Shinshū daizōkyō.* 85
   vols. Taishō issaikyō kankōkai, 1924–32.
Takehana Isao. "Sanekata." In Inukai Kiyoshi, Inoue Muneo, Ōkubo Tadashi,
   Ono Hiroshi, Tanaka Yutaka, Hashimoto Fumio, and Fujihira Haruo, eds.,
   Waka daijiten, p. 398. Meiji Shoin, 1986.
Tamagami Takuya, ed. *Genji monogatari. Kanshō Nihon koten bungaku* 9.
   Kadokawa Shoten, 1975.

————, ed. *Genji monogatari kenkyū: Genji monogatari hyōshaku.* 14 vols. Kadokawa Shoten, 1964–1969.

Tamai Kōsuke. *Nikki bungaku no kenkyū.* Hanawa Shobō, 1965.

————, ed. *Sanuki no suke nikki zenchūkai.* Yūseidō, 1969. First published in 1936 as *Sanuki no suke no nikki tsūshaku.*

————. *Sarashina nikki sakkan kō.* Ikuei shoin, 1925.

Torikaebaya monogatari. Suzuki Hiromichi, ed. *Kōchū Torikaebaya monogatari.* Kasama Shoin, 1988.

Tosa nikki, ed. Matsumura Seiichi. In Matsumura Seiichi and Kimura Masanori, eds., *Tosa nikki, Kagerō nikki. NKBZ* 9: 5–73. Shōgakkan, 1973.

Towazugatari, ed. Fukuda Hideichi. *SNKS* 20. Shinchōsha, 1978.

Tsumoto Nobuhiro. *Sarashina nikki no kenkyū.* Waseda Daigaku Shuppanbu, 1982.

Tsunoda Bun'ei. *Taikenmon'in Tamako no shōgai.* Asahi Shinbunsha, 1985.

Tsurezuregusa, ed. Nagazumi Yasuaki. In Kanda Hideo, Nagazumi Yasuaki, and Yasuraoka Kōsaku, eds., *Hōjōki, Tsurezuregusa, Shōbōgenzō zuimonki, Tannishō. NKBZ* 27: 85–286. Shōgakkan, 1971.

Tsuzuki Kimiko. "Yorimichi seiji to joryū bungei saron: sono ichi." *Daiichi Hō iku Tandai kenkyū kiyō* 1 (Apr. 1984): 1–29.

Uemura Etsuko. *Kagerō nikki kaishaku taisei.* 8 vols. to date. Meiji Shoin, 1983–94.

————. *Kagerō nikki no kenkyū.* Meiji Shoin, 1972.

————. "Michitsuna no haha." In Waka bungakkai, ed., *Ōchō no kajin, waka bungaku kōza* 6, pp. 200–230. Ōfūsha, 1970.

Ujishūi, Kojidan, Jikkunshō, ed. Kuroita Katsumi. *Kokushi taikei* 18. Yoshikawa Kōbunkan, 1932.

Ury, Marian. Review of *The Emperor Horikawa Diary by Fujiwara no Nagako, "Sanuki no Suke Nikki,"* trans. Jennifer Brewster. *HJAS* 39 (1979): 220–25.

Utsuho monogatari, ed. Kōno Tama. 3 vols. *NKBT* 10–12. Iwanami Shoten, 1959–1960.

Wakashi kenkyūkai, ed. *Shikashū taisei.* 7 vols. plus supplement. Meiji Shoin, 1973–1976.

Wakita Haruko. "Marriage and Property in Premodern Japan from the Perspective of Women's History." *Journal of Japanese Studies* 10, no. 1 (Winter 1984): 73–99.

Watanabe Minoru. *Heianchō bunshōshi.* Tokyo Daigaku Shuppankai, 1981.

Willig, Rosette, trans. *The Changelings: A Classical Japanese Court Tale.* Stanford: Stanford University Press, 1983.

Wixted, John Timothy. "Chinese Influences on the *Kokinshū* Prefaces." In Laurel Rodd with Mary Henkenius, trans., *Kokinshū: A Collection of Poems Ancient and Modern*, pp. 387–402. Princeton: Princeton University Press, 1984.

————. "The *Kokinshū* Prefaces: Another Perspective." *HJAS* 43, no. 1 (June 1983): 215–38.

Woolf, Virginia. *A Room of One's Own*. New York: Harcourt, Brace & World, 1957 [1929].

———. "The Tale of Genji." *Vogue* (London) 66, no. 2 (July 1925).

Yamato monogatari, ed. Takahashi Shōji. In Katagiri Yōichi, Fukui Teisuke, Takahashi Shōji, Shimizu Yoshiko, eds., *Taketori monogatari, Ise monogatari, Yamato monogatari, Heichū monogatari. NKBZ* 8: 267–438. Shōgakkan, 1972.

Yowa no Nezame, ed. Suzuki Kazuo. *NKBZ* 19. Shōgakkan, 1974.

Yuzawa Shōji. "*Sanuki no suke nikki* no buntai to ishiki: seikaku ya hyōka no saiko o kiten ni." *Heian bungaku kenkyū* 77 (May 1987): 213–19.

Zenkindai Joseishi Kenkyūkai, ed. *Kazoku to josei no rekishi: kodai, chūsei.* Yoshikawa Kōbunkan, 1989.

☞ Index

In this index an "f" after a number indicates a separate reference on the next page, and an "ff" indicates separate references on the next two pages. A continuous discussion over two or more pages is indicated by a span of page numbers, e.g., "57–59." *Passim* is used for a cluster of references in close but not consecutive sequence.

Library of Congress Cataloging-in-Publication Data

Sarra, Edith
   Fictions of femininity : literary inventions of gender in Japanese
court women's memoirs / Edith Sarra.
    p. cm.
   Includes bibliographical references and index.
   ISBN 0-8047-3378-3 (cloth : alk. paper)
   1. Japanese diaries—Heian period, 794–1185—History and
criticism. 2. Japanese diaries—Women authors—History and criticism. 3. Femininity in literature. 4. Gender identity in literature.
I. Title.

PL741.2.S26   1999
895.6'8140309—dc21   98-33910
                                                     CIP

Original printing 1999
Last figure below indicates year of this printing:
08 07 06 05 04 03 02 01 00 99

CPSIA information can be obtained
at www.ICGtesting.com
Printed in the USA
LVHW101022240722
724266LV00022B/844/J